Fodor's
Costa Rica,
Belize,
Guatemala

PRAISE FOR FODOR'S GUIDES

"Fodor's guides . . . are an admirable blend of the cultural and the practical."
—The Washington Post

"Researched by people chosen because they lived or have lived in the country, well-written, and with good historical sections . . . Obligatory reading for millions of tourists."
—The Independent, *London*

"Usable, sophisticated restaurant coverage, with an emphasis on good value."
—Andy Birsh, Gourmet restaurant columnist, quoted by Gannett News Service

"Packed with dependable information."
—Atlanta Journal Constitution

"Fodor's always delivers high quality . . . thoughtfully presented . . . thorough."
—Houston Post

"Valuable because of their comprehensiveness."
—Minneapolis Star-Tribune

Fodor's Travel Publications, Inc.
New York • Toronto • London • Sydney • Auckland

Fodor's Costa Rica, Belize, Guatemala

Editor: Elaine Robbins
Editorial Contributors: Kurt Aguilar, Jacob Bernstein, Bob Blake, Craig Cabanis, David Dudenhoefer, Philip Eade, Echo Garrett, Bevin McLaughlin, Richard Nidever, Tracy Patruno, Maria Sacchetti, Mary Ellen Schultz, Annelise Sorenson, Nancy Van Itallie, Simon Worrall
Creative Director: Fabrizio La Rocca
Cartographer: David Lindroth
Illustrator: Karl Tanner
Cover Photograph: Luis Castañeda/Image Bank

Design: Vignelli Associates

Special Sales

Contents

6 Belize   *225*

Spanish Vocabulary   *277*

Index   *283*

Maps

Foreword

While every care has been taken to ensure the accuracy of the information in this guide, the passage of time will always bring change, and consequently the publisher cannot accept responsibility for errors that may occur.

All prices and opening times quoted here are based on information supplied to us at press time. Hours and admission fees may change, however, and the prudent traveler will avoid inconvenience by calling ahead.

Fodor's wants to hear about your travel experiences, both pleasant and unpleasant. When a hotel or restaurant fails to live up to its billing, let us know and we will investigate the complaint and revise our entries where the facts warrant it.

Send your letters to the editors of Fodor's Travel Publications, 201 East 50th Street, New York, NY 10022.

Highlights
and
Fodor's Choice

Highlights

Costa Rica

Small Hotels The nation's tourism boom, which has made the industry Costa Rica's second-leading moneymaker, has led to a seemingly unquenchable thirst for hotel rooms. However, large chains have all but ignored Costa Rica, leaving room for smaller operators to remodel existing buildings, especially old homes, into hotels and bed-and-breakfasts of fewer than 20 guest rooms. A booming area for such renovations in San José is Barrio Amón, northeast of the city center.

Infrastructure Road repairs on the Pacific coast should make beach access in that region easier this year. A rugged stretch of road leading to the port town of Quepos, near the popular Manuel Antonio beach area, was under repair in early 1994. A new highway farther south toward the Dominical area was being built, and the dirt roads on the wild Nicoya Peninsula were being improved in early 1994.

Horse Racing Horse racing with parimutuel betting has returned to Costa Rica after a two-year hiatus. The $5 million **Hipodromo El Sol** (Sun Racetrack) at Ojo de Agua, Alajuela, near the Juan Santamaría airport, was expected to open in 1994. A small track, the **Hipodromo Panorama** near the town of Cartago, has reopened and is offering limited racing.

Tourism Information On-Line Tourism information is now available on-line through **INFOTUR** (tel. 223–4481), a free information and reservations service that uses the same database as the Costa Rican Tourism Institute.

Belize

Marine Recreation More tour companies are offering package trips to Belize's 350-mile Barrier Reef, the world's second largest after Australia's. The reef, which has been proposed as a UNESCO World Heritage Site, is home to a spectacular array of marine life and still largely unscathed by human impacts. The trips feature world-class diving, fishing, and sailing; *see* Tour Companies in Chapter 1, Essential Information.

Cultural Immersion in Southern Belize The **Toldedo Eco-Tourism Association** (TEA), under the direction of William "Chet" Schmidt, has launched a dynamic project known as the **Village Guest Eco-Trail Program,** which immerses visitors for 24 hours into a household in a traditional Mayan village. It should be stressed that these village stays are not just a casual tourist attraction with play-acting indigenes, but a real immersion into a traditionally functioning village. The project is gaining increasingly wide respect and popularity, and since the number of guests is limited to just a handful in each village, stays should be booked well in advance. At press time the price for two people was US$105, which includes walking tours, participation in village rituals and meals, and transportation from Punta Gorda. *Toledo Eco-Tourism Association (TEA), 65 Front St., Box 75, Punta Gorda, tel. 07/22119.*

Guatemala

Cultural Festival Antigua's third biennial Cultural Festival (February 1995) features an array of Central American and Mexican artists presenting concerts, theater, exhibitions, and seminars—all amid the ancient ruins and churches of that timeless city.

El Petén Continuing restoration of ruins, improved access to natural and archaeological sites, and an array of new travel services are opening more and more of the jungle region of El Petén to foreign visitors. Tourists continue to flock to the spectacular, ancient city of Tikal, but there is much more for the visitor to discover in El Petén, including many other Mayan ruins, jungle lakes, and rivers, plus a treasure trove of rain forest and fauna.

Wilderness Exploration Ecological and adventure tourism is opening Guatemala's wilderness to more visitors every year. Jungle treks, white-water rafting, cave exploration, volcano ascents, river trips, and deep-sea fishing can all be combined with visits to striking Indian villages or ancient ruins.

Fodor's Choice

No two people will agree on what make a perfect vacation, but it's fun and helpful to know what others think. We hope you'll have a chance to experience some of Fodor's Choices yourself while visiting Central America. For detailed information about each entry, refer to the appropriate chapters within this guidebook.

Archaeological Sites

Costa Rica Guayabo National Monument near Turrialba

Teatro Nacional (National Theater) in San José

Belize Altun Ha

Lamanai

Caracol

Xunantunich

Guatemala Tikal, El Petén

Seibal, El Petén

Quiriguá, Atlantic & Verpaces

Dining

Costa Rica Barba Roja, Manuel Antonio (*$$–$$$*)

Ponte Vecchio, San Pedro (*$$*)

Miss Edith's, Cahuita (*$*)

Belize Elvi's Kitchen, Ambergris Cay (*$$*)

Estel's, Ambergris Cay (*$*)

GG's, Belize City (*$*)

Guatemala Jake's, Guatemala City (*$$$*)

El Bistro, Panajachel (*$$*)

Jean François, Guatemala City (*$$$*)

Lodging

Costa Rica Hotel La Mariposa, Manuel Antonio (*$$$$*)

Le Bergerac, San José (*$$$*)

Turrialtico, Turrialba (*$*)

Belize Chaa Creek, The Cayo (*$$$*)

Maruba Resort, near Belize City (*$$$*)

Rum Point Inn, Placencia (*$$$*)

Chan-Chich Lodge, Corozal and the North (*$$$*)

Guatemala Hotel Las Americas, Guatemala City (*$$$$*)

Posada Santiago, Santiago Atitlán (*$$*)

Hotel Mesón Panza Verde, Antigua (*$$*)

Casa Santo Domingo, Antigua (*$$$$*)

Special Moments and Views

Costa Rica Watching Arenal volcano erupting at night

Watching turtles arrive on the beaches of Tortuguero, Ostional, Playa Grande, and Nancite

Spotting quetzals near San Gerardo de Dota and at Monteverde

Belize Scuba diving at the Blue Hole on Lighthouse Reef

Swimming at the Rio On pools at the Mountain Pine Ridge

Sunrise over the New River Lagoon at Lamanai

Night diving at Hol Chan Marine Reserve

Guatemala Sunset on Lake Atitlán

Good Friday in Antigua

Any highland village festival

Taste Treats

Costa Rica *Ceviche* (raw sea bass marinated in lemon juice)

Ensalada de Palmito (heart of palm salad)

Gallos (tortillas with a variety of fillings)

Flan de coco (coconut custard)

Belize Stewed armadillo or iguana at Macy's Café in Belize City

Serre at BJ's in Plancencia

Death by Chocolate for dessert at the Fort Street Guest House in Belize City

Guatemala *Tapado* (seafood stew, served along Caribbean coast)

Pollo Pepián (chicken in sauce)

Robalo (snook, prepared in finer restaurants)

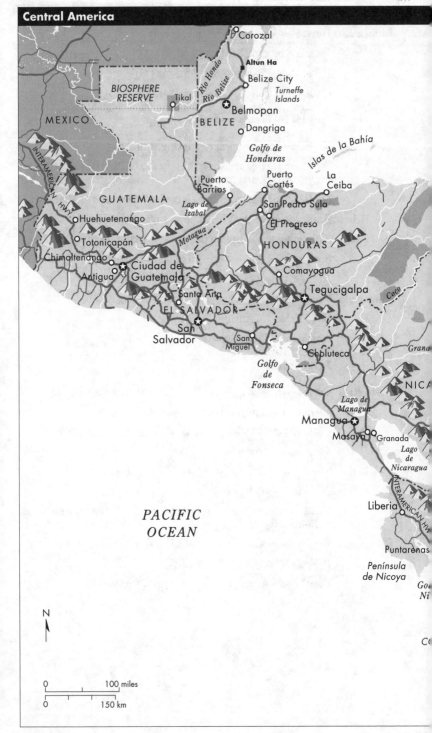

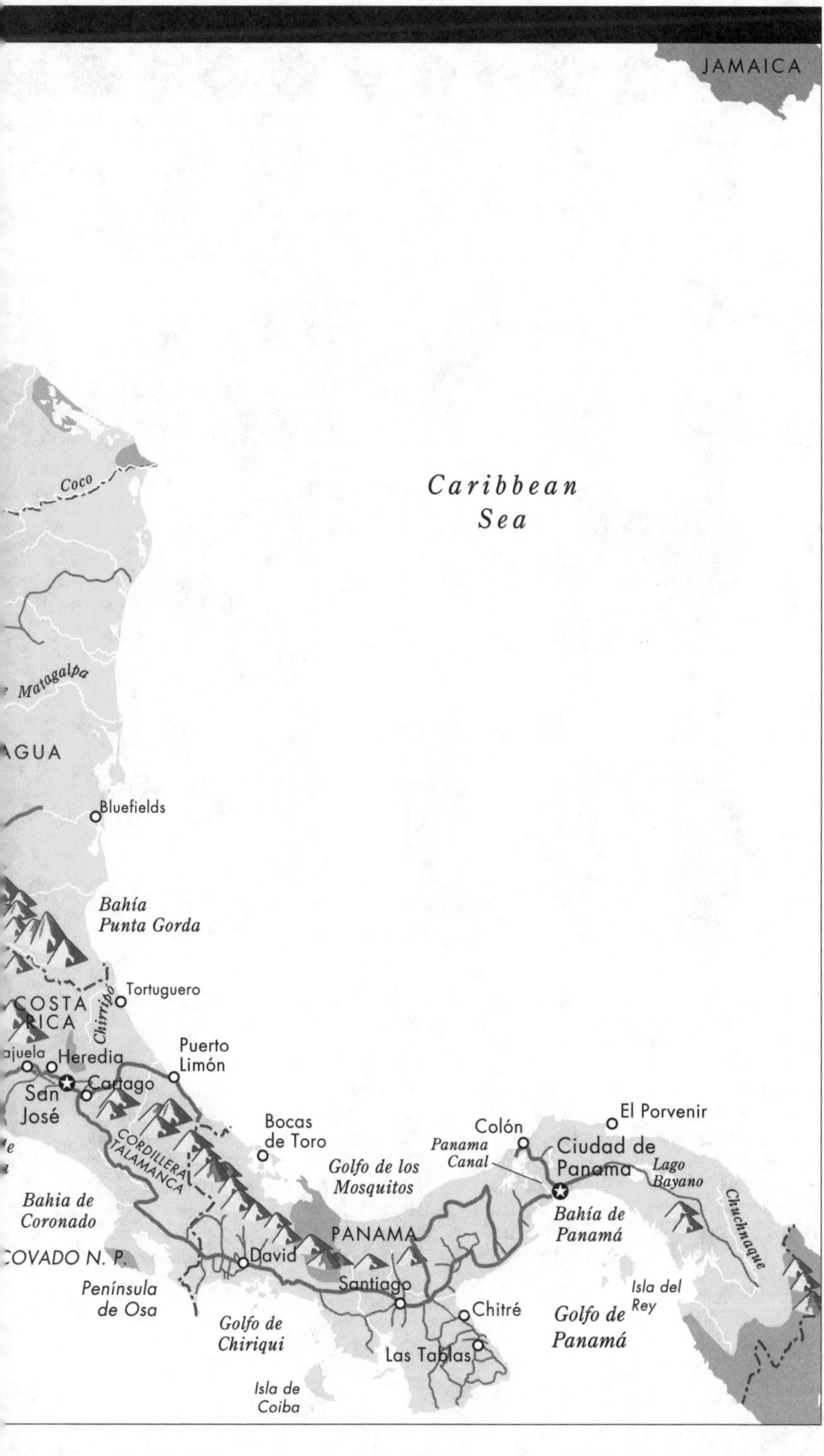

JAMAICA

Caribbean
Sea

Coco

Matagalpa

AGUA

Bluefields

Bahía
Punta Gorda

COSTA
RICA

Chirripó

Tortuguero

Puerto
Limón

juela Heredia

San   Cartago
José

CORDILLERA
TALAMANCA

Bocas
de Toro

Colón

Panama
Canal

El Porvenir

Ciudad de
Panama

Lago
Bayano

Chuchnaque

Golfo de los
Mosquitos

Bahía de
Coronado

COVADO N. P.

Bahía de
Panamá

PANAMA

David

Península
de Osa

Golfo de
Chiriqui

Santiago

Isla del
Rey

Chitré

Golfo de
Panamá

Las Tablas

Isla de
Coiba

World Time Zones

Numbers below vertical bands relate each zone to Greenwich Mean Time (0 hrs.).
Local times frequently differ from these general indications,
as indicated by light-face numbers on map.

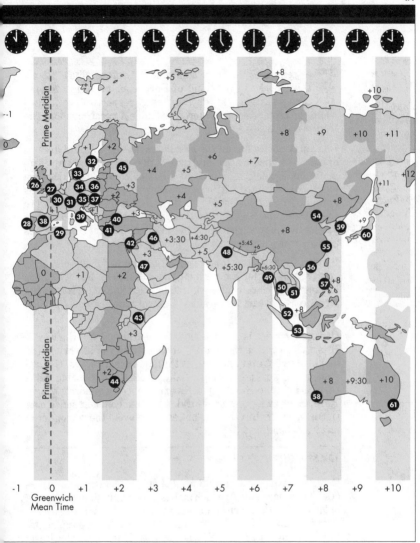

Introduction

By John Mitchem

John Mitchem has covered Latin America for a variety of publications, including the Philadelphia Inquirer, *the* Denver Post, *and* Américas *magazine.*

For centuries the tropics have held a unique allure. Something clicks in the mind of Europeans or North Americans—particularly during their respective winters—when the tropics are considered as an ideal vacation spot. The tropics are paradise.

Central America has all the attributes needed to fulfill dreams of equatorial bliss. A languid pace of life; compelling, polychromatic landscapes; hundreds of miles of coast where the sea meets beaches lined with coconut trees, and jungle foliage spills down nearby mountains. From the rain forests of Costa Rica to the volcanic lakes of Guatemala and the offshore cays and islands strung like jewels from Panama to Belize, Central America has always been a sensory paradise of color and climate.

Central America today is a region that can fulfill any vision. If you are looking for the conflict, you will find it. But if you are looking for a place where you can lie back and luxuriate in the pleasures of an earthly paradise, Central America can offer this, too.

Central America is a compelling, fascinating part of the world. It is a place where the texture and electricity of history in the making are felt every moment of the day. In many ways, Central America is working through many of the same growing pains that Europe and North America experienced a generation ago. Here, as elsewhere in the world, a certain common-sense caution is in order. But there is no reason to avoid the region, or in any way abandon it.

The Geography of Influence

Central America has a total area of 507,772 square kilometers (196,000 square miles), which makes it about one-fourth the size of Mexico, its northern neighbor. The area is packed with a variety of terrain that rivals the continent of South America: mountain peaks at more than 4,200 meters (14,000 feet); jungles in the Darien and the Mosquito Coast that have never been surveyed; deserts, plains, and vast pine barrens; high-altitude hardwood forests that resemble northern Europe more than the tropics.

The narrow isthmus, as narrow in some places as 80 kilometers (50 miles), is, in its entirety, smaller than Texas. But the placement of the isthmus has opened the area to incredible amounts of foreign influence. It has always tended to stand between things: between the gold and silver of Peru and Spain; between the East and West coasts of the United States when, during the California gold rush, Nicaragua was the preferred transit route for westward migration; between Mexico and South America; and—at least politically—between the United States and the Soviet Union. The Panama Canal, an added factor, served to raise the strategic stakes in the region and brought to bear incredible political pressure.

Economically, culturally, and politically, Central America has been washed by repeated waves of foreign influence. Never isolated like Africa or the jungles of the Amazon Basin, its great ancient cultures were in decline before the European Conquest and were easy prey for the economic and cultural exploitation of Spain. It is today a melange of various African, Amerindian, and European cultures with, for the most part, only the Spanish language and the Catholic church to give it a sense of unity. And even Spanish is not universal, as thousands of Central Americans prefer to speak English or indigenous dialects. And as the coasts of Central America and its placement on the globe have exposed it to the outside world, its mountains have hindered communication within.

The Barrier Mountains

The overwhelming geographic fact of life in Central America is the continuous, relentless chain of mountains that dominates nearly every republic. The mountains that run the north–south length of the isthmus are volcanic and young. There are more than 20 active volcanoes in the region. These pressure points of geothermal energy constantly threaten havoc, but ironically it is the rich ash of volcanic eruptions that have given Central American soil its legendary fertility. Virtually the entire region is an active earthquake zone, and on numerous occasions (as recently as 1976 for Guatemala City), large sections of capital cities have had to be substantially rebuilt.

Over the centuries the mountains have served to divide population groups to the degree that today the cultural landscape of the region is more of a quilt than a melting pot. The terrain of the isthmus, which made roads and communications problematic right into the 1980s, can still be blamed for much of the economic underdevelopment of the region. Trade among the Central American republics has always been difficult, and attempts at regional political integration have failed repeatedly. It was only under President Kennedy's Alliance for Progress that a highway linking the republics of Guatemala, Honduras, El Salvador, Nicaragua, Costa Rica, and Panama was constructed. Belize is still cut off from the rest of Central America, with poor mountain roads across to Guatemala and irregular shipping down the coast to Honduras. Even within nations, the mountains and jungles of Central America have kept populations separate: Mountain Indians in Guatemala often speak no Spanish, and the peoples of the Caribbean coasts of Honduras and Nicaragua generally have more relatives in New Orleans or Miami than they do in Tegucigalpa or Managua.

The ocean has always been a reliable transit route for the Central American economies, and as a result, Europe and the United States have overwhelmingly influenced the isthmus. Intraregional contact remains a problem. An extractive, agricultural economic system has developed in which most economic activity involves the export of commodities and the import of goods and services from outside the region. Foreign economic powers have brought their cultural and political influences with them, and as a result, Central America today has profound difficulties with regional unity.

The mountains have also stood as a barrier to social equality and the development of the Central American people. When the riches of the Maya were looted and the gold and silver mines played out, the Spanish conquerors turned to export-oriented agriculture as the primary economic activity of the Central American colonies. The indigenous inhabitants of the land were driven to the mountains or barren coasts, where they scratched out whatever subsistence could be had. Even today it is on the coasts and in the highest mountains that one finds concentrations of native inhabitants. The Spanish built their plantations on the richest soil, and the Indians came down to work these fields as day laborers. Indigo, cacao, and then sugar, cotton, coffee, tobacco, and bananas were the primary crops. Few of these products are actually cultivated to feed the people of Central America.

The struggle over land has been at the root of most Central American conflicts in the 500 years since the arrival of the first Europeans, and it remains the principal cause of the struggle today. Early in its history, Central America divided into two distinct classes of people—those who had the land, and those who worked the land on their behalf.

The Receding Forests

The Caribbean and Pacific coasts, the high mountain cloud forests, even the supernatural desolation of the volcanoes in Central America, have a transcendent quality. The popular conception of Central America is of jungle, dense with color and the omnipresent roar of insects, reptiles, and multicolored birds.

Despite this fantastic popular view, the hand of man is everywhere apparent. Central America has a dense and rapidly growing population. Beyond the agro-industrial tracts of bananas, cotton, and coffee, most agriculture is of a rudimentary nature. Agriculture is principally of the slash-and-burn type—the most primitive form of planting on earth. Land is cleared, trees cut down, and the biomass is burned. The soil, often deceptively meager under the canopy of natural growth, rapidly loses its nutrients as minerals are leached away. The patch of land is then abandoned for another. Scrub weeds take over and underfed cattle graze where forests once stood. This type of destruction is complicated by the need to cultivate even extremely steep tracts of land to keep up with the demands of a rapidly growing population. The slash-and-burn technique produces alarming erosion and land destruction from which there is little hope of recovery.

Belize was once a logging colony where fine hardwoods like mahogany were harvested for nearly two centuries. As a result, much of the nation was covered by a meager scrub of gnarled trees and undergrowth. Now, however, the land is starting to recover, and forests cover some 60% of the area. In some countries, overcultivation and erosion are complicated by rocketing populations, which further tax the exhausted soil. Water tables are dropping at dangerous rates, and international aid agencies finance the digging of ever-deeper wells to perform rudimentary irrigation. The rain forests that once characterized the isthmus are, sadly, vanishing. In northern Costa Rica the pressure comes from large-scale cattle ranching, which produces cheap meat for American fast-food chains. In northern Guatemala and southern Mexico population pressures are driving subsistence farmers farther and farther into the wilderness in search of new land to slash and burn. The destruction of natural habitats for wildlife in the region is driving many species of animals, notably exotic birds and wildcats, to the brink of extinction.

The struggle over land feeds this Central American conflict, too. Since the best lands are occupied by the tiny minority of the population that controls the national economics, it is politically expedient to encourage peasant occupation of unused wilderness lands. Throughout the isthmus there are unoccupied lands with seemingly great agricultural potential. But, on closer inspection, these rain forests and mountains are ill-suited to commercial development. Their occupation merely hastens the ecological crisis.

Central American People

Central America is an ethnic patchwork—a blend of virtually every racial type known to the New World. A foundation of indigenous population built upon by waves of European, Afro-Caribbean, Middle Eastern, and even Asian immigration has created a modern mixture of races known as the mestizo.

The indigenous population of pre-Conquest Central America was in itself a blend of Indians from North and South America. Mezoamerican Indians were the product of highly developed, often urban cultures. The Olmecs, Toltecs, and Aztecs of Mexico and the Maya of Guatemala, Belize, Honduras, and El Salvador are examples of advanced Indian groups living in developed, hierarchical states. Indians migrating north from South America included the Chibcha of Colombia; the Cuna, Chocó, and Guaymí of Panama; the Huetares, Borucas, and Chorutegas of Costa Rica; and the Rama, Suma, and Miskito of Nicaragua. These groups lived in less complex societies that were based on hunting, primitive agriculture, and fishing. Between these two distinct groups were the Lenca, Jicaque, and Paya of Honduras and El Salvador.

The Spanish who settled in Central America soon subdivided into various social strata founded on degrees of racial purity and even place of birth. The Spanish crown dictated that only the *peninsulares* born in Spain could occupy key posts such as governors, judges, and administrators, and these Spaniards came to monopolize wealth and power. The Creoles, born in the colonies, were relegated to inferior positions, but eventually had their day when independence destroyed the aristocracy.

Continuing down the social ladder of colonial Central America were the mestizos, who soon came to represent the majority. The mestizos fell in where the "pure" bloods left off—in small business and small-scale plantation farming. For the most part, they spoke Spanish, culturally embraced Europe, and passed social aggression down the scale to the full-blood Indians, who were held in contempt by all. The Indians served as serfs and slaves, oppressed and put down by every religious, political, and economic institution created by colonialism.

Indians in Central America, even in the present day, have had to make a bitter choice in their lives—to live in Indian communities and withdraw from advancement along the economic scale or to ignore their cultural heritage by assuming the Spanish language and European dress, abandoning traditional lands and moving to urban areas, and even discarding their indigenous names. This choice between isolation and assimilation is increasingly evident in Central America as Indian communities continue to languish in social and economic poverty.

Africa also lives in Central America—in the thousands of black Central Americans, the vast majority of whom live on the Caribbean coast of the isthmus. Blacks were first brought to the region in the 16th century when indigenous slave populations working the mines and plantations of the colonies needed to be replenished. Later groups of blacks from the West Indies were brought to the isthmus for plantation work or, in the case of Panama, for large-scale engineering projects. Many of these black Central Americans speak English as their primary language.

Blacks in the coastal region have intermingled with indigenous groups. The Miskito, Suma, and Rama Indians of Nicaragua are examples of this. A smaller subgroup are the Black Caribs of Belize, Honduras, and Nicaragua, the product of a racial mix of Africans and Carib Indians on the island of Saint Vincent, who were exported en masse by the British to Central America in the late 18th century.

Various new strains have been added to this mixture. Asians are evident in virtually every Central American city. European-descended Jews are a small but economically dynamic ethnic group, as are the Palestinians sprinkled throughout the region. North Americans of various ethnicities are evident in every Central American nation.

Central America's geography is a mirror of its multiracial history. Guatemala today is overwhelmingly indigenous, with the minority of mestizos and whites concentrated in the cities. Belize is primarily black, with various blends in the principal cities and Maya communities in the south. Costa Rica is the only country in Central America with a largely "pure" European ethnicity.

1 Essential Information

Before You Go

Government Tourist Offices

Costa Rica, Guatemala, and Belize all have their own U.S.-based tourist board. *See* Before You Go in the individual country chapters that follow.

The Department of State's **Citizens Emergency Center** issues Consular Information Sheets, which cover crime, security, and health risks as well as embassy locations, entry requirements, currency regulations, and other routine matters. (Travel Warnings, which counsel travelers to avoid a country entirely, are issued in extreme cases.) For the latest travel advisories, stop in at any passport office, consulate, or embassy; call the interactive hotline (tel. 202/647–5225); or, with your PC's modem, tap into the Bureau of Consular Affairs' computer bulletin board (tel. 202/647–9225).

Tours and Packages

Should you buy your travel arrangements to Central America packaged or make them yourself? There are advantages either way. Buying packaged arrangements saves you money, particularly if you can find a program that includes exactly the features you want. You also get a pretty good idea of what your trip will cost from the outset. For most destinations, you have two options: fully escorted tours and independent packages. There is a wide variety of independent packages for every budget and taste, whether you want river trips, Mayan expeditions, or rain-forest exploration, as well as a number of special-interest programs.

Travel agents are your best source of recommendations. They will have the largest selection, and the cost to you is the same as buying direct. Whatever program you ultimately choose, be sure to find out exactly what is included: taxes, tips, transfers, meals, baggage handling, ground transportation, entertainment, excursions, sports or recreation (and rental equipment for any sport you plan to pursue). Ask about the level of hotel used, its location, the size of its rooms, the kind of beds, and its amenities, such as pool, room service, or programs for children, if they're important to you.

Find out the operator's cancellation penalties. Nearly everyone charges them, and the only way to avoid them is to buy trip-cancellation insurance (*see* Insurance, *below*). Also ask about the single supplement, a surcharge assessed to solo travelers. Some operators do not make you pay it if you agree to be matched up with a roommate of the same sex, even if one is not found by departure time. Remember that a program that has features you won't use, whether for rental sporting equipment or discounted museum admissions, may not be the most cost-efficient choice for you. Note that when you are pricing different packages, it sometimes pays to purchase the same arrangements separately, as when a rock-bottom promotional airfare is being offered. Base your choice on what's available at your budget for the destinations you want to visit.

Tour Companies

Listed below is a sample of the tours and packages available. Most tour operators request that you book through a travel agent (there is no additional charge for doing so). For additional resources, contact your travel agent or tourist office.

In the United States **Forum Travel** (91 Gregory La., No. 21, Pleasant Hill, CA 94523, tel. 510/671–2900) invites you to share the "Belize Explorer," a one-week or 12-day tour that includes overnight camping and visits to classic Mayan sites, rain forests, caves and waterfalls, barrier reefs, and more.

Gadabout Tours (700 Tahquitz Canyon Way, Palm Springs, CA 92262, tel. 619/325–5556 or 800/952–5068) offers an eight-day tour of Costa Rica, including visits to rain forests, the Poás volcano, and the Ujarras Mayan ruins.

Tara Tours (6595 NW 36th St., Suite 306-A, Miami, FL 33166, tel. 305/871–1246 or 800/327–0080) follows the "Mayan Path" for an eight-day tour that visits Guatemala City, Lake Atitlán, Antigua, and the Mayan pyramids of Tikal.

Travcoa (Box 2630, Newport Beach, CA 92658–2630, tel. 714/476–2800 or 800/992–2004) offers a 22-day tour of Costa Rica, Honduras, and Guatemala, including a rail trip through lush rain forests and visits to Turtuguero and the Mayan sites of Copan and Tikal. A 15-day tour of Guatemala and the Yucatán is also available.

In the United Kingdom **Bales Tours Ltd.** (Bales House, Junction Rd., Dorking, Surrey RH4 3HB, tel. 306/76881) has a 10-day "Highlights of Guatemala" tour and longer tours that also take in Mayan sites in Honduras and the Yucatán.

British Airways Holidays (Atlantic House, Hazelwick Ave., Three Bridges, Crawley, West Sussex RH10 1NP, tel. 0293/518022) offers a 10-night discovery tour of Guatemala.

Exodus Expeditions (9 Weir Rd., Balham, London SW12 0LT, tel. 081/675–5550) offers a two-week Costa Rica expedition exploring the jungles, rivers, and coastline, and a 24-day Ruta Maya adventure camping tour of the landscapes and Mayan remains of Mexico, Guatemala, and Belize.

Steamond Latin American Travel (278 Battersea Park Rd., London SW11 3BS, tel. 071/978–5500) has packages to Belize, an 8-day Costa Rican Scenery tour, and longer tours that include Guatemala, Mexico, and Honduras.

Special-Interest Tours Conservationists point out that the Central American governments don't have the resources to enforce existing laws that protect the environment, or even to effectively manage their national parks and protected areas. Environmentalists are looking for ways to motivate people to protect the forests, and the best way they've found is to teach those responsible for the destruction that conservation pays. Promoting "ecotourism" is a potential means of making conservation profitable, the idea being that as more tourists visit a country's natural areas, the government and rural dwellers will become more interested in protecting them.

Many tourists want to do more than just visit Central America's natural wonders; they would like to help assure that those wild areas don't disappear before their children or grandchildren have a chance to see them. Some of the basic rules that tourists and tour operators should follow are: don't disturb wildlife, don't litter, and don't eat or purchase wild animals or products made from them. Since most tourists head to the same national parks, it helps to travel to less-visited areas, thereby decreasing the human impact on any one area, and to enjoy a more natural experience. It is also important to make sure that your visit benefits the people who live near the wilderness, by using local guides or services, visiting local restaurants, or buying local handicrafts or fruits.

Certain tour operators are very interested in protecting the tropical nature they take people to see, and they arrange tours that benefit local conservation efforts, sometimes even donating part of their profits to environmental groups. The Ecotourism Society (Box 755, North Bennington, VT 05257, tel. 802/447–2121) can provide some information about tour operators in the United States who run environmentally friendly tours to Central America, as can the Center for Responsible Tourism in Costa Rica. The Department for Responsible Tourism (San José, Costa Rica, tel. 33–7112) offers a similar service within that country. You can also donate money to environmental groups working to protect the region's natural treasures. Tour operators in each country may be able to suggest local groups that need your financial support, or if you want to make a tax-deductible donation, Conservation International, the World Wildlife Fund, and the Nature Conservancy are aiding ecological efforts in the isthmus.

See individual chapters for information on specific tours offered within each country. *See below* for operators in the United States.

Adventure **Journeys** (Box 2658, Ann Arbor, MI 48106, tel. 800/255–8735, fax 303/665–2945) features WAWA (Week-After-Week), small-group, nature- and culture-oriented adventure trips, including eight-day guided explorations of Costa Rica and Belize. **Lost World Adventures** (1189 Autumn Ridge Dr., Marietta, GA 30066, tel. 404/971–8586 or 800/999–0558) specializes in South American and Central American adventures, including mountain biking, deep-sea fishing, and scuba diving.

Archaeology The **American Museum of Natural History** (Central Park West at 79th St., New York, NY 10024, tel. 212/769–5700 or 800/462–8687 outside NY) has all-inclusive discovery tours of the reefs, the rain forests, and Mayan ruins throughout the region. **Archaeological Tours** (271 Madison Ave., New York, NY 10016, tel. 212/986–3054, fax 212/370–1561) explores the scenic splendors of Belize and Guatemala, with visits to famous Mayan temples and rarely visited ruins, ongoing excavation sites, colorful market towns, and colonial villages.

Canoeing **American Wilderness Experience** (Box 1486, Boulder, CO 80306, tel. 303/444–2622 or 800/444–0099) organizes canoeing and kayaking explorations into the lushest and least-explored corner of tropical Costa Rica along the Pacific coast. **Battenkill Canoe, Ltd.** (Box 65, Arlington, VT 05250, tel. 802/362–2800 or 800/421–5268) specializes in river trips through north-central Costa Rica.

Diving **Tropical Adventures** (111 2nd Ave. N, Seattle, WA 98109, tel. 206/441–3483 or 800/247–3483) has dive packages to Cocos Island (the world's largest uninhabited island) off the coast of Costa Rica and to Belize's Barrier Reef.

Environment **Earthwatch** (680 Mount Auburn St., Watertown, MA 02272, tel. 617/926–8000) recruits volunteers to serve in its EarthCorps as short-term assistants to scientists on research expeditions. **National Audubon Society** (700 Broadway, New York, NY 10003, tel. 212/979–3000, fax 212/979–3188) explores the exotic wonders of Central America's Pacific coast on a cruise, with stops in Antigua in Guatemala, and Poás and Santa Rosa national parks in Costa Rica. **Lindblad's Special Expeditions** (720 5th Ave., New York, NY 10019, tel. 212/765–7740 or 800/762–0003) uses smaller (usually no more than 110-passenger) expedition ships on journeys exploring the tropical rain forests of Costa Rica, Belize's Barrier Reef, and the beautiful islands and remote shorelines of the Mayan coast. **Oceanic Society Expeditions** (Ft. Mason Center, Bldg. E, San Francisco, CA 94123, tel. 800/326–7491) provides specialized nature expeditions focusing on educational experiences with expert naturalists. **Tauck Tours** (11 Wilton Rd., Box 5027, Wilton, CT 06881, tel. 800/468–2825) combines land exploration and small-ship cruising of Costa Rica and Panama on a nine-day itinerary in a natural wonderland.

Horseback **Fits Equestrian** (685 Lateen Rd., Solvang, CA 93463, tel. 805/688–
Riding 9494 or 800/666–3487) has six-, nine-, and 11-day jungle tours based in Belize, combining horseback riding with visits to archaeological sites, swimming at Five Sister Falls, and shopping across the border in Guatemala.

Package Deals for Independent Travelers

American Airlines/Latour (tel. 800/832–8383) offers packages for a minimum of three days to destinations in Costa Rica, such as San José, La Cruz, Puntarenas, Jacó Beach, and Quepos. The packages include airfare, accommodations, and sightseeing options such as island cruises, white-water rafting, and excursions to a wildlife reserve.

Best of Belize (Box 1266, Point Reyes, CA 94956, tel. 415/663–8022) offers a variety of packages to sites in Belize, as well as personalized itineraries, including diving expeditions, rain-forest excursions, and a trip to Mayan sites.

Brendan Tours (15137 Califa St., Van Nuys, CA 91411, tel. 818/785–9696 or 800/421–8446) offers four different itineraries for one-week "freelance tours" to Costa Rica, as well as packages to Guatemala for four or eight days. The trips combine plenty of free time with organized activities. Packages to Belize for a minimum of three days are also available.

Cavalcade Tours (450 Harmon Meadow Blvd., Secaucus, NJ 07096, tel. 201/617–8922 or 800/356–2405) has a six-night package to Costa Rica that includes three nights in a five-star hotel in San José and three nights on the Pacific coast. Included in the fee are use of golf courses, horseback riding, snorkeling, round-trip airfare, a city tour of San José, and transfers.

Costa Sol International (1717 N. Bayshore Dr., Suite 3333, Miami, FL 33132, tel. 800/245–8420) offers independent tours and à la carte "discover packages" to Costa Rica, from three nights to two weeks. Optional sightseeing tours and activities are available.

Forum Travel (*see* Tour Companies, *above*) offers many exciting packages to Costa Rica, Belize, and Guatemala, including "Eco-adventures," bed-and-breakfast stays, tours with naturalists, "design-it-yourself" packages, and the option to string together two- and three-day expeditions to a variety of sites.

Magnum Americas (718 Washington Ave., Box 1560, Detroit Lakes, MN 56503, tel. 218/847–3012 or 800/447–2931) will customize itineraries to Belize, including dive and snorkeling trips, rafting, caving, and inland excursions to Mayan sites in Belize and Guatemala.

PCI Tours (Box 4324, Homestead, FL 33092, tel. 305/242–9504 or 800/255–2508) will customize packages for independent travelers to Costa Rica and Guatemala.

Tara Tours (*see* Tour Companies, *above*) offers a tremendous variety of packages to Guatemala, Belize, and Costa Rica, including a five-day "Mayan Odyssey," an eight-day tour of "Markets and Colonial sites," and other excursions to the beaches, islands, and mountains of Costa Rica and Belize.

Travel Belize (637B S. Broadway, Boulder, CO 80303, tel. 303/494–7797 or 800/626–3483) offers myriad inland and island packages for three to eight days. Hotel, meals, and sightseeing options are available, as well as day trips to destinations in Guatemala.

When to Go

The Central American climate is marked by a two-season year. The rainy season, called *invierno* (winter), lasts April through November; the dry season, called *verano* (summer), runs November through April. During the rainy season the vegetation is at its most lush and gorgeous, but many roads—especially nonasphalt ones—are washed out. The best time to visit Central America is at the tail end of the rainy season, when everything is still green and most parts of the region are accessible. Most visitors head to Central America during the dry season; consequently, hotel and restaurant prices are at their highest during this time. If you want to escape the tourist crowds and the tourist prices and don't mind getting very wet, visit during the rainy season. Temperatures in the rainy season are virtually the same as those in the dry season. Keep in mind that during the rainy season some restaurants may close and hotels may offer limited facilities; but reservations are easy to get, even at top establishments, and you'll have the Mayan ruins and beaches to yourself. Note that Guatemala's busiest time of the year is around Holy Week, from Palm Sunday to Easter Sunday, and that hotels in Antigua, Panajachel, and Chichicastenango book up months ahead of time.

Climate Central America's climate varies greatly between the lowlands and the mountains. Guatemala's Caribbean coast, for example, sees sweltering humid weather with soaring temperatures while the mountains in the northern Western Highlands (as with Costa Rica's and Belize's peaks) can have downright chilly evenings. Bring a light sweater or jacket if you plan to spend a lot of time in the mountains. Central America's rainy season is marked by sporadic downpours that occur without warning. Generally, rainfall is heavier in the afternoon than in the morning, so you may want to do the majority of your sightseeing and shopping in the morning hours, leaving your afternoons flexible. Belize has a particularly heavy rainy season. In the far south, you'll need an umbrella most of the year (as much as 160 inches of rain fall annually) except during a brief respite between February and April. On the cays, the wet season is often accompanied by lashing northerly winds known in Creole as Joe North. In a bad year, Joe North can turn into Hurricane Hattie.

Central America's tropical temperatures generally hover between 70°F and 85°F. The high humidity, however, is the true sweat culprit. Remember to drink plenty of bottled water to avoid dehydration.

For More Information For current weather conditions for cities in the United States and abroad, plus the local time and helpful travel tips, call the **Weather Channel Connection** (tel. 900/WEATHER; 95¢ per minute) from a touch-tone phone.

What to Pack

Pack light because baggage carts are scarce at airports and luggage restrictions are tight.

Clothing Your best bet is to bring casual, comfortable, hand-washable clothing. T-shirts and shorts are acceptable near the beach and in heavily touristed areas. Loose-fitting long-sleeved shirts and pants are good to have in the smaller towns (where immodest attire is frowned upon) and to protect your skin from the ferocious sun and mosquitoes. Bring a large hat to block the sun from your face and neck. If you're heading into the mountains—the Guatemalan highlands, for example—tote a light sweater and a jacket because the nights and early mornings can be chilly. A pair of sturdy sneakers or hiking boots is essential if you plan to do a lot of sightseeing and hiking. Sandals or other footwear that lets your feet breathe is good for strolling about town.

Miscellaneous Bring an extra pair of eyeglasses or contact lenses in your carry-on luggage. If you have a health problem that requires a prescription drug, pack enough to last the duration of the trip or have your doctor write a prescription using the drug's generic name because brand names vary from country to country. Always carry prescription drugs in their original packaging to avoid problems with customs officials, and don't pack these drugs in luggage that you plan to check; your bags may go astray. Also pack a list of the offices that supply refunds for lost or stolen traveler's checks.

Electricity The electrical current in Costa Rica and parts of Belize is 220 volts, 50 cycles alternating current (AC); Guatemala and the United States run on 110-volt, 60-cycle AC current. Unlike wall outlets in the United States, which accept plugs with two flat prongs, some outlets in Belize take continental-type plugs, with two round prongs. Outlets in Costa Rica use U.S.-style plugs but run at 220V. You'll need an adapter (*see below*) even though the sockets look like 110V outlets. If you plan to take electric appliances to Central America, inquire with your hotel or the tourist office about the local current and outlets.

Adapters, Converters, Transformers To use U.S.-made electric appliances in countries with a different current, you'll need an adapter plug. Unless the appliance is dual-voltage and made for travel, you'll also need a converter. Hotels sometimes have 110-volt outlets for low-wattage appliances marked "For Shavers Only" near the sink; don't use them for a high-wattage appliance like a hair dryer. If you're traveling with an older laptop computer, carry a transformer. New laptop computers are auto-sensing, operating equally well on 110 and 220 volts, so you need only the appropriate adapter plug. For a copy of the free brochure "Foreign Electricity Is No Deep Dark Secret," send a stamped, self-addressed envelope to adapter-converter manufacturer the **Franzus Company** (Customer Service, Dept. B50, Murtha Industrial Park, Box 142, Beacon Falls, CT 06403, tel. 203/723–6664).

Luggage Regulations Airline baggage allowances depend on the airline, the route, and the class of your ticket; ask in advance. In general, on domestic flights and international flights between the United States and foreign destinations, you are entitled to check two bags—neither exceeding 158 centimeters, or 62 inches (length + width + height) or weighing more than 32 kilograms (70 pounds). A third piece may be brought aboard; its total dimensions are generally limited to less than 114 centimeters (45 inches) so it will fit easily under the seat in front of you or in the overhead compartment. In the United States, the Federal Aviation Administration (FAA) gives airlines broad latitude for carry-on allowances and tailors limits to different aircraft and operational conditions. Charges for excess, oversize, or overweight pieces vary.

If you are flying between two foreign destinations, note that baggage allowances may be determined not by piece but by weight— generally 40 kilograms (88 pounds) of luggage in first class, 30 kilograms (66 pounds) in business class, and 20 kilograms (44 pounds) in economy. If your flight between two cities abroad *connects* with your transatlantic or transpacific flight, the piece method still applies.

Safeguarding Your Luggage Before leaving home, itemize your bags' contents and their worth in case they go astray. To minimize that risk, tag them inside and out with your name, address, and phone number. (If you use your home address, cover it so that potential thieves can't see it.) Put a copy of your itinerary inside each bag so that you can be easily tracked. At check-in, make sure that the tag attached by baggage handlers bears the correct three-letter code for your destination. If your bags do not arrive with you or if you detect damage, immediately file a written report with the airline before you leave the airport.

Taking Money Abroad

Traveler's Checks Traveler's checks are preferable in metropolitan centers, although you'll need cash in rural areas and small towns. The most widely recognized are **American Express, Citicorp, Diners Club, Thomas Cook,** and **Visa,** which are sold by major commercial banks. Both American Express and Thomas Cook issue checks that can be countersigned and used by you or your traveling companion. Typically the issuing company or the bank at which you make your purchase charges 1% to 3% of the checks' face value as a fee. Some foreign banks charge as much as 20% of the face value as the fee for cashing traveler's checks in a foreign currency. Buy a few checks in small denominations to cash toward the end of your trip, so you won't be left with excess foreign currency. Record the numbers of checks as you spend them, and keep this list separate from the checks.

Currency Exchange Banks offer the most favorable exchange rates. If you use currency-exchange booths at airports, rail and bus stations, hotels, stores, and privately run exchange firms, you'll typically get less favorable rates, but you may find the hours more convenient.

You can get good rates and avoid long lines at airport currency-exchange booths by getting a small amount of currency at **Thomas Cook Currency Services** (630 5th Ave., New York, NY 10111, tel. 212/757–6915 or 800/223–7373 for locations in major metropolitan areas throughout U.S.) or **Ruesch International** (tel. 800/424–2923 for locations) before you depart. Check with your travel agent to make sure that the currency of your destination country can be imported.

Getting Money from Home

Cash Machines Although automated-teller machines (ATMs) are proliferating worldwide, they are not readily available in Central America. **Cirrus** and **Plus** are the two biggest international networks, and they may expand service to Central America soon. If you do come across an ATM machine, you can use your bank card to withdraw money from an account and get cash advances on a credit-card account if your card has been programmed with a personal identification number, or PIN. Check in advance for limits on withdrawals and cash advances within specified periods. Ask whether your bank-card or credit-card PIN will need to be reprogrammed for use in the area you'll be visiting. Four digits are commonly used overseas. (Note that Discover is accepted only in the United States.) On cash advances you are charged interest from the day you receive the money from ATMs as well as from tellers. Although transaction fees for ATM withdrawals abroad may be higher than fees for withdrawals at home, Cirrus and Plus exchange rates are excellent because they are based on wholesale rates offered only by major banks. They also may be referred to abroad as "a withdrawal from a credit account."

Wiring Money You don't have to be a cardholder to send or receive a **MoneyGram from American Express** for up to $10,000. Go to a MoneyGram agent in retail and convenience stores and American Express travel offices, and pay up to $1,000 with a credit card and anything over that in cash. You are allowed a free long-distance call to give the transaction code to your intended recipient, who only needs to present identification and the reference number to the nearest MoneyGram agent to pick up the cash. MoneyGram agents are located in more than 70 countries (call 800/926–9400 for locations). Fees range from 3% to 10%, depending on the amount and your method of payment.

You can also use **Western Union;** to wire money, bring either cash or a cashier's check to the nearest office, or call and use your MasterCard or Visa. Money sent from the United States or Canada will be available for pickup at agent locations in Costa Rica, Belize, and Guatemala within minutes. Once the money enters the system, it can be picked up at *any* of 22,000 locations (call 800/325–6000 for the one nearest you).

Long-Distance Calling

AT&T, MCI, and Sprint have several services that make calling home or your office more affordable and convenient when you're traveling. Use one of them to avoid pricey hotel surcharges. The **AT&T** Calling Card (tel. 800/225–5288) and the AT&T Universal Card (tel. 800/662–7759) give you access to the service. With AT&T's USADirect (tel. 800/874–4000 for codes in countries you'll be visiting), you can reach an AT&T operator with a local or toll-free call. **MCI's** Call USA (MCI Customer Service, tel. 800/444–4444) allows that service from 85 countries or from country to country via MCI WorldReach. **Sprint** Express (tel. 800/793–1153) has a toll-free number that travelers abroad can dial to reach a Sprint operator in the United States.

Passports and Visas

If your passport is lost or stolen abroad, report the loss immediately to the nearest embassy or consulate and to the local police. If you can provide the consular officer with the information contained in the passport, he or she will usually be able to issue you a new passport promptly. For this reason, keep a photocopy of the data page of your passport separate from your money and traveler's checks. Also leave a photocopy with a relative or friend at home.

U.S. Citizens All U.S. citizens, even infants, need a valid passport and a return ticket to enter Costa Rica or Belize for stays of up to 90 days in Costa Rica or 30 days in Belize. U.S. citizens require a valid passport with either a tourist card or a visa to enter Guatemala. Tourist cards can be purchased for $5 through airlines serving Guatemala, through

Guatemalan consulates, or at the border. To obtain a visa, valid for one year, contact the Guatemalan embassy (2220 R St. NW, Washington, DC 20008, tel. 202/745–4952) or the nearest consulate.

You can pick up new and renewal passport application forms at any of the 13 U.S. Passport Agency offices and at some post offices and courthouses. Although passports are usually mailed within four weeks of your application's receipt, allow five weeks or more from April through the summer. Call the Department of State Office of Passport Services' information line (tel. 202/647–0518) for fees, documentation requirements, and other details.

Canadian Citizens Canadian citizens need a valid passport and a return ticket to enter Costa Rica or Belize for stays of up to 90 days in Costa Rica, 30 days in Belize. Canadian citizens require a valid passport with either a tourist card or a visa to enter Guatemala. Tourist cards can be purchased for $5 through airlines serving Guatemala, through Guatemalan consulates, or at the border.

Passport application forms are available at 23 regional passport offices as well as post offices and travel agencies. For both a first or a subsequent passport, you must apply in person. Children under 16 may be included on a parent's passport but must have their own to travel alone. Passports are valid for five years and are usually mailed within two weeks of an application's receipt. For fees, documentation requirements, and other information in English or French, call the passport office (tel. 514/283–2152 or 800/567–6868).

U.K. Citizens Citizens of the United Kingdom need a valid passport to enter Costa Rica or Belize. U.K. citizens visiting Guatemala require a passport and either a tourist card or a visa to enter Guatemala. Tourist cards can be purchased for $5 through airlines serving Guatemala, through Guatemalan consulates, or at the border. Visa forms are available from the Guatemala Tourist Board (13 Fawcett St., London SW10 9HN, tel. 071/351–3042).

Applications for new and renewal passports are available from main post offices as well as the six passport offices located in Belfast, Glasgow, Liverpool, London, Newport, and Peterborough. You may apply in person at all passport offices or by mail to all except the London office. Children under 16 may travel on an accompanying parent's passport. All passports are valid for 10 years. Allow a month for processing.

Customs and Duties

On Arrival *See* individual country chapters for specifics on customs information.

Duty-free allowances for visitors entering Belize include 3 liters of liquor and one carton of cigarettes. All electrical appliances, cameras, jewelry, or other items of value must be declared at the point of entry.

Visitors entering Costa Rica may bring in 500 mg of tobacco, three liters of wine or spirits, two kilos of sweets and chocolates, and the equivalent of $100 worth of merchandise. Two cameras, six rolls of film, binoculars and electrical items for personal use only are also allowed; these will be noted in your passport at customs and must be in your possession when you leave the country.

Duty-free allowances for visitors entering Guatemala include 500 mg of tobacco, 3 liters of spirits, and 2 bottles of perfume.

Returning Because Belize, Costa Rica, and Guatemala are part of the Caribbe-
Home an Basin Initiative's beneficiary countries, the customs exemption
U.S. Customs for returning U.S. citizens is raised from $400 to $600.

If you've been out of the country for at least 48 hours and haven't
already used the exemption or any part of it in the past 30 days, you
may bring home $600 worth of foreign goods duty-free. So can each
member of your family, regardless of age; and your exemptions may
be pooled, so that one of you can bring in more if another brings in
less. A flat 10% duty applies to the next $1,000 worth of goods; above
$1,600, the rate varies with the merchandise. (If the 48-hour or 30-
day limit applies, your duty-free allowance drops to $25, which may
not be pooled.) Please note that these are *general* rules, applicable
to most countries; more generous allowances are in effect for certain
developing countries that benefit from the Generalized System of
Preferences (GSP). These include Costa Rica, Belize, and Guatemala, but the GSP program is set to expire at the end of September
1994.

Travelers who are 21 or older may bring back 1 liter of alcohol duty-
free, provided the beverage laws of the state through which they reenter the United States allow for it. In addition, 100 non-Cuban cigars and 200 cigarettes are permitted, regardless of your age.
Antiques and works of art more than 100 years old are duty-free.

Gifts valued at less than $50 may be mailed to the United States
duty-free, with a limit of one package per day per addressee, and do
not count as part of your exemption (do not send alcohol or tobacco
products or perfume valued at more than $5). Mark the package
"Unsolicited Gift," and write the nature of the gift and its retail value on the outside; most reputable stores will handle the mailing for
you.

For a copy of "Know Before You Go," a free brochure detailing what
you may and may not bring back to the United States, rates of duty,
and other pointers, contact the **U.S. Customs Service** (Box 7407,
Washington, DC 20044, tel. 202/927–6724). A copy of "GSP and the
Traveler" is available from the same source.

Canadian Once per calendar year, when you've been out of Canada for at least
Customs seven days, you may bring in C$300 worth of goods duty-free. If
you've been away fewer than seven days but more than 48 hours, the
duty-free exemption drops to C$100 but can be claimed any number
of times (as can a C$20 duty-free exemption for absences of 24 hours
or more). You cannot combine the yearly and 48-hour exemptions,
use the $300 exemption only partially (to save the balance for a later
trip), or pool exemptions with family members. Goods claimed under the C$300 exemption may follow you by mail; those claimed un-
der the lesser exemptions must accompany you.

Alcohol and tobacco products may be included in the yearly and 48-
hour exemptions but not in the 24-hour exemption. If you meet the
age requirements of the province through which you reenter Canada, you may bring in, duty-free, 1.14 liters (40 imperial ounces) of
wine or liquor *or* two dozen 12-ounce cans or bottles of beer or ale. If
you are 16 or older, you may bring in, duty-free, 200 cigarettes, 50
cigars or cigarillos, and 400 tobacco sticks or 400 grams of manufactured tobacco. Alcohol and tobacco must accompany you on your
return.

An unlimited number of gifts valued up to C$60 each may be mailed
to Canada duty-free. These do not count as part of your exemption.

Label the package "Unsolicited Gift—Value Under \$60." Alcohol and tobacco are excluded.

For more information, including details of duties on items that exceed your duty-free limit, ask the **Revenue Canada Customs and Excise and Taxation Department** (2265 St. Laurent Blvd. S, Ottawa, Ont., K1G 4K3, tel. 613/957–0275) for a copy of the free brochure "I Declare/Je Déclare."

U.K. Customs From countries outside the European Community such as Costa Rica, Belize, and Guatemala, you may import duty-free 200 cigarettes, 100 cigarillos, 50 cigars or 250 grams of tobacco; 1 liter of spirits or 2 liters of fortified or sparkling wine; 2 liters of still table wine; 60 milliliters of perfume; 250 milliliters of toilet water; plus £136 worth of other goods, including gifts and souvenirs.

For further information or a copy of "A Guide for Travellers," which details standard customs procedures as well as what you may bring into the United Kingdom from abroad, contact **HM Customs and Excise** (Dorset House, Stamford St., London SE1 9PY, tel. 071/928–3344).

Traveling with Cameras, Camcorders, and Laptops

About Film and Cameras If your camera is new or if you haven't used it for a while, shoot and develop a few test rolls of film before leaving home. Store film in a cool, dry place—never in the car's glove compartment or on the shelf under the rear window.

Airport security X-rays generally aren't harmful to film with ISO below 400. To protect your film, carry it with you in a clear plastic bag and ask for a hand inspection. Such requests are honored at U.S. airports, and are up to the inspector abroad. Don't depend on a lead-lined bag to protect film in checked luggage—the airline may increase the radiation to see what's inside. Call the **Kodak Information Center** (tel. 800/242–2424) for details.

About Camcorders Before your trip, put camcorders through their paces, invest in a skylight filter to protect the lens, and check all the batteries. Most newer camcorders are equipped with batteries that can be recharged with a universal or worldwide AC adapter charger (or multivoltage converter) usable whether the voltage is 110 or 220. All that's needed is the appropriate plug.

About Videotape Videotape is not damaged by X-rays, but it may be harmed by the magnetic field of a walk-through metal detector, so ask for a hand-check. Airport security personnel may ask you to turn on the camcorder to prove that it's what it appears to be, so make sure the battery is charged.

About Laptops Security X-rays do not harm hard-disk or floppy-disk storage, but you may request a hand-check, at which point you may be asked to turn on the computer to prove that it is what it appears to be. (Check your battery before departure.) Most airlines allow you to use your laptop aloft except during takeoff and landing (so as not to interfere with navigation equipment). For international travel, register your foreign-made laptop with U.S. Customs as you leave the country. If your laptop is U.S.-made, call the consulate of the country you'll be visiting to find out whether it should be registered with customs upon arrival. Before departure, find out about repair facilities at your destination, and don't forget any transformer or adapter plug you may need (*see* Electricity, *above*).

Staying Healthy

Shots and Medications   The major health risk in Central America is posed by the contamination of drinking water and fresh fruit and vegetables by fecal matter, which causes the intestinal ailment known facetiously as "Montezuma's Revenge" and more mundanely as traveler's diarrhea. Fortunately it usually lasts only a day or two. Paregoric, a good antidiarrheal agent that dulls or eliminates abdominal cramps, does not require a doctor's prescription in Central America. Two drugs recommended by the National Institutes of Health for mild cases of diarrhea can be purchased over the counter: Pepto-Bismol and loperamide (Imodium). If you come down with the malady, rest as much as possible and drink lots of fluids (such as tea without milk—chamomile is a good folk remedy for diarrhea). In severe cases, rehydrate yourself with a salt-sugar mixture added to purified water (½ teaspoon salt and 4 tablespoons sugar per quart/liter of purified water). The best defense is a careful diet. Stay away from unbottled or unboiled water, as well as ice, uncooked food, and unpasteurized milk and milk products.

According to the Centers for Disease Control (CDC), Central America presents a limited risk of malaria, hepatitis A and B, dengue fever, typhoid fever, and rabies. Guatemala, much more so than Costa Rica and Belize, is where you should be careful. Travelers to the major tourist areas need not worry. However, if you plan to visit remote regions or stay for more than six weeks, check with the CDC's **International Travelers Hotline** (Center for Preventive Services, Division of Quarantine, Traveler's Health section, 1600 Clifton Rd., MSE03, Atlanta, GA 30333, tel. 404/332–4559). The hot line recommends chloroquine (Analen) as an antimalarial agent. Malaria-bearing mosquitoes bite at dusk and night, so travelers visiting susceptible regions should take mosquito nets, wear clothing that covers the body, and carry repellent containing Deet and a spray against flying insects for living and sleeping areas. No vaccine exists against dengue, so if this disease is in the area, travelers should use aerosol insecticides indoors as well as repellents against the mosquito.

Rabies is carried through dogs, so be alert around dogs that appear homeless. Guatemala, particularly in rural areas, has a large number of wild, potentially rabid dogs. In recent years, Peace Corps volunteers have been stationed near Guatemala's Lake Panajachel to vaccinate inhabitants against rabies. If you are bitten, immediately look for the dog or the dog's owner and contact a physician.

Children traveling to Central America should have current innoculations against measles, mumps, rubella, and polio. And scuba divers take note: PADI recommends that you do not dive and fly within a 24-hour period.

Finding a Doctor   The **International Association for Medical Assistance to Travellers** (IAMAT, 417 Center St., Lewiston, NY 14092, tel. 716/754–4883; 40 Regal Rd., Guelph, Ontario N1K 1B5; 57 Voirets, 1212 Grand-Lancy, Geneva, Switzerland) publishes a worldwide directory of English-speaking physicians whose qualifications meet IAMAT standards and who have agreed to treat members for a set fee. Membership is free.

Assistance Companies   Pretrip medical referrals, emergency evacuation or repatriation, 24-hour telephone hot lines for medical consultation, dispatch of medical personnel, relay of medical records, cash for emergencies, and other personal and legal assistance are among the services provided by several organizations specializing in medical assistance to travelers. Among them are **International SOS Assistance** (Box 11568, Philadelphia, PA 19116, tel. 215/244–1500 or 800/523–8930; Box 466, Pl. Bonaventure, Montréal, Qué. H5A 1C1, tel. 514/874–7674 or 800/363–0263), **Medex Assistance Corporation** (Box 10623, Baltimore, MD 21285, tel. 410/296–2530 or 800/874–9125), **Near Services** (450 Prairie Ave., Suite 101, Calumet City, IL 60409, tel. 708/868–6700 or 800/654–6700), and **Travel Assistance International** (1133 15th St. NW, Suite 400, Washington, DC 20005, tel. 202/331–1609 or 800/821–2828). Because these companies will also sell you death-and-dismemberment, trip-cancellation, and other insurance coverage, some overlap with travel-insurance policies is discussed under Insurance, *below.*

Publications *The Safe Travel Book* by Peter Savage ($12.95; Lexington Books, 866 3rd Ave., New York, NY 10022, tel. 212/702–4771 or 800/257–5755, fax 800/562–1272) is packed with handy lists and phone numbers to make your trip smooth. *Traveler's Medical Resource* by William W. Forgey ($19.95; ICS Books, Inc., 1 Tower Plaza, 107 E. 89th Ave., Merrillville, IN 45410, tel. 800/541–7323) is also an authoritative guide to care overseas.

Insurance

For U.S. Residents Most tour operators, travel agents, and insurance agents sell specialized health-and-accident, flight, trip-cancellation, and luggage insurance as well as comprehensive policies with some or all of these features. Before you make any purchase, review your existing health and homeowner policies to find out whether they cover expenses incurred while traveling.

Health-and-Accident Insurance Specific policy provisions of supplemental health-and-accident insurance for travelers include reimbursement for $1,000 to $150,000 worth of medical and/or dental expenses caused by an accident or illness during a trip. The personal-accident, or death-and-dismemberment, provision pays a lump sum to your beneficiaries if you die or to you if you lose one or more limbs or your eyesight; the lump sum awarded can range from $15,000 to $500,000. The medical-assistance provision may reimburse you for the cost of referrals, evacuation, or repatriation and other services, or it may automatically enroll you as a member of a particular medical-assistance company (*see* Assistance Companies, *above*).

Flight Insurance Often bought as a last-minute impulse item at airports, flight insurance pays a lump sum when a plane crashes to a beneficiary if the insured dies or sometimes to a surviving passenger who loses eyesight or a limb. Like most impulse buys, flight insurance is expensive and basically unnecessary. It supplements the airlines' coverage described in the limits-of-liability paragraphs on your ticket. Charging an airline ticket to a major credit card often automatically entitles you to coverage and may also embrace travel by bus, train, and ship.

Baggage Insurance In the event of loss, damage, or theft on international flights, airlines' liability is $20 per kilogram for checked baggage (roughly about $640 per 70-pound bag) and $400 per passenger for unchecked baggage. On domestic flights, the ceiling is $1,250 per passenger. Excess-valuation insurance can be bought directly from the airline at check-in for about $10 per $1,000 worth of coverage. However, you cannot buy it at any price for the extensive list of excluded items shown on your airline ticket.

Trip Insurance **Trip-cancellation-and-interruption insurance** protects you in the event you are unable to undertake or finish your trip, especially if your airline ticket, cruise, or package tour does not allow changes or cancellations. The amount of coverage you purchase should equal the cost of your trip should you, a traveling companion, or a family member fall ill, forcing you to stay home, plus the nondiscounted one-way airline ticket you would need to buy if you had to return home early. Read the fine print carefully, especially sections defining "family member" and "preexisting medical conditions." **Default** or **bankruptcy insurance** protects you against a supplier's failure to deliver. Such policies often do not cover default by a travel agency, tour operator, airline, or cruise line if you bought your tour and the coverage directly from the firm in question. Tours packaged by one of the 33 members of the **United States Tour Operators Association** (USTOA, 211 E. 51st St., Suite 12B, New York, NY 10022, tel. 212/750–7371), which requires each member to maintain $1 million in an account to reimburse clients in case of default, are likely to present the fewest difficulties. Even better, pay for travel arrangements with a major credit card, so that you can refuse to pay the bill if services have not been rendered—and let the card company fight your battles.

Comprehensive Companies supplying comprehensive policies with some or all of the
Policies above features include **Access America, Inc.** (Box 90315, Richmond, VA 23230, tel. 800/284–8300); **Carefree Travel Insurance** (Box 310, 120 Mineola Blvd., Mineola, NY 11501, tel. 516/294–0220 or 800/323–3149); **Tele-Trip** (Mutual of Omaha Plaza, Box 31762, Omaha, NE 68131, tel. 800/228–9792); **The Travelers Companies** (1 Tower Sq., Hartford, CT 06183, tel. 203/277–0111 or 800/243–3174); **Travel Guard International** (1145 Clark St., Stevens Point, WI 54481, tel. 715/345–0505 or 800/826–1300); and **Wallach and Company, Inc.** (107 W. Federal St., Box 480, Middleburg, VA 22117, tel. 703/687–3166 or 800/237–6615).

U.K. Most tour operators, travel agents, and insurance agents sell poli-
Residents cies covering accident, medical expenses, personal liability, trip cancellation, and loss or theft of personal property. You can also buy an annual travel-insurance policy valid for every trip (usually of less than 90 days) you make during the year in which it's purchased. Make sure you will be covered if you have a preexisting medical condition or are pregnant.

For advice by phone or "Holiday Insurance," a free booklet that sets out what to expect from a holiday-insurance policy and gives price guidelines, contact the **Association of British Insurers** (51 Gresham St., London EC2V 7HQ, tel. 071/600–3333; 30 Gordon St., Glasgow G1 3PU, tel. 041/226–3905; Scottish Providence Bldg., Donegall Sq. W, Belfast BT1 6JE, tel. 0232/249176; call for other locations).

Car Rentals

Renting cars is not common among Central American travelers. The reasons are clear: In capital cities, traffic and car theft are rampant (look for guarded parking lots or hotels with lots); in rural areas, roads are often unpaved, muddy, and dotted with potholes; and often the cost of gas is steep. However, for obvious reasons, a car can be a wonderful asset to your trip. You don't have to worry about unreliable bus schedules, you have a lot more control over your itinerary and the pace of your trip, and you can head off to explore on a whim.

Most car-rental companies are represented in Central America, including **Avis** (tel. 800/331–1212 or 800/879–2847 in Canada); **Budget** (tel. 800/527–0700); **Dollar** (tel. 800/800–4000); **Hertz** (tel. 800/654–3131 or 800/263–0600); and **National** (tel. 800/227–7368). In Guatemala, five local companies have offices in Guatemala City, and most have representatives at the airport. These are **Ahorrent** (Blvd. Liberación 4–83, Zona 9, tel. 320544); **Rental** (11 Calle 2–18, Zona 9, tel. 341416); **Tabarini** (2 Calle A 7–30, Zona 10, tel. 319814 or 316108); and **Tally** (7 Avenida 14–74, Zona 1, tel. 514113 or 23327). Local car-rental companies in Belize include **Smith & Sons** (12 Banak St., Belize City, tel. 02/73779) and **Elijah Sutherland** (127 Neal Pen Rd., Belize City, tel. 02/73582).

In cities, unlimited-mileage rates range from $30 to $60 per day for an economy car to $60 to $85 for a large car; weekly unlimited-mileage rates range from $200 to $400. This includes VAT tax, which in Guatemala is 7%–10% on car rentals. Costa Rica and Belize generally don't have a tax tacked on. It's often more expensive to rent a car outside major cities. Special packages, such as fly/drive combinations in conjunction with your international airline ticket, offer discount rental rates. A four-wheel-drive (*doble-tracción*) vehicle is often essential in order to reach many parts of Central America, especially during the rainy season. They can cost roughly twice as much as an economy car and should be booked well in advance. A four-wheel-drive vehicle (Land Rover is an excellent choice) is crucial in Belize, where paved roads are at a minimum. However, Belize is a particularly expensive spot to rent a car—prices are generally $20 more per day than in Costa Rica or Guatemala.

Requirements Most rental companies will accept your driver's license, but some require an International Driver's Permit, available from the American or Canadian Automobile Association.

Extra Charges Picking up a car in one city or country and leaving it in another may entail drop-off charges or one-way service fees, which can be substantial. The cost of a collision or loss-damage waiver can be high, too. Automatic transmissions and air-conditioning are not universally available abroad; ask for them when you book, and check the cost before you commit to the rental.

Cutting Costs Major international companies have programs that discount their standard rates by 15% to 30% if you make your reservation before departure (anywhere from 24 hours to 14 days), rent for a minimum number of days (typically three or four), and prepay the rental. More economical rentals may be part of fly/drive or other packages, even bare-bones deals that combine only the rental and an airline ticket (*see* Tours and Packages, *above*).

Several companies operate as wholesalers; they do not own their own fleets but rent in bulk from those that do and offer advantageous rates to their customers. Rentals through such companies must be arranged and paid for before you leave the United States. One company offering such service is **Auto Europe** (Box 1097, Camden, ME 04843, tel. 207/828–2525 or 800/223–5555; in Canada, 800/458–9503). You won't see these wholesalers' deals advertised, and they're even better in summer, when business travel is down. Always ask whether the prices are guaranteed in U.S. dollars or foreign currency and if unlimited mileage is available. Also find out about any required deposits, cancellation penalties, and drop-off charges, and confirm the cost of any required insurance coverage.

Student and Youth Travel

Central America is a fantastic place for students and youths on a budget. In Guatemala and Costa Rica you can live well on $15 a day. Belize is more expensive; expect to shell out $35–$45 a day. Although to date only Costa Rica has youth hostels, Guatemala and Belize are also packed with cheap lodging possibilities. Any option near the bus station is usually a good bet moneywise. One of the cheapest ways to spend the night is camping. As long as you have your own tent, it's easy to set up camp anywhere. (If it looks like you're near someone's home, it's always a good idea to inquire first.) Central America is a popular travel destination for adventurous backpackers, so you'll have no problem hooking up with other like-minded travelers in any major city or along the popular travel routes. Chatting with other backpackers is the best way to pick up tips and advice on how to live and play within a lean budget. Both Guatemala City and San José have major universities with thriving student populations.

Travel Agencies **Council Travel Services (CTS),** a subsidiary of the nonprofit Council on International Educational Exchange, specializes in low-cost travel arrangements abroad for students and is the exclusive U.S. agent for several discount cards. Also newly available from CTS are domestic air passes for bargain travel within the United States. **CIEE**'s twice-yearly *Student Travels* magazine is available at the CTS office at CIEE headquarters (205 E. 42nd St., 16th Floor, New York, NY 10017, tel. 212/661–1450) and in Boston (tel. 617/266–1926), Miami (tel. 305/670–9261), Los Angeles (tel. 310/208–3551), and at 43 branches in college towns nationwide (free in person, $1 by mail). **Campus Connections** (1100 E. Marlton Pike, Cherry Hill, NJ 08034, tel. 800/428–3235) specializes in discounted accommodations and airline fares for students. The **Educational Travel Centre** (438 N. Frances St., Madison, WI 53703, tel. 608/256–5551) offers low-cost domestic and international airline tickets, mostly for flights departing from Chicago, and rail passes. Other travel agencies catering to students include **TMI Student Travel** (1146 Pleasant St., Watertown, MA 02172, tel. 617/661–8187 or 800/245–3672), and **Travel Cuts** (187 College St., Toronto, Ontario M5T 1P7, tel. 416/979–2406).

Discount Cards For discounts on transportation and on museum and attractions admissions, buy the **International Student Identity Card** (ISIC) if you're a bona fide student or the **International Youth Card** (IYC) if you're under 26. In the United States the ISIC and IYC cards cost $16 each and include basic travel-accident and -illness coverage and a toll-free travel-assistance hot line. Apply to **CIEE** (*see* address *above;* tel. 212/661–1414; the application is in *Student Travels*). In Canada the cards are available for $15 each from **Travel Cuts** (*see above*). In the United Kingdom they cost £5 and £4 respectively at student unions and student travel companies, including Council Travel's London office (28A Poland St., London W1V 3DB, tel. 071/437–7767).

Lodging No International Youth Hostels exist in Central America. To find out about cheap accommodations, ask at the university in the city you are visiting. The **Belize Tourist Board** (tel. 212/268–8798 or 800/624–0686) maintains lists of guest houses and property rentals throughout the country.

Traveling with Children

Publications *Newsletter*	*Family Travel Times,* published 10 times a year by **Travel with Your Children** (TWYCH, 45 W. 18th St., 7th Floor Tower, New York, NY 10011, tel. 212/206–0688; annual subscription $55), covers destinations, types of vacations, and modes of travel. TWYCH also publishes *Cruising with Children* and *Skiing with Children.*
Books	*Traveling with Children—And Enjoying It,* by Arlene K. Butler ($11.95 plus $3 shipping; Globe Pequot Press, Box 833, 6 Business Park Rd., Old Saybrook, CT 06475, tel. 800/243–0495, or 800/962–0973 in CT) helps you plan your trip with children from toddlers to teens.
Getting There *Air Fares*	On international flights, the fare for infants under age 2 not occupying a seat is generally either free or 10% of the accompanying adult's fare; children ages 2 to 11 usually pay half to two-thirds of the adult fare. On domestic flights, children under 2 not occupying a seat travel free, and older children currently travel on the "lowest applicable" adult fare.
Baggage	In general, infants paying 10% of the adult fare are allowed one carry-on bag, not to exceed 70 pounds or 45 inches (length + width + height) and a collapsible stroller; check with the airline before departure because you may be allowed less if the flight is full. The adult baggage allowance applies for children paying half or more of the adult fare.
Safety Seats	The FAA recommends the use of safety seats aloft and details approved models in the free leaflet **"Child/Infant Safety Seats Recommended for Use in Aircraft"** (available from the Federal Aviation Administration, APA–200, 800 Independence Ave. SW, Washington, DC 20591, tel. 202/267–3479; Information Hotline, tel. 800/322–7873). Airline policy varies. U.S. carriers allow FAA-approved models bearing a sticker declaring their FAA approval. Because these seats are strapped into regular passenger seats, airlines may require that a ticket be bought for an infant who would otherwise ride free. Foreign carriers may not allow infant seats, may charge the child's rather than the infant's fare for their use, or may require you to hold your baby during takeoff and landing, thus defeating the seat's purpose.
Facilities Aloft	Some airlines provide other services for children, such as children's meals and freestanding bassinets (only to those with seats at the bulkhead, where there's enough legroom). Make your request when reserving. The annual February–March issue of *Family Travel Times* details children's services on dozens of airlines ($10; *see above*). "Kids and Teens in Flight" (free from the U.S. Department of Transportation's Office of Consumer Affairs, R-25, Washington, DC 20590, tel. 202/366–2220) offers tips for children flying alone.
Lodging *Home Exchange*	You can find a house, apartment, or other vacation property to exchange for your own by becoming a member of a home-exchange organization, which then sends you its annual directories listing available exchanges and includes your own listing in at least one of them. Arrangements for the actual exchange are made by the two parties, not by the organization. For more information contact the **International Home Exchange Association** (IHEA, 41 Sutter St., Suite 1090, San Francisco, CA 94104, tel. 415/673–0347 or 800/788–2489).
Apartment and Villa Rentals	If you want a home base that's roomy enough for a family and has cooking facilities, a furnished rental may be the solution. It's gener-

ally cost-efficient, too, although not always—some rentals are luxury properties (economical only when your party is large). Home-exchange directories do list rentals—often second homes owned by prospective house swappers—and some services search for a house or apartment for you (even a castle if that's your fancy) and handle the paperwork. Some send an illustrated catalogue, and others send photographs of specific properties, sometimes at a charge. Up-front registration fees may apply.

Among such companies are **Vacation Home Rentals Worldwide** (235 Kensington Ave., Norwood, NJ 07648, tel. 201/767–9393 or 800/633–3284) and **Villas International** (605 Market St., Suite 510, San Francisco, CA 94105, tel. 415/281–0910 or 800/221–2260). **Hideaways International** (767 Islington St., Box 4433, Portsmouth, NH 03802, tel. 603/430–4433 or 800/843–4433) functions as a travel club. Membership ($99 annually per person or family at the same address) includes two annual guides plus quarterly newsletters; rentals are arranged directly between members, not by the club staff.

Hints for Travelers with Disabilities

In general, provisions for people with disabilities in Central America are extremely limited. Outside major cities, roads are unpaved, making wheelchair travel difficult. Exploring most of Central America's attractions implies walking down cobblestoned streets and, sometimes, steep trails and muddy paths. Buses are not equipped to carry wheelchairs, so wheelchair users should hire a van to get about. However, there is a growing awareness of the needs of the disabled, and the friendly, helpful attitude of people helps somewhat to make up for the lack of provisions. For information on accessibility in Costa Rica, contact the **National Tourists Institute** (Calle 5, Aves. Central y Segunda, San José, Costa Rica, tel. 506/221733 or 506/2211090). For general information on facilities for the disabled in Belize, contact the **Central American Information Center** (Box 50211, San Diego, CA 92105, tel. 619/262–6489). In Guatemala, contact the **Guatemala Tourist Commission** (1–17 Ave. 7, Central Cívico, Guatemala City, Guatemala, tel. 2/31133).

Accommodations The **Holiday Inn** (reservations tel. 800/465–4329) in San José, Costa Rica; the **Westin Camino Real** (reservations tel. 800/228–3000) in Guatemala City, Guatemala; and the **Ramada Inns** (reservations tel. 800/228–2828) in Antigua, Guatemala, and Belize City, Belize, have rooms equipped for the disabled. The Westin also provides wheelchairs for disabled guests.

Organizations Several organizations provide travel information for people with disabilities, usually for a membership fee, and some publish newsletters and bulletins. Among them are the **Information Center for Individuals with Disabilities** (Fort Point Pl., 27–43 Wormwood St., Boston, MA 02210, tel. 617/727–5540 or 800/462–5015 in MA between 11 and 4, or leave message; TDD 617/345–9743); **Mobility International USA** (Box 10767, Eugene, OR 97440, tel. and TDD 503/343–1284, fax 503/343–6812), the U.S. branch of an international organization based in Britain (*see below*) that has affiliates in 30 countries; **MossRehab Hospital Travel Information Service** (tel. 215/456–9603, TDD 215/456–9602); the **Travel Industry and Disabled Exchange** (TIDE, 5435 Donna Ave., Tarzana, CA 91356, tel. 818/344–3640, fax 818/344–0078); and **Travelin' Talk** (Box 3534, Clarksville, TN 37043, tel. 615/552–6670, fax 615/552–1182).

In the United Kingdom Important information sources include the **Royal Association for Disability and Rehabilitation** (RADAR, 25 Mortimer St., London

W1N 8AB, tel. 071/637–5400), which publishes travel information for people with disabilities in Britain, and **Mobility International** (228 Borough High St., London SE1 1JX, tel. 071/403–5688), an international clearinghouse of travel information for people with disabilities.

Travel Agencies and Tour Operators
Flying Wheels Travel (143 W. Bridge St., Box 382, Owatonna, MN 55060, tel. 507/451–5005 or 800/535–6790) is a travel agency specializing in domestic and worldwide cruises, tours, and independent travel itineraries for people with mobility impairments. Adventurers should contact **Wilderness Inquiry** (1313 5th St. SE, Minneapolis, MN 55414, tel. and TDD 612/379–3838), which orchestrates action-packed trips such as white-water rafting, sea kayaking, and dog sledding for those challenged with disabilities. Tours are designed to bring together people who are physically challenged and those who aren't.

Publications
Several free publications are available from the U.S. Consumer Information Center (Pueblo, CO 81009): "New Horizons for the Air Traveler with a Disability" (include Dept. 608Y in the address), a U.S. Department of Transportation booklet describing changes resulting from the 1986 Air Carrier Access Act and from the 1990 Americans with Disabilities Act; and the Airport Operators Council's *Access Travel: Airports* (Dept. 5804), which describes facilities and services for people with disabilities at more than 500 airports worldwide.

Travelin' Talk Directory (*see* Organizations, *above*) was published in 1993. This 500-page resource book ($35) is packed with information for travelers with disabilities. **Twin Peaks Press** (Box 129, Vancouver, WA 98666, tel. 206/694–2462 or 800/637–2256) publishes the *Directory of Travel Agencies for the Disabled* ($19.95), listing more than 370 agencies worldwide, and *Wheelchair Vagabond* ($14.95), a collection of personal travel tips. Add $2 per book for shipping.

Information Sources
Several organizations provide travel information for people with disabilities, usually for a membership fee, and some publish newsletters and bulletins. Among them are the **Information Center for Individuals with Disabilities** (Fort Point Pl., 27–43 Wormwood St., Boston, MA 02210, tel. 617/727–5540 or 800/462–5015 in MA between 11 and 4, or leave message; TDD/TTY tel. 617/345–9743); **Mobility International USA** (Box 3551, Eugene, OR 97403, voice and TDD tel. 503/343–1284), the U.S. branch of an international organization based in Britain and present in 30 countries. **MossRehab Hospital Travel Information Service** (1200 W. Tabor Rd., Philadelphia, PA 19141, tel. 215/456–9603, TDD tel. 215/456–9602); The **Society for the Advancement of Travel for the Handicapped** (SATH, 347 5th Ave., Suite 610, New York, NY 10016, tel. 212/447–7284, fax 212/725–8253); the **Travel Industry and Disabled Exchange** (TIDE, 5435 Donna Ave., Tarzana, CA 91356, tel. 818/368–5648); and **Travelin' Talk** (Box 3534, Clarksville, TN 37043, tel. 615/552–6670).

Hints for Older Travelers

Organizations
The **American Association of Retired Persons** (AARP, 601 E. St. NW, Washington, DC 20049, tel. 202/434–2277) provides independent travelers who are members of the AARP (open to those age 50 or older; $8 per person or couple annually) with the Purchase Privilege Program, which offers discounts on lodging, car rentals, and sightseeing, and arranges group tours, cruises, and apartment living through AARP Travel Experience from American Express (400

Pinnacle Way, Suite 450, Norcross, GA 30071, tel. 800/927–0111 or 800/745–4567).

Two other organizations offer discounts on lodgings, car rentals, and other travel products, along with such nontravel perks as magazines and newsletters: the **National Council of Senior Citizens** (1331 F St. NW, Washington, DC 20004, tel. 202/347–8800; membership $12 annually) and **Mature Outlook** (6001 N. Clark St., Chicago, IL 60660, tel. 800/336–6330; $9.95 annually).

Note: Mention your senior-citizen identification card when booking hotel reservations for reduced rates, not when checking out. At restaurants, show your card before you're seated; discounts may be limited to certain menus, days, or hours. If you are renting a car, ask about promotional rates that might improve on your senior-citizen discount.

Tour Operators If you want to take your grandchildren, look into **Grandtravel** (*see* Traveling with Children, *above*). **Saga International Holidays** (222 Berkeley St., Boston, MA 02116, tel. 800/343–0273) caters to those over age 60 who like to travel in groups.

Publications *The 50+ Traveler's Guidebook: Where to Go, Where to Stay, What to Do* by Anita Williams and Merrimac Dillon ($12.95; St. Martin's Press, 175 5th Ave., New York, NY 10010) is available in bookstores and offers many useful tips. "The Mature Traveler" (Box 50820, Reno, NV 89513, tel. 702/786–7419; $29.95), a monthly newsletter, contains many travel deals for older travelers.

Hints for Gay and Lesbian Travelers

Organizations The **International Gay Travel Association** (Box 4974, Key West, FL 33041, tel. 305/292–0217, 800/999–7925, or 800/448–8550), which has 700 members, will provide you with names of travel agents and tour operators who specialize in gay travel. The **Gay & Lesbian Visitors Center of New York Inc.** (135 W. 20th St., 3rd Floor, New York, NY 10011, tel. 212/463–9030 or 800/395–2315; $100 annually) mails a monthly newsletter, valuable coupons, and more to its members.

Travel Agencies and Tour Operators The dominant travel agency in the market is **Above and Beyond** (3568 Sacramento St., San Francisco, CA 94118, tel. 415/922–2683 or 800/397–2681). Tour operator **Olympus Vacations** (8424 Santa Monica Blvd., Suite 721, West Hollywood, CA 90069; tel. 310/657–2220 or 800/965–9678) offers all-gay and lesbian resort holidays. **Skylink Women's Travel** (746 Ashland Ave., Santa Monica, CA 90405, tel. 310/452–0506 or 800/225–5759) handles individual travel for lesbians all over the world and conducts two international and five domestic group trips annually.

Publications The premiere international travel magazine for gays and lesbians is **Our World** (1104 N. Nova Rd., Suite 251, Daytona Beach, FL 32117, tel. 904/441–5367; $35 for 10 issues). **Out & About** (tel. 203/789–8518 or 800/929–2268; $49 for 10 issues) is a 16-page monthly newsletter with extensive information on resorts, hotels, and airlines that are gay-friendly.

Credit Cards

The following credit-card abbreviations are used in this guide: AE, American Express; D, Discover; DC, Diners Club; MC, Master-Card; V, Visa.

Arriving and Departing

From North America by Plane

Several airlines fly to major Central American cities. Consult your travel agent on which bargains are currently available. For airline and flying time information, *see* Arriving and Department in individual country chapters.

Flights are either nonstop, direct, or connecting. A **nonstop** flight requires no change of plane and makes no stops. A **direct** flight stops at least once and can involve a change of plane, although the flight number remains the same; if the first leg is late, the second waits. This is not the case with a **connecting** flight, which involves a different plane and a different flight number.

Cutting Costs The Sunday travel section of most newspapers is a good source of deals. When booking, particularly through an unfamiliar company, call the Better Business Bureau and your local or state Consumer Protection Bureau to find out whether any complaints have been registered against the company, pay with a credit card if you can, and consider trip-cancellation and default insurance (*see* Insurance, *above*).

Promotional Less expensive fares, called promotional or discount fares, are
Airfares round-trip and involve restrictions, which vary according to the route and season. You must usually buy the ticket—commonly called an APEX (advance purchase excursion) when it's for international travel—in advance (7, 14, or 21 days are usual), although some of the major airlines have added no-frills, cheap flights to compete with new bargain airlines on certain routes.

With major airlines, the cheaper fares generally require minimum- and maximum-stays (for instance, over a Saturday night or at least seven and no more than 30 days). Airlines generally allow some return-date changes for a $25 to $50 fee, but most low-fare tickets are nonrefundable. Only a death in the family would prompt the airline to return any of your money if you cancel a nonrefundable ticket. However, you can apply an unused nonrefundable ticket toward a new ticket, again with a small fee. The lowest fare is subject to availability, and only a small percentage of the plane's total seats will be sold at that price. Contact the **U.S. Department of Transportation's Office of Consumer Affairs** (I–25, Washington, DC 20590, tel. 202/ 366–2220) for a copy of "Fly-Rights: A Guide to Air Travel in the U.S." *The Official Frequent Flyer Guidebook* by Randy Petersen ($14.99, plus $3 shipping; 4715-C Town Center Dr., Colorado Springs, CO 80916, tel. 719/597–8899, 800/487–8893, or 800/485– 8893) yields valuable hints on getting the most for your air-travel dollars.

Consolidators Consolidators or bulk-fare operators—"bucket shops"—buy blocks of seats on scheduled flights that airlines anticipate they won't be able to sell. They pay wholesale prices, add a markup, and resell the seats to travel agents or directly to the public at prices that still undercut the airline's promotional or discount fares (higher than a charter ticket but lower than an APEX ticket and usually without the advance-purchase restriction). Moreover, some consolidators sometimes give you your money back. Carefully read the fine print detailing penalties for changes and cancellations. If you doubt the reliability of a company, call the airline once you've made your booking to confirm that you do, indeed, have a reservation on that flight.

The biggest U.S. consolidator, C.L. Thomson Express, sells only to travel agents. Well-established consolidators selling to the public include **UniTravel** (Box 12485, St. Louis, MO 63132, tel. 314/569–0900 or 800/325–2222), which has domestic flights as well as service to Central America.

Discount Travel Clubs Travel clubs offer members unsold space on airplanes, cruise ships, and package tours at as much as 50% below regular prices. Membership may include a regular bulletin or access to a toll-free hot line giving details of available trips departing from three or four days to several months in the future. Most also offer 50% discounts off hotel rack rates, but double check with the hotel to make sure it isn't offering a better promotional rate independent of the club. Clubs include **Discount Travel International** (114 Forrest Ave., Suite 203, Narberth, PA 19072, tel. 215/668–7184; $45 annually, single or family), **Entertainment Travel Editions** (Box 1014 Trumbull, CT 06611, tel. 800/445–4137; $28–$48 annually), **Great American Traveler** (Box 27965, Salt Lake City, UT 84127, tel. 800/548–2812; $29.95 annually), **Moment's Notice Discount Travel Club** (425 Madison Ave., New York, NY 10017, tel. 212/486–0503; $45 annually, single, or family), **Privilege Card** (3391 Peachtree Rd. NE, Suite 110, Atlanta, GA 30326, tel. 404/262–0222 or 800/236–9732; domestic annual membership $49.95, international, $74.95), **Travelers Advantage** (CUC Travel Service, 49 Music Sq. W, Nashville, TN 37203, tel. 800/548–1116; $49 annually, single or family), and **Worldwide Discount Travel Club** (1674 Meridian Ave., Miami Beach, FL 33139, tel. 305/534–2082; $50 annually for family, $40 single).

Publications The newsletter "Travel Smart" (40 Beechdale Rd., Dobbs Ferry, NY 10522, tel. 800/327–3633; $44 annually) has a wealth of travel deals in each monthly issue.

Enjoying the Flight Fly at night if you're able to sleep on a plane. Because the air aloft is dry, drink plenty of fluids while on board. Drinking alcohol contributes to jet lag, as do heavy meals. Bulkhead seats, in the front row of each cabin—usually reserved for people who have disabilities, the elderly, or those traveling with babies—offer more legroom, but trays attach awkwardly to seat armrests, and all possessions must be stowed overhead.

Smoking Since February 1990, smoking has been banned on all domestic flights of fewer than six hours' duration; the ban also applies to domestic segments of international flights aboard U.S. and foreign carriers. On U.S. carriers flying to destinations in Central America, a seat in a no-smoking section must be provided for every passenger who requests one, and the section must be enlarged to accommodate such passengers if necessary as long as they have complied with the airline's deadline for check-in and seat assignment. If smoking bothers you, request a seat far from the smoking section.

Foreign airlines are exempt from these rules but do provide no-smoking sections, and some nations—including Canada as of July 1, 1993—have gone so far as to ban smoking on all domestic flights; other countries may ban smoking on flights of less than a specified duration. The International Civil Aviation Organization has set July 1, 1996, as the date to ban smoking aboard airlines worldwide, but the body has no power to enforce its decisions.

2 Portraits of Costa Rica, Belize, Guatemala

The Natural Splendors of Central America

By David Dudenhoefer

David Dudenhoefer is an environmental and travel writer based in Central America and the author of The Panama Traveler (Windham Bay Press).

Banana republics and revolutions. Those are the first things that come to mind when most people think about Central America. It's been the news media's business to familiarize the public with the region's social strife, but not to relate the glory of its ancient ruins, pristine beaches, colorful textiles, and friendly inhabitants. Only recently has a more sophisticated populace begun to associate the inter-American isthmus with its greatest attributes: a treasure trove of tropical nature and an extraordinary variety of scenery.

Comprising an area slightly larger than Spain, and considerably smaller than the state of Texas, the slip of land that connects the North and South American continents claims more species of birds than are found in the United States and Canada combined, and more species of moths and butterflies than exist in the entire continent of Africa. You can find rolling pine forests; rumbling volcanoes; lush cloud forests; serene volcanic lakes; primeval mangrove swamps; stunning palm-lined beaches; sultry lowland rain forests; colorful coral reefs; spectacular cascades; tumultuous white-water rivers; rugged mountain ranges; rare tropical dry forests; scrubby deserts; slow-moving jungle rivers; and stretches of rocky coastline. And because of its compactness, all these diverse landscapes and varied wildlife occur in convenient proximity.

In geological terms, the inter-American land bridge is a rather recent phenomenon. Until a few million years ago, the North and South American continents were separated by a canal the likes of which Teddy Roosevelt—the father of the Panama Canal—couldn't have conjured up in his wildest dreams. In the area that is now occupied by Panama, Costa Rica, and southern Nicaragua, the waters of the Pacific and Atlantic oceans flowed freely together for unfathomable millennia. Geologists have named this former canal the Straits of Bolívar, after the Venezuelan revolutionary who wrested much of South America from Spain.

Beneath the Straits of Bolívar and the continents themselves, the incremental movement of tectonic plates slowly pushed North and South America closer. Geologists speculate that as the continents approached one another, a chain of volcanic islands began to bridge the gap. A combination of volcanic activity and plate movement led to the completion of a land bridge, which closed the inter-oceanic canal and opened a terrestrial corridor between the Americas about 3 million years ago.

Because several tectonic plates meet beneath Central America, the isthmus has long been a geologically unstable area; earthquakes and volcanic eruptions still hit the headlines occasionally. A curse it may seem, but the fact is there wouldn't be much of a Central America if not for both of these phenomena. Much of the region's best soil was once spewn from the volcanoes, and the upward movement of the Caribbean Plate as the Cocos Plate slipped beneath it pushed many parts of the southern isthmus up out of the sea. A recent example of this upward movement can be seen along Costa Rica's southern Caribbean coast, where an earthquake on April 22, 1991, thrust the coastline up more than 3⅓ feet (a meter), pushing large coral formations out of the water and adding up to 33 yards (30 meters) of land to the coast.

The continental connection 3 million years ago had profound biological consequences, since it both separated the marine flora and fauna of the Pacific and Atlantic oceans and simultaneously created a pathway for interchange between the American continents. Three million years is a long time by biological standards, and the region's plants and animals have changed considerably since the gap was closed. Evolution took slightly different paths in the Atlantic and Pacific waters that flank the isthmus. Organisms that evolved in separate continents made their way into the opposite hemisphere, and the resulting interaction eventually determined what exists in the Americas today. It is important to understand, however, that the plants and animals that live in Central America are more than just the sum of what passed between the continents; the corridor also acts as a filter, so the region is home to many species that couldn't make the journey from one hemisphere to the other. Thus the rain forests of the eastern and southern portions of Central America comprise the most northerly distribution of southern species like the great green macaw and the poison dart frogs, while the dry forests on the western side of the isthmus define the southern limit for northern species like the Virginia opossum and coyote. To top it all off, the many physical barriers and the variety of environments on the isthmus may foster the development of numerous native species.

What all this biological balderdash means for visitors to Central America is that they might be able to spot a South American spider monkey and a North American raccoon sharing the shade of a rain tree, which is native to Central America. On a larger scale, it means that the region is home to a disproportionately high percentage of the planet's plant and animal species. Though Central America covers only one-half of one percent of the earth's land area, about 10% of the world's species live here, so it's no wonder scientists have dubbed it a "biological superpower."

Nearly all of these biological endowments are stored within the region's forests. Though many physical forces combine to determine the characteristics of these forests, the two most important factors are altitude and rainfall. Altitude plays an important role in determining what lives where, and often defines the distribution of different types of forests and the wildlife that inhabits them. Although temperature in the tropics doesn't change much through the course of the year, the highlands stay consistently cooler than the lowlands. This means that you can spend a morning sweating in a sultry coastal forest, then drive a couple of hours up into the mountains, where you will need a warm jacket. In a more temperate area of the world, the cold weather merely hits the mountaintops a month or two before the lowlands, but eventually old man winter gets his icy grip on everything. In the tropics, things are different: The only place it ever freezes is at the top of the highest mountains, so the high-altitude flora tends to be very different from what's found in a nearby valley. Many lowland plants and animals used to a warm climate can't survive the cold-weather journey over tropical mountains, a circumstance that limits the realms of many species and improves the likelihood of new species evolving.

Altitude also plays an important role in determining the humidity of a forest. Clouds tend to accumulate around the highest mountains and volcanoes, providing not only regular precipitation up top, but also shade, which slows evaporation. This creates the conditions for the luxuriant cloud forests that cover the upper slopes of many mountains, which spend most of their time enveloped in a thick mist. As you climb higher on either side of a mountain range or volcano, the vegetation becomes more lush; hit the peaks of the highest mountains protruding up from the cloud cover, however, and you'll find fairly arid conditions.

Rainfall patterns may surprise you: Though people tend to associate the tropics with rain, many areas of Central America receive very little. This too is a result of the region's precipitous topography, and a phenomenon called "rain shadow," during which one side of a mountain range receives much more rain than the other because clouds heading from one direction lose most of their moisture as they hit the mountains and rise. The Pacific slope of much of Central America experiences a seasonal rain-shadow effect, and the Guatemalan region of Zacapa, a valley almost surrounded by high mountains, is so well shielded from most rainstorms that it has a desert landscape.

Thanks to the relentless nature of the tradewinds, the eastern side of Central America receives much more rain than the western half. The tradewinds pump a steady supply of moisture-laden clouds southwest over the isthmus, where they encounter warm air and mountains, which makes them rise. The clouds cool as they rise, which leaves them able to hold less moisture and causes them to dump most of their liquid luggage on the Caribbean slope.

During Central America's rainy season, which runs from May to November, regular storms roll off the Pacific Ocean and soak the western side of the isthmus on a near-daily basis. During the rainy season, the entire isthmus gets wet, and the Pacific slope sometimes receives more rain than the Atlantic. But in the dry season, from November to May, the tradewinds take over, and hardly a drop falls on the land bridge's western side. The two seasons have a profound effect on the forests of the Pacific lowlands, which receive almost no rainfall from December to May and consequently acquire a desert visage, with many trees dropping their foliage. Those forests quickly regain their verdure when the annual rains return in May, the beginning of a springlike season that is nonetheless referred to as winter by Central Americans.

The net result of all this variation in precipitation and altitude is a virtual mosaic of forests studding the isthmus. Biologists have dutifully identified these different forest types and grouped them into categories—rain, cloud, dry, pine, and mangroves— but because conditions often change within a short distance, many forests are considered "transitional," or caught between two categories. Of the major forest types, however, the one that best exemplifies the complexity of tropical nature is the rain forest.

A pristine rain forest is quite an impressive sight, with massive trees towering overhead—most of the leaves and branches are more than 100 feet above the ground—and thick vines and lianas hanging down from the treetops. Most of the foliage in a virgin rain forest is found in the canopy, which is the uppermost spread of the giant trees' leaves and branches plus the many plants that live upon them. Those branches provide platforms for a multitude of epiphytes—plants that grow on other plants but don't draw their nutrients from them—such as ferns, orchids, bromeliads, and vines. This is also where most of the forest's animals spend the majority, if not all, of their time.

Because the canopy foliage filters out most sunlight before it can reach the ground, the forest floor is usually a dim and quiet place, with not nearly as much undergrowth as in those old Tarzan movies. But many of the plants that do grow down below look familiar to northern visitors: since the light level of the rain-forest floor resembles that of the average North American living room, your basic popular house plant thrives here. The exception to the sparse vegetation rule is found wherever an old tree has fallen over, an event that is invariably followed by a riot of growth, with an excess of plants fighting over the newfound sunlight.

A lack of light characterizes the floor of the rain forest, but a shortage of water is the case up in the canopy. Plants that live here have developed a series of adaptations to cope with the aridity of the canopy environment, such as thick leaves that resist evaporation and spongy roots that soak up large amounts of water in a short period of time. Both traits are common among the thousands of species of colorful orchids that grow in Central America's forests. In the case of tank bromeliads, the plant's funnel shape helps it collect a pool of water at the center of its leaves. As tiny oases of the canopy, they attract plenty of arboreal animals, which drink from, hunt at, or live in the plant's pool. There is even a kind of tree frog whose tadpoles develop in the reservoirs, where they subsist on resident insects and larvae. While the plant provides vital water for an array of animals, the waste and carcasses of many of these animals in turn provide the plants with nutrients, another necessity in short supply up high.

Unfortunately, the great variety of plant and animal life that resides in the rain-forest canopy is difficult to observe from the forest floor, and most animals spend a great deal of their time and energy trying not to be seen. Still, you can catch distant glimpses of many species, such as the very still forms of sloths, furry figures amid the foliage, or the brilliant regalia of parrots, macaws, and toucans. You can't miss the arboreal acrobatics or chatter of monkeys, who leap from tree to tree, hang from branches, or throw fruit and sticks at intruders below. And hikers may occasionally encounter earth-bound creatures like the coati mundi, a narrow-nosed relation of the raccoon, or the agouti, a terrier-size rodent that resembles a giant guinea pig. The iridescent blue morpho butterfly, hummingbirds, and the tiny lizards that stand guard on tree trunks or scurry off into the leaf litter are some of the animals one is likely to spot in the rain forest.

An untrained eye can miss the details, however, so a good nature guide is invaluable. You may be standing in front of 100 different species of plants, and see only an incomprehensible green mesh. Tropical rain forests are among the richest, most complex, and most productive ecosystems in the world. Their biological diversity is so vast that scientists haven't even named most of the plant and insect species found there, and they have completed thorough studies of only a small fraction of the species that they have identified. Though tropical moist forests cover only 7% of the earth's surface, it has been estimated that they contain about half the planet's plant and animal species, which means a small patch of rain forest can consist of thousands of different kinds of plants and animals.

Aside from the heat and humidity, the rain-forest ecosystem is characterized by intense predation. While animals spend much of their time trying to find their next meal, both plants and animals dedicate a great deal of energy to the goal of not being eaten. Animals tend to accomplish this by hiding or fleeing, but those options aren't available to plants, which have devised a series of defenses such as thorns, leaf hairs, and other substances that make their leaves less than appetizing. Because of the relative toxicity of a large part of the rain-forest foliage, many insects eat only a small portion of any given leaf before moving on to another plant, so as not to ingest a lethal dose of any one poison. The consequence of this can be seen by staring up toward the canopy—almost every leaf is full of little holes that allow the sunlight to shine through the verdure. Some insects develop an immunity to one toxin and eat only the plant that contains it. This is a common strategy of caterpillars, since mobility isn't their strong point.

Popular tactics that animals use to keep from being eaten include staying on the move, keeping quiet and alert, and, of course, hiding. Though they are a chore to spot, the few camouflaged critters that you'll discover are invariably intriguing.

Some animals actually advertise: Bright colors help them find a mate amid the mesh of green but can also serve as a warning to potential predators. Take poison dart frogs, for instance: Their skins are so toxically laced with deadly poisons that South American Indians use them to make their darts and arrows more deadly. Another trick for scaring off predators is mimicry. Commonly, harmless creatures impersonate venomous ones, but, more rarely, acts of deception reach an amazing level of intrigue. One caterpillar has a tail that resembles the head of a snake, and a butterfly exists that looks like the head of an owl when it opens its wings.

The rain forest is the stage for a constant contest between the eaters and the eaten, as well as for plants' and animals' competition against other species that have similar niches—the biological equivalent of jobs. This competition has fostered cooperation between noncompetitive organisms. Plants need to get their pollen and seeds distributed as far as possible, and every animal requires a steady food supply. Tropical plants are pollinated by everything from fruit flies and hummingbirds to bees and bats, and since they have to feed the animals that deliver their pollen, their flowers are usually designed so nectar is easily available to their pollinators but protected from freeloaders who do nothing for the plant. Some of the more extreme examples of this can be found in the thousands of species of orchids that grow in Central America's forests; many of them are pollinated by only one species of bee or beetle. There is even an orchid that hides its nectar and pollen behind a petal door, which only its pollinator can open.

Competition for limited resources is a predominant force in the rain forest, which keeps trees growing taller, roots reaching farther, and everything mobile working on some way to get more for less. The battle for light has sent most of the rain-forest foliage sky high, whereas the battle for nutrients has caused the process of decay and recycling that follows every death in the forest to take place at breakneck pace. One result of this high-speed decomposition is that most of the nutrients in a rain forest are found within living things, and the soil beneath them retains very little of the essential elements. As a consequence, rain-forest soils tend to be nutrient-poor, and less than ideal sites for farming.

Rain forests aren't the only types of tropical forests in Central America. The region's rare dry forests are similar to rain forests in many ways, especially during the rainy season. But when the rains stop, the dry forest acquires a seasonal aridity; most of the trees lose their leaves but simultaneously burst into full, colorful flower. Containing many of the plants, animals, and exclusive relationships found in the rain forest, the tropical dry forest is also home to groups associated with the forests and deserts of Mexico and the southern United States, such as cacti, coyotes, white-tailed deer, and diamondback rattlesnakes. Because dry forests are not as dense as rain forests, there is less foliage to hide behind, and you'll find it easier to observe animals here than in the other forest types. This is especially true during the dry season, when the forest's fauna can be found congregating around available water supplies and fruit or flowers.

The upper reaches of many mountains and volcanoes are draped with cloud forest, a more luxuriant, precipitous version of the rain forest. Cloud forests are the epitome of lushness—so lush that it can be difficult to find the bark on a cloud-forest tree for all the growth on its trunk and branches. Plants grow on plants growing on plants: Vines, orchids, ferns, and bromeliads are everywhere, and moss proliferates on the vines and leaves of other epiphytes.

Because cloud forests tend to grow on steep terrain, the trees grow on slightly different levels, which means the canopy forms a less continuous cover than that experienced in a lowland rain forest. Consequently, more pale light reaches the ground, where you'll encounter plenty of undergrowth, like prehistoric-looking tree-ferns and "poor-man's umbrellas," which consist of little more than a few giant leaves.

Cloud forests are home to a multitude of animals, ranging from delicate glass frogs, whose undersides are so transparent that you can see many of their internal organs, to the spectacular quetzal, one of the most beautiful birds in the world. The male quetzal has a bright crimson belly and iridescent green back, with two-foot tail feathers that float behind the bird when it flies, ample inspiration for the name the ancient Mayas gave it— "winged serpent." While the tangle of foliage and almost constant mist can make it difficult to get a good look at much of the cloud forest's wildlife, you should be able to catch a glimpse of plenty of other flying objects, including an array of brightly colored hummingbirds.

Since the cloud forest is almost constantly enveloped in mist, its canopy doesn't suffer the water shortage that plagues other kinds of forests. In fact, the cloud-forest canopy is practically the wettest part of the woods. The upland portions, while receiving few downpours, gain their moisture from a perpetually mobile, moisture-laden mist, which moves through the forest and deposits a condensation on the billions of leaves that make up the mosses, orchids, ferns, vines, bromeliads, and other epiphytes. This condensation results in a sort of secondary precipitation, with droplets forming on the epiphytic foliage and falling regularly down from the branches to the forest floor. Cloud forests thus function like giant sponges, soaking up the humidity from the clouds and sending it slowly downhill to feed the streams and rivers that many regions and cities depend upon for water. And because some of the precipitation that falls on the cloud forests flows west, it usually feeds streams and rivers that run through arid regions, even at the height of the dry season.

Though they may not seem exotic to the visitor from the north, pine forests cover a large part of Central America, especially the highlands of Guatemala and Honduras. The Central American pine forests don't boast the kind of biological diversity found in most other forest types, but they are undeniably beautiful and are home to numerous species of birds and other animals. An interesting aspect of the Guatemalan highlands is that the hilltops and most mountainsides are covered with pine, while secluded valleys that maintain higher average temperatures are draped with luxuriant cloud forests, which contain much more diversity than the adjacent pine forests.

A more exclusively tropical forest is the mangrove, a regularly flooded, primeval-looking profusion that can be found along both of Central America's coasts. Mangrove forests grow in the tidal zone, usually near river mouths, and often surround lagoons or river deltas. Trees in these forests grow propped up on stilt roots, which keeps leaves out of salt water and helps the trees absorb carbon dioxide during high tide. The roots also provide protection for a variety of marine species and serve as props for many kinds of shellfish.

Mangroves are homogenous forests, with stands of one species of tree that often stretch off as far as the eye can see, but they are also productive ecosystems that play an important role in estuaries. Many marine animals—oysters, snapper, and shrimp, for instance—spend particular stages of their lives in mangrove estuaries, while other species are born and die here. This means that mangroves are not only vital to the health of the ocean beyond them, but they are also attractive sites for animals that feed on small fish. You'll find a vast assortment of fish-eating birds, including herons, pelicans, ospreys, kingfishers, and rare creatures like the great jabiru—a massive stork and the largest bird inhabiting the isthmus—or the roseate spoonbill, an elegant pink wader.

In the ocean beyond the mangroves lie coral reefs, another distinctly tropical phenomenon that supports one of the most diverse ecosystems in the world. Coral reefs occur off both of Central America's coasts, from the crystalline waters that wash against Cocos Island, some 589 kilometers (365 miles) southwest of Costa Rica, to the aquamarine sea along the shore of Ambergris Cay, in northeast Belize. Though the Pacific has some impressive coralline congregations. the most spectacular reef in the region—in the Americas, for that matter—lines the eastern edge of Belize. Here is the second largest barrier reef in the world (number one is Australia's Great Barrier Reef), an impressive collection of oceanic organisms and a vital ecological organ of the Caribbean Sea's marine body.

On the other geographical extreme—about as far as one could travel from Central America's coastal reefs and still remain in the region—is the paramo, a tundralike ecosystem that covers the tops of the Talamanca Mountain Range, in southern Costa Rica. A combination of shrubs and grasses that grow above the tree line, the paramo is common in the heights of South America's Andes, with Costa Rica's patches being the most northerly point in its distribution.

With such remarkable diversity in such a small area of land, one would expect any trip in Central America to pass everchanging natural panoramas packed with a variety of living things. But it soon becomes clear that the region's predominant landscapes are not cloud forests and rain forests, but the coffee and banana plantations that have replaced them. The ancient Mayas may have revered animals like the jaguar and quetzal, but much of their former realm has become the home of less illustrious beasts: the cow and cattle egret, which are perhaps the two animals that visitors to Central America see more of than any others.

The fact is that more than two-thirds of Central America's original forests have already been destroyed, and most of those trees fell during the past 40 years. It has been estimated that between 3,000 and 3,500 square kilometers (1,158 and 1,351 square miles) of the region's forests were cut every year during the past decade, a rate of deforestation that could leave Central America devoid of pristine forests by the year 2020. Such a fate would not only mean the demise of the jaguars and quetzals, but would have grave consequences for the region's human inhabitants as well. The forests regulate the flow of rivers, by absorbing rains and releasing the water slowly, and deforestation often results in severe soil erosion, which decreases the productive capacity of the land. But the destruction of Central America's forests is a loss for the entire world, since hidden within the flora and fauna are unknown substances, which could eventually be extracted to cure diseases and serve humankind.

Central America's remaining forests face increasing pressure from a growing and impoverished human population. People hunt within them, cut down their valuable hardwoods, and completely destroy many wooded areas in order to establish farms. Forests are cut and burned to make room for banana and coffee plantations, or to become pasture for cattle whose meat is often shipped north. Much of the destruction is the work of small farmers, who fell patches of forest to plant their beans and corn, and after a few years of diminishing harvests, sell their land to cattle ranchers or speculators and move on to cut more forest. The cycle of destruction is fueled by poverty and greed, and though Central American governments have established protected areas and passed laws to limit deforestation, the region's wildlands continue to disappear.

Conservationists point out that the Central American governments don't have the resources to enforce existing laws that protect the environment, or even to effectively manage their national parks and protected areas. Environmentalists are looking for ways to motivate people to protect the forests, and the best way they've found is to teach those responsible for the destruction that conservation pays. Promoting "ecotourism"—increasing the number of tourists who visit a country's natural areas, so the government and rural dwellers will become more interested in protecting them—is a potential means of making conservation profitable.

A River Trip to Lamanai

By Simon
Worrall

Simon
Worral is a
British-born
writer. He
writes
regularly for
the London
Sunday
Times
Magazine,
Geo, and
many other
European
and
American
publications
on travel,
technology,
culture, and
politics. He
currently
makes his
home in East
Hampton,
New York.

E ven though I spent the entire boat ride huddled under a tarpaulin trying to keep dry, this journey along the New River to Lamanai, the longest-occupied Mayan site in Belize, was one of the high points of my visit. We started from just south of Orange Walk, where the Maruba Resort has a boat that takes people up the river.

The town itself is one of the least attractive in Belize—a run-down market town, with six or seven third-rate Chinese restaurants and a lot of bars of dubious renown (Orange Walk has a reputation as being both the drug-distribution center and prostitution capital of Belize). Paradoxically, it is also the center for the Mennonites, and you will often see the lean, fit-looking men running errands in the town—the women are not allowed to "mix"—dressed in the almost standard Mennonite uniform: plaid shirt, suspenders, work boots, and straw hat. With their straw-blond hair, blue eyes, and startlingly Germanic looks, they are the most unusual of the many ethnic groups that have settled in Belize.

Originally a radical splinter group of the Lutheran Reformation in 16th-century Europe, the Mennonites had, metaphorically speaking, many stamps in their passports before they finally got here. From Holland, where their spiritual godfather and namesake, Menno Simons, called the movement into being, they went to Switzerland, and then to Prussia. Like the Amish, whom they resemble in many ways, the Mennonites strongly opposed warfare in any form, and they paid for their treasonable pacificism with banishment. In 1663, a small group traveled to North America. Another group went east, settling in western Russia, until the witch hunts of the 1917 Revolution once again forced them into exile. Many traveled to Canada, and from there, to Mexico. The first settlers to make Belize their home arrived in 1958, and they immediately filled a vacant economic niche as dairymen and farmers. Today, most of Belize's vegetables, milk, and dairy produce are produced by Mennonites. They are also the most skilled carpenters and house-builders in the country.

From Orange Walk, the journey up the river to Lamanai is like a scene from Peter Matthiessen's novel *At Play in the Fields of the Lord*. At first the river is broad and straight, then it contracts to a maze of narrow tributaries that wind in and out of the mangroves. For much of the time, it is no more than a few boat widths across, so you can almost reach out and touch the tangled mass of vegetation on the bank. Many of the trees are covered in a squashy cactus known as "devil's guts" or by huge, black termite nests hanging from the trunks like dollops of Christmas Pudding, some of them as much as two or three feet in circumference. As we passed a tree at the water's edge, a colony of bats flew off. Numerous birds took flight as we approached—white herons; diminutive jacana; hawks; and even the rare jabiru stork, the largest bird in the New World, with a wingspan of up to eight feet. Here and there, brilliant, lilac-colored morning glories dotted the dense green undergrowth.

After about an hour, we emerged into a broad lake area the size of the Hudson at Annandale. I could see why the Maya built a settlement here. From the water, the limestone cliffs on which they built their temples would have been impregnable, with a commanding view of the river and the surrounding countryside. As well as providing an abundant supply of fish, turtles, and snails, the New River also served as a trade route, linking Lamanai with most of northwestern Belize, from its source on a line with Belize City, to its estuary near Corozal, and the Yucatán Peninsula beyond.

L amanai was a miniature Venice, a powerful port-city that lived by river trade and fishing. The river also gave Lamanai its name. In Mayan, it means "submerged crocodile," and this densely forested waterway is still home to hundreds of their descendants. To the Maya, the crocodile was a sacred animal, and when archaeologists excavated Lamanai, they found masks depicting a man wearing a crocodile headdress.

Unlike all other sites in Belize, Lamanai was occupied by the Maya until well after Columbus arrived in the New World. Archaeologists have found signs of continuous occupation from 1500 BC until the 16th century, its people carrying on a way of life that had been passed down for millennia until Spanish missionaries arrived to separate them from their past and lure them to Catholicism. The ruins of the church the Spaniards built can still be seen at the nearby village of Indian Church. In the same village, there is also an abandoned sugar mill from the 19th century. With its immense drive-wheel and steam engine—on which you can still read the name of the manufacturer, Leeds Foundry in New Orleans—swathed in strangler vines and creepers, it is a haunting sight.

In all, 50 or 60 Mayan structures were spread over the 950-acre Archaeological Reserve. The most impressive of them is the largest Preclassic structure in Belize: a massive, stepped temple built into the hillside overlooking the river. A ball court, numerous dwellings, and several other fine temples remain. One of the finest stelae found in Belize, an elaborately carved depiction of the ruler Smoking Shell, can be seen here, as well as the only archaeological museum in Belize, where site caretakers will be glad to show you a 2,500-year progression of pottery, carvings, and small statues.

Archaeologists also found the grave of a seven-year-old child, believed to have been a royal personage. He was buried in an upright sitting position on a bench; at his feet are the bones of five two-year-olds, all with their necks broken. The discovery suggested that the people of Lamanai practiced human sacrifice.

Most of the structures at Lamanai have only been superficially excavated. Trees and vines grow from the top of temples, the sides of one pyramid are covered with vegetation, and another rises abruptly out of the forest floor. At Lamanai, no tour buses, no cold drink stands, intrude: you'll find only ruins, forest, and wildlife.

The path to the ruins leads up through lush forest from the grassy riverbank. We passed huge guanacaste trees, mahogany trees, rubber trees, and even an allspice, with its pungent leaves and fruit. Here and there were magnificent cahoune palms, growing out of the ground like quivers of arrows. After about a 10-minute walk, we reached the first temple, a massive structure of weathered limestone ascending a hill. At the base a moss-covered stone throne is built into the wall, where the ruler would have sat for blood-letting rituals. Remarkably, the throne at Lamanai is embellished with what looks like the Chinese symbol for male and female, the yin-yang, suggesting a possible connection with the Orient. Halfway up is a carving that depicts a man's face inside the mouth of a jaguar. From the top, a spectacular view unfolds through the treetops to the river below and the surrounding countryside.

As we stood looking down at the throne, a sound, something between a donkey's braying and the roar of a jaguar, shattered the silence. Ahead of us rose the Jaguar Temple, a massive stepped pyramid at the end of a grassy plaza, three of its sides still overgrown with trees and bushes. As we looked over to it, a toucan burst into view and roosted on a giant guanacaste tree. Then we heard the same piercing cry that had moments earlier immobilized us. Another call answered it, then another, until the forest was echoing with the wails of a group of black howler monkeys. Later, we found a group of seven or eight, including a mother and her baby, feeding in a stand of breadnut trees by the ruined foundations of Mayan houses. To the Maya, the monkey was a sacred animal—the god of writing—and thanks to the conservation of the land, they are back at Lamanai.

3 National Parks and Wildlife Reserves

Costa Rica, Belize, and Guatemala together possess an almost unfathomable wealth of natural and archaeological assets. Spread among them are hundreds of important pre-Columbian ruins, more species of plants and animals than scientists have been able to count, and a variety of scenery that ranges from barren mountain peaks to lush forests and vibrant coral reefs. Moreover, the governments of all three countries have had the foresight to protect a significant portion of their ecological and archaeological wealth as national parks and preserves of various other categories.

In Costa Rica, the best-protected wild areas are the national parks and the biological reserves; wildlife refuges are not nearly as well protected. In Guatemala, protected areas created specifically for the conservation of nature are called *biotopos*, and archaeological sites are called national parks (although the extensive Tikal National Park is also one of the most impressive nature reserves in the isthmus). Belize has sanctuaries or reserves.

Though the names may change from country to country, there is one characteristic that all but a few well-developed protected areas have in common—lack of infrastructure. Only a few of the region's parks can be reached by paved roads, many require four-wheel-drive vehicles to visit, and some can only be reached by boat, on horseback, or on foot. Some parks don't have much of a visitor center and trails aren't well marked, but getting in and out of them is half the adventure.

Although the protected areas of Costa Rica, Belize, and Guatemala contain spectacular scenery and wildlife, don't expect to come face to face with a jaguar. Jaguars, tapirs, giant anteaters, and quetzals inhabit many of the region's parks and preserves, but it's unlikely that you will ever see these animals. You are, however, pretty likely to catch glimpses of monkeys, toucans, iguanas, and noisy flocks of parrots and parakeets. Because of the thick foliage and prevalent mist, cloud forests in particular are not the best places to see birds or wildlife. (For an in-depth discussion of rain forests, cloud forests, and other Central American habitats, *see* "The Natural Splendor of Central America" in Chapter 2.)

Many tour companies offer trips to the national parks and reserves (*see* Tours and Packages in Chapter 1, Essential Information, and Tour Companies in individual country chapters). Whether you travel on your own or with a tour group, make sure your visit benefits the people who live near the wilderness areas: Use local guides or services, visit local restaurants, and buy local handicrafts or fruits. To ensure these areas will be preserved for future generations, make donations to local conservation groups; tour operators in each country may be able to make suggestions. A few foreign environmental organizations, including Conservation International, World Wildlife Fund, and the Nature Conservancy, are also aiding ecological efforts in the isthmus.

Costa Rica

Costa Rica has done a remarkable job of conserving part of its natural heritage. Just three decades ago, there was hardly a protected area in the country; today the parks system covers more than 11% of the territory. Thanks to the foresight of local conservationists, its parks and reserves contain examples of nearly all the country's ecosystems, among them mangrove estuaries, lowland rain forests, tropical dry forests, beaches, coral reefs, cloud forests, caves, freshwater swamps and lagoons, active volcanic craters, and transition forests. In addition to the national parks, a variety of other wild areas enjoy some degree of protection. Costa Ricans are coming to realize that conservation pays, and the country is slowing moving away from many of the destructive habits that have already claimed most of its wilderness.

During the first two decades of parks system's development, conservationists raced against rampant deforestation to purchase and protect as much of the country's vital wildlands as possible. The National Parks Service is now concentrating on consolidating management of those parks, improving their infrastructure, and facing a new challenge—controlling the crowds of visitors that are flocking to the protected areas. Because some the country's most popular parks receive so many visitors during the high season, it can be worth your while to head to less popular protected areas, where you'll be treated to a more private and natural experience.

The **National Parks Service** sells a guide to the parks, which is in Spanish and contains little practical information but has decent maps and lists the facilities at each protected area. The parks office is in San José, on Calle 25 between Avenidas 8 and 10 (tel. 257–0922; open weekdays 8–4).

For Dining and Lodging information, *see* the end of each regional section.

Central Valley National Parks

Since the Central Valley was the first part of Costa Rica to be settled, and is now home for more than half of its burgeoning population, Mother Nature has had to retreat to the region's mountaintops and a few isolated river valleys. Most of the wilderness that remains has been declared protected, so there are several parks that can be easily visited on day trips from San José. The Central Valley parks have good access, with paved roads, albeit with a few potholes, leading to all of them, and most (all but Guayabo and Barva) are accessible for people who can't walk far. Because the floor and lower slopes of the Central Valley are covered with coffee plantations and cities and towns, the region's parks are predominantly high-elevation cloud forest ecosystem—extremely luxuriant and often shrouded in a thick mist.

Braulio Carrillo This amazing, accessible expanse of pristine wilderness is one of Costa Rica's largest protected areas (44,534 hectares/110,000 acres). Stretching from the misty mountaintops north of San José to the Atlantic lowlands, **Braulio Carrillo National Park** protects a series of ecosystems that range from the cloud forests that cover the park's upper slopes to the tropical wet forest of the Magsasay sector. The Guapiles Highway, the main route to the Atlantic coast, cuts though one of Braulio's most precipitous areas, passing countless breathtaking views of the rugged, forest-cloaked landscape. There is a ranger station near the Ziriquí Tunnel, where a short but steep trail loops through the cloud forest. Another trail leads into the forest to the right about 17 kilometers (10 miles) after the tunnel and heads to a stream with a cascade and swimming hole. The vegetation is beautiful around the highway, and you may see a few of the 350 bird species that inhabit the park. (Although Braulio is home to most of the mammals found in Costa Rica, they tend to avoid the forest near the highway.) There are no camping areas in this part of the park.

Hikers may want to explore the Barva Volcano sector of Braulio, which features a trail that leads through the cloud forest to two crater lakes. Camping is allowed at the Barva ranger station, which is far from any traffic and thus is a good area to see birds and animals. Quetzals can be spotted in the area during the dry season, which is the only time you'll want to camp there, but it's a good place for a morning hike any time of year. Stay on the trail when hiking anywhere in Braulio; it's easy to get lost in the cloud forest, and the rugged terrain makes wandering through the woods very dangerous.

Getting There **By Car.** Take the road from San José to Heredia. The route to Braulio Carrillo heads north out of Heredia through the communities of Barva, San José de la Montaña, Paso Llano, and Sacramento. At Sacramento the road becomes dirt and gets worse as it nears the ranger station. Although a four-wheel-drive vehicle is needed to make it all the way, a standard automobile will get you most of the way there in the dry season.

By Bus. There is frequent bus service from San José to Braulio Carrillo (*see* Getting Around in San José and the Central Valley in Chapter 4, Costa Rica). Buses from Heredia go to Paso Llano, about 6 kilometers (4 miles) from the park.

Guayabo Although the ruins here don't compare with the those of the Maya cities in Guatemala and Belize, **Guayabo National Monument** is Costa Rica's most significant archaeological site. Most of the original buildings were made of wood, so only their bases remain. Rangers give guided tours (in Spanish) of the ruins, which include an aqueduct and communal well. On your own, you can hike along a trail that loops through the surrounding rain forest, where there is excellent bird-watching. Camping is permitted.

Getting There **By Car.** Guayabo sits on the lower slopes of Turrialba Volcano and is most easily reached by taking the old Atlantic Highway to the town of Turrialba, then heading 19 kilometers (12 miles) north to Guayabo.

By Bus. Hourly buses head from San José to Turrialba, where you can hire a cab to Guayabo. There is only one bus a day between Turrialba and Guayabo.

Irazú Volcano Smaller than Poás, **Irazú Volcano National Park** protects little more than the summit of the higher Irazú Volcano (3,433 meters/11,260 feet). The landscape at the top of the crater is bleak but beautiful, still scarred by the volcano's violent eruptions in 1963, when it covered the Central Valley with several feet of ash. It's best to head up Irazú as early in the morning as possible, before the summit becomes enveloped in clouds, so that you can catch a glimpse of its cream-of-asparagus crater lake and, if you're lucky, views of nearby mountains and of either the distant Pacific or Caribbean. There are no trails or visitor center at the summit, but a paved road leads all the way to the top, past pastoral landscapes that look more like the Alps than what you'd expect to see in Central America.

Getting There **By Car.** Head east from San José on the Interamerican Highway. At the Cartago intersection, turn left; the road continues all the way to the summit.

By Bus. A bus departs San José for the park on Saturday and Sunday.

Poás Volcano A vast and desolate crater dominates **Poás Volcano National Park,** one of the country's most popular and best developed preserves. A paved road leads all the way to the crater, and there are well-maintained trails and an elaborate visitor center. The park protects the summit of that mildly active volcano, which regularly spews a plume of sulfuric smoke, and the surrounding cloud forest. The road that heads off the parking lot ends at a nearby overlook of the crater, which is usually at least partially hidden by clouds. Two short trails lead into the forest from that road; the first is a nature trail with a series of signs displaying nature poetry, the second leads to an inspiring turquoise lake in an extinct crater surrounded by lush vegetation. The visitor center, near the parking lot, has an extensive exhibit about volcanoes (in Spanish) that includes information about Poás's history of activity. During the rainy season, it's best to visit Poás early in the morning. Camping is not permitted.

Getting There **By Car.** Take Interamerican Highway to Alajuela; from there, ask directions for Poás.

By Bus. There is a bus departing San José for Poás every Sunday. *See* Getting Around in San José and the Central Valley in Chapter 4, Costa Rica.

Tapantí The Grande de Orosi River flows through the middle of **Tapantí National Park,** a protected cloud forest that covers the mountain slopes at the far end of the Orosi Valley, and the emerald waters of that boulder-strewn stream pour into some brisk but inviting swimming holes near the park's picnic area. There's a modest visitor center by the entrance, and 1.6 kilometers (1 mile) up the road is a parking area with trails that head into the woods on both sides of the street. The Sendero Oropéndola trail leads to two loops, one that passes the picnic and swimming areas and another that winds through the forest nearby. The trail across the road does a loop along a forested hillside, and La Pava trail, 2½ kilometers (1½ miles) farther up the road on the right, leads down a steep hill to the riverbank. Several kilometers farther up the road from La Pava is a view of a long, slender cascade on the other side of the valley.

There are no campsites or lodgings in Tapantí, but it's the perfect destination for a morning swim and a picnic, although it tends to get cloudy and cool in the afternoon. The road is paved all the way into the park; however, the last few kilometers have more potholes than pavement.

Getting There **By Car.** Head east on the Interamerican Highway to Cartago. Drive through town, and take the road to Paraíso (the road isn't well-marked, so you may need to ask directions). Take a right to Orosi; after passing through town, take the right fork to Tapantí National Park.

Dining and Lodging All the parks listed above can be easily visited on day trips from San José or nearby towns. If you do choose to stay overnight, Río Palomo in Orosi is the nearest lodge to Tapantí, and Hotel El Pórtico is the closest hotel to the Barva sector of Braulio Carillo (*see* Dining and Lodging in San José and the Central Valley in Chapter 4, Costa Rica). Though most of Braulio Carrillo's wilderness is practically inaccessible, both La Selva and Rara Avis biological reserves are contiguous with the lower reaches of the park, which means you can experience the area's biological diversity from those convenient lodges (*see* Dining and Lodging in the Atlantic Lowlands in Chapter 4, Costa Rica). Guayabo lies very close to the Turrialba hotels (*see* Dining and Lodging in the Atlantic Lowlands in Chapter 4, Costa Rica).

Atlantic Lowlands

The hot and humid Atlantic lowlands are like a giant greenhouse, and with their lush vegetation, the parks on Costa Rica's Caribbean slope are the kind of wilderness you might envision when you hear the word "jungle." In these Atlantic forests live South American species that you won't find in the rest of Costa Rica—poison dart frogs, the crab-eating raccoon, and the great green macaw.

The Atlantic region's most popular protected areas are coastal parks, where the rain forest meets the beach, which means that marine wonders complement diverse flora and fauna. Aside from the surf and sand, the prime natural attractions along the southern Caribbean coast are coral reefs, while the northern beaches are famous for the sea turtles that climb onto them at night to lay their eggs in the sand.

The protected areas on the Caribbean side have the added convenience of being close to good dining and lodging; in some cases restaurants and hotels stand just a stone's throw from the park entrance. And the trip there can be an adventure in its own right, since the Atlantic Highway passes through the heart of Braulio Carrillo National Park, and the boat trip up the canals to Tortuguero is one of the best opportunities to see wildlife in Costa Rica.

Cahuita The 240-hectare (600-acre) coral reef that surrounds Cahuita Point is a natural treasure, so **Cahuita National Park** was set up to protect its 35 species of coral and its even greater number of sponges and seaweeds, which provide food and refuge for hundreds of species of colorful tropical fish and crustaceans. This alone would be ample attraction for visitors; most, however, come for Cahuita's luxuriant coastal forest and idyllic palm-lined beaches, which are straight out of a travel poster.

The path that winds in and out of the forest along the beach, from the town of Cahuita around the point to Puerto Vargas, offers a good look at the park's coastal and jungle wonders. The hike can be completed in a few hours if you don't stop to swim and enjoy the scenery. The forest and swamps are home to troops of monkeys, kingfishers and herons, kiskadees, sloths, snakes, and lots of crabs and lizards. The beach nearest to the town of Cahuita has a regular rip tide, so swim farther into the park, where the beach curves toward the point. This is also a good snorkeling area, though the best diving is off the point. Unfortunately, the park's coral reef is slowly being killed by sediment, runoff from deforested areas such as the banana plantations in the nearby Estrella Valley.

Getting There Cahuita National Park starts at the southern edge of Cahuita, which is served by bus from San José; there is also regular service to Puerto Viejo (*see* Getting Around in the Atlantic Lowlands in Chapter 4, Costa Rica). Five kilometers (3 miles) south of Cahuita on the left is the road to Puerto Vargas, the ranger station, and the camping area. If you stay in town, you can take a bus or catch a ride into Puerto Vargas and hike back around the point in the course of a day. If you camp at Puerto Vargas, you can also hike south along the beach to Puerto Viejo and catch a bus or taxi back to the park. Be sure to bring plenty of water, food, and sunscreen on these hikes.

Caño Negro **Caño Negro Wildlife Refuge** offers a river trip that can be an interesting alternative to the Tortuguero canal trip and that is more easily combined with travel to the Arenal area and Guanacaste. Another lowland rain-forest reserve, Caño Negro has suffered severe deforestation over the years, but most of the Frio River remains lined with trees, so the boat trip up the river to the reserve provides an opportunity to see a variety of wildlife. The lagoon at the heart of the reserve also attracts a wealth of waterfowl from November to January.

Getting There Boats can be hired for trips to Caño Negro in the town of Los Chiles, near the Nicaraguan border. The larger hotels in the Arenal–La Fortuna area offer day tours to the refuge.

Gandoca– Although less pristine than Cahuita National Park, **Gandoca-**
Manzanillo **Manzanillo Wildlife Refuge** stretches along the southeastern coast from the town of Manzanillo to the border of Panama, offering plenty of rain forest and many good dive spots. Because of weak laws governing the conservation of refuges and the value of coastal land in the area, Gandoca-Manzanillo has suffered steady environmental degradation over the years and continues to be developed. For now, the easiest way to explore it is by hiking along the coast south of Manzanillo, which also has some good snorkeling offshore. You can hike back out the way you head in, or arrange in Puerto Viejo to have a boat pick you up at Monkey Point (a 3–4 hour walk from Manzanillo) or Gandoca (6–8 hours from Manzanillo). Boat trips to dive spots and beaches in the refuge can also be arranged in Puerto Viejo.

Getting There **By Car.** Take the Atlantic Highway to Moín, then the Coastal Highway south to the Puerto Viejo turnoff. Continue through Puerto Viejo and head south via Punta Uva to Manzanillo.

By Bus. There is sporadic bus service to Manzanillo from Puerto Viejo.

Tortuguero The Spanish word for turtle is *tortuga,* so it isn't surprising that
and Barra **Tortuguero National Park** was created to protect the sea turtles that
del Colorado nest by the thousands on its beach. The park comprises a variety of ecosystems, including lowland rain forest, estuaries, and swampy areas dominated by yolillal palms. The park's palm-lined beach stretches off as far as the eye can see; you can wander there alone, but rip currents make swimming dangerous. This spectacular beach is even more intriguing at night, when four species of endangered sea turtles nest there. If you want to watch them, contact your hotel or the parks office to hire a certified local guide. (You won't be permitted to use a flashlight or camera on the beach, since the lights may deter the turtles from nesting.)

The jungle-lined canals that lead to Tortuguero have been called the Amazon of Costa Rica, and the boat trip up to the park, which leaves from the docks at Moín, is an excellent opportunity to see the area's wildlife, including several species of kingfishers and herons, sloths, monkeys, and crocodiles. Hire a dugout canoe with guide to explore some of the rivers that flow into the canal; these waterways contain less boat traffic and often have more wildlife. You can also continue up the canals to the **Barra del Colorado Wildlife Refuge,** an immense protected area that is connected with the park via a biological corridor. Barra del Colorado is a less-visited area that protects significant expanses of wilderness.

Getting There Although there are no roads to Tortuguero, getting there is easy enough—either with a tour (*see* Guided Tours in the Atlantic Lowlands in Chapter 4, Costa Rica) or by flying or taking a bus to Moín then catching a boat up (*see* Getting Around in the Atlantic Lowlands in Chapter 4, Costa Rica). There are fewer boats to Barra del Colorado, but you can also fly there directly from San José. Plenty of companies offer tours there, and all the big hotels provide transportation to the park.

Dining and The communities of Tortuguero and Cahuita, at the northern edges
Lodging of the parks of the same name, offer a variety of dining and lodging options (for Tortuguero, *see* Dining and Lodging in the Atlantic Lowlands in Chapter 4, Costa Rica). **Costa Rica Expeditions** (tel. 222–0333) has its own lodge on the northern border of Tortuguero National Park. Caño Negro is best explored on a day trip from the Arenal–Fortuna area, which also has plenty of hotels and restaurants (*see* Dining and Lodging in the Northwest in Chapter 4, Costa Rica). The Gandoca-Manzanillo Reserve actually has some hotels and restaurants within its borders, and there is a wide range of dining and accommodations in the nearby Puerto Viejo de Limón area (*see* Dining and Lodging in the Atlantic Lowlands in Chapter 4, Costa Rica).

Northwest Costa Rica

The several parks in the province of Guanacaste protect some of the last remnants of the Mesoamerican tropical dry forest that once covered the Pacific lowlands from Costa Rica to the Mexican state of Chiapas. Because Spanish colonists found the climate on the Pacific slope of the isthmus more hospitable than its humid Atlantic side, most of the development that followed the conquest of Central America took place at the cost of the Pacific forests, and today hardly any wilderness remains on that half of the land bridge. The protected dry forests of Guanacaste are, consequently, of extreme importance to conservationists.

During the rainy season, the tropical dry forest looks very much like the lowland forests in other parts of the country, but as soon as the daily deluges subside in December, the landscape enters a transition. As the dry season progresses, most of the trees drop their foliage and the region resembles a desert. Many trees flower during the dry season, however, and the yellow, white, and pink blossoms of the tabebuia add splashes of color to the leafless landscape.

Because of the sparse foliage and partial deforestation, Costa Rica's dry forest parks are some of the best places in the country to see wildlife. Many animals native to North America are common in Guanacaste's protected areas—white-tailed deer, coyotes, magpie jays, diamondback rattlesnakes—but they are also home to predominantly South American animals like collared peccaries, armadillos, parrots, and broad-beaked vultures called *caracaras*.

Perhaps due to the wide open spaces one encounters in the Northwest, the region's parks tend to lie away from bus routes, which means you're best off visiting most of them in rental cars or on tours. The big tour companies in San José offer trips to northwest parks: **Guanacaste Tours** (tel. 666–0306) in Liberia knows the region best. **Horizontes** (tel. 222–2022) has the best guides. **Fantasy Tours** (tel. 220–2126) offers a boat tour to Palo Verde on Saturday.

Barra Honda Rocky hills that contain an extensive network of caves dominate **Barra Honda National Park,** an area of protected dry forest farther south. Local guides lower spelunkers into the caverns using ropes and a climber's ladder—a descent into darkness that is not for the fainthearted but is rewarding for the adventurous. If you're not up for the drop, you can trek into the forest-covered hills, which are full of wildlife and where scenic overlooks offer views of the Gulf of Nicoya and surrounding countryside. The Cascada Trail begins near the ranger's office and makes a loop near the caves that should take two or three hours to walk; serious hikers will want to continue on to the Boquete Trail, which, together with the Cascada Trail, takes the better part of a day to hike down and back. A community tourism association provides guides and climbing equipment and runs a simple restaurant and lodge by the park entrance. Camping is permitted.

Getting There **By Car.** Take the Interamerican Highway northwest from San José, turn left for the Tempisque Ferry. The turnoff to Barra Honda is on the right shortly after you cross the river.

By Bus. There is regular bus service to Nicoya from San José; in Nicoya, take a taxi to Barra Honda.

Palo Verde– The adjoining **Palo Verde National Park** and **Lomas Barbudal Biolog-**
Lomas **ical Reserve** protect some significant expanses of dry forest, and
Barbudal since both areas receive fewer visitors than Santa Rosa, they offer a more natural experience. Palo Verde's major attraction is the swampland that becomes the temporary home for thousands of migratory birds toward the end of the rainy season. An important part of these lagoons lies near the ranger station, where a raised platform has been built for bird-watchers. From December to March you can spot dozens of species of aquatic birds in the area, including several kinds of herons, ducks, wood storks, and elegant roseate spoonbills.

Palo Verde's forests are home to most of the species you can find in Santa Rosa, and the road that leads to the ranger station from the town of Bagaces passes some wooded patches where you're bound to spot birds and mammals if you drive slowly. There are also trails that head away from the ranger station—one short path into the hills behind it, and a longer one that goes to the river. The road south from Bagaces is long and rough and passes a lot of pasture before it gets to the park. An alternative route between Palo Verde and the Interamerican Highway passes through Lomas Barbudal, which means it passes more forest, though it's longer. The ranger station in Lomas Barbudal stands by the Cabuya River, which has a small swimming hole nearby, and the road that crosses the stream becomes a trail that winds around the forested hillside. The road that heads north from Lomas is pretty bad, but it's only 15 kilometers (9 miles) to the highway. Camping is permitted at Palo Verde.

Getting There **By Car.** Both Palo Verde and Lomas Barbudal are best reached by car. The road to Palo Verde heads south off the Interamerican Highway at Bagaces. The turnoff from the Interamerican Highway to Lomas Barbudal is about 15 kilometers (9 miles) south of Liberia.

Rincón de la **Rincón de la Vieja National Park** was created to protect the upper
Vieja slopes of the volcano of the same name, with forests that stay greener than those in the drier lowland and a series of steam geysers, bubbling mud pots, hot springs, and several cascades. This extensive protected area has entrances at Hacienda Santa María and Las Pailas. There's a camping area by the old farmhouse of Santa María, and a 2-kilometer (1¼-mile) hike away is Bosque Encantado, where the Zopilote River pours over a cascade in the forest forming an enticing pool. Three kilometers (2 miles) farther is a hot sulfur spring that is a popular spot for a dip, and four kilometers (2½ miles) beyond that are the boiling mud pots and fumaroles in an area called Las Pailas. If you're not with a guide, don't get too close to the mud pots; their edges are brittle, and several people have slipped in and been severely burned. The trail to the summit of the volcano heads into the forest above Las Pailas, but it's a trip for serious hikers, best done in the dry season (and by those prepared for cold weather

at the top). The nearby Rincón de la Vieja Mountain Lodge (*see* Dining and Lodging in the Northwest in Chapter 4, Costa Rica) offers horseback tours of the park.

Getting There   **By Car.** Take the Interamerican Highway northwest from San José to Liberia and drive through town to the dirt road that leads to the Santa Maria sector of the park. The road to the Las Pailas sector and the Rincon de la Vieja Mountain Lodge heads east from the Interamerican Highway just a few kilometers north of Liberia. A four-wheel-drive vehicle is recommended for either of these bone-rattling rides.

Santa Rosa   **Santa Rosa National Park** combines a variety of attractions, which makes it one of the country's most impressive protected areas. The dry forest that covers much of the park draws biologists and nature lovers, and while one of the park's beaches (Nancite) is a vital nesting area for the olive ridley sea turtle, the beach next to it (Naranjo) is known among surfers for its world-class waves.

The forested slopes of Orosí Volcano, which are protected within Guanacaste National Park, can be seen from the Interamerican Highway as you approach the entrance to Santa Rosa. A couple of kilometers after you enter Santa Rosa, there is a scenic overlook on the right that offers the first good look at the park's dry forest. La Casona, the old farmhouse and former battle site, houses a small museum that includes exhibits about the battle and the area's ecology. A small nature trail loops through the woods near La Casona, and there is a large camping area nearby. The road that passes the campground heads to Playa Naranjo, a spectacular, pristine beach that offers great animal-watching and surfing. There is a camping area at Playa Naranjo, but no potable water, and it can only be reached in a four-wheel-drive vehicle or by hiking a 12-kilometer (7-mile) hike from La Casona. Be aware that Santa Rosa's campgrounds sometimes fill up during the dry season, especially during the first week of January and Holy Week (Palm Sunday–Easter Sunday).

If you don't have time to go to Playa Naranjo, there are two good animal-watching trails that head off the road before it becomes too steep for anything but four-wheel-drive vehicles. The Patos Trail, on the left a few kilometers after the campgrounds, heads through the forest past a water hole and several scenic overlooks. A kilometer farther down the road on the right is a short trail that leads to an overlook from which you can see distant Playa Naranjo, and the massive Witch's Rock, which stands offshore.

Nancite, to the north of Naranjo, is an important turtle-nesting beach. The *arribadas*—mass nestings—that Nancite is famous for can also be seen at **Ostional Wildlife Refuge,** near Nosara. Another important nesting beach is Playa Grande, protected within **Las Baulas Marine National Park,** near the resort town of Tamarindo. Las Baulas is visited by thousands of leatherback turtles—the world's largest—every year during the October–March nesting season. The adjacent **Tamarindo Wildlife Refuge** protects a mangrove estuary that is an excellent bird-watching area.

Getting There   **By Car.** Take the Interamerican Highway north all the way to Santa Rosa National Park; the park is west of the highway at Km 269. Las Baulas lies north of Tamarindo, on the other side of an estuary; from Liberia, head south to Santa Cruz, then west to the coast.

By Bus. Buses leave San José at 5 and 7:45 AM and 4:15 PM for Peñas Blancas, passing the entrance to Santa Rosa about 5 hours later.

Dining and Lodging Liberia is the most convenient town from which to visit Guanacaste's parks, but nearby beach resorts such as Coco and Ocotal are almost as close and much more comfortable. Ostional lies near Nosara and Carrillo. Barra Honda is close to Nicoya and can be easily visited from Carrillo and Nosara, but there is a small, community-run lodge near the park entrance, which has several simple, comfortable rooms for rent. (There's no phone, so you'll have to show up and see if there's a vacancy.) Las Baulas is easy to visit from Tamarindo and Flamingo, but Hotel Las Tortugas, *below*, is right there. *See* Dining and Lodging in the Northwest in Chapter 4, Costa Rica.

Hotel Las Tortugas. This hotel stands at the edge of Las Baulas National Park right on the beach. The restaurant has an impressive ocean vista, and although the rooms don't have great views, they are comfortable, with good beds and air conditioning, as well as stone floors and stucco walls. Las Tortugas stands in front of the surf break and sometimes has dangerous rip currents, but most people who stay there come to see the turtles nesting. Local guides escort visitors along the beach at night, and the hotel also offers canoe trips in the wildlife refuge during the day. *Apdo. 164, Santa Cruz de Guanacaste, tel. and fax 680–0765. 11 rooms with bath. Facilities: restaurant, pool, parking. No credit cards. $$$*

Los Inocentes Lodge. Though Guanacaste National Park is closed to tourists, you can explore the wilderness on the north side of the park from this nature lodge on a working ranch. Guest rooms are in the old ranch house, along with an open-air restaurant and a long veranda that offers views of the ranch and nearby Orosí Volcano. Rooms are well-ventilated, with screens, wooden floors, and separate bathrooms. The restaurant serves hearty, set meals. Horseback or wagon tours of the dry forest are the main attraction; you can also see a remarkable amount of wildlife just by strolling along the stream near the lodge. *Apdo. 1370–3000, Heredia, tel. 265–5484. 12 rooms with bath. Facilities: restaurant, parking, pool, horses available. MC, V. $$$*

Southwest Costa Rica

The Southwest's varied ecosystems range from coral reef to lowland rain forest and highland paramo, a habitat of shrubs and herbs common to the upper Andes. There are animals in this region that you'd have a hard time finding in other parts of the country, such as scarlet macaws and squirrel monkeys. Although it has some of the country's most pristine wilderness, some of its parks have been receiving more visitors than the rangers can handle.

Carara The **Carara Biological Reserve,** on the road between Puntarenas and Jacó Beach, comprises one of the last remnants of a transition zone between the dry forests of the north and the humid forests of the south, and it is one of the most popular natural reserves in Costa Rica. Its tall trees don't drop their foliage during the dry season, but the sylvan scenery is much less luxuriant than what you'll encounter farther south. Carara is one of two areas in the country where you'll find scarlet macaws, which are easiest to see in the early morning or late afternoon. The Tarcoles River, which defines its northern border, is a good place to see crocodiles.

Unfortunately, Carara's proximity to San José and several resort beaches has brought tour buses of visitors to the park on a daily basis. At press time, the Parks Service threatened to close the park to visitors if the tour companies didn't pay the salaries of extra rangers needed to manage the crowds. For independent travelers, the presence of tour buses usually means that most of the animals probably have been frightened farther into the forest. If you catch Carara when there are few visitors—very early or late in the day—you can see a lot. The trail that starts near the ranger station makes a loop through the forest that should take an hour to hike. A longer trail, several kilometers to the north, is better for animal-watching, but cars parked at the trail head have been broken into. Camping isn't permitted at Carara.

Chirripó Centered around Costa Rica's highest peak, **Chirripó National Park** is a wild and scenic area that is different from what you'll find anywhere else in the country. And it's so remote that there is no easy way in. On the hike up from San Gerardo de Rivera, you'll take in some gorgeous scenery, but it's a grueling climb. There is a cabin near the top, so you don't have to pack a tent, but you'll need food, a camp stove, a good sleeping bag, and warm clothes. It's best to head out of San Gerardo with the first light of day, since the hike takes between 6 and 12 hours, depending on your physical condition. You can spend the night in the refuge halfway up if you're moving slowly or get a late start. You'll want at least a day at the cabin, since you have to hike up from there to explore the peaks, glacier lakes, and paramo—a highland ecosystem common to the Andes that consists of shrubs and herbaceous plants. Trails lead to the top of Chirripó and the nearby peak of Terbi, both of which offer unforgettable views. Camping isn't allowed at Chirripó, and reservations for the cabin must be prepaid at the parks office in San José or San Isidro (tel. 771–3155). Be prepared for very cold weather on top.

Corcovado An expanse of wilderness covering one third of the Osa Peninsula, in the country's southwest corner, **Corcovado National Park** is among the most impressive and pristine of Costa Rica's protected areas, safeguarding virgin rain forest, deserted beaches, jungle-edged rivers, and a vast swamp that hardly anyone visits. Corcovado is home to all the big animals—boa constrictors, jaguars, harpy eagles, tapirs—and if you're lucky enough to see these critters, it's most likely to happen in Corcovado. You will definitely see flocks of scarlet macaws, troops of squirrel monkeys, colorful poison dart frogs, and countless other interesting wildlife.

But the park's tropical nature has survived intact because it is in such a remote area, which means you have to spend either a good bit of money or time and energy if you want to go there. The easiest way to visit the park is on a day trip from one of the lodges in the nearby Drake Bay area, but if you have a backpack and strong legs, you can spend days deep within its wilderness. There are several trails into the park, along the beach starting from La Leona or San Pedrillo ranger stations, or through the forest from Los Patos ranger station. Though hiking is always tough in that tropical heat, the forest route is easier than the beach hike (especially the walk between La Leona and Sirena, which can only be done on the beach at low tide). You don't have to carry a tent or much food, though, since bunks and meals are available at the Leona, San Pedrillo, Los Patos, and Sirena ranger stations if you reserve and pay in advance at the parks office in San José or Puerto Jimenez. You can hire a boat in Sierpe or Drake Bay to take you to San Pedrillo, or hire a taxi in Puerto Jimenez to take you most of the way to Los Patos or La Leona. It's a hard, all-day hike between any two stations, and you'll want at least a day to rest between hikes. There is potable water at every station; don't drink stream water.

Manuel The popularity of **Manuel Antonio National Park** is not surprising.
Antonio But the assets of this beautiful patch of wilderness—exuberant forest, idyllic beaches, and coral reefs—have made the area too popular
for its own good. The road between the town of Quepos and Manuel
Antonio is lined with hotels, and when their guests head to the park,
its magic wanes. In an attempt to manage the crowd, the Parks
Service only allows 600 visitors to enter per day, which means you
might not get in during the afternoon in high season. It is closed
Monday.

The park entrance is on the beach just across a little estuary (don't
swim there—it's polluted) from the end of the road. A trail heads
through the forest just behind the beach, although most people walk
on the sand. Another trail that does a loop on Punta Catedral, the
point at the end of the beach, offers a good look at the rain forest and
a fantastic view of nearby islands. The second beach, on the other
side of the point, is in a deep cove that is safe for swimming. From
the simple visitor center here, one trail leads to the nearby cove of
Puerto Escondido and a lookout point beyond; a second, the Perzoso,
heads back through the forest to the park's entrance. Camping is not
permitted.

Getting There **By Car.** For Carara, take the Interamerican Highway west, and
turn left at the sign for Jacó; Carara will appear on the left immediately after crossing the Tarcoles River. For Manuel Antonio, take a
left at the Jacó turnoff, continue south on the Coastal Highway another 47 kilometers (28 miles) past Jacó, to Quepos; Manuel Antonio
lies several kilometers south of Quepos. For Chirripó, take the
Interamerican Highway south to San Isidro (136 kms [84 miles]),
where a road heads north to the town of San Gerardo de Chirripó (15
kms [9 miles]) and the trailhead.

By Bus. There are regular buses from San José to Manuel Antonio
and Puerto Jiménez (get a taxi from Puerto Jiménez to the
trailhead). Buses depart hourly from San José to San Isidro and several times a day from San Isidro to San Geraldo de Chirripó.

By Plane There are regular flights from San José to Manuel Antonio and
Puerto Jiménez.

Guided Tours Most of the big San José operators run tours to Carara, but **Geotur**
(tel. 234–1867) is the most experienced. Tours to Carara or Manuel
Antonio can also be booked through the big hotels in Jaco Beach.
The hotels in the Drake Bay area run regular boat trips to Corcovado, and **Costa Rica Expeditions** (tel. 222–0333) can fly you to their
tent camp on the other end of the park. You'll have to climb Chirripó
on your own.

Dining and Carara is just a 30-minute drive from the selection of restaurants
Lodging and lodgings in Puntarenas (*see* Dining and Lodging in the Northwest in Chapter 4, Costa Rica) and Jacó Beach (*see* Dining and Lodging in the Southwest in Chapter 4, Costa Rica). Manuel Antonio lies
near more lodging and dining options than you'll find in both those
towns combined (*see* Dining and Lodging in the Southwest in Chapter 4, Costa Rica). The nature lodges in Drake Bay on the Osa Peninsula (*see* Dining and Lodging in The Southwest in Chapter 4, Costa
Rica) offer day trips to Corcovado that bring you back to a comfortable room in time for a hearty dinner; otherwise you'll have to pack
your food and bedding, as is the case with Chirripó.

Guatemala

By Jacob Bernstein

Jacob Bernstein has covered Guatemala for Reuters, the San Francisco Examiner, and other publications from his base in Guatemala City.

Guatemala's rich natural diversity makes it a fascinating destination for nature lovers. Unlike the Costa Rican government, Guatemala's has not invested nearly enough in protecting the country's natural wonders or in making them accessible to tourists; travel to some areas is nearly impossible. One good way to see the local flora and fauna is on river trips or other adventure tours. Try **Maya Expeditions** (tel. 947–951) or **Izabal Adventures** (tel. 340–323), both of which are experienced and committed to ecotourism.

Guatemala's protected areas are called *biotopos*. Administered by the San Carlos National University, the biotopos were first established in the late 1970s to protect specific threatened animals or ecosystems. Today they represent the last stand for many endangered plants and animals, presenting a window on a marvelous spectrum of Guatemala's diversity. Although they are chronically underfunded, biotopos are staffed with friendly, helpful rangers committed to conservation. For more information contact the **Center for Conservation Studies** (Avenida La Reforma 0–63, Zona 10, tel. 327–612). Admission to the biotopos is usually free, but in order to help fund the upkeep of these magnificent areas, there are donation boxes at the entrances.

Cerro Cahui

Cerro Cahui Wildlife Preserve, with more than 3,703 hectares (1,500 acres) of rain forest, is one of the most accessible biotopos in El Petén, protecting a portion of a mountain that extends into the eastern edge of Lake Petén Itzá. A hike along either of two easy, well-maintained trails offers the opportunity to see ocellated turkeys, toucans, parrots, spider monkeys, and tepezcuintle (the large rodents hunted for their flavorful meat). Tzu'unte, a 3-kilometer (1¼-mile) trail, leads to two lookout points with views of nearby lakes. The upper lookout, Mirador Moreletii, is known by the locals as Crocodile Hill because from the other side of the lake it looks like the eye of a half-submerged crocodile. Los Ujuxtes, 400 meters (437 yards) long, offers a panoramic view of three lakes. Both begin at the ranger station, where interpretive guides in English are sporadically available.

Getting There

From Guatemala City, head for the Atlantic coast and turn left after the town of Franceses (there will be a sign for Flores or the Petén; be prepared for a rough road). Cerro Cahui is located after El Remate on the road to Tikal. Turn left at the sign for Camino Real, and follow the dirt road to the park entrance.

Dining and Lodging

Cerro Cahui is close to Camino Real Tikal and El Gringo Perdido (*see* Dining and Lodging in Tikal and El Petén in Chapter 5, Guatemala).

Chocón Machacas

Chocón Machacas Wildlife Reserve is commonly known as the Manatee Biotopo, and although manatees are said to inhabit the area, it is almost impossible to see these shy but endangered marine mammals. What one can see easily in the 7,205-hectare (17,790-acre) reserve is mangrove swamp, spectacular rain forest, and a variety of bird and animal life. The park consists of a small island surrounded by rivers, and there is only one land trail of a little less than 1 kilometer. The trail is well maintained, easily walked, and presents interesting examples of old-growth trees and rain-forest plants. There is a good chance that Pancho, a harmless but rather annoying spider monkey that rangers brought to the park from another area, will accompany you on your walk and try to hitch a ride on your leg.

The real beauty of the reserve can be seen in a boat ride through the dozens of creeks and lagoons that circle the park, where otters and many bird species can be seen. Most of the major hotels in Rio Dulce rent boats with guides for individual or group tours (*see* Getting There, *below*). Some of the creeks go through thick forest, under giant mahogany, ceiba, and mangrove trees, which overhang the water to form tunnels. There is a visitor center at the park entrance, where interpretive guides in English can be purchased when in stock.

Getting There   The only way to reach Chocón Machacas is by boat, either from Rio Dulce, Livingston, or Puerto Barrios. It's a 45-minute trip from Rio Dulce, where boat tours can be arranged at most major hotels or at the **Rio Dulce Travel Warehouse** (in El Relleno by the water, under the concrete bridge; make reservations with Izabal Adventures in Guatemala City, tel. 340–323), which offers boat tours through the park and along the Polochic and Oscuro, two beautiful rivers teeming with wildlife that flow into Lake Izabal.

Dining and   Catamaran Island and Marimonte Inn, on the banks of the Dulce
Lodging   River, are the closest accommodations to the park (*see* Dining and Lodging in the Verpaces and Atlantic Lowlands in Chapter 5, Guatemala).

Monterrico   **Monterrico Natural Reserve,** which offers a nice beach and excellent bird-watching, encompasses 2,800 hectares (6,916 acres) of mangrove swamp and tropical dry forest that jut up against the Pacific Ocean. Turtles swim ashore from July to February to lay their eggs; walking along the beach at night, you might encounter them digging their nests. Monterrico has a nice beach, but be careful: The ocean can be rough.

The park has a splendid aquatic trail, which can be followed by boat, and a land trail, which is not worth the effort. The aquatic trail winds its way through swamps with three types of mangrove. A trip here is an excellent opportunity for viewing more than 100 species of migratory and indigenous birds; fisher eagles, pelicans, and herons abound. The best time to go is at dawn or sunset, when enormous flocks of birds flap across a blood-red sky on their way to bed down for the night. From the swamps, there's a magnificent view of four of Guatemala's volcanos, including the active Pacaya. Guided boat tours ($2 per person for two hours) through the swamp trail can be arranged with park guards.

San Carlos University's center inside the reserve is well worth a visit. A project to raise animals for local villagers to sell or eat in lieu of capturing wild ones brings the visitor face to face with caimans (relatives of crocodiles), iguanas, and turtles in various stages of development. The *aldea* of Monterrico, located within the reserve, is a rustic town of about 1,100 people, where most residents relax in their hammocks in the afternoon and where it's easy to leave the pressures of civilization behind.

Getting There   **By Car.** Take the highway to Escuintla from Guatemala City. From Escuintla, take the left to Taxisco and follow the road to the village of La Avellana, where a ferry regularly takes travelers to Monterrico Beach.

By Bus. Buses depart the main bus station in Guatemala City for Taxisco every half hour. From Taxisco, microbuses depart regularly for La Avellan, where there's a ferry that goes to Monterrico Beach.

Dining and   There are several moderately priced hotels along the beach, most of
Lodging   which are little more than concrete rooms with cold showers and

beds covered with mosquito netting. They have no addresses but are easy to find along the small beach. **El Kaiman** (no phone) is one of the cleanest; it has a simple restaurant. **Hotel Baule Beach** (tel. 736–196 in Guatemala City) also has a good restaurant. A fancier hotel, **Hotel Paradise** (no phone), with a pool, restaurant, and 32 bungalows, was under construction at press time (spring 1994).

Divino Maestro. The best restaurant in the village of Monterrico, this simple establishment has tables under a thatched roof in an open-air room. There is no fixed menu, but you can choose from four types of fresh fish as well as crab, shrimp, meat, or chicken. The *caldo de mariscos* (seafood stew) is delicious. *In the aldea of Monterrico, no phone. No credit cards.* $$

Quetzal The **Quetzal Reserve** offers the chance to see the Guatemalan national bird, the resplendent quetzal, in its natural habitat. The male quetzal is magnificent, with its 2-foot-long train of tail feathers and brilliant, metallic-green body with red and white underparts. You can see its antics between April and June during mating season; the best place to watch, oddly enough, is not in the park itself but in the parking lot of the hotel Ranchito El Quetzal, 1½ kilometers (1 mile) north of the biotopo.

The Quetzal Reserve is also one of the last cloud forests in Guatemala and represents a vital source of water for the region's rivers. A walk along its trails gives the sense of being in a giant sponge. Water, evaporated from Lake Izabal and the Honduran Gulf, comes down in the form of rain and condensed fog, which is then collected by the towering old growth trees and verdant, dense vegetation. The loss of cloud forests such as this one is turning adjacent lowland areas into desert.

Once inside the forest, breathe deep; the air is rich with moisture and oxygen. Epiphytes, lichens, hepaticas, mosses, bromeliads, ferns, and orchids abound. If you're lucky, you can catch howler monkeys swinging above the well-maintained trails.

The biotopo is not large and can be visited in a day, although the best time to see the quetzal is early morning or late afternoon. The park offers two trails: Los Helechos ("the ferns"), which takes about an hour to walk, and Los Musgos ("the moss"), which takes two hours and makes a short detour to a series of beautiful waterfalls. The last part of both trails crosses a river with concrete bathing pools where you can take a swim if you don't mind the cold. An interpretive guide is available at the stand at the trailheads.

Getting There **By Car.** Take the Atlantic Highway to El Rancho (Km 84), then follow the road to the left, which heads toward Cobán. The Quetzal Reserve is about 75 kilometers (46 miles) north of El Rancho.

By Bus. Take any bus going to Cobán and ask the driver to let you off at the Quetzal Reserve.

Dining and Posada Montana del Quetzal and Ranchito del Quetzal are the closest
Lodging lodges to the reserve (*see* Dining and Lodging in the Verpaces and Atlantic Lowlands in Chapter 5, Guatemala).

Sierra de las The **Sierra de las Minas Biosphere Reserve,** said to be named for the
Minas Mayan jade and obsidian quarries that once were active in the area, represents one of the last truly unexplored places of Central America. Recently declared a biosphere reserve, it is loosely modeled after the Maya Biosphere Reserve (*see* Tikal, *below*). Within its territory—which cuts across four departments in the Atlantic region: Progreso, Baja Verapaz, Zacapa, and Izabal—are at least four

types of forest and more than 70% of the species of vertebrates found in Guatemala. Biologists working in the area continue to discover new plant and insect varieties. Unfortunately, there is no tourism infrastructure, and it is almost impossible to arrive without the aid of a four-wheel-drive vehicle or helicopter. If you are undaunted by the challenge, contact **Tamandua** (tel. and fax 322–690), an environmental group with a special interest in the area, to obtain the most up-to-date information.

Tikal **Tikal National Park** is located in the Maya Biosphere Reserve, which covers the upper third of El Petén, the department that boasts Guatemala's largest concentration of primary growth forest and its most important archaeological ruins. Surrounded by a multiple-use buffer zone, Tikal National Park is at the biosphere reserve's sacrosanct core and is supposed to be off-limits to human development. Tikal is easily visited and presents excellent opportunities for animal- and bird-watching while one walks among the ruins. There are several nature trails, both within the ruins and outside them. In particular, the short interpretative Benil-Ha Trail is excellent for identifying old-growth trees and rain-forest plants. Outside the park there is a somewhat overgrown trail halfway down the old airplane runway on the left. It leads to the remnants of several old rubber-tappers' camps, and because few people go there, it presents an excellent opportunity to see animals and birds.

Getting There Tikal National Park is an hour's drive northeast of Flores on the road to Tikal. Buses depart from the Hotel San Juan in Santa Elena at 6:30 AM and 1 PM. Taxis headed for the park depart from Santa Elena and the airport regularly.

Dining and The lodges in Tikal are close to the park (*see* Dining and Lodging in
Lodging Tikal and El Péten in Chapter 5, Guatemala).

Belize

By Richard Nidever

Richard Nidever is the former editor of the Belize Review, *an ecotourism magazine.*

The backbone of Belize's efforts to promote ecotourism is its marvelous collection of national parks, nature reserves, and wildlife sanctuaries. Since the creation of the first such area, Half Moon Cay National Monument, in 1982, Belize has jumped on the conservation bandwagon with unabashed enthusiasm, putting over 30% of its land under some form of protection. The most interesting and accessible of Belize's many protected areas are described here; for more information about these and others, contact the **Belize Audubon Society** (Box 282, 29 Regent St., Belize City, tel. 02/77369) or the **Belize Center for Environmental Studies** (Box 666, 55 Eve. St., Belize City, tel. 02/45739).

Belize Zoo The **Belize Zoo and Tropical Research Education Center** is a good place to learn about the country's conservation efforts and see some native species that you aren't likely to spot in the wild. The Belize Zoo could fit into a small corner of the San Diego Zoo, and it has only a fraction of the animals. So why is it considered by some to be the world's best? Because the natural settings for the animals and the zoo's commitment to wildlife protection make it (and its founder, Sharon Matola) perhaps the single strongest force in Belizean conservation.

Matola originally came to Belize in 1983 to manage a band of local animals for a wildlife film. When the film's budget dried up, she was left with the animals and, knowing that releasing them back into the wild would be a death sentence, decided to start a zoo. From these humble beginnings, Matola slowly built up the zoo while embarking on an ambitious education program aimed especially at children. For the first time, Belizeans were able to see the wild animals who share their country and learn how valuable the preservation of the animals' habitat could be for a developing nation. Many conservation leaders credit Matola with developing a new appreciation for local wildlife that has been instrumental in the fight to protect and preserve their habitats.

The zoo houses the elusive jaguar, the endangered Baird's tapir (the national animal of Belize and the largest land mammal in Central America), howler monkeys, and many other species. The enclosures replicate as close as possible the animals' natural environment, which sometimes makes spotting them difficult, so the best time to visit (as well as the coolest) is early morning or late afternoon, when most of the animals are fed.

Getting There **By Car.** From Belize City, take the Western Highway to Mile 30.

By Bus. Buses from Belize City to San Ingacio stop at the Belize Zoo.

Cockscomb Basin The mighty jaguar, once the undisputable king of the Central American and South American jungles, is now extinct or endangered in most of its original range. But it has found a sanctuary in **Cockscomb Basin Wildlife Sanctuary** on 41,310 hectares (102,000 acres) of lush rain forest in the Cockscomb range of the Maya Mountains. Because of the Jaguar Reserve, as this area is commonly called, as well as other protected areas in the country, Belize has the highest concentration of jaguars in the world.

Jaguars are shy, nocturnal animals that prefer to keep their distance from humans, so the possibility of sighting a jaguar in the wild is almost nil. Still, a visit here is rewarding in other ways. The reserve boasts Belize's best-maintained system of jungle and mountain trails, most of which have at least one outstanding swimming hole. The sanctuary also offers spectacular views of the Cockscomb range and Victoria Peak and the chance to see many other endangered flora and fauna, including over 300 bird species. If you plan to do any extensive hiking, pick up a trail map at the visitor center and bring insect repellent, a long-sleeved shirt, and long pants. Keep in mind that the best time to hike anywhere in Belize is early morning or late afternoon/early evening, when temperatures are lower and more wildlife can be seen.

Getting There **By Car.** The Cockscomb Basin Wildlife Sanctuary is most easily reached by four-wheel-drive vehicle from either Dangriga or Placencia. Take the Southern Highway to Maya Center, where you'll find the visitor center and an 11-kilometer (7-mile) dirt road that leads into the reserve.

Dining and Lodging Campsites are available in the park ($5 night), but most people spend the night in the Dangriga or Placencia (*see* Dining and Lodging in Placencia and the South in Chapter 6, Belize).

Half Moon Cay **Half Moon Cay National Monument,** Belize's easternmost island, although difficult to reach and lacking accommodations, offers one of the greatest wildlife encounters in Belize. Part of the Lighthouse Reef system, Half Moon Cay owes its protected status to the presence on the island of the red-footed booby in such stunning profusion that it's hard to believe that the species has only one other nesting colony in the entire Caribbean (on Tobago Island off the coast of Venezuela). Some 4,000 of these rare seabirds call the island home, along with more than 90 other bird species, iguanas, lizards, and loggerhead turtles. The entire 16-hectare (40-acre) island is a nature reserve, and visitors can explore the beaches or head into the bush on the narrow nature trail. Along this trail, above the trees at the center of the island, is a small viewing platform. Climb up, and you're suddenly in a sea of birds; they fill the branches of the surrounding trees so completely that it's hard not to be reminded of a certain Hitchcock movie.

Getting There   Because there are no accommodations and no regular boat service to the island, most people come to Half Moon Cay National Monument on a tour. A visit is usually combined with dives at the legendary Blue Hole and Half Moon Cay Wall, considered by many to be the two best dive sites in Belize. One-day or overnight camping trips can be arranged through several dive operators in San Pedro on Ambergris Cay or through dive resorts on the Turneffe Islands or the Belize Barrier Reef (*see* Dining in The Cays and Atolls in Chapter 6, Belize).

Dining and   The nearest accommodations are at the Lighthouse Reef Resort,
Lodging   which offers a trip here as part of a week-long package (*see* Dining and Lodging in The Cays and Atolls in Chapter 6, Belize).

Hol Chan   **Hol Chan** (Mayan for "little channel") is a 13-square-kilometer (5-square-mile) marine reserve about 6 kilometers (4 miles) southeast of Ambergris Cay. Because fishing is off limits, divers and snorkelers can see teeming marine life, including green moray eels and spotted eagle rays. A special treat for adventurous divers is a night dive: The water lights up with bioluminescence, and many nocturnal animals, such as octopus and spider crabs, can be observed going about their activities. You need above-average swimming skills; the strong tidal current has caused at least one drowning.

Getting There   San Pedro on Ambergris Cay is the jumping-off point for trips to Hol Chan Marine Reserve. Before you go, stop in at the Hol Chan office in San Pedro (Barrier Reef Dr.), where you can find information on Belize's underwater flora and fauna. All of San Pedro's dive operators offer trips to Hol Chan (*see* Diving in Chapter 6, Belize), which generally last about two hours and are reasonably priced (about $15 for snorkeling and $30 for a single-tank dive). **Ramon's Dive Shop** (tel. 026/2071) and **Amigos del Mar** (tel. 026/2706) offer glass-bottom-boat tours of the marine reserve—perfect for those who want to see marine life without getting wet.

Terra Nova   **Terra Nova Medicinal Plant Reserve,** the first in the world set aside exclusively for traditional healers, covers 2,430 hectares (6,000 acres) of old-growth forest in the Yalbac Hills, in the Cayo District. Visitors can see how traditional healers harvest and prepare their herbal medicines. The reserve is a good place to see wildlife since it is an oasis for deer, monkeys, tropical birds, jaguars, and tapir driven from surrounding lands that have been clearcut for agriculture. Terra Nova was created to rescue and replant seedlings of endangered medicinal rain forest plants, to encourage sustainable harvesting of these plants for use by traditional healers, and to encourage respect for traditional herbal healing through its educational programs. Classes will eventually be offered on traditional healing with medicinal plants, and there will be a demonstration site for a reforestation project that will show how "abandoned" land is slowly transformed back into rain forest.

Getting There   To find out about road conditions (the road is sometimes closed in the rainy season, from June to September) and to get directions to Terra Nova, stop at the **Ix Chel Farm and Tropical Research Center** (in Cayo, next to the Chaa Creek Resort, no phone, fax in San Ignacio); the reserve is about an hour's drive north of Ix Chel. There is an interesting medicinal plant trail at the Tropical Research Center that provides information about the work of Dr. Rosita Arvigo, the prime mover behind the creation of Terra Nova, and Don Eligio Panti, Belize's legendary Maya medicine man.

Dining and Lodging There are no accommodations near Terra Nova; *see* Dining and Lodging in the Cayo in Chapter 6, Belize.

4 Costa Rica

By Philip Eade

Born and raised in Shropshire, Philip Eade lives in a gray-green-terraced house in Shepherd's Bush, London, which he uses as a base for his life as an itinerant writer, barrister, and amateur painter. He is also an author of Fodor's Spain '93.

Defining what it is that sets Costa Rica apart from neighboring Central American republics is a popular game with Costa Ricans and outsiders alike. With Nicaragua to the north and Panama to the south, Costa Rica is seen as a tranquil haven amid its turbulent surroundings. It is the region's purest democracy by a long chalk, with no army, a deep-rooted respect for human rights, well-educated people, and excellent hospitals. For visitors, however, the most striking feature of Costa Rica is the remarkable variety of flora, fauna, landscape, and climate within its frontiers—all tucked into an area roughly the size of West Virginia (31,248 square kilometers [19,530 square miles]).

These protected tracts of wilderness, encompassing a vast array of habitats, presently make up around 12% of Costa Rica's territory—the target is 25%—and help to ensure the survival of its 560 species of mammals, amphibians, and reptiles, 850 species of birds, 130 species of freshwater fish, and 9,000 species of plants.

Rife deforestation has so far permitted the creation of Guanacaste's vast parched cattle ranches to the northeast and sprawling banana and African palm plantations in the southern and western lowlands. The park system is pitted against this sweeping tide, and is one of the main reasons why large areas of undulating terrain still remain cloaked in dense tropical jungle, seen to especially dramatic effect when clinging to the slopes of smoking semi-active volcanos—a line of which form an arc northeast of the Central Valley.

To the south, much of the 12,000-foot Cordillera de Talamanca—the highest mountain range in southern Central America—now comprises the contiguous Chirripó and La Amistad national parks, whose trails enable one to experience the breathtaking transition from tropical rain forest up through oak forests to a high-altitude Andean blend of shrubs and bare rock, and to glimpse the amazing resplendent quetzal, by wide repute the prettiest bird in the Americas.

While on this subject, one oughtn't omit mention of Costa Rica's famous whitewater rivers and its Caribbean and Pacific coasts, with mile upon mile of varied pristine beaches backdropped by lush palms and rain forest. Some of the beaches are venues for the spectacular *arribadas* of nesting sea turtles; others are playgrounds for beachcombers, surfers, divers, and anglers.

Costa Rica's comparative social and racial homogeneity stems back to early colonial intermarriage between the Spaniards and Indians. The vast majority of Costa Ricans are now *mestizos* (mixed blood), unlike in Guatemala, where 65 percent of the population are Indians. Ninety percent of Costa Ricans are Catholics, yet the church remains relatively poor and weak. Catholicism accounts in part of their strong family ties and somewhat fatalistic attitudes—a tendency to qualify conclusions by a *"si Dios quiere"* ("God willing"). On the other hand, Ticos (as Costa Ricans refer to themselves, on account of their tendency to use *tico* as a diminutive ending) have rejected other articles of faith and doubt the authority of priests to a far greater extent than in other Latin American countries. This all no doubt owes something to the trend in modernizing societies to eschew religion, but it is also explicable by reference to Ticos' tendency to be fence-sitters. They favor moderation and hate to be thought of as fanatics. By abolishing the army in 1949, Ticos not only saved themselves money to spend on hospitals and schools, but they also removed the specter of fanatical militarism.

Costa Rica has enjoyed a long history of political stability. In 1889 it held what is considered the first free election in Central American history, marked by press freedom, frank debates by rival candidates, honest vote counting, and the first peaceful transition of power from a ruling group to the opposition. The nascent democratic system was carefully nurtured during the early 20th century. The only serious threat came in 1948, when Rafael Angel Calderón refused to acknowledge his defeat at the polls. The ensuing popular revolt was led by José Figueres, who on May 8, 1948, accepted the position of president. The new constitution abolished the army in order to preclude a repeat of the episode. (Ironically, Figueres's son, José María, succeeded Calderón's son, Rafael Angel Calderón Fournier, as president in May 1994.)

Peace and democracy are the cardinal tenets of modern Costa Rica. Former president Oscar Arias Sánchez epitomized the working of these principles in 1986 by closing down the Contra bases in northern Costa Rica, enforcing Costa Rica's neutrality, and initiating the Central American Peace Plan aimed at ending the war in Nicaragua, achievements for which he was awarded the Nobel Peace Prize in 1987.

With the war in Nicaragua over, the new challenge facing Costa Rica is how best to cope with the booming tourism industry, which will soon surpass banana exports as the country's top earner. While tourism provides a much needed injection of foreign exchange into the flagging economy, it has yet to be fully decided which direction it should take. The buzzwords now are "ecotourism" and "sustainable development," and with so much in the way of natural beauty to protect, it is hoped that Costa Rica will find it possible to continue down these roads rather than opt for something akin to the Acapulco or Cancun styles of development.

Before You Go

Government Tourist Offices

In the United States **Costa Rican National Tourist Bureau** (1101 Bricknell Ave., BIV Tower, Suite 801, Miami, FL 33131, tel. 800/327–7033).

In Canada and the U.K. Although there are no tourists offices as such, the Costa Rican embassies in Ontario and London can provide travelers with limited tourist information (*see* Passports and Visas, *below*, for addresses).

When to Go

The best time to visit Costa Rica is during the dry season, which runs from December through April. From late November until early February, in particular, you have the combined advantages of good weather, lush vegetation, and lower prices. If you want to visit the beach during the rainy season, it is often dry and sunny in Guanacaste, but more rarely so in the south or on the Caribbean. Bear in mind that hotels are much more likely to be booked up during the dry season.

Despite the fact that Costa Rica lies well inside the northern hemisphere, the dry season (December–April) is referred to as *verano* (summer) and the rainy season as *invierno* (winter). Temperatures vary little from season to season: The elevated Central Valley has an average daytime temperature of 72°F (22°C) and nights are cool all year round. The Caribbean and Pacific coasts are some 10°–15°F hotter than this; the Caribbean is more humid. During the dry season, Guanacaste is the hottest place of all, with temperatures frequently up in the 90s; as for its rainy season, mornings are generally warm and sunny and afternoons cool and wet.

The following are the average daily maximum and minimum temperatures for San José.

Jan.	75F	24C	May	80F	27C	Sept.	79F	26C
	58	14		62	17		61	16
Feb.	76F	24C	June	79F	26C	Oct.	77F	25C
	58	14		62	17		60	16
Mar.	79F	26C	July	77F	25C	Nov.	77F	25C
	59	15		62	17		60	16
Apr.	79F	26C	Aug.	78F	26C	Dec.	75F	24C
	62	17		61	16		58	14

The following are the average daily maximum and minimum temperatures for Golfito.

Jan.	91F	33C	May	91F	33C	Sept.	91F	33C
	72	22		73	23		72	22
Feb.	91F	33C	June	90F	32C	Oct.	90F	32C
	72	22		73	23		72	22
Mar.	91F	33C	July	90F	32C	Nov.	91F	32C
	73	23		72	22		72	22
Apr.	91F	33C	Aug.	90F	32C	Dec.	91F	33C
	73	23		72	22		72	22

Festivals and Seasonal Events

National holidays are known as *feriados;* there are 15 each year. On these days government offices, banks, and post offices are all closed and public transport is severely restricted. Religious festivals are characterized by colorful processions in the countryside. The following is a list of feriados:

January 1: New Year's Day; **March 19:** St. Joseph's Day (San José's patron saint); **Good Friday–Easter Sunday; April 11:** Anniversary of Battle of Rivas (defeat of William Walker); **May 1:** Labor Day; **June 10:** Corpus Christi; **June 29:** St. Peter and St. Paul; **July 25:** Annexation of Guanacaste; **August 2:** Virgin of Los Angeles (Costa Rica's patron saint); **August 15:** Mother's Day; **September 15:** Independence Day; **October 12:** Columbus (Colón) Day; **December 8:** Immaculate Conception; **December 24–25:** Christmas; **December 26–31:** Nonstop carnivals and festivals (San José only). For festivals peculiar to each region, *see* The Arts and Nightlife in regional sections.

Costa Rican Currency

The currency of Costa Rica is the colón (plural: colones). The exchange rate floats in relation to the U.S. dollar, with the colón subject to small devaluations; at press time (spring 1994) the colón stood at 177 to the dollar. Major credit cards are accepted at many of the larger hotels and more expensive restaurants. Cash in dollars and traveler's checks can be exchanged in banks, some hotels, and unofficially in restaurants, bars, and on the street. The black market is illegal, unsafe, and highly discouraged because of rising crime. Stick to the banks.

Costa Rica

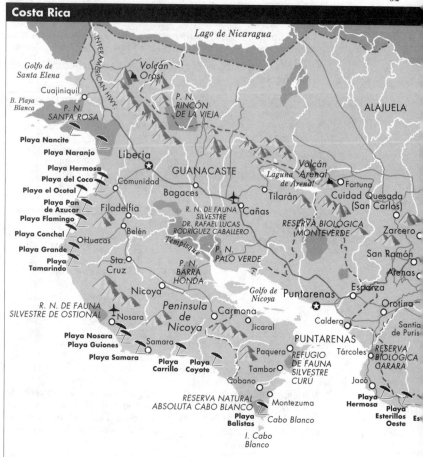

Lago de Nicaragua

Golfo de
Santa Elena

Cuajiniquil

B. Playa
Blanca

P. N.
SANTA ROSA

Playa Nancite

Playa Naranjo

Playa Hermosa

Playa del Coco

Playa el Ocotal

**Playa Pan
de Azucar**

Playa Flamingo

Playa Conchal

Playa Grande

**Playa
Tamarindo**

R. N. DE FAUNA
SILVESTRE DE OSTIONAL

Playa Nosara
Playa Guiones

Playa Samara

Volcán
Orosi

P. N.
RINCÓN
DE LA VIEJA

INTER-AMERICAN HWY

Liberia

GUANACASTE

Comunidad

Bagaces

Filadelfia

Belén

Huacas

Sta.
Cruz

Nicoya

Nosara

Samara

**Playa
Carrillo**

**Playa
Coyote**

R. N. DE FAUNA
SILVESTRE
DR. RAFAEL LUCAS
RODRÍGUEZ CABALLERO

Tempisque

P. N.
PALO VERDE

P. N.
BARRA
HONDA

Península
de
Nicoya

Carmona

Jicaral

Paquera

Tambor

Cobano

ALAJUELA

Volcán
Arenal

Laguna
de Arenal

Tilarán

Fortuna

Cuidad Quesada
(San Carlos)

RESERVA BIOLÓGICA
MONTEVERDE

Zarcero

San Ramón

Atenas

Cañas

Golfo de
Nicoya

Puntarenas

Esparza

Orotina

Caldera

Santia
de Puris

PUNTARENAS

Tárcoles

RESERVA
BIOLÓGICA
CARARA

Jacó

**Playa
Hermosa**

**Playa
Esterillos
Oeste**

Es

REFUGIO
DE FAUNA
SILVESTRE
CURÚ

RESERVA NATURAL
ABSOLUTA CABO BLANCO

Montezuma

**Playa
Balistas**

Cabo Blanco

I. Cabo
Blanco

PACIFIC OCEAN

N

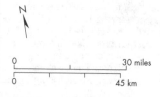

0	30 miles
0	45 km

What It Will Cost

Costa Rica's economy is much more stable than those of neighboring states, and inflation remains comparatively in check. The cost of living is also correspondingly higher, but visitors will find that eating and drinking out can be very inexpensive. Foreign electrical goods have punitive tariffs and are thus very expensive.

Taxes The VAT equivalent currently stands at 10%. To this is added a 3% hotel tax and usually 10% for service in smarter restaurants. Golfito is a duty-free port, but you need to stay there at least 24 hours to take advantage of it.

Sample Costs Cup of coffee, 60 colones; bottle of beer, 150 colones; 1½-kilometer (1-mile) taxi ride, 150 colones; bus from San José to Limón, 500 colones; plane from San José to Golfito, 7,700–9,600 colones.

Passports and Visas

U.S., Canadian, and British citizens must have a valid passport to enter Costa Rica for a stay of up to 90 days. U.S. citizens planning a stay of under 30 days, however, do not need a passport; upon presenting an original birth certificate and two forms of identification, they will be issued a tourist card at the airport when they leave the United States. Visas and health certificates are not required. If you lose your passport, go to the police immediately and report it. Bring the report, with positive ID and a photocopy of the passport's photo page (do this before you leave home, and keep it separate from your passport), to the embassy in San José (*see* Important Addresses and Numbers in San José and the Central Valley, *below,* for embassy addresses).

U.S. Citizens For more information, contact the **Costa Rican Embassy** (1825 Connecticut Ave., NW, Suite 211, Washington, DC 20009, tel. 202/234–2945). There are also consulates in Chicago, Dallas, Houston, Miami, Los Angeles, New Orleans, and New York.

British Citizens **Costa Rican Embassy** (36 Upper Brook St., London W1Y 1PE, tel. 071/495–3985).

Canadian Citizens **Costa Rican Embassy** (150 Argyle Ave., Suite 115, Ottawa, Ont. K2P 1B7, tel. 613/562–2855).

Customs and Duties

On Arrival U.S., Canadian, and British citizens entering Costa Rica may bring in half a kilo of manufactured tobacco and 3 liters of liquor duty free. Any amount of foreign or local currency may be taken in or out. Tourists are permitted to bring two cameras, binoculars, and electrical items for personal use only. Word processors and the like can be held in customs and taxed unless you can produce proof that they are for personal use.

On Departure If your passport has been stamped indicating you have brought valuable goods into the country, you will need to show that you are taking them away with you. An $8 airport tax is payable on departure.

Language

Spanish is the official language of Costa Rica. While some Costa Ricans do speak English, especially those on the Caribbean coast, your stay will be much better if you learn some Spanish before you go, and bring your phrase book with you. Do at least attempt to learn the rudiments of polite conversation such as "please" (*por favor*) and "thank you" (*gracias*), as Ticos (Costa Ricans) appreciate this kind of thing.

Car Rentals

Major international and local car rental firms vie for business in San José, at the airport, and in most of the larger towns. Decide what type of vehicle you want to rent; a four-wheel-drive (*doble-tracción*) is essential for reaching many parts of the country, especially during the rainy season. They cost roughly twice as much as small cars and are frequently booked well in advance. Be sure to read the small print on the hire agreement and note that you will be liable to pay a sizable amount ($1,000–$1,500) in the event of a crash or theft. In San José, most car rental agencies are located along Paseo Colón. The best deals (approximately $40–$60 per day, including mileage, for cars; $80 for 4WD) are at **Avis** (Calle 42 and Ave. Las Americas, tel. 232–9922) and **Hertz** (Paseo Colón at Calle 38, tel. 223–5959), but shop around.

Further Reading

Culture and History   *The Costa Ricans,* by Richard, Karen, and Mavis Biesanz, contains the best description of the national character. In *Costa Rica, The Unarmed Democracy*, by Leonard Bird, you'll find a thorough political history of the country. *The Costa Rica Reader*, edited by Mark Edelman and Joanne Kenen, is an insightful collection of essays on Costa Rican topics, and *What Happen*, by Paula Palmer, relates the folk history, dreams, and legends told by the people of the Talamanca coast.

Natural History   *A Guide to the Birds of Costa Rica*, by F. Gary Stiles and Alexander F. Skutch, is an absolute must for bird-watchers; it is lavishly illustrated by Dana Gardner and remains the most comprehensive treatment of migrant and resident bird species. Other helpful texts include *The Butterflies of Costa Rica and Their Natural History*, by Philip J. Devries; *A Naturalist in Costa Rica*, by Alexander F. Skutch; *Costa Rican Natural History*, edited by Daniel H. Janzen; and *Journey Through a Tropical Jungle*, by Adrian Forsyth. *The National Parks of Costa Rica*, by Mario A. Boza, contains descriptions of each park in the system, accompanied by superb color photography.

Novels   *One Hundred Years of Solitude*, by Gabriel García Márquez, describes the impact of the United Fruit Company on a small fictitious town similar to Golfito.

Arriving and Departing

From North America by Plane

Airports and Airlines   The main tourist season in Costa Rica, from Thanksgiving to Easter, coincides with vacation times, like Thanksgiving and Christmas. Hence flights often become fully booked months ahead. Check through fares from your city to San José as well as fares from your city to a gateway and from the gateway into San José; the latter can be cheaper. Gateway cities in the United States are Dallas, Houston, Los Angeles, Miami, New Orleans, and New York. If your ticket combines airlines, try to get it issued on the ticket stock of the airline that has an office in San José, making it easier to make changes on the return leg. There are charter flights from Canada, but those from the United States had been suspended at press time.

At present, all flights arrive at and depart from **Juan Santamaría International Airport,** 16 kilometers (10 miles) north of downtown San José.

The following airlines fly to San José from the United States: **Aero Costa Rica** (tel. 800/237–6274), **American** (tel. 800/433–7300), **Aviateca Guatemala** (tel. 800/327–1225), **Continental** (tel. 800/231–0856), **Lacsa–Costa Rican** (tel. 800/225–2272), **Mexicana** (tel. 800/531–7921), **Taca–El Salvadoran** (tel. 800/535–8780), **Tan Sahsa–Honduran** (tel. 800/327–1225), and **United** (tel. 800/827–7777). Shop around for the best current deal, and bear in mind that some airlines allow interesting stopovers for no extra charge in places such as Mexico, Belize, or Guatemala.

Flying Time From New York, flights to San José take 5½ hours (via Miami); from Los Angeles, 8½ hours (via Mexico); from Houston, 4½ hours (via Guatemala); from Miami, two hours (direct).

From the United States by Car, Boat, and Bus

By Car The trip down the Interamerican Highway from the U.S. border states to Costa Rica requires time, patience, and preparation. From Brownsville, Texas, it is 3,700 kilometers (2,300 miles) to the Costa Rican border. Driving at night is not recommended. You should allow three weeks in each direction, which will give you time enough each day to find your hotel in daylight, with a little time left over for sightseeing. Two weeks will probably be spent in Mexico; from there it is a five-day drive to Costa Rica. Don't leave home without valid insurance: This may mean having to insure through a Mexican company such as **Sanborn** (tel. 210/686–0711) in McAllen, Texas. If the 1992 Peace Agreement in El Salvador holds, it may become safe to take the shorter route through there—check with the U.S. State Department. The alternative is to go via Guatemala City (*see* Chapter 5, Guatemala) and straight to the border with Honduras.

By Boat Cruises are the most restful way of traveling. The U.S.–Costa Rica cruise season runs September–May with trips lasting from three days to a week. Luxury liners equipped with swimming pools and gymnasiums sail from Fort Lauderdale, Florida, to Limón and from Los Angeles to Caldera, south of Puntarenas. On board you can sign up for tours for when you arrive. Packages include the cost of flying to the appropriate port in the United States. Cruise lines operating these routes include **Carnival** (tel. 800/327–9501), **Holland America** (tel. 800/426–0327), **Royal Viking** (tel. 800/422–8000), **Cunard** (tel. 800/221–4770), **Sunline** (tel. 800/872–6400), **Seaborne** (tel. 800/351–9595), **Regency** (tel. 800/388–5500), **Ocean Cruise** (tel. 800/556–8850), **Sitmar Cruise** (tel. 305/523–1219), and **Crystal Cruises** (tel. 800/446–6645). Your travel agent will be able to give you details of prices, which range from $1,000 to $5,000.

By Bus There is bus service between Managua, Nicaragua, and San José, and between Panama and San José. **Tica** (Calle 9 and Ave. 4, tel. 221–9229) buses leave Panama City daily at 8 PM and arrive at 5 PM. Tica buses also run between San José and Managua. **TRACOPA** (Ave. 18 and Calle 4, tel. 221–4214) buses leave San José daily at 7:30 AM, arriving at David, Panama, at 4 PM. From there, onward buses go to Panama City, seven hours away.

From the United Kingdom by Plane

Most routes from the United Kingdom to Costa Rica go via the United States, using the airlines listed above. The best current deal is with **Continental** (tel. 0293/776464), whose return fare is around £550; there's a six-hour stopover in Houston. A faster option is to fly with **KLM** (tel. 081/750–9000), which has direct flights from Amsterdam (around 10 hours). Charter flights are due to start soon from Germany. Contact **Journey Latin America** (16 Devonshire Rd., London W4 2HD, tel. 081/747–3108) for the best current deals.

Staying in Costa Rica

Getting Around

By Plane Considering the nation's often difficult driving conditions, flying can be a convenient way to get around. Two domestic airlines serve Costa Rica. **Sansa** (Calle 24, between Ave. Central and Ave. 1, tel. 221–9414 or 233–0397) flies out of **Juan Santamaría International Airport** near Alajuela (*see* Arriving and Departing, *above*). **Travelair** (tel. 220–3054 or 232–7883) uses **Tobias Bolaños Airport** in the San José suburb of Pavas. At press time, Sansa flew to the following destinations: Quepos (Mon.–Sat.), Nosara/Carrillo (Mon.–Wed., Fri. and Sat.), Tamarindo (Mon.–Wed., Fri. and Sat.), Barra del Colorado (Tues., Thurs., and Sat.), Golfito/Coto 47 (Mon.–Sat.), Palmar Sur (Mon., Wed., and Fri.). The airline will not carry surfboards, so surfers generally rent vehicles to get around or rent boards when they arrive at a surfing venue. At press time, Travelair had daily flights to the following destinations: Barra del Colorado/Tortuguero, Tarmarindo, Nosara/Carrillo, Tambor, Quepos, Palmar Sur, and Golfito/Puerto Jiménez. Several charter companies in San José will fly you to places where scheduled airlines won't go, including Limón and the remote Osa Peninsula; check the yellow pages under *taxis aereos* (air taxis).

By Train Though the government has recently commenced limited commuter rail service in the San José metropolitan area (*see* Getting Around in San José and the Central Valley, *below*), intercity train travel has all but ceased. What remains is a short tour between the Atlantic lowlands towns of Siquirres and Guapiles, meant to replicate part of the spectacular but departed Jungle Train route between Turrialba and Siquirres (*see* Tour Companies, *below*).

By Bus Reliable and inexpensive bus service covers most of the country. On longer routes, buses stop midway at *sodas* (inexpensive cafés). Tickets are sold either at the bus station or on the buses themselves. A patchwork of private companies operates out of San José from a variety of departure points. For detailed information, consult the Getting Around sections of individual regions. Note that although this information was current at press time, it is worthwhile asking the tourist office in San José for an update to make sure. Reservations are not usually necessary and often not possible, but if you want to be sure of a seat, phone ahead.

By Car Roads range from paved highways to badly rutted tracks, often impassable during the wet season without a four-wheel-drive vehicle. Distances may look small on the map but can take a deceptively long time to cover. Allow, for example, four hours for the 140-kilometer (88-mile) journey to Manuel Antonio and five hours for the 285-kilometer (178-mile) trip to Tamarindo. Signposts are virtually nonexistent, and you will probably have to ask for the right road out whenever you enter a town.

Rules of the Road With the exception of the Central Valley, there isn't much traffic on the roads. This comes as a relief because there are plenty of would-be Mario Andrettis on Costa Rica's highways; watch out for hare-brained passing on blind corners, tailgating, and failures to signal. Watch out, too, for two-lane roads that feed into one-lane bridges with specified rights of way.

Parking Car theft is rife in Costa Rica, and at night it is foolish to leave your car in an unlocked parking place. It is one of the idiosyncrasies of insurance here that if you do otherwise, you may well be liable to pay for the car. Most hotels, except for the least expensive, therefore offer secure parking with a guard or locked gates.

Gasoline Gasoline costs around $2 per gallon.

Telephones

Local Calls Costa Rica's phone system is very good by Third World standards. For calls within the country it is also very cheap—local calls from pay phones cost 10 colones per minute, but you will pay more if you use a hotel's phone, and more still from your room. In rural areas where pay phones don't exist as such, look for the yellow "telefono publico" signs, indicating phones from which you can make calls for the same rates as pay phones. You will often find them in the village *pulpería* (grocery). No area codes exist within Costa Rica. At press time, the national phone company was undertaking an ambitious expansion that included changing every telephone number in the country from six digits to seven. Call 113 for domestic directory inquiries and 110 for domestic collect calls.

International Calls The Guía Telefónica (phone book) contains numbers for various services as well as rates for calling different countries. To call overseas direct, dial 00, then the country code (1 for the United States and Canada, 44 for Great Britain), the area code, and the number. It is more expensive to phone from your hotel. Calls through the operator are more than twice as expensive, the only advantage being that if the person you need to speak to isn't in, there is no charge even if somebody answers. Discount times for calling the United States and Canada are weekdays 10 PM–7 AM and weekends; for calling the United Kingdom the only discounted time is between Friday at 10 PM and Monday at 7 AM. Good places to make international calls and to send faxes, telexes, or telegrams in San José are the **ICE office** (Ave. 2 between Calles 1 and 3; open daily 7 AM–11 PM) and **Radiographica Costarricense** (Ave. 5 between Calles 1 and 3; open daily 7 AM–10 PM).

U.S. visitors can call home directly through three telecommunications companies from any phone, including pay phones. You can make collect calls or charge it to your credit card. The companies are **AT&T** (dial 114), **Sprint International** (dial 163), and **MCI** (dial 162). Operators speak English and Spanish.

Dial 116 if you want an operator (English spoken) for international calls, collect or otherwise; dial 124 (English spoken) for information on tariffs; and dial 123 to send telegrams by phone.

Mail

The postal service does not measure up to the telephones. Mail from the States or Europe can take a lifetime to arrive, occasionally it never does, and even within the country it is fairly unreliable. Outgoing mail is marginally quicker. Always use airmail for overseas; it might take anywhere from 10 days to two weeks or more. The rates are very low, although they are set to rise. In 1993, letters to the United States cost just 45 colones; to the United Kingdom, 55 colones. Mail theft is a chronic problem, so do not send checks, money, or anything else of value through the mail.

You can have mail sent to your hotel or use poste restante at the post office (Correos). Most Costa Ricans have to go to the post office to pick up their mail, because of the absence of both street names and any house-to-house service. *Apartado* and the abbreviation *Apdo.*, which you will see in many addresses, means post office box.

American Express (tel. 800/528–2121) cardholders can have mail sent to them at the local American Express office.

Tipping

In most restaurants 10% is included for service, so don't feel obliged to tip; however, don't hesitate if the service has been especially good. Taxi drivers do not expect tips either, although it is customary to add on a little to round out the fare; add on more still if your driver has been especially helpful. You can safely assume that if the driver refuses to use his meter, his quoted fare will include a tip. Tips for hotel bellboys and porters are about 100 colones per bag. Tour guides also expect tips—around $1 per day—and don't forget the bus driver.

Opening and Closing Times

Banks Most banks are open weekdays 9–3. A branch of **Banco Nacional de Costa Rica** (in the San José suburb of San Pedro, across from the church) is open until 6. A branch of **Banco Anglo Costarricense** (200 meters, or 218 yards, east of the San Pedro church) is open until 7.

Museums Generalizing about Costa Rican museum opening times is unwise. Opening times appear next to the museums in the exploring sections of the text.

Shops As a rule, shops are open weekdays 9–7, although some still observe the long lunch hour from noon to 2 PM. Saturday opening times vary; some close at noon, others later. A handful of stores, especially souvenir shops, have Sunday hours.

Shopping

Ceramics, wood, leather, jewelry, and coffee make up the bulk of visitors' shopping lists. Pots are made in pre-Columbian designs in many parts of the country and are sold from roadside houses, especially in the Nicoya Peninsula, as well as in town markets. Different woods are used in a range of kitchen implements including salt and pepper shakers, coffee filter stands, cutting boards, and fruit and salad bowls. Painted boxes for odds and ends, masks, carved birds, and miniature ox carts may further tempt you. The elaborately patterned hammocks tend to be rather heavy due to the large wooden ends and the thickness of the string; if you are visiting Mexico or Guatemala, you can find cheaper and more portable ones there. All those Guanacaste cattle mean a thriving leather industry, which turns out a range of bags, suitcases, and belts, mostly well made and of good value. There is also a thriving folk jewelry industry with thousands of innovative designs; a good place to browse for these is the Plaza de la Cultura in San José. Most of San José's *artesanía* (handicraft) shops sell products from throughout Central and South America, but prices are inevitably rather inflated, if cheaper than back home. Lastly, don't forget to buy some coffee before you leave, preferably from a market rather than a souvenir shop.

Sports and Outdoor Activities

Bicycling — True, much of Costa Rica is mountainous, but also abundant are plains that are ideal for cycling. A few tour agencies now offer guided bike tours that allow visitors to sample the country's divergent landscapes and climatic zones. Tours range in length from a single day to much longer. You can also hire your own bicycles in many places.

Bird-watching — Bird-watchers flock to Costa Rica in the knowledge that this tiny country boasts an avifauna of 830 species, more than the United States and Canada put together. High on most people's lists are the resplendent quetzal and the scarlet macaw. F. Gary Stiles and Alexander F. Skutch's illustrated *A Guide to the Birds of Costa Rica* is an invaluable guide.

Fishing — Costa Rica is a magnet for anglers worldwide. The silvery tarpon and snook attract sportfishermen to the northern Caribbean shore. January through May is the best time for tarpon, August through November for snook. On the Pacific side, game fish include billfish, marlin, tuna, dorado, and sailfish. Inland, you'll find stream and river fishing: Lake Arenal, for example, is a good spot for rainbow bass. Freshwater and beach permits are sold at most branches of **Banco de Costa Rica, Banco Nacional de Costa Rica, Banco Anglo Costarricense,** and **Banco Popular.** Deep-sea permits are provided by fishing guides. Tackle, tide tables, and advice can all be obtained in San José from **La Casa del Pescador** (Calle 12 between Aves. 4 and 6) or **Deportes Keko** (Calle 20 between Aves. 4 and 6).

Hiking — Costa Rica's system of national parks has endless hiking potential, from tough mountain climbing in the Cordillera de Talamanca to gentler rambles around the rain forests. Hiking possibilities are detailed in individual exploring sections and in Chapter 3, National Parks and Native Reserves.

Horse Riding — Companies that offer horseback tours include **Tipical Tours** (tel. 233–8486), **Saragundi Specialty Tours** (tel. 255–0011), and **Magic Trails** (tel. 253–6146). You can also rent horses in various locations to go exploring on your own (*see* Sports in the Atlantic Lowlands and in the Northwest, *below*).

Water Sports — Scuba diving, snorkeling, surfing, and white-water rafting are among the excellent water sports that Costa Rica offers. *See* Sports in regional sections, *below*, for details.

Spectator Sports

Bullfighting — The unique feature of Costa Rican bullfights is that the bull is never injured, let alone killed. A popular festival takes place at the end of each year in the Zapote Bullring in eastern San José.

Soccer — Costa Rica's national sport is played everywhere. First Division league games are usually played on Sundays. The largest stadiums are the Saprissa stadium in Tibas, on the left of the Guapiles highway just outside San José, and National Stadium in La Sabana Park.

Beaches

With two long coastlines, the Pacific one very indented, Costa Rica has an embarrassment of beaches that is almost impossible to log in its entirety. The vast majority are completely undeveloped and virtually unspoiled. They are fringed by lush tropical vegetation on the Caribbean and southern Pacific coasts, and by less dense, shrubbier dry forest vegetation in Guanacaste. Guanacaste is recommended for reliable weather during the rainy season. On all of these beaches, riptides are a potential hazard (*see* Beaches in The Southwest, *below*, for tips on how to deal with them).

Tour Companies

Most of the burgeoning number of tour companies in San José offer roughly the same lineup of one- to three-day trips around the Central Valley and to a few coastal and mountain tourist spots. A few venture out of the rut and offer adventure, nature, bird-watching, and photography tours. **Serendipity Adventures** (tel. 450–0318) has an extraordinary week-long trip that includes hot-air ballooning, white-water rafting, jungle biking, and windsurfing. **Jungle Trails** (tel. 255–3486) has an excellent variety of hiking, camping, and bird-watching trips for one to 15 days. **Explore Costa Rica** (tel. 220–2121) specializes in natural-history tours. **Guanacaste Tours** (tel. 666–0306) offers day trips to the protected areas in Guanacaste province. **Ríos Tropicales** (tel. 233–6455) is Costa Rica's top white-water-rafting outfitter. **Aventuras Naturales** (tel. 225–3939) has a number of popular mountain-biking trips. **Henchoz Tours** (tel. 233–9658) offers a nine-day photography expedition and several week-long nature trips nationwide. **Costa Rica Adventours** (tel. 220–2627) offers tours to farms that breed caiman (the Central American relative of the alligator) and butterflies. **Swiss Travel** (tel. 231–4055), one of the nation's oldest tour agencies, organizes a scuba-diving trip to Cocos Island, 418 kilometers (260 miles) offshore, and a train trip to a banana plantation in the Atlantic lowlands. **Tikal Tours** (tel. 233–2811), another well-established company, offers ecotourism trips throughout the country.

Dining

Costa Rica is a veritable garden of fresh vegetables and fruit, which means most cooking tastes good whatever the recipe. Just don't expect anything spicy. Indigenous cuisine is available from the ubiquitous and inexpensive *sodas*, while a string of higher-priced restaurants serve an international smorgasbord of recipes—Italian, French, German, Japanese, Chinese, Korean, you name it. Normal eating hours are noon–3 and 7–midnight.

Bocas, or appetizers, are served with drinks in most bars. They are either free or very cheap, but you have to ask for them. Ceviche and *gallos* (*see below*) are common ones.

The typical Costa Rican main course is *casado*—a plate of rice, black beans, shredded raw cabbage and tomato salad, meat or egg, and sometimes *plátanos* (fried plantains). The national breakfast dish is *gallo pinto*—fried rice and beans, with optional fried or scrambled egg. Maize is another staple, especially for snacks: Options include *guiso de maíz* (corn stew), *empanadas* (corn turnovers filled with beans, cheese, potatoes, and meat), *gallos* (meat, beans, or cheese in a sandwich of tortillas or maize pancakes), and *elote*, which is corn on the cob, *asado* (roasted) or *cocinado* (boiled). *Sopa negra* is a black broth made from beans, vegetables, and boiled eggs. *Picadillo* is a vegetable stew with a touch of meat, often accompanying *casado*. *Olla de carne* is a hearty beef stew with cassava, squash, plantains, and other vegetables. *Corvina* (sea bass), *camarones* (shrimps), and *langosta* (lobster, also called *bogavante*) are all widely available. Ceviche is a delicious cold stew consisting of raw sea bass cured in lemon juice with onions and coriander. Opinions vary as to whether you should risk this during a cholera outbreak—some say the lemon juice kills any germs. Guanacaste is Costa Rica's T-bone heartland, but you will find good quality *lomito* (beef tenderloin) at amazingly low prices in most places. Most Costa Rican dishes come with shredded raw cabbage and carrots, and sliced tomatoes. Fried plátanos, *yuca* (cassava), and boiled *pejibaye* (palm fruit tasting like a cross between avocado, chestnut, and pumpkin) are also popular and often eaten on their own. Good as a starter is *ensalada de palmito* (heart of palm salad), a real delicacy in most countries but relatively inexpensive here due to the profusion of palm trees. Common fruits here are mango, papaya, *piña* (pineapple), and the ubiquitous banana. Lesser-known and therefore more exciting options include the *marañon* (the orange fruit of the cashew tree), *granadilla* (passion fruit), *mamón chino* (similar to a litchi with a spiky red skin), and *carambola* (star fruit). You can get virtually any of these in the form of delicious juices, called *refrescos*, made with either water or milk. Recommended desserts include *tres leches*, a Nicaraguan specialty made of treacle sponge and three kinds of milk; *queque seco*, the same as pound cake; and *flan de coco*, a sweet coconut flan.

Ratings   Meal prices range enormously from the sodas to the sophisticated restaurants of San José. While approximate ratings are given below, remember that careful ordering can get you a moderately priced meal at a $$$$ restaurant. Prices are per person, including a first course, entrée, and dessert. Drinks, taxes, and gratuities are not included. Highly recommended restaurants are indicated by a star ★.

Category	Cost
$$$$	over $20
$$$	$10–$20
$$	$5–$10
$	under $5

Lodging

Hotels are going up fast to keep pace with the growth in the popularity of Costa Rica as a vacation destination. The Ministry of Tourism has made the creation of 2,000 first-class rooms and 2,000 of a lesser category a top priority. Reserve well in advance during the dry season—two to three months ahead to be sure of a room—and be sure to send the deposit lest you arrive and find your reservation has disappeared.

Luxury international hotels are mainly confined to San José, where a handful of modern high-rise operations offer all the facilities business travelers have come to expect. Many visitors will prefer the smaller one-of-a kind hotels set in colonial bungalows with verdant courtyards; again, these are most numerous in and around San José.

In outlying areas, including the coast, lodging is predominantly in *cabinas*, a sort of rustic equivalent of U.S. motels (motels here, by the way, are mostly short-stay sex hotels). These are places where the bedrooms are in individual units, often detached and set apart from or around the central area, which comprises a reception area, restaurant, and swimming pool. Cabinas range from very basic indigenous-style huts with few if any creature comforts, to flashier units equipped with all modern conveniences, where the time-worn rusticity is purely cosmetic. Many have cooking facilities. Often designed along cabina lines, a series of lodges have sprung up in recent years in outlying areas to cater to naturalist vacationers.

Most national parks have campsites with varying degrees of facilities. Call the **Parques Nacionales** (tel. 257–0962) for more information. Camping at the beach is often possible (many beaches offer no other option), but be careful of your belongings when you leave your tent unattended.

Ratings Prices are for a double room, excluding service and 14.4% tax. Highly recommended lodgings are indicated by a star ★.

Category	San José
$$$$	over $90
$$$	$50–$90
$$	$25–$50
$	under $25

San José and the Central Valley

Most trips to Costa Rica start in San José. Downtown, this is a busy grid-plan city—population estimates range from 300,000 to more than a million, depending on how many suburbs you include—with a rather untidy hodgepodge of building styles ranging from mirror-glass high rises to elegant stuccoed colonial bungalows. You'll find a lot of prefabricated office blocks of very dubious architectural distinction, and a block or so away, brightly colored terraces of one- or two-story houses of wood or adobe. In the affluent suburbs at the edges, middle-class bungalow-dwelling Ticos barricade themselves behind high-security metal fencing and tend their tidy gardens.

San José's best points are its location and climate. It stands in a broad fertile bowl at an altitude of just over 915 meters (3,000 feet), overlooked to the west by the jagged Cerros de Escazú and to the north by the twin volcanoes of Barva and Poás. These green uplands are almost never out of view. On clear days you can make out the lofty Irazú volcano in the east. The climate is excellent, with cool nights and daytime temperatures ranging from 15°C to 26°C (59°F–79°F). The rainy season lasts from May until November, although mornings and late afternoons are often sunny and brilliantly clear.

The city was founded in 1737 and replaced Cartago as the country's capital shortly after independence. It stayed relatively small for over a century, before the coffee and banana industries caused it to mushroom after World War II. San José now truly dominates national life. Roughly one-third of the entire population lives within its metropolitan area. National government, diplomats, industry, and agribusiness have their headquarters here, and all the institutions required of a capital city—good hospitals, schools, the main university, theaters, restaurants, and nightclubs—flourish within its limits.

All in all, it ranks as a fairly pleasant place—excepting the car exhaust fumes that stifle the city at times—but with so much else to see in the country, it would be unwise to spend a lot of time here. Rather, make some easy excursions to the Central Valley while you're here. A ring of spectacular volcanoes, all of which you can visit with varying degrees of ease, defines the boundaries of the Meseta Central. This is a densely populated area, heavily planted with neat rows of coffee. Coffee is invested with a certain amount of cultural mystique and folklore. Costa Rican artists have long venerated coffee workers; the painted ox cart, which was once used to transport coffee to Puntarenas, is now almost a national symbol.

Arriving and Departing

By Plane
Airports and Airlines
All international and some domestic flights arrive at **Juan Santamaría Airport,** 16 kilometers (10 miles) northwest of downtown San José. Other domestic flights depart from **Tobias Bolaños Airport** in the suburb of Pavas, 3 kilometers (1.8 miles) west of downtown San José. (For airlines serving San José, *see* Arriving and Departing, *above.)*

Between the Airport and Downtown
Taxis from the airport to downtown cost around $10. Far cheaper and almost as quick is the bus marked "Ruta 200 San José," which will drop you at the west end of Avenida 2, close to the heart of the city. The other option is to pick up a vehicle from one of the car-rental offices. Driving time is about 20 minutes, but allow 40 minutes to be safe. Note that some hotels provide a free shuttle service—inquire when you book.

By Car
San José is the hub of the national road system. Paved roads fan out from Paseo Colón to Escazú, the airport, the Pacific coast, and Nicaragua; from Calle 3 to Limón and the Atlantic coast; and through San Pedro to Cartago, the Southwest, and Panama.

By Bus
San José has no central bus station. For arrival and departure depots for various destinations, *see* Getting Around, *below.*

Getting Around

By Car
All of the streets in downtown San José are one-way. Traffic gets surprisingly congested at peak hours, when you are ill-advised to attempt to drive through the city.

By Bus
In San José
Bus service within San José is absurdly cheap (less than 30 colones per ride) and easy to use. For Paseo Colón and La Sabana take buses marked "Sabana-Cementerio" from stops along Avenida Central, and for Los Yoses/San Pedro take those marked "San Pedro" or "Lourdes" from Avenida 2.

To Central Valley from San José
Bus service to Central Valley from San José is listed here according to destination point, followed by information on the appropriate bus's departure point in the capital, telephone numbers for the bus company, time schedules, and length of ride, in this order: to the **airport** and **Alajuela,** departures from Avenida 2 between Calles 12 and 14 (Tuasa, tel. 222–5325) daily every 10 minutes 5:30 AM–7 PM (20-minute ride), every 40 minutes 7 PM–midnight, every hour midnight–5 AM; to **Braulio Carrillo** (bus marked GUAPILES), departures from

Calle 12 between Avenidas 7 and 9 (Coopetrangua, tel. 223–1276) daily every 30 minutes 5:30 AM–7 PM (35-minute ride); to **Cartago,** departures from Calle 5 and Avenida 18 (SACSA, tel. 233–5350) daily every 10 minutes (45-minute ride); to **Irazú volcano,** departures from Avenida 2 between Calles 1 and 3, outside Gran Hotel Costa Rica (Metropoli, tel. 272–0651) at 8 AM and returning at 1 PM Saturday and Sunday (90-minute ride); to **Poás volcano,** departures from Calle 12 between Avenidas 2 and 4 on Sunday at 8:30 AM and returning at 2:30 PM (90-minute ride); to **Zarcero,** departures from Calle 16 between Avenidas 1 and 3 (Auto Transportes Ciudad Quesada, tel. 255–4318) daily every hour on the hour 5 AM–7 PM.

Around To **Lankester Gardens,** departures from the south side of Central
Central Valley Park in Cartago (Coopepar, tel. 544–6127) daily every 30 minutes 4:30 AM–10:30 PM; to **Orosí Valley,** departures from one block east and three blocks south of Las Ruinas in Cartago (Mata, tel. 551–6810) weekdays every 90 minutes (every hour on weekends) 6 AM–10 PM; to **Sarchí,** departures from Calle 8 between Avenidas Central and 1 in Alajuela daily (Tuan, tel. 441–3781) every 30 minutes 5 AM–10 PM; to **Sacramento** (Barva volcano), take Paso Llano bus from Heredia (first bus 6:30 AM), get off at Sacramento crossroads (note: some go only as far as San José de la Montaña, adding an hour to the hike; check first).

By Taxi Taxis are a good deal in the capital. You can hail them in the street or call beforehand. Companies include **San Jorge** (tel. 221–3434), **Coopetaxi** (tel. 235–9966), and **Taxis Unidos** (tel. 221–6865). A 3-kilometer (1.9-mile) ride costs around 200 colones. By law, all cabbies must use their meters. If one refuses, negotiate a price before going anywhere.

By Train The new **Intertren** service connects the capital with the suburb of Pavas and the towns of Cartago and Heredia. Trains for **Pavas** depart from Pacific Station (Calle Central and Avenida 20) weekdays 6 AM, 12:15 PM, and 5:15 PM; Sunday 10 AM and 11:15 AM. **Cartago** trains depart from Atlantic Station (Avenida 3 between Calles 19 and 21) weekdays 5 AM, 7:15 AM, 1:45 PM, and 5:30 PM; Sunday 9 AM, 11:30 AM, and 1:50 PM. **Heredia** trains depart from Atlantic Station weekdays 5:45 AM, noon, and 5:15 PM; Sunday 10 AM and noon.

Important Addresses and Numbers

Tourist The main **ICT** (Instituto Costarricense de Turismo, Plaza de la
Information Cultura, tel. 222–1090) tourist office for the entire country is beneath Plaza de la Cultura. Walk down the steps across from the Burger King on Calle 5. It's open weekdays 9–5, Saturday 9–1. There is also a tourism information desk at Juan Santamaría International Airport (open daily 6 AM–9 PM).

Embassies U.S. **Embassy** (Rohrmoser, Pavas, tel. 220–3939). **Canadian Embassy** (Edificio Cronos, Calle 3 and Ave. Central, tel. 255–3522). U.K. **Embassy** (Centro Colón, Paseo Colón between Calles 38 and 40, tel. 221–5816).

Emergencies **Police** (tel. 117, or 127 outside cities); **Traffic Police** (tel. 227–8030); **Ambulance** (Cruz Roja, tel. 128); **Fire** (Bomberos, tel. 118).

Hospitals Those open to foreigners include **Clínica Bíblica** (Ave. 14 between Calles Central and 1, tel. 223–6422) and **Clínica Católica** (Guadalupe, attached to San Antonio Church on Esquivel Bonilla Street, tel. 225–5055).

Pharmacy The **Clínica Bíblica** (*see above*) also operates a 24-hour pharmacy.

Bookstores *See* Shopping, *below* for English-language bookstores.

Travel **American Express** (Calle Central, Aves. 3 and 5, tel. 223–3644) and
Agencies **Universal** (Calle 5 and Ave. 1, tel. 257–0181).

Guided Tours

Orientation San José does not really warrant a tour in itself, but if you do want to
Tours be shown around, **Swiss Travel** and **Tikal Tours** (*see* Tour Companies,
above) both have good city tours.

Special- **Geotur** (tel. 234–1867) runs an excellent day tour to Braulio Carrillo
Interest and National Park for around $45. **Jungle Trails** (tel. 255–3486) takes
Walking Tours groups hiking for the day on Barva volcano and also offers numerous
other well-designed tours of the Central Valley.

Exploring San José and the Central Valley

Because San José is the heart of the nation's transportation system,
most travelers cannot avoid spending at least a couple of days there.
The following tours will help visitors while away the time in the un-
spectacular city as they await connections to more inviting parts of
the country.

Tours 1 and 2 cover downtown San José. The city is laid out on a grid:
Avenidas (avenues) run east and west; *calles* (streets), north and
south. Avenidas that are north of Avenida Central have odd numbers while those to the south are even. Avenidas 2 and Central
merge in the west and become Paseo Colón. Calles to the east of
Calle Central have odd numbers, those to the west have even. Calle 3
leads to the Guapiles Highway, which heads for the Atlantic coast.
Sounds simple, but it isn't. Usually Ticos don't use avenue–street
descriptions when giving directions, but instead will say that somewhere is "two blocks north of the Correos, and two blocks east, next
to the Mercedes garage."

The remaining tours cover Central Valley excursions. Tour 3 takes in
Cartago; Irazú volcano, with its view of both coasts; and the verdant
Orosi Valley. Tour 4 goes through Alajuela to Poás volcano, with
stunning views of a sulfur-laden crater lake and trails through a
dwarf cloud forest. Tour 5 heads through Heredia to Barva volcano,
the crater of which is reached after a brisk, 30-minute hike.

Highlights for **Central Market** (*see* Tour 1)
First-time **Gold Museum** (*see* Tour 1)
Visitors **Irazú Volcano** (*see* Tour 3)
Jade Museum (*see* Tour 2)
National Museum (*see* Tour 2)
National Theater (*see* Tour 1)
Orosi Valley (*see* Tour 3)
Poás Volcano (*see* Tour 4)

*Numbers in the margin correspond to numbers on the Tours 1 and 2:
San José map.*

Tour 1: Start with the **Tourist Office** beneath **Plaza de la Cultura,** where you
San José, can pick up a map and other tourist information. Steps lead down
Central West from Calle 5. The bustling plaza above is San José's cultural and
❶ shopping hub; stalls hawk a fine but overpriced selection of jewelry.
At the southwest corner is the venerable Gran Hotel Costa Rica
with a 24-hour Parisienne café that offers the best people-watching
in town. *Plaza de la Cultura, tel. 222–1090. Open weekdays 9–5,
Sat. 9–1.*

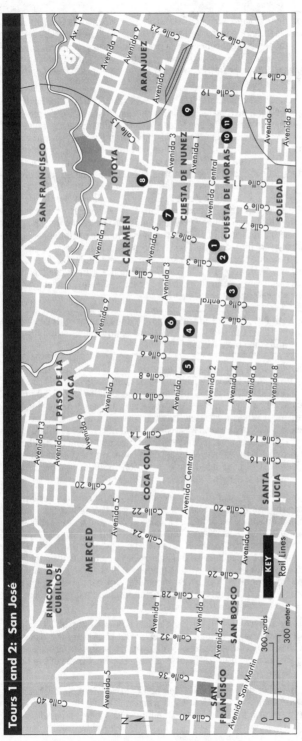

Tours 1 and 2: San José

KEY
— Rail Lines

Banco Central, **4**
Catedral Metropolitana, **3**
Correos (Central Post Office), **6**
Mercado Central, **5**
Museo de Jade (Jade Museum), **8**
Museo Nacional, **11**

Parque Morazán, **7**
Parque Nacional, **9**
Plaza de la Democracia, **10**
Teatro Nacional, **2**
Tourist Office/Plaza de la Cultura, **1**

Next door to the Tourist Office is the Banco Central's **Gold Museum.** This dazzling, modern, well-lighted museum is well worth seeing; it contains the largest collection of pre-Columbian gold jewelry in Central America: 20,000 troy ounces of gold in more than 1,600 individual pieces. *Plaza de la Cultura, no phone. Admission free. Open Fri. 1–5; weekends 9–5.*

Diagonally across from the Gran Hotel Costa Rica on the Plaza is the **②** **Teatro Nacional** (National Theater), easily Costa Rica's most enchanting building. The sandstone facade is decorated by statues of Beethoven and Spanish 17th-century Golden Age playwright Calderón de la Barca, marble columns with bronnze capitals, and Italianate arched windows. The Muses of Dance, Music, and Fame stand aloft against the sky and a maroon iron cupola. Chagrined at being bypassed by the touring prima donna Adelina Patti in 1890, wealthy coffee merchants raised export taxes in order to pay for the Belgian architects, cast iron, Italian marble, and decorators. Frescoes depicting coffee and banana production grace the stairway. The theater was inaugurated in 1894 with a performance of Gounod's *Faust,* starring an international cast. The sumptuous baroque interior looks new due to a two-year restoration project undertaken after the theater was damaged in the 1991 earthquake. Check the box office on the east side of the theater for upcoming performances. *Admission: 350 colones. Open Mon.–Sat. 9–5:30.*

Time Out The **National Theater Cafe** off the lobby has a stunning Belle Époque setting. It serves exotic coffees, good sandwiches, exquisite pastries, and some main dishes.

Avenida 2 is to your left as you emerge from the theater, and invariably it is chock-a-block with fume-belching traffic. This is the main east-west street, flanked by ugly office buildings and huge billboards. Ahead, you can see the white corrugated dome of the uninteresting **③** **Catedral Metropolitana** (Metropolitan Cathedral), one block west on the left. Cream-colored and neoclassical outside, it is decorated inside with patterned floor tiles and framed polychrome bas-reliefs. It is undergoing an ambitious three-year restoration project that is scheduled for completion in 1996, but part of the building remains open for Mass. *Open Sun. 8–1 and 3–9.*

Parque Central, an ordinary tree-planted square with benches to watch the world go by, fronts the cathedral. By night it is notorious as a pickup spot. Its spiderlike kiosk was donated by former Nicaraguan dictator Anastasio Samoza. Renegotiate yourself across Avenida 2 and pass by the Melico Salazar Theater, San José's other leading venue. The venerable Soda Palace, a restaurant cum black market exchange, comes next. Street money changing is technically illegal and there is little profit incentive, but money changers here are notorious for circulating counterfeit bills and using doctored calculators to shortchange customers.

④ Turn right here down Calle 2 to the large **Banco Central.** This financial hub experiences a lot of street crime and is, therefore, patrolled by Canadian-style mounties. Notice the 10 sculpted figures of bedraggled *campesinos* (peasants) outside the west front of the bank. *Open weekdays 9–3.*

⑤ One block west of here is the **Mercado Central** (Central Market), between Avenidas 1 and Central, a warren of dark, narrow passages flanked by stalls selling exotic-smelling spices (some labeled according to their medicinal uses); fish; fruit; vegetables; and wood and leather handicrafts. More than anywhere, it feels like the melting pot of San José.

Time Out Seafood, fried rice, fruit juices, and more are on offer at the many café stalls inside the market. **Soda Ciudades de Italia** on the corner of Calle 6 and Avenida 1 is a rough-and-ready saloon bar decorated with suspended bottles of local liquor; order an Imperial, saddle up to the bar, and listen to the *machista* (menfolk) whistling.

Walk two blocks east along Avenida 1 and, on your left, you'll find ❻ the white stuccoed **Correos building** (Central Post Office). Upstairs is a display of first-day stamp issues. Also, here's your opportunity to look down on the activity of loading *apartado* (post office) boxes. A pretty dull pastime, you say? The fact is, street addresses barely exist in this country, and Ticos fall over themselves to get a post office box here. *Open weekdays 8 AM–midnight, Sat. 8–noon.*

Opposite the Post Office is the marble facade of the exclusive **Club Unión** (members only). Continue down Avenida 1 and back to Plaza de la Cultura.

Tour 2: Two blocks north of the Plaza de la Cultura, you arrive at the quar-
San José, tered **Parque Morazán,** enlarged and relandscaped in 1990 and 1991,
Central East and featuring a central neoclassical bandstand. A quiet, serene
❼ place for young lovers and families to walk on weekends, it is a hang-out for hookers and pickpockets at night and is deafening and smog-choked when weekday traffic rolls into San José. Ahead stands the Aurola Holiday Inn, a mirror-sided monstrosity; at 17 stories, it is downtown San José's tallest building. Walk east along Avenida 3 and turn left through the shady Parque de España to the tall modern INS (National Insurance Institute) building, which unexpectedly houses San José's second-most-interesting museum on its 11th floor.

❽ The **Museo de Jade Marco Fidel Tristan** (Jade Museum) contains the world's largest collection of American jade. When it was produced in pre-Columbian times, from around 300 BC to AD 700, in the Nicoya and South Pacific or Diquis regions, jade was considered more valu-able than gold. Mostly it was carved into pendants depicting human and animal figures. It was also used for tooth fillings and for deco-rating pots and vases. A series of drawings explain how jade, an ex-tremely hard stone, was cut using string saws with quartz and sand abrasive. The museum also contains other pre-Columbian artifacts such as polychrome vases and three-legged metates (low tables for grinding corn). The final room displays a startling array of carved fertility symbols. *Admission free. Open weekdays 8–3.*

Adjacent to the INS building stands the colonial Casa Amarilla, once owned by Andrew Carnegie and now used by the Foreign Min-istry to impress outsiders. If you ask at the door they should let you in to see the elegant series of patios, elaborate plasterwork, and hardwood floors. Walk a block east and then turn right past the mod-
❾ ern National Library and the **Parque Nacional.** The latter is the most pleasant of all San José's downtown parks. As you cross Avenida 1, look right to the row of old colonial housing that has barely changed in the past hundred years; it's one of the few visible remnants of the colonial era still standing in San José. Next on the left is the mock-Mudéjar Legislative Assembly building, home to Costa Rica's Con-gress. You can look around, although there isn't much to see apart from a chart recording the more momentous moments in Costa Rican history.

⑩ The terraced open space across Avenida Central, the **Plaza de la Democracia,** was created by President Oscar Arias to mark 100 years of democracy and to receive visiting dignitaries during the hemispheric summit in October 1989. It will look much better once the trees grow, but the view west toward the jagged Cerros de Escazú is tremendous already. Standing over the eastern side of the plaza is the coral-colored Bellavista Fortress, with bullet scars in the turrets to remind citizens of the 1948 Civil War.

⑪ The well-organized **Museo Nacional** (National Museum), housed in the whitewashed colonial interior, gives first-time visitors a quick and insightful lesson into Costa Rica's culture from pre-Columbian times to the present. Heavy-beamed display rooms lead off a veranda and pleasant manicured courtyard garden. Rooms are devoted to pre-Columbian artifacts, period costumes, colonial furniture, and photos of Costa Rican life through the ages. *Admission: 100 colones. Open Tues.–Sat. 8:30–5, Sun. 9–5.*

Tour 3: Cartago, Irazú, Paraíso, and the Orosi Valley

Numbers in the margin correspond to points of interest on the The Central Valley map.

Travelers trying to do this trip in one day should be prepared to be on the road from dawn until well past dusk. For a more leisurely pace, break it into two parts, visiting Irazú volcano or Cartago one day and tackling the rest of the trip on another.

⑫ The 22 kilometers (15 miles) to **Cartago** goes by quickly on the two-lane Interamerican Highway. Cradle of Costa Rican culture and capital for 260 years until 1823, Cartago lost almost all its historic buildings as a result of earthquakes in 1841 and 1910. The last of these prevented completion of the central cathedral, whose ruins (Las Ruinas) now form a pleasant garden, cultivated with pines and bougainvillea.

Visit the **Basílica de Nuestra Señora de Los Angeles** (Basilica of Our Lady of the Angels), 10 blocks east of the main square. A Byzantine hodgepodge of styles, the basilica is the focus of an amazing annual pilgrimage from San José. During the night of August 1 and well into the early-morning hours of the 2nd, the road from San José becomes a river of people on their way to celebrate the appearances in 1635 of La Negrita, Costa Rica's patron saint, at the spring which flows out behind the church. The faithful come here to fill bottles. Miraculous healing powers are attributed to the saint; along with the thousands of symbolic crutches, ears, eyes, and legs placed next to her diminutive statue sit trophies in recognition of her gifts. The constant arrival of tour buses and school groups, along with shops selling candles and bottles of holy water in the shape of the saint, add a bit of circus atmosphere to the scene. La Negrita has twice been stolen, most recently in 1950 by José León Sanchez, now one of Costa Rica's best known novelists, who spent 20 years on the prison island of San Lucas for his crime.

Time Out Duck into **Pops**, a half-block north of the market on the main street, for an ice cream or a cool drink and a view of the always bustling strip.

⑬ The drive up **Irazú volcano,** Costa Rica's highest at 3,433 meters (11,260 feet) and one of its most active, is very exciting (*see* Chapter 3, National Parks and Wildlife Reserves). Leave San José very early in the day during the dry season so as not to be thwarted by low clouds. Bear left where Irazú is signposted, 4 kilometers (2½ miles) short of Cartago, to bypass the city. Driving time from San José to

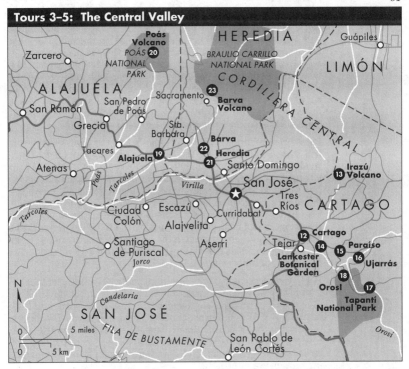

the summit is comfortably short of 1½ hours. Looming high above Cartago, Irazú's eruptions have dumped a considerable quantity of ash and mud on the city over the years. The most recent occasions were from 1963 through 1965, beginning on the day that John F. Kennedy arrived in Costa Rica for a presidential visit. Vast boulders and mud rained down on the countryside, damming rivers and causing serious flooding. While farmers who cultivate its slopes live in fear of the frequent chaos that Irazú causes, they are also grateful for the soil's richness, a direct upshot of the volcano's deposits.

The road up passes strawberry fields and native oak forests. You pass through the villages of Potrero Cerrado and San Juan de Chicoá, both with lookout points, before reaching the bleak, gaping craters at the summit. Although currently dormant, gases and steam billow out from fumaroles on Irazú's northwestern slope, scarcely visible from the crater lookouts. The gray, moonscapelike peak of Irazú is one of the few places from which both the Pacific Ocean and the Caribbean Sea can be viewed, although clouds frequently obscure both from view. The Area Recreativa de Prusia, halfway down, has trails for beautiful walks through oak and pine forest. Picnic areas are available if you want to bring your own supplies; warm, waterproof clothing is advisable for the summit.

To reach Paraíso, a small market town with an interesting botanical garden, go through the center of Cartago, keeping the basilica to your left. The road isn't well marked, so ask a passerby if in doubt. After 6 kilometers (4 miles), an orange sign on the right-hand verge marks the turn to Jardín Lankester (**Lankester Botanical Garden**). Created in the 1940s by the English naturalist Charles Lankester to help preserve the local flora, it is now under the auspices of the University of Costa Rica. The lush garden and greenhouses contain the world's largest orchid collection, more than 800 species, both native and introduced. Orchids are mostly epiphytes, meaning they use other plants for support without damaging them in the process. The best time to visit the always interesting garden is March–May, when the orchids are in full bloom. Bromeliads and aroids also abound, along with 80 species of trees, including hardwoods, fruit, bamboo, and cacti. The diversity of plants attracts a wide variety of birds as well. *Dulce Nombre, Cartago. Admission: 500 colones. Open daily 8:30–3:30. 1-hr guided tours available on the hour.*

⑮ Pass through **Paraíso,** turn right just before the town's shady central park, and look out for the *bomberos* (fire station) on your left. Aside from housing splendid old-style fire engines, this marks the left turn to Ujarrás, somewhat obscurely signed. After 4.6 kilometers (3 miles) of snaking through coffee plantations, you arrive at a mirador (vantage point) overlooking one of the prettiest valleys in Costa Rica, fed in the west by the confluence of the Navarro and Orosi rivers and drained in the east by the ferocious Reventazón. The valley has been dammed in the east for hydroelectricity, forming a lake. Alongside the water, the highly fertile red soil supports a patchwork of tidily cultivated crops.

⑯ Begin your descent and turn right 1 kilometer (⅗ mile) after the mirador. The road ends at **Ujarrás,** the ruins of the oldest church in Costa Rica, a structure surrounded by well-kept gardens. Built between 1681 and 1693 in honor of the Virgin of Ujarrás, the church, together with the surrounding village, was abandoned in 1833 after a series of earthquakes and floods. An unlikely victory by the Spaniards over a superior force of invading British pirates was attributed to a prayer stop here.

Time Out The lakeside **Charrara recreation area** is 1 kilometer (⅗ mile) east of Ujarrás. Past basketball courts, a soccer field, and barbecue stands you'll reach a poolside restaurant. It overlooks a swimming pool and the meandering river. New management is remodeling the restaurant, which is scheduled to reopen in 1994. *Tel. 240–7253. Admission: adults 100 colones, plus 50 colones for your car, children 50 colones.*

Continue east to the large Cachí dam, to the left of which the Reventazón dashes away down a bottomless chasm. Rounding this corner you can see the valley in reverse. Another 12 kilometers (7½ miles) along the smooth, paved road brings you to the Hotel Río Palomo, whose pool nonguests can use for 150 colones (*see* Dining and Lodging, *below*). Cross the wooden suspension bridge over the Orosí River and, shortly after, turn left to Tapantí.

⑰ Courtesy of the hydroelectric power station, the 10-kilometer (6-mile) track to **Tapantí National Park,** a 4,694-hectare (11,600-acre) reserve of cloud forest, is in excellent condition (*see* Chapter 3, National Parks and Wildlife Reserves). The track follows the course of the Orosi past coffee plantations, elegant *fincas* (farmhouses), and seasonal barracks for coffee workers, before being hemmed in by steep slopes of thick jungle. The green rangers' office is on your left; stop here and pay the small entry fee. The Forest Service oversees this humid premontane forest refuge where 211 species of birds reside. The graceful, shy, and endangered quetzal nests here in late spring; look into the laurel trees to the left of the road near the entry, and you may spot one. Jaguar and ocelot also live here, but very discreetly. You can often see howler monkeys on the far bank of the

Orosi. The track continues through the reserve, and you can leave your vehicle by the start of various trails, one of which leads to a swimming spot on the Orosi, best in the dry season between November and June. This is also a good place for trout fishing (Apr. 1–Oct. 31), but you will need a permit. Taxis carrying up to six people do runs to the reserve from beside the football pitch in the town of Orosi for about $15 per round-trip. *Admission: 200 colones. Open daily 7–4.*

On the way into the town of Orosi are thermal swimming pools, full of mineral water, and a poolside bar. *Admission: 200 colones. Open Tues.–Sun. 8–4.*

® **Orosi** itself is a tiny village with a beautiful restored colonial church but not much else to attract tourists. Built in 1743, the structure has a squat, whitewashed facade; the roof is made of sugarcane overlaid with terra-cotta barrel tiles. Inside, canvases depict the Stations of the Cross. The museum in the cloister alongside houses old religious regalia and multicolored wood carvings. Opening times fluctuate, but ask around and somebody should open up. From Orosi you can complete the loop uphill back to Paraíso.

Tour 4: The quickest route to Poás volcano is via the city of Alajuela. Unless
Alajuela and a traveler has an unquenchable thirst for run-of-the-mill towns,
Poás there is no reason to stop in Alajuela. Turn right at the west end of Paseo Colón and follow signs along the divided highway. While it is Costa Rica's second city (population 50,000) and only a 30-minute
® bus ride from the capital, **Alajuela** has a provincial feel. Architecturally it differs little from the bulk of Costa Rican towns: A low-rise grid plan with structures painted in primary colors is the norm. The stuccoed colonial cathedral, badly damaged by the 1991 quake, has pretty capitals decorated with local produce motifs.

Alajuela's chief claim to fame is as birthplace of Juan Santamaría, the national hero who did away with William Walker (*see* The Northwest, Tour 2, *below*). His deeds are celebrated in the **Museo Juan Santa María** in the old prison building, one block north of the central square. It contains maps, compasses, weapons from both sides, and paintings, including one of Walker's men filing past to lay down their weapons. The colonial-style building is more interesting than its displays inside, however. *Admission free. Open Tues.–Sun. 2–9 PM.*

Ask directions for the road to Poás, since there are no signs—aim for Vara Blanca and then Poasito. The road winds its way up past coffee and sugarcane fields, fruit trees, and pine forests. It is paved all the
® way to the top of the 2,683-meter (8,800-foot) **Poás volcano.** Poás's multicolored crater, at nearly 1½ kilometers (1 mile) across and 305 meters (1,000 feet) deep, is said to be the second largest in the world, and the sight of the smoking fumaroles and greenish-turquoise sulfurous lake at the bottom is breathtaking. All sense of scale is absent because of the lack of any vegetation within the crater. The summit is frequently enshrouded in mist, and many who come up see little beyond the lip of the crater. But wait a while, especially if there is some wind, because it can clear miraculously. If you're lucky, you will see the famous geyser in action, spewing a column of black mud high into the air. Poás last erupted properly in 1953 and is thought to be approaching another active phase; at any sign of danger it is closed to visitors, as it was in 1989. The earlier in the day you go, the better. It can be very cold and wet at the summit, so dress accordingly. If you come ill-equipped, you can avail yourself of the plant commonly known as the poor man's umbrella. Bring a handkerchief, because the sulfurous gases can play havoc with your

eyes; soaking it in vinegar is supposed to neutralize the sulfuric acid and so ease your breathing. It is forbidden to venture down the side of the crater. A last note of warning: This is a popular site and, because of the crowds, is not a good choice for those who like solitude.

The 5,670-hectare (14,000-acre) **Poás National Park** (*see* Chapter 3, National Parks and Wildlife Reserves), created in 1971, protects epiphyte-laden cloud forest on the volcano's slopes and dwarf shrubs near the summit. One trail, which leads off to the right of the main crater trail, goes through thick dwarf shrubs toward the large and eerie Botos Lake, occupying an extinct crater some 15 minutes away. Another leads from the car park through a taller stretch of cloud forest; boards along the way feature sentimental ecopoetry. Mammals are almost absent because of the volcano's recent active cycle, but you should see frogs, toads, and various birds, including insect-size hummingbirds. On occasion, quetzals have also been spotted. On Sundays, audiovisual displays can be viewed in the auditorium located near the parking area. *No phone. Admission free. Open daily 7–4.*

Time Out On the way down, find time to stop at the **Chubascos Restaurant,** a great favorite for Costa Rican cooking; their casados and *refrescos* (fruit juices) are top-drawer. If it's warm, you can sit out in the garden.

There is an alternative return route: a battered, bone-crunching one-lane road to San José through the towns of Heredia and Barva, with a trip to Barva volcano. While pretty, it takes quite a bit longer.

Tour 5: Heredia and Barva Volcano **Heredia** has a population of around 30,000 and is home to an attractive colonial stone church that dates back to 1763. The barrel-tile roofs and whitewashed verandas of the municipal buildings surrounding the shady central park give off a vague colonial whiff, but really no more than that. They call this Costa Rica's most colonial city, but in a country that has lost almost all its old architecture to earthquakes, Heredia bears witness to just how little that means.

㉑

㉒ Head next to **Barva,** many of whose old barrel-tile adobe houses have recently been restored, and then on to Sacramento via San José de la Montaña and Porrosatí (or Paso Llano). Halfway up this steep ascent, 4 kilometers (2.4 miles) past San José, you pass the crossroads for Hotel El Pórtico (*see* Dining and Lodging, *below*). Go left for 1 kilometer (½ mile) to El Pórtico, or bear right to keep heading toward the volcano. The countryside consists of pastures divided by woods of oak, pine, and cedar. The air is usually cool up there; coupled with the mixed forest, the atmosphere is a surprise for those who expect only rain forest, bananas, and coffee beans to grow in Costa Rica.

㉓ The extinct 2,896-meter (9,500-foot) **Barva volcano** is the highest point in the **Braulio Carrillo National Park** (*see* Chapter 3, National Parks and Wildlife Reserves), whose entrance is about a 30-minute walk from the crater. Buses go as far as San José de la Montaña, leaving a four-hour hike to the crater. Bring rain gear, boots, and a compass; even experienced hikers who know the area have lost their way up here. The main crater lake is about 200 yards across. Its almost vertical sides are covered in poor man's umbrellas and oak trees laden with epiphytes. Nearby are other smaller lakes. You may just see quetzals if you arrive in the early morning. *Admission: 150 colones. Open daily 7–4.*

What to See and Do with Children

The **Modern Puppet Theater** has been entertaining kids for a quarter century. *100 meters (328 feet) east, 100 meters north of Santa Teresita Church; tel. 225–6926. Admission: 350 colones. Performances Sun. at 11 and 3.*

Bearing in mind the country's amazing wildlife, the **Parque Zoológico Simón Bolivar** is rather modest in scope, but there is no denying its convenience as a way of introducing children to what lives here. *Avenida 11 and Calle 11. Admission: 200 colones. Open daily 9–4.*

Two kilometers away from the Fiesta Maíz (*see* Off the Beaten Track, *below*), the **Bosque Encantado** (open weekends only) is an amusement park with swimming pools, horses, and motorized swans. *Admission: 200 colones. Open weekends 9–4.*

In the San José suburb of La Uruca, the **Parque Nacional de Diversiones** (National Amusement Park) has vintage rides, such as roller coasters and Ferris wheels. *2 km (1.2 mi) west of Hospital México, tel. 231–6823. Admission: 300 colones. Open Mar.–June and Nov. daily; July–Oct. and Dec.–Feb., weekends.*

Off the Beaten Track

Don't be confused by the absence of motion within the display cases in the **Serpentarium**—all of the snakes and lizards here are very much alive. Most notorious are the *terciopelo* (fer-de-lance viper), which is responsible for over half of the poisonous snakebites in Costa Rica; boa constrictors; and the newly acquired group of man-eating piranha. *Tel. 255–4210. Ave. 1 between Calles 9 and 11. Admission: 300 colones. Open daily 9–6.*

Start a small loop to the west of San José with a visit to the **Butterfly Farm** in La Guácima. Head out toward the airport and turn left at the Cariari Hotel to San Antonio de Belén. Turn right after the church here, and shortly left. From here signs with butterflies show the way. The farm contains a variety of habitats holding forty rare species of butterflies. Guided tours allow you to see butterflies at various stages of development. *Tel. 438–0115. Admission: 1350 colones. Open daily 9–3.*

Have lunch at the **Fiesta Maíz** (open Fri.–Sun. 6:30 AM–8:30 PM) in La Garita. This lively restaurant serves exclusively maize-based recipes and is popular with Ticos on weekends.

Continue across the Interamerican Highway toward Alajuela to the **Zoo Ave,** a recently remodeled bird zoo with enlarged cages. *Tel. 433–9140. Admission: 700 colones. Open daily 9–4:30.*

Shopping

Arts and Crafts The Central Market has the best range and prices for leather bags, belts, and shoes, as well as hammocks, but shop around and haggle before digging out your wallet. The best place for bags and belts is next to the northwestern entrance. **Boutique Annemarie** in the lobby of the Don Carlos Hotel (*see* Lodging in San José, *below*) is particularly strong in small objects carved in wood and imitation pre-Columbian stoneware. **Taymarú** (Ave. 8, 230 meters/250 yards west of ICE, Los Yoses, tel. 234–2225) is recommended for wooden salad bowls and patterned pottery. **La Casona** (Calle Central between Aves. Central and 1) is a minimarket with just about every craft typical of Central America. **Atmosfera** (Calle 5 between Aves. 1 and 3) is good for jewelry, masks, wall hangings, and dishes with bright, primitive designs. Look out in all these places for the jewelry by Sr. y Sra. Ese, who specialize in polished wooden pieces made from carpenters' scraps; they sell here for a fraction of what they go for in the United States. **Casa del Sonador,** just west of the Cachí Dam, sells whimsical handcarved woodwork at half the price you'd pay in San José.

Antiques **Boutique la Puerta** (Calle 7, 9 meters/10 yards north of Ave. 2; open Mon.–Sat. 8–noon and 2:30–6) sells high-quality antiques from colonial times and is strong on decorative lamps and candlesticks.

Books and **The Bookshop** (Ave. 1 between Calles 1 and 3, tel. 221–6847) sells a
Maps wide selection of books in English at rather inflated prices.

Universal (Ave. Central between Calles Central and 1, tel. 222–2222) has a similarly good selection as well as a stock of large-scale topographical maps.

Coffee and You can see your coffee being roasted at **El Trébol** (Calle 8, on west
Liquor side of Central Market), and the rates are good. **Yamuni** (Ave. 2 and Calle 7) is San José's largest liquor store; it's a good place to buy local liqueurs, picnic gear, and kitchenware.

Sports

Golf Nine-hole courses are open to nonmembers at the **Costa Rica Country Club** in Escazú and **Los Reyes Country Club** in La Guácima (southwest of Alajuela). Unfortunately, you have to be a guest at either the Cariari or the Herradura hotel to play the **Cariari Country Club's** 18-hole course.

Gymnasiums Gyms attached to all the large luxury hotels are reliable; the one at the Corobicí is recommended. The National Gymnasium in the southeast corner of La Sabana is the city's largest. For others, look under "Gymnasios" in the *Paginas Amarillas* (*Yellow Pages*).

Hiking Hiking trails can be found at Braulio Carrillo, Poás, and Irazú (*see* Exploring, *above*).

Jogging La Sabana, at the end of Paseo Colón, once the airport but now a eucalyptus-shaded park, is the best place to jog in San José, with 5-kilometer (3-mile) routes along cement paths.

Tennis Public tennis courts can be found at **La Sabana** and the country clubs referred to under Golf, *above*. Hotels with courts include the **Cariari** and **Tara,** but the facilities are not available to nonguests.

White-water White-water trips start from San José, but the action takes place in
Rafting and other parts of the country. *See* Sports in The Atlantic Lowlands, *be-*
Canoeing *low.*

Dining and Lodging

Dining Almost all of the various dishes peculiar to regional Costa Rica plus a true smorgasbord of international recipes can be found somewhere in the capital. Good dining areas include the Paseo Colón zone to the west, and the suburb of San Pedro, to the east. Dress is casual unless otherwise stated. For ratings, *see* Dining and Lodging in Staying in Costa Rica, *above*. Highly recommended restaurants are indicated by a star ★.

Lodging San José hotels vary from luxurious and basic. You can choose between high rises with all modern conveniences and older colonial buildings with tons more atmosphere but fewer creature comforts. For ratings, *see* Dining and Lodging in Staying in Costa Rica, *above*. Highly recommended hotels are indicated by a star ★.

Escazú
Dining and Lodging
★

Tara Resort Hotel. Patterned after the house of the same name in *Gone with the Wind* and decorated in antebellum style, this hotel near the top of Pico Blanco could be the country's most luxurious. Hardwood floors throughout the three-story, white-and-green building are covered with patterned area rugs. A 10-foot-wide veranda encircles the second floor, offering 180-degree views of the Central Valley. Guest rooms are decorated with floral spreads and lace curtains; French doors open onto the veranda. The presidential suite features a canopied bed, a large dressing room, and a fireplace. The restaurant solidifies its good reputation with specialties such as beef tenderloin in green pepper sauce and chicken Tara in a mango-avocado sauce. There is an extensive wine list, with a good choice of French reds and California whites. *Apdo. 1459, Escazú, 1250, tel. 228–6992, fax 228–9651. 12 rooms with bath, 1 suite, 1 bungalow. Facilities: restaurant, Jacuzzi, pool, tennis court, massage. AE, DC, MC, V. $$$$*

Orosí
Dining and Lodging

Río Palomo. Next to the bridge across the Orosí, the restaurant of this hotel property enjoys close proximity to the stony river. The large open-sided dining room has a cane ceiling, a tile floor, and spindly white metal chairs. The best option is the fresh fish. The other bonus is the large pool with high board, open to nonresidents/diners for 150 colones. Farther along the riverbank you come to the secluded modern *cabinas* (cottages) with white walls, wood ceilings, and modern furniture. Larger units have well-equipped kitchens. *Apdo. 220, 7050 Cartago, tel. 533–3128, fax 533–3173. 7 cabinas with bath. Facilities: restaurant, bar, pool. AE, DC, MC, V. Restaurant serves lunch only. $–$$*

San José de la Montaña
Dining and Lodging

Hotel El Pórtico. This place is 9 kilometers (5.4 miles) up a steep, battered, sometimes paved track from Barva and 27 kilometers (16 miles) from the capital. The small redbrick hotel's long sloping roof is vaguely reminiscent of a Swiss chalet; the interior decor blends brick, hardwood, and terra-cotta tiles to achieve a rustic effect, and soft leather chairs, sofas, and a log fire warm the central areas. Bedrooms have carpeting, paneled walls, and patterned bedspreads. The food is good, though portions are on the small side. Surrounding the hotel is a garden with pine trees and geese—a great place for hiking and bird-watching, or just relaxing in the fresh mountain air. *Apdo. 289, 3000 Heredia, tel. 260–6000, fax 260–6002. 13 rooms with bath. Facilities: restaurant, bar, sauna, Jacuzzi, pool. AE, MC, V. $$*

Santa Barbara de Heredia
Dining and Lodging

Finca Rosa Blanca. The white Gaudíesque architecture and decorative touches of this small bed-and-breakfast hotel make it the most unusual in Costa Rica. The honeymoon suite has a waterfall above the tub and a 360-degree view from the rooftop tower. The other units echo this eccentric, frilly approach. A sitting room, dotted with pre-Columbian-style statuettes, has white upholstery set against dark wood and Ecuadorian tapestries. Finca Rosa Blanca lies at 1,300 meters (4,264 feet), 15 kilometers (9 miles; 45 minutes) north of San José. Tours to the nearby volcanoes, coffee plantations, and rivers make it an ideal base for exploring the Central Valley. *Apdo. 41, 3009 Santa Barbara de Heredia, tel. 239–9392, fax 441–3009. 8 suites with bath. Facilities: breakfast room. AE, V. $$$$*

San José
Dining

Le Chandelier. In terms of decor, ambience, and cooking, this is San José's classiest restaurant. The Swiss chef, Claude Dubuis, has been

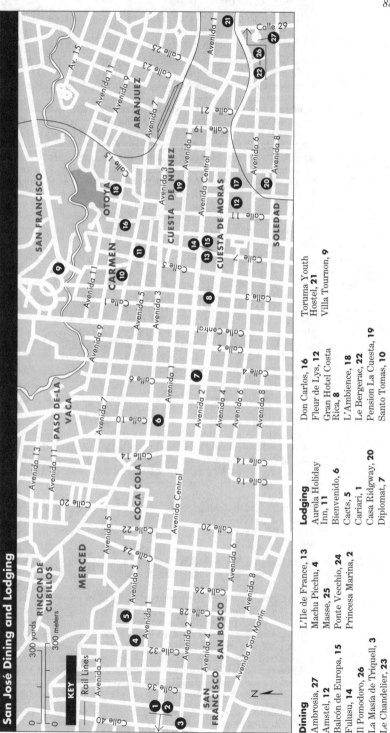

San José Dining and Lodging

KEY

— Rail Lines

Dining
Ambrosia, **27**
Amstel, **12**
Balcón de Europa, **15**
Fulusu, **14**
Il Pomodoro, **26**
La Masía de Triquell, **3**
Le Chandelier, **23**
L'Ile de France, **13**
Machu Picchu, **4**
Masse, **25**
Ponte Vecchio, **24**
Princesa Marina, **2**

Lodging
Aurola Holiday Inn, **11**
Bienvenido, **6**
Cacts, **5**
Cariari, **1**
Casa Ridgway, **20**
Diplomat, **7**
Don Carlos, **16**
Fleur de Lys, **12**
Gran Hotel Costa Rica, **8**
L'Ambience, **18**
Le Bergerac, **22**
Pensión La Cuesta, **19**
Santo Tomas, **10**
Toruma Youth Hostel, **21**
Villa Tournon, **9**

delighting businesspeople and visitors over the past 13 years. His *menú de degustación* (tasting menu) offers the best way to sample his range; highlights include the *filet de truchas al pernod y repollo* (trout fillet in pernod with cabbage) and *pato à la naranja* (duck à l'orange). The wicker chairs, tile floor, paneling, mirrors, original paintings, and formal service all complement the cooking. *San Pedro, from ICE, 1 block west and 100 meters (328 feet) south, tel. 225–3980. Reservations advised. AE, DC, MC, V. Closed Sun., Holy Week, and Dec. 24–27. $$$$*

★ **L'Ile de France.** Proprietor-chef Jean Claude, who hails from Paris, has overseen this intimate downtown restaurant for 17 years. The design is simple but elegant, with a tile floor, table-high wood paneling, padded leather chairs, and white walls adorned with framed Toulouse-Lautrec posters. The sauce-based cooking is superb, and there is a very extensive list of French wines. *Calle 7 between Aves. Central and 2, tel. 222–4241. Reservations advised. AE, DC, MC, V. Closed Sun. $$*

La Masía de Triquell. In 1979, Catalan Francisco bought this old colonial house near the end of Paseo Colón and converted it into San José's most authentic Spanish restaurant. Since his death, his widow (Emerita) and son (also named Francisco) have kept the restaurant on the same course. The dining room has a tile floor, wood beams, hanging fans, white walls adorned with antique weaponry, white tablecloths, and leather-and-wood Castilian-style chairs. Start with *champiñones al ajillo* (mushrooms sautéed with garlic and parsley), and as a main course try the *camarones Catalana* (shrimps in a tomato, onion, and garlic sauce with whipped cream). The wine list is long and international, strongest in the Spanish and French departments. Francisco is planning to move the restaurant to a new locale sometime in 1994, so call ahead to find out where it ends up. *Ave. 2 and Calle 40, tel. 221–5073. Reservations advised. AE, DC, MC, V. Closed Sun. afternoon and Mon., Holy Week, and Dec. 25–Jan. 2. $$$*

★ **Ambrosia.** A navy-blue canopy at the entrance of an open-air shopping mall heralds this chic restaurant in San Pedro. The menu is international and ranges across salads, soups, pancakes, pasta, and fish. Start with the *sopa Neptuna* (mixed fish soup with tomato, onion, bacon, and cream); follow with either the light fettuccine ambrosia (pasta with white sauce, cheese, ham, and oregano) or *corvina troyana* (steamed sea-bass fillet covered with sauce of mushrooms, shrimps, and tarragon, and served with rice and vegetables). The atmosphere is relaxed and informal, the decor well chosen to complement the adventurous cooking: tile floor, coral walls, watercolors, wood and cane chairs, and plants. *Centro Comercial de la Calle Real, San Pedro, tel. 253–8012. Dinner reservations advised. AE, DC, MC, V. Closed Sun. afternoons, Holy Week, and Dec. 23–Jan. 4. $$*

Amstel. Amstel functions as a hotel, but the renowned restaurant is really what makes the place. Pristine coral tablecloths, wicker chairs, and soldierly white-uniformed waiters create a classy ambience to complement the excellent and very reasonably priced Costa Rican and international cuisine. All of the *a la parilla* (grilled) fish dishes are worth trying, as are the Steak Cafe Paris and Steak Diane. *Calle 7 and Ave. 1, tel. 222–4622. Dinner reservations advised. MC, V. $$*

Balcón de Europa. Italian-owned and in existence since 1909, this is San José's oldest restaurant. The central location has changed several times due to seismic activity. The cuisine is international and wide-ranging, although not always consistent; the best choices are the pasta dishes. The paneled interior features a hardwood floor, white-and-green tablecloths, ceiling fans, and abundant plants. Old sepia photos of Costa Rica, including the first ones taken in San José, cover the walls. The ambience is relaxed. *Avenida Central and Calle 9, tel. 221–4841. Dinner reservations advised. No credit cards. $$*

Machu Picchu. On a quiet street just north of Paseo Colón, this small restaurant set in a converted house is the place to go if you want excellent Peruvian cuisine or a good pisco sour. A few Peruvian travel posters and some fish netting holding plastic crabs and lobsters are about the only concessions the management makes to decor. The food, however, is anything but plain. The *pique especial de mariscos* (special seafood platter), which is big enough for two people, features shrimp, conch, and squid cooked four ways. The *causa limonesa*, a lemon-accented potato salad with shrimp, is a good starter. A blazing Peruvian hot sauce served on the side adds zip to any dish. *Calle 32, 125 meters (410 feet) north of Kentucky Fried Chicken, Paseo Colón, tel. 222–7384. AE, DC, MC, V. Closed Sun. $$*

★ **Ponte Vecchio.** Affable chef-owner Tony D'Alaimo has applied what he learned from his New York Italian restaurant to this cozy and popular San Pedro spot. The garish sign in the colors of the Italian flag belies the tasteful interior, which features soft lighting and candles and fresh flowers on the coral-pink tablecloths. The menu isn't particularly creative, but fresh local meats and vegetables, homemade pasta, and imported cheeses help create high-quality classic Italian cuisine. Start out with antipasti, followed with rich cheese ravioli, and finish things off with veal saltimbocca. *100 meters (328 feet) west and 10 minutes north of San Pedro Church, tel. 225–9399. Reservations advised. AE, DC, MC, V. Closed Sun., Christmas, New Year's Day, and Thurs. and Fri. of Holy Week. $$*

Fulusu. This Chinese place across from L'Ile de France is one of the very few restaurants in the country where you can get spicy food. The decor is mundane, with black cafeteria-style chairs and Chinese-style paper light shades, but the *vainicas con cerdo* (green beans with pork) and *pollo estilo sichuan* (Szechuan chicken) are the best hot food plates in town. *Calle 7, Aves. Central and 2, tel. 223–7568. No reservations. No credit cards. Closed Sun., Dec. 24–Jan. 3, and Holy Week. $*

Il Pomodoro. In San Pedro, across the street from Masse (*see below*), is San José's best pizzeria. The pizza menu is long (*capricciosa*, with artichokes, ham, sausage, and olives, is especially recommended), and you'll find a medium-size pizza ample for two moderately hungry people. Alternatives to the humble pie are calzone, *focaccia* (a stuffed bread), spaghetti, and lasagna. The maroon-and-white tiled floor, dark paneling, round wooden tables, and low-hanging lamps cast a bistro spell on the place. *91 meters (100 yards) north of San Pedro Church, tel. 224–0966. No reservations. No credit cards. Closed Dec. 15–Jan. 31. $*

Masse. Here's to Sargis Yousefi, the friendly Iranian emigré who runs this popular locale in the university neighborhood of San Pedro—this is a man who knows how to serve a good and cheap *plato del día* (daily special). His specialty is *pollo al carbon* (chicken cooked on charcoal, marinated with lemon, onions, and garlic). A neon Rex cigarette sign and striped canopy are out front, so you can't miss it. Patrons savor the verdant terrace, decorated with primary-colored chairs, wooden tables, and jolly murals. *136 meters (150 yards) north of San Pedro Church, tel. 225–9763. No reservations. V. Closed Sun. and Dec. 19–Jan. 7. $*

Princesa Marina. Somehow this workers' place on the west side of La Sabana Park has found a way to serve fresh seafood for less than half the prices found elsewhere in San José. That's probably why it's usually crowded with middle-class Costa Rican families and less-than-affluent couples on dates. Though not particularly creative, the offerings, including conch and lobster, are a dream for hardcore seafood lovers, and it also serves the largest plates of ceviche and palmito salads around. Friendly, efficient waiters in white shirts and black ties add a touch of class. The sprawling, open-air north dining room is less noisy than the inside one, though it can get chilly. *Sabana West, 150 meters (492 feet) south of Channel 7, tel. 232–0481. AE, DC, MC, V. $*

Dining and Lodging **Fleur de Lys.** This elegant, chic establishment is run by Swiss International Hotels, but you'd never guess that it's part of a chain. Guest rooms in this restored lavender mansion are small but bright, with big closets, floral bedspreads, Tiffany-style table lamps, and paintings by Costa Rican artists; junior suites are more spacious. The prime location between the museum and the Plaza de la Cultura is marred a bit by its proximity to a railroad track (fortunately, trains don't run too late at night). Buffet breakfast, served in an intimate restaurant in the back, is included in the price. The French chef has won accolades for his Swiss-Italian creations, including chicken with wine and herbs, and shrimp flambéed with whiskey. Fish lovers who are getting tired of corvina will light up at a specialties list that includes sole in tomato and basil sauce and squid in champagne sauce. *Calle 13 between avenidas 2 and 4, San José, tel. 223–1206, fax 257–3637. 20 rooms with bath, 1 suite. Facilities: restaurant, bar, parking. AE, DC, MC, V. $$$*

★ **L'Ambience.** L'Ambience is, by a long shot, San José's most elegant hotel, located in a quiet, upscale residential neighborhood five blocks from the city center. Each bedroom in this restored colonial manor house overlooks the central courtyard, where tropical potted plants drape themselves over multicolored *azulejos* (glazed tiles). The antique furniture, gilt mirrors, and old prints in the bedrooms are from the owner's personal collection. The presidential suite has a large drawing room attached. The restaurant offers a menu with a markedly French accent. Try the *tournedos Dijonnaise* (fillets of beef with a mustard cream sauce). Even if you can't afford to stay here, it is worth coming to sample the very good value lunches. *Calle 13 at Avenida 9, Apdo. 1040–2050 San José or c/o Interlink 179, Box 526770, Miami, FL 33152; tel. 222–6702, fax 223–0481. 6 rooms with bath, 1 suite. Facilities: restaurant, bar. No credit cards. $$$*

Lodging **Aurola Holiday Inn.** From the upper floors of this 17-story mirror-glass edifice three blocks north of Plaza de la Cultura, you get the best views in town. Bedrooms are decorated with cream-striped wallpaper, deep-pile brown carpets, patterned bedspreads, and attractive local prints. The beds themselves are conspicuously wide and roomy. Ask for a room facing south, or better still, one on the southwest corner for the best views of all. Rooms on the upper floors come equipped with minibars and VCRs. Public areas are high-ceilinged, modern, and airy to complete the appealing tone of this all-amenity hotel. *Ave. 5 and Calle 5, Apdo. 7802, 1000 San José, tel. 233–7233 or 800/465–4329 in the U.S., fax 255–1036. 188 rooms with bath, 13 suites. Facilities: top-floor restaurant, bar, cafeteria, casino, indoor pool, Jacuzzi, sauna, gymnasium, parking. AE, DC, MC, V. $$$$*

Cariari. The modern, low-rise Cariari is many people's choice due to its range of facilities, which include an 18-hole golf course. Redecorated in 1990, typical bedrooms have blue carpets, white walls, watercolors, sloping wood ceilings, and beds with striped covers and bulging circular headboards. Restaurants range from the relaxed poolside bar, with cane chairs and mustard tablecloths, to posh Los Vitrales, whose green velvet chairs overlook a tropical rock garden. There is always something going on at this out-of-town property (it's on the highway to the airport), meaning you can just stay put if you like. Many do. *Apdo. 737 Centro Colón, San José, tel. 239–0022 or 800/227–4274 in the U.S. 220 rooms with bath. Facilities: 3 restaurants, bar, cafeteria, casino, gymnasium, outdoor pool, Jacuzzi, tennis, golf, parking. AE, DC, MC, V. $$$$*

Gran Hotel Costa Rica. Opened in 1930, the dowager of San José hotels remains a focal point of the city. All bedrooms have recently been redone with beige walls, pastel-patterned bedspreads, subdued carpets, and individual abstract watercolors; rooms overlooking the noisy Plaza de la Cultura have the best views. The bathrooms have old-fashioned taps and modern comfort. A drawback: The size combined with the flow of nonguests frequenting the hotel's glitzy ground-floor casino and bars reduce the intimacy quotient to zero. *Ave. 2 at Calle 3, Apdo. 527, 1000 San José, tel. 221–4000, fax 221–3501. 106 rooms with bath, 13 suites. Facilities: restaurant, 24-hr cafeteria, 24-hr casino, bars, parking. AE, DC, MC, V. $$$*

Le Bergerac. Set in a quiet residential neighborhood east of downtown, this hotel, occupying what was once a block of private homes, is the cream of a growing crop of small, upscale San José hotels. Public areas are eclectically furnished with antiques; guest rooms have custom-made stone and wood dressers and writing tables along with tropical-print bedspreads. Deluxe rooms, with large bathrooms and sitting areas on the garden terraces or balconies, are worth the extra $10. The Aux Fine Herbes restaurant serves French country food in the alfresco dining area. *Apdo. 1107–1002, San José, tel. 234–7850, fax 225–9103. 10 rooms with bath. Facilities: restaurant, parking, meeting room. MC, V. $$$*

★ **Santo Tomas.** Architecturally similar to the Don Carlos but on a busier street, the ceilings here are taller, the walls whiter, the fittings more elegant, and the prices marginally higher. You can get a feeling for how the coffee barons must have lived in this restored, turn-of-the-century, 650-square-meter (7,000-square-foot) plantation house that features mahogany floors and handmade tile. Select an upstairs room for a view north toward Heredia, although tall people may find the eaved ceiling a hazard. It's also a good idea to request a room with a window—rooms that open onto the corridor are gloomy. *Ave. 7 between Calles 3 and 5, San José, tel. 255–0448, fax 222–3950. 20 rooms with bath, 5 suites. Facilities: bar, breakfast room. No credit cards. $$$*

★ **Don Carlos.** A rambling gray villa two blocks north of the Aurola houses this eclectically decorated hotel–cum–crafts shop. Public areas are a split-level maze of polished hardwood floors, greenery-draped courtyards, and tiled patios, intermittently adorned with colorful crafts for sale in the shop on the premises. Bedrooms vary greatly, so if you are here for a few days, shop around for your favorite room on arrival. You'll pay an extra $5 for a superior room in the Colonial wing; rooms here have polished wood floors, high white ceilings, and heavy furniture. Another $5 buys yet more space. *Calle 9 between Aves. 7 and 9, Apdo. 1593, 1000 San José, tel. 221–6707, fax 255–0828. 19 rooms with bath, 6 suites. Facilities: restaurant, cocktail lounge, breakfast room. AE, MC, V. $$–$$$*

★ **Villa Tournon.** Just a few minutes' walk north of downtown or a two-block jaunt from El Pueblo shopping center will take you to this modern, businessman's hotel, noted for its true-value accommodations. Sloping wooden ceilings and bare redbrick walls recall the construction of a ski chalet. Bright landings lead to snug bedrooms painted in pastel shades and adorned with prints. The restaurant serves a wide variety of meat and fish dishes, brought to the tables by white-jacketed waiters. The small garden is attractively laid out with lawns, shrubs, and a kidney-shaped pool. *Barrio Tournon, Apdo. 69, 2120 San José, tel. 233–6622, fax 222–5211. 80 rooms with bath. Facilities: restaurant, parking, pool. AE, MC, V. $$–$$$*

★ **Cacts.** Cacts is located in a quiet residential neighborhood three blocks north of Paseo Colón. Guest rooms are carpeted, with bedside lamps, Japanese prints on the walls, and modern bathrooms. In the bright breakfast room, free coffee is available all day, and the futuristic sitting room is equipped with American cable TV. Canaries in a floor-to-ceiling cage off the reception area serenade you when you come and go. Not all the bedrooms have windows, so specify when you book; Nos. 1 and 9 have reasonable views. The hotel also functions as a tour/travel agency and offers a taxi service to and from the airport. The remote location, a 15- to 20-minute walk from downtown, is a possible drawback, but downtown-destined buses do ply along Paseo Colón. *Ave. 3 Bis between Calles 28 and 30, Apdo. 379, 1005 San José, tel. 221–2928, fax 221–8616. 16 rooms with bath. Facilities: breakfast room, TV room. AE, MC, V. $$*

Diplomat. This colorless place on a commercial street a half block from the busy Avenida 2 is popular among bargain hunters who want to be in the middle of the action. The impeccably clean, quiet, boxlike rooms, with tan walls, worn carpets, twin beds, and tiny bedside tables, have all the charm of an army barracks. Sitting areas and huge tropical murals on each floor add a bit of flair to the otherwise drab surroundings. *Apdo. 6606–1000, San José, tel. 221–8133, fax 233–7474. 30 rooms with bath. Facilities: restaurant, bar. MC, V. $$*

★ **Pension la Cuesta.** Staying here is probably as close as you'll get to sampling a private Tico home. The eight rooms occupy part of a centrally located old wooden villa. The works of Otto Apvy Sirias, one of the country's foremost painters, hang on all walls of his centrally located house, including the bedrooms. The decor throughout is very unhotellike: wicker chairs, hardwood floors, and brightly painted walls. At the rear of the house is a bright, sunken sitting room/breakfast room. Rooms in back are darker but quieter than those in front. *Ave. 1 between Calles 11 and 15, San José, tel. 255–2896, fax 257–2272. 8 rooms, 3 shared bathrooms. Facilities: breakfast room. MC, V. $$*

Bienvenido. Converted from an old movie theater in 1991, Bienvenido has rapidly become a backpacker's favorite. In the hectic area between the Central Market and Borbón, you don't get too much peace, but the rates here are rock-bottom bargains considering the perfectly adequate clean rooms with tile floors, large metal-frame windows, firm wooden beds, and powerful, hot showers. The somewhat prisonlike corridors are brightened by sitting areas with plants and cane chairs. Make use of the valuables room, because thefts are not uncommon in this zone. The new, adjacent restaurant, Meylin, serves good typical Costa Rican food. *Calle 10 between Aves. 1 and 3, tel. 233–2161, fax 221–1872. 48 rooms with bath. Facilities: restaurant. No credit cards. $*

★ **Casa Ridgway.** Affiliated with the Quaker Peace Center next door, Casa Ridgway is the budget option for itinerants concerned with peace, the environment, and social issues in general. Installed in an old wood villa, the bright, clean premises include a planted terrace, lending reference library, and kitchen where you can cook your own food. There are rooms for couples and bunk dormitories for larger groups and individuals. *Ave. 6 Bis 1336 off Calle 15, Apdo. 1507, 1000 San José, tel. 233–6168. 6 rooms, 2 shared bathrooms. Facili-*

ties: kitchen, workshop/lecture area, resource library. No credit cards. $

Toruma Youth Hostel. The headquarters of Costa Rica's expanding hostel network is housed in an elegant blue-and-white colonial bungalow, situated in Los Yoses. The tiled lobby and veranda are ideal spots where backpackers can assemble to swap travel tips. The open bunks in the marginally more costly new section are preferable to the coffinlike boxes toward the back. An on-site information center offers discounts on tours. *Ave. Central between Calles 29 and 31, tel. 224–4085. 105 beds with shared bath. Facilities: dining hall, kitchen area. MC, V. $*

The Arts and Nightlife

The Arts
Festivals

The second Sunday in March is **Día del Boyero** (Oxcart Driver Day), when a colorful procession of carts parades through San Antonio de Escazú. The **International Arts Festival** goes on for two weeks in March and features dancers, theater groups, and musicians from around the world performing at several locales in the San José area. April 11 is **Juan Santamaría Day**, celebrated in Alajuela with marching bands, majorettes, and parades. A dance festival is held in April and May at the Teatro Melico Salazar. In Alajuela in July, the **Festival of Mangoes** involves nine days of music, parades, markets, and general merrymaking. *See also* Festivals and Seasonal Events in Before You Go, *above.*

Theater and Music

The Baroque **Teatro Nacional** (Plaza de la Cultura, no phone) hosts performances of the excellent National Symphony orchestra, whose season runs from April to the end of December, with concerts on Thursday and Friday evenings and Sunday afternoons. It also stages performances from visiting opera companies and dance troupes. The other main theater is the **Teatro Melico Salazar** (Ave. 2 between Calles Central and 2, tel. 221–4952). Dozens of theater groups, including two that perform in English, put on shows at smaller theaters around town; check the English-language *Tico Times* for theaters ads.

Cinemas

Dubbing is rare in Costa Rica, so cinema goers can see films in their original language, usually English, and brush up on their Spanish by reading the subtitles. The film scene is dominated by U.S. movies, which reach San José about a month after their release in the United States. **Sala Garbo** (Ave. 2 and Calle 28) is San José's only arts cinema. The University of Costa Rica in San Pedro shows a wide array of classic U.S. and European-made films. For listings look in any local paper.

Nightlife
Bars and Discotheques

Blending white walls, bare brickwork, and timber, **La Esmeralda** (Ave. 2 between Calles 5 and 7) is a late-night mariachi bar where visitors get serenaded and gaze at paintings depicting old scenes of San José. Vans sit outside ready to carry mariachi bands to and fro. The food isn't bad either. A trendy place to be seen is **El Cuartel de la Boca del Monte** (Ave. 1 between Calles 21 and 23), a large low-ceilinged bar where young artists and professionals gather to eat bocas and sip San José's fanciest cocktails. **Río** in Los Yoses is always rocking and crowded with young Ticos on weekends. In San Pedro, lively bars line the streets around the university; turn left two blocks after the church. CantoAmerica, the country's most popular calypso and folk band, keeps things lively nearly every week at the bohemian **Contravia** bar, two blocks farther east and a block south (turn right at Nueva China restaurant). The privileged young, or *chicos plásticos*, as they're known here, can be encountered at **Tequila**

Willy's, a Mexican restaurant bar farther down the road toward Cartago. **El Pueblo** is a shopping arcade in the style of a quaint Spanish village and home to a range of bars, restaurants, and discos. Recommended are **Cocoloco,** which has a live salsa band, and **La Plaza,** with its huge dance floor. **Key Largo** (Calle 7 between Aves. 1 and 3) mainly appeals to men. It is installed in an elegant old mansion with beautiful carved ceilings, but don't imagine that the prime surroundings have miraculously boosted your sex appeal—the women who approach you here are almost certainly prostitutes. **La Torre** (Calle 7 between Aves. 1 and Central) is a gay bar where women can go to escape the relentless attentions of men.

Cabaret **Josephine's** (Ave. 8 between Calles 2 and 4, tel. 257–2269) is a Vegas-style theater-nightclub presenting a cabaret show called "San José Nights." It is open from 9 PM until 3 AM.

Casinos The **Casino Colonial** (Ave. 1 and Calle 9) is in a restored old mansion and is open 24 hours a day. Other possibilities are the **Aurola Casino,** atop the Aurola Holiday Inn, and the **Cariari** (*see* Dining and Lodging, *above*).

The Atlantic Lowlands

Adjacent to the Caribbean Sea and separated from the Central Valley by the lofty spine of the Cordillera Central (Central Mountains), the Atlantic Lowlands area described here lies between the provinces of Limón and Heredia, scenically dominated by sprawling banana plantations and thick tropical jungle. The widespread, largely untamed region stretches from the dense rain forests of the Sarapiquí region northeast of San José, home to the private La Selva and Rara Avis reserves, east through banana-growing areas, and down to the pristine beaches at Cahuita and Puerto Viejo on the southern Caribbean. In between are the untouched jungle of Braulio Carrillo National Park and Costa Rica's most important archaeological site, Guayabo National Monument.

The distinctive and colorful Afro-Caribbean character of this region is what most obviously sets it apart. Roughly a third of Limón province's population are Afro-Caribbeans, descendants of early 1800s turtle fishermen and the West Indians who arrived in the late 1800s to construct the Atlantic Railroad and then work on banana and cacao plantations. They had to withstand extreme hardship—some 4,000 Jamaicans are reputed to have died from yellow fever, malaria, and snakebites during the construction of the first 40 kilometers (25 miles) of railroad to San José. They were paid relatively well, however, and their lot gradually improved. By the 1930s many had obtained their own small plots of land, and when the price of cacao rose in the 1950s, they emerged as comfortable landowners employing migrant, landless Hispanics. However, until the Civil War of 1948, Afro-Caribbeans were forbidden from crossing to the Meseta Central, for fear of upsetting the country's racial balance, and they were thus prevented from following work when United Fruit abandoned many of its blight-ridden plantations in the 1930s for green-field sites on the Pacific plain. Although Jamaican immigrants brought some aspects of British colonial culture, such as maypole dancing and cricket, these habits have long since given way to reggae, salsa, and baseball.

Laid-back coastal villages to head for include Cahuita, whose extra pull stems from its readily accessible protected rain forest and coral reef, and Puerto Viejo, renowned as a surfer's paradise. Locals and travelers amble about the dirt streets, between brightly painted wooden bungalows, barefoot or in flip-flops, exchanging the odd "Wh'appen man?"

Coastal Talamanca's way of life has changed from one based upon farming and fishing to one based on tourism. A severe earthquake in April 1991, followed by widespread flooding in August, came as a cruel blow to the fragile economy of the region. Although locals still speak in awe of the earthquake, damaged bridges and roads have all been repaired and repaved, making access to Talamanca the best it's ever been.

To the north is the Tortuguero region, whose centerpiece is Tortuguero National Park, where turtles arrive in the hundreds of thousands to lay their eggs on the beaches. And farther north still, sportfishing folk will find tarpon and snook aplenty to detain them off the shores of Barra del Colorado.

Important Addresses and Numbers

Tourist Information The tourist office in San José has information covering the Atlantic Lowlands (*see* Important Addresses and Numbers in San José and the Central Valley, *above*).

Emergencies **Police** (tel. 117 in towns or 127 in rural areas); **Traffic Police** (tel. 227–8030); **Fire** (Bomberos, tel. 118); **Ambulance** (Cruz Roja, tel. 128).

Arriving and Departing by Plane

See Getting Around in Staying in Costa Rica, *above*.

Arriving and Departing by Car and Bus

By Car The paved two-lane Guápiles highway runs from Calle 3 in San José to Limón. South of Limón, a recently improved paved road goes past the Cahuita turnoff and proceeds toward Puerto Viejo. The pavement gives out near Puerto Viejo, but the road remains navigable as far as Punta Uva year-round.

By Bus Bus service to the Atlantic Lowlands from San José includes daily service to **Limón** from Avenida 3 between Calles 19 and 21 (tel. 223–7811) every hour between 5 AM and 7 PM (2½-hour trip); to **Cahuita** and **Sixaola** from Avenida 11 between Calles Central and 1 (tel. 221–0524) daily at 6 and 8:30 AM and 1:30 and 3:30 PM (four-hour trip); to **Turrialba** from Calle 13 between Avenidas 6 and 8 (tel. 556–0073) daily every hour between 5 AM and 10 PM; to **Río Frío** and **Puerto Viejo de Sarapiquí** via Braulio Carrillo from Ave. 11 between Calles Central and one daily at 7, 9, and 10 AM and 1, 3, and 4 PM (four-hour trip).

Getting Around

By Car There are no roads to Tortuguero (*see* By Boat, *below*). At press time the paved road running down the Talamanca coast was in good shape past Cahuita and then gave way to a passable dirt track as far as Punta Uva.

By Bus Buses leave Radio Casino in Limón for Cahuita, Puerto Vargas, Puerto Viejo, and Sixaola daily at 5 and 10 AM and 1 and 4 PM.

By Boat Many private operators will take you from the docks at Moín, just outside of Limón, to Tortuguero, but there is no scheduled public transportation. **Modesto Watson** (tel. 226–0896; *see* Guided Tours, *below*), an eagle-eyed Miskito Indian guide, will take you upstream if he has room on his boat. You can hire boats to travel between Tortuguero and Barra del Colorado, but prices are quite high. Boats leave Puerto Viejo de Sarapiquí to travel upstream but times vary— contact **El Gavilan Lodge** (tel. 234–9507; *see* Dining and Lodging, *below*).

By Train The famous Jungle Train from San José to Limón via Turrialba is out of operation, taking with it the last rail transportation in the area. **Swiss Travel** (tel. 231–4055) offers a one-day tour that includes a train trip between Siquirres and Guápiles.

By Bicycle Several companies rent bicycles in both Cahuita and Puerto Viejo— ask around when you arrive.

Guided Tours

Orientation Tours Tortuguero National Park comes high on most people's agendas, and choosing the right tour is crucial. **Cotur's** (Paseo Colón and Calles 34/36, tel. 233–0155) three-day, two-night tour with a bus to Port Hamburgo, a canal trip, and accommodations at the comfortable prefab Jungle Lodge is a good value at $210 per person, double occupancy. **Mawamba** (tel. 223–2421) is slightly more expensive for the same length tour if you stay at the nicer Mawamba Lodge, but cheaper if you stay in the basic Sabina's Cabinas; their launch from Moín is somewhat faster. **Costa Rica Expeditions** (Calle Central and Ave. 3, tel. 257–0766) flies guests directly to the relatively upscale Tortuga Lodge for three days and two nights at a price of about $300. **Fran and Modesto Watson** (tel. 226–0896) give visitors a feel for the history and ecology of the area on their $125 two-day, one-night tour; guests stay at the comfortable Manatí Lodge. **Adventure Tours** (Hotel Corobicí, tel. 232–4063) operates a two-day, one-night trip up the Sarapiquí, San Juan, and Colorado rivers to Barra del Colorado, staying at the Río Colorado Lodge and returning via Tortuguero and Limón. The cost is around $200.

Special-Interest Tours **Cahuita Tours** (Cahuita, tel. 758–1515, ext. 232) offers glass-bottom-boat tours of the Cahuita National Park coral reef; diving and snorkeling equipment is also available for rent. **Moray's** (Cahuita, tel. 758–1515, ext. 216) runs snorkeling expeditions and tours by boat of the beaches to the south. **ATEC** (across the street from Soda Tamara, Puerto Viejo, no phone), a cooperative of knowledgeable local guides, runs excellent natural-history tours out of Puerto Viejo de Talamanca.

Excursions **Swiss Travel** (tel. 231–4055) has a day trip that includes a train ride between Siquirres and Guápiles and a visit to a banana plantation.

Exploring the Atlantic Lowlands

Tour 1 visits Braulio Carrillo National Park on the way to Limón and the Caribbean Sea. Tour 2 forms a loop around the northern lowlands featuring lush tropical rain forests at Rara Avis and La Selva research stations. Tour 3 is an alternative route to the Caribbean on a scenic road via Turrialba and the Guayabo ruins. Tour 4 covers Tortuguero and Barra del Colorado, and Tour 5 moves south along the Talamancan shore past the beaches of Cahuita and Puerto Viejo.

Highlights for First-time Visitors **Braulio Carrillo** (*see* Tour 1)
Cahuita (*see* Tour 5)
Guayabo (*see* Tour 3)

La Selva (*see* Tour 2)
Rara Avis (*see* Tour 2)
Tortuguero (*see* Tour 4)

Tour 1:
Via Braulio
Carrillo to the
Caribbean

Numbers in the margin correspond to points of interest on the Atlantic Lowlands map.

The quickest route from San José to the Atlantic coast runs through the magnificent cloud forest of Braulio Carrillo National Park before reaching the Caribbean Sea and the lively port town of Limón. The 160-kilometer (100-mile) trip along the Guápiles highway takes 2½ hours, all being well—the highway, carved out of mountainous jungle, is susceptible to landslides. Make sure it's not blocked before heading out.

From San José, follow signs along Calle 3 marked north to Guápiles. After a few miles of divided highway the road narrows and begins its twisty ascent up into the cloud forest, almost perpetually enshrouded in mist. In a country where deforestation has been and still is rife, **Braulio Carrillo National Park** provides the opportunity to see dense primary tropical cloud forest as far as the eye can see. It owes its foundation in 1978 to the storm provoked by the construction of the highway, when the government bowed to pressure from environmentalists. With the highway running through it, the park's rain forest is the most accessible in the country for those traveling from the San José area. It is well worth a visit, even if seen only through a car window. Covering 44,534 hectares (110,000 acres), the park's extremely diverse terrain realizes altitudes varying between 30 and 2,896 meters (100 and 9,500 feet) above sea level, and it extends from the central volcanic range down the Atlantic slope to La Selva research station near Sarapiquí. Six thousand species of trees, 500 of birds, and 135 of mammals have been catalogued here.

① The **Zurquí ranger station** is on the right of the road, 455 meters (500 yards) before the Zurquí tunnel. Ascents start here and are steep, so the paths inevitably involve a lot of ups and downs. The main mile-long trail through primary forest culminates in a mirador (vantage point); unfortunately the highway is included in the view. Wear boots to protect you from the mud and the snakes. An early start, preferably before 8 AM, lessens the risk of mist. Monkeys, tapirs, jaguars, kinkajous, sloths, raccoons, margays, and porcupines all live in the forest, although most animals are very shy. Resident birds include the quetzal and the eagle. Orchids, bromeliads, heliconias, fungi, and mushrooms are easily viewed.

② From the **Carrillo ranger station,** 22 kilometers (14 miles) farther along the highway, the trails are less steep and make for an easier jaunt. For access to the 2,896-meter (9,500-foot) Barva volcano you need to start from Sacramento, north of Heredia (*see* San José and the Central Valley, Tour 5, *above*). The walk to the crater takes two to three hours, but your efforts are rewarded by great views. *Park admission: 200 colones. Open daily 7–4.*

As the highway descends and straightens toward Guápiles, you enter the province of Limón, and cloud forest gives way to banana plantations and deforested pastureland.

Time Out

Shortly after descending to the flatlands, immediately after the Río Corinto bridge, is the **Restaurant Corinto,** where truckers and locals linger over their gallo pinto and eggs in the open-air dining room.

③ After passing through villages with names like Bristol, Stratford, and Liverpool, you arrive in the provincial capital, Limón. **Puerto**

The Atlantic Lowlands

Limón's promontory setting, overlooking the Caribbean, is inherited from an ancient Indian village, Cariari, which lay close to the Isla Uvita, where Christopher Columbus laid anchor on his final voyage in 1502. The colorful Afro-Caribbean flavor of Costa Rica's most important port (population 50,000) gives visitors their first glimpse of life on Costa Rica's east coast. It is a lively town with a 24-hour street life. The houses are largely wooden and brightly painted, although the grid-plan streets now have a worn appearance, worsened by damage from the 1991 earthquake.

On the left of the highway as you enter Limón is a large Chinese cemetery: Chinese made up another part of the railroad construction team. Follow the railroad as far as the palm-lined promenade that runs around Parque Vargas. From the promenade you can see the raised dead coral left stranded by the quake. Nine Hoffman's two-toed sloths live in the trees of Parque Vargas; ask a passer-by to point them out, as sighting them requires a trained eye. From here, find the lively market on Avenida 2, between Calles 3 and 4; fruit can be bought here for the road onward. Staying overnight in Limón is not recommended: Street crime is far from uncommon.

Tour 2: Follow Tour 1, taking a left turn at Santa Clara just after the high-
Rara Avis, La way has completed its descent onto the Caribbean plain. The recent-
Selva, and ly paved road leads through flat, deforested pasture.
Puerto Viejo
de Sarapiquí After 25 kilometers (16 miles) you reach Las Horquetas, which is the
jumping-off point for the 1,337-hectare (3,300-acre) private reserve
❹ of **Rara Avis** (tel. 253–0884; *see* Dining and Lodging, *below*). The 16-
kilometer (10-mile) journey up from here to the reserve is accom-
plished in three hours on horseback, two hours by tractor, or one

hour by Jeep. The trails are steep and rugged, but seeing the flora and fauna is worth the hard work. Rara Avis was started by an ecologist named Amos Bien to combine research, tourism, and sustainable extraction of forest products. Bilingual guides are on hand to take visitors along the muddy trails and to help spot wildlife, which includes toucans, green macaws, howler and spider monkeys, vested anteaters, tapirs, and sloths; they will also convincingly explain their means of harvesting: a process that minimizes forest destruction. The reserve's lacy double waterfall is one of Costa Rica's most photographed sites. The site is open only to overnight guests. All-inclusive package tours, with a three-day minimum stay, cost about $250.

⑤ La Selva, a 1,498-hectare (3,700-acre) reserve at the confluence of the Puerto Viejo and Sarapiquí rivers, comes next: Look for the sign for the Sarapiquí Ecoadventure Lodge on the left some 14 kilometers (9 miles) farther on. It will lead you to La Selva. La Selva is a much more agreeable locale than Rara Avis for those who prefer to see wildlife without sweating or getting dirty. This OTS (Organization for Tropical Studies) biological research station is designed for scientists but welcomes visitors in the daytime and also overnight when space permits—January–March and June–July are the busiest times. Extensive and well-marked trails and swing bridges connect habitats as varied as tropical wet forest, swamps, creeks, rivers, secondary regenerating forests, and pasture. Sundry plants are tagged along the route, and there is plenty of wildlife to interest you. Buy one of the superb self-guide pamphlets based on ongoing scientific research available at park headquarters, which is at the entry point. The OTS has a van that carries visitors here from San José, or you can arrive by public bus or rental car. *OTS, Apdo. 676, 2050 San Pedro, tel. 240–6696. Admission: $18 per day, including lunch; $88 overnight, with 3 meals.*

⑥ During the last century **Puerto Viejo de Sarapiquí** was a thriving river port and the only link with Barra del Colorado and Tortuguero. Fortunes nosedived with the construction of the coastal canal from Moín, and today it has a rundown air. The activities of the Contras also made this a dangerous zone during the 1980s, but with the political situation now improved, boats once again ply the old route up the Sarapiquí River to the San Juan River on the Nicaraguan frontier. There's really not much here to grab the attention of tourists.

⑦ Head west from Puerto Viejo along the paved road past **Selva Verde Lodge** in Chilamate (*see* Dining and Lodging, *below*) to La Virgen, where the Centro Turistica has a swimming pool. Nearby are clear stone-bottomed pools in the Sarapiquí River for bathing.

Time Out **Rancho Leona** (*see* Dining and Lodging, *below*) is in La Virgen on the left; it is the best refreshment stop in the area.

In San Miguel there is a right turn toward Arenal. The road straight on toward San José climbs steeply alongside the Sarapiquí River's deep forested gorge. **⑧** Stop at the factory in **Cinchona** to buy tasty jam or dried fruits. Two kilometers farther, the road passes the spectacular La Paz waterfall. To return to San José, continue south for 40 kilometers (24 miles).

Tour 3: The alternative route from San José to the Caribbean coast through
Turrialba and Cartago and Turrialba takes around four hours. A pretty drive
Guayabo heads from Cartago to Turrialba via Pacayas and Santa Cruz. Take the Irazú road and turn right just before Cot, next to a large white statue of Jesus. The road is twisty, but the hillside scenery is stun-

ning. Pollarded jaul trees line the road to form pretty avenues, and white girder bridges traverse crashing streams. From Santa Cruz a track leads up to within hiking distance of the 3,323-meter (10,900-foot) summit of Turrialba volcano. As you begin the descent to Turrialba, the temperature rises and neatly farmed coffee crops cover the slopes.

9 **Turrialba** is a relatively well-to-do grid-plan agricultural center with a population of 30,000 that suffered when the main San José–Limón route was diverted through Guápiles. The demise of the Jungle Train has been an additional blow. Although lively enough, the town itself doesn't have much to offer, but there are still interesting places to investigate. Kayakers and white-water rafters, for instance, flock here to ride the Reventazón and Pacuare rivers; serious aficionados stay all winter.

10 Nineteen kilometers (12 miles) north by bumpy road, on the slopes of Turrialba volcano, is the **Guayabo National Monument,** Costa Rica's most significant archaeological site. In 1968 a local landowner was out walking her dogs when she discovered what she thought was a tomb. Her friend, archaeologist Carlos Piedra, began excavating and unearthed the base wall of the chief's house in a large city (around 20,000 inhabitants) covering 20 hectares (49 acres). The city was abandoned in AD 1400, probably due to disease and/or starvation. A guided tour (in Spanish only) takes you through premontane rain forest to a mirador from where you can see the layout of the excavated circular buildings. Only the raised foundations survive since the conical houses themselves were built of wood. Descending into the city ruins, observe the well-engineered surface and covered aqueducts leading to a drinking-water trough that still functions; next you'll pass the end of an 8-kilometer (5-mile) paved walkway used to transport the massive building stones. Carved abstract patterns on stones continue to baffle archaeologists, although some clearly depict jaguars, which were revered by the Indians as deities. The hillside jungle setting is captivating, and the trip is further enhanced by the bird-watching possibilities; sacklike nests of *oropéndolas* hang from many of the trees. *Admission: 200 colones. Open daily 8–3.*

11 Five kilometers (3 miles) southeast of Turrialba, on the way to Siquirres, is the **Centro Agronómico Tropical de Investigación y Enseñanza** (CATIE), one of the world's leading tropical research centers. The 810-hectare (2,000-acre) premises include pristine white offices, landscaped grounds, seed conservation chambers, greenhouses, orchards, experimental agricultural projects, and lodging for students and teachers. CATIE is also a good bird-watching spot; a trail leads from behind the administration building to the Reventazón River and around the lagoon. You might catch sight of the brilliant, yellow-winged *jacana spinosa*. Phone ahead for more information; the center has presently suspended guided tours but these may again be available in the future. *Tel. 556–6431.*

Shortly after the turn to CATIE, the road crosses the raging Reventazón River and roughly follows its course. The twisting road offers alternating views toward Irazú volcano and the Caribbean. Grass and sugarcane grow on the valley bottom, while the slopes above are neatly planted with coffee; you pass the occasional elegant *finca* (farmhouse) on the way to Siquirres. Here you meet the Guápiles highway and Tour 1.

**Tour 4:
Tortuguero
and Barra del
Colorado**

⑫

Tortuguero means "turtle region," and this area tucked into north-eastern Costa Rica remains one of the world's prime spots for viewing the awesome though excruciatingly difficult life cycle of sea turtles. The stretch of beach between the Colorado and Matina rivers was first mentioned as a nesting ground for sea turtles in 1592, in a Dutch chronicle. Due to its isolation—there isn't a road to this day—the turtles were able to get on with their nesting virtually undisturbed for centuries. By the 1950s, however, the harvesting of eggs and catching of turtles had increased to such an extent that the turtles faced extinction. In 1963 an executive decree regulated the hunting of turtles and the gathering of eggs, and in 1970 the Tortuguero National Park was established (*see* Chapter 3, National Parks and Wildlife Reserves).

Four species of turtle nest here: the green turtle, the hawksbill, the loggerhead, and the giant leatherback. Green turtles reproduce in large groups, and Tortuguero is one of the sites they choose for nesting from July to October every year. They lay eggs on average every two to three years and produce two or three clutches each time. In between, they feed as far away as Florida and Venezuela. Their meat is considered the best of all turtle species, and there have been attempts to breed them artificially. Hawksbills are small in comparison with other sea turtles and are threatened by hunters because of tortoise-shell, a valuable transparent brown substance from the surface of turtle shells that is much sought after to make jewelry in countries like Japan. Loggerheads, as their name implies, have outsize heads as well as shorter fins; they are very rare at Tortuguero, though, and you are extremely unlikely to see one. The giant leatherback is the largest of all turtle species; individuals grow up to 2 meters (6½ feet) long. They have a tough outer skin instead of a shell, hence their name. From mid-February through April, leatherbacks nest mainly in the southern sector of the park. At the right time of year, there is no reason why you shouldn't witness firsthand the remarkable spectacle of this mass emergence. Most nesting turtles come ashore at night, plowing an uneven furrow with their flippers to propel themselves to the high-tide line, beyond which they employ their hind flippers to scoop out a hole in which to lay their eggs. A couple of months later, the hatchlings struggle out of the nests and make their tortuous, danger-ridden way to the sea.

With around 5 meters (200 inches) of rainfall a year, the Tortuguero region is one of the wettest in Costa Rica. Almost all of the park is flat alluvial plain; the 305-meter (1,000-foot) Sierpe Heights in the west provide the only relief. Vegetation is mainly tropical wet forest. Next to the beach, herbaceous plants such as seagrapes and beach bean flourish. Along the rivers and canals grow water hyacinth and tall palm groves. You can rent dugout canoes to explore this waterway network.

Freshwater turtles live in the rivers, as well as crocodiles, which are most prevalent in the Agua Fría River, and the endangered manatees, also called sea cows. Manatees, which consume huge quantities of aquatic plants, are endangered mainly because their lack of speed renders them easy prey for hunters. Inhabitants of the forests include tapirs (look out for these in the jolillo groves), jaguars, anteaters, ocelots, howler monkeys, collared and white-lipped peccaries, raccoons, otters, skunks, and coatis. There are also some 350 species of birds and countless butterflies (including the iridescent blue Morpho) in the area.

Most people visit Tortuguero as part of a tour (*see* Guided Tours, *above*), but it is possible to hitch a ride with a tour group or hire a boat at the dock in Moín.

Farther up the coast, bordered in the north by the San Juan River and the frontier with Nicaragua, is the vast 92,340-hectare

⑬ (228,000-acre) **Barra del Colorado Wildlife Refuge** (*see* Chapter 3, National Parks and Wildlife Reserves). Approach is by air or boat from Tortuguero, and transport once you get there is almost exclusively waterborne; there are virtually no paths in this swampy terrain. Apart from the route via Tortuguero, another possibility is to come from Puerto Viejo up the Sarapiquí and San Juan rivers. The list of species that you are likely to see from your boat is virtually the same as for Tortuguero; the main difference is the greater feeling of being off the beaten track. Most who make it as far as this are attracted by the sportfishing potential (*see* Sports, *below*). The hamlet of Barra del Colorado, with its stilted, plain wooden houses and dirt paths, remains without motorized land vehicles, although some locals have added outboard motors to their hand-hewn canoes.

Tour 5: The flat, well-paved road to Cahuita branches off to the right at the
Coastal railroad tracks at the second traffic light as you head into Limón.
Talamanca The Caribbean crashes to shore on your left. The climate gets steamier. And you begin to understand why nobody moves too quickly in this part of the country. Apart from a few brief indents, the road hugs the palm-fringed coast. Watch carefully for the left

⑭ turn to **Cahuita** about 8 kilometers (5 miles) out of Limón; it is quite easy to miss. Turn right at the end of the first of three entrance roads to get to Cahuita's main dirt street, flanked by wooden-slat cabins. The turquoise Salón Vaz emits lively reggae, soca, and samba 24 hours a day; the assemblage of dogs dozing on its veranda encapsulates the laid-back pace of life here. Cahuita is a backpackers' holiday town with something of a druggy reputation, a hippie hangout with additional Afro-Caribbean spice.

At the southern end of the main street is the start of **Cahuita National Park** (*see* Chapter 3, National Parks and Wildlife Reserves). Its completely undeveloped curving white-sand beach stretches for 3 kilometers (2 miles). Lush rain forest extends to the brink of the coconut palm–fringed beach. A trail follows the coastline within the forest to Cahuita point, which is encircled by a 243-hectare (600-acre) coral reef. Fish such as blue parrot fish and angelfish weave their way among the various species of coral and sponge. The reef escaped the 1991 earthquake with little damage, but biologists are worried that the coral has stopped growing due to silt and blue plastic bags washed down the Estrella River from banana plantations upstream. Glass-bottom-boat tours operate out of Cahuita to see this aquatic garden (*see* Guided Tours, *above*). Visibility is best in September and October. To snorkel independently, swim out from the beach on the Puerto Vargas side.

⑮ The trail extends as far as **Puerto Vargas,** the park's main headquarters. Along the trail there are opportunities for spotting howler monkeys, coatis, armadillos, and raccoons. Some stretches of beach have much worse currents than others; ask the rangers at either end for advice. There are campsites carved out of the jungle along the beach at Puerto Vargas.

⑯ **Puerto Viejo,** 16 kilometers (10 miles) south of Cahuita, is quieter but has a clutch of *cabinas* (cottages) and hotels. Watch for the left turn 8 kilometers (5 miles) before Bribri; the last 6 kilometers (4 miles) are unpaved. Many visitors come here with only one thing on their mind: surfing. Waves are at their best between December and April and again in June and July. A decent dirt track leads south from Puerto Viejo to **Punta Uva,** where some of the region's first luxurious tourism developments have opened in the last two years, and on to Manzanillo.

The **Gandoca-Manzanillo Wildlife Refuge** protects orey and jolillo swamps, 10 kilometers (6 miles) of beach where four species of turtle lay their eggs, and 300 hectares (741 acres) of cativo forest and coral reef (*see* Chapter 3, National Parks and Wildlife Reserves). The Gandoca estuary is a nursery for tarpon and a wallowing spot for crocodiles and caimans. Administrators Benson and Florentino Grenald can tell you more and recommend a local guide. If you ask when you enter Manzanillo village, you will be pointed toward them.

From the frontier with Panama, retrace your steps to the main road and head left through Bribri to Sixaola, the border town. There are no roads to connect this isolated area northwest of Panama with the rest of the country.

What to See and Do with Children

Beaches provide the best entertainment for children in this area (*see* Beaches, *below*). The sight of the giant turtles at Tortuguero is also sure to excite their imaginations. Also consider a snorkeling or horseback tour run by **Moray's** (tel. 758–1515, ext. 216) or **Cahuita Tours** (tel. 758–1515, ext. 232) in Cahuita.

Off the Beaten Track

The remote 9,153-hectare (22,600-acre) **Hitoy Cerere Biological Reserve** occupies the head of the Valle de la Estrella. The park's limited infrastructure was badly damaged by the 1991 quake, whose epicenter was precisely there. Paths that do exist are very overgrown due to their limited use—visitors scarcely ever get here. Jaguars, tapirs, peccaries, porcupines, anteaters, and armadillos all live in the forest, along with more than 115 species of birds. Look out for the so-called Jesus Christ lizards, which can walk on water. The moss-flanked rivers have clear bathing pools and spectacular waterfalls. To get there, take a Valle de la Estrella bus from Limón and get off at Finca Seis; hire a jeep here and you'll be able to get within 1 kilometer (⅗ mile) for $5. Check beforehand with the park service in San José if you want to stay overnight.

From Turrialba, drive or catch a bus 30 kilometers (20 miles) southeast to Moravia de Chirripó. Nearby are a handful of **Talamancan Indian settlements,** only recently in touch with mainstream Costa Rican life. You will pass through Tuís close to the Rancho Naturalista (*see* Dining and Lodging, *below*).

Shopping

Shopping is not the star attraction of the Atlantic Lowlands. The owners of **Rancho Leona** (*see* Dining and Lodging, *below*) make and sell stained glass, necklaces, earrings, and painted T-shirts. On the track running north from Cahuita to Playa Negra, **Tienda de Artesania** is a women's craft cooperative producing painted T-shirts and jewelry.

Sports

Fishing Tarpon and snook attract sportfishermen to the northern Caribbean shore—January through May is the best time for tarpon, August through November for snook. Lodges offering fishing trips include **Isla de Pesca** (tel. 223–4560), **Casamar** (tel. 343–8834), and **Río Colorado Lodge** (*see* Dining and Lodging, *below*).

Horseback Riding **Moray's** (tel. 758–1515, ext. 216) in Cahuita offers guided horseback tours.

Scuba Diving and Snorkeling Cahuita has Costa Rica's largest reef (*see* Guided Tours, *above*, for dive trips).

Other dive spots include the coral reef at Isla Uvita off Limón, and sea caverns off Puerto Viejo. The water is clearest during the dry season.

Surfing Although some point breaks were badly affected by coastal uplift in 1991, other new ones were created—a left at Cocles and a right at Punta Uva. Puerto Viejo's famous Salsa Brava is still ridable. December to March and June to August are the best times for surfing this coast.

White-water Rafting and Kayaking The Atlantic side of the Cordillera Central is Costa Rica's white-water heartland. The Reventazón River is probably the fiercest, with many Class IV and V (most advanced skills required) rapids, suitable only for more experienced rafters and kayakers. The Pacuare River, which runs parallel to it, has intermediate-level rapids and prettier, wooded-canyon scenery. Three companies operate similar rafting/kayaking trips out of San José of varying length and grade: **Costa Rica Expeditions** (tel. 222–0333), **Rios Tropicales** (tel. 233–6455), and **Aventuras Naturales** (tel. 225–3939). The cost is around $70 for one day. **Rancho Leona** (*see* Dining and Lodging, *below*) offers gentler kayaking excursions down the Sarapiquí River.

Beaches

The Atlantic coast is characterized by long swaths of palm-fringed white sand. During the rainy season it is probably the least-reliable area in terms of weather, although mornings are often sunny. The attraction of beaches here is the laid-back atmosphere of the villages along the coast, such as Cahuita and Puerto Viejo. Cahuita's best beach is the long curve fronting the rain forest of the national park—this has soft white sand, in contrast to the hard black stuff at Playa Negra. Puerto Viejo is often overrun by the surfing fraternity (*see* Sports, *above*), but you'll find some great beaches down the coast, especially just north of Punta Uva.

Dining and Lodging

Dining Much of the cooking along the Caribbean coast derives from old Jamaican recipes. *Rondon* is a stew that needs hours of preparation, so you have to notify your restaurateur in advance. Rice and beans are flavored with coconut, meat is fried with hot spices to make *paties* (pies), and fish or meat, yams, plantains, breadfruit, peppers, and spices are boiled in coconut milk to prepare a "rundown." Popular buns are johnny (or journey) cakes and pan bon. Various medicinal herbal teas are another ubiquitous feature. Seafood is, of course, readily available. Dress is casual in all the restaurants we list. Highly recommended restaurants are indicated by a star ★. For ratings, *see* Staying in Costa Rica, Dining and Lodging, *above*.

Lodging With a couple of exceptions, the Atlantic Lowlands have no luxury hotels. Most places to stay are rustic *cabinas* (cottages) or nature lodges. Highly recommended hotels are indicated by a star ★. For ratings, *see* Staying in Costa Rica, Dining and Lodging, *above*.

Barra del **Río Colorado Lodge.** This jungle lodge caters almost exclusively to
Colorado sportfishing folk, as the property runs a modern fleet of 16- and 23-
Dining and foot sportfishing vessels. Bedrooms have twin beds with patterned
Lodging bedspreads, paneled ceilings, white curtains, and basket lamp-
shades. Expensive all-inclusive tours include the flight here, all meals, and fishing. *Apdo. 5094, 1000 San José, tel. 710–6879 or 800/ 243–9777 in the U.S., fax 231–5987. 18 rooms with bath. Facilities: restaurant, bar, tackle store. AE, MC, V. $$$*

Cahuita **Jaguar.** These white cabinas on Playa Negra provide the roomiest
Dining and accommodations plus the classiest cooking in Cahuita. The naturally
Lodging ventilated cabins have high ceilings, large wooden beds, mosquito
★ blinds, and terra-cotta floors, and you'll be delighted by the assort-
ment of fruit trees and virtual menagerie of exotic birds on the 7-hectare (17-acre) grounds. The rooms nearest the road enjoy a view of the Caribbean through palm trees. The owners tend an herb garden whose produce they use in their most popular recipe, *dorada en salsa de herbas* (dorado fish in an herb sauce). Phone ahead to see if transportation is available from Limón. *Tel. 758–1515, ext. 238, or 226–3775; fax 226–4693. 45 rooms with bath. Facilities: restaurant, garden. MC, V. $$*

★ **Miss Edith's.** Miss Edith is revered for her outrageous Caribbean cooking, vegetarian meals, and herbal teas for whatever ails you. Don't expect to get anything in a hurry; most of her dishes are made to order. But her rondon and smoked chicken are worth the wait. Her restaurant is at the north end of town, near the *guardia rural* (police station). *No phone. No reservations. No credit cards. Closed Tues. and Sun. lunch. $*

Vista de Mar. The main attraction of this open-air, aluminum-roofed eatery is its proximity to Cahuita National Park. After a hard day of sunbathing, you need walk only about 10 steps past the park exit to sample its traditional Costa Rican food and seafood. The *pescado en salsa* (fish in sauce) is always fresh. *Tel. 758–1515, ext. 228. No reservations. No credit cards. $*

Lodging **Atlántida.** Atlántida's main asset is its attractively landscaped grounds. Located up the street from Jaguar, the yellow bedrooms of this hotel are quite small and have heavy wood furniture, fans, and mosquito blinds. They encircle a thatched restaurant that provides breakfast with the price of the room. You can also cook your own food. The managers cultivate a younger and trendier ambience than Jaguar's. *Apdo. K, Limón, tel. 758–1515, ext. 213, fax 228–9467. 30 rooms with bath. Facilities: restaurant. AE, MC, V. $$*

★ **Aviarios del Caribe.** As you head south from Limón, myriad signs lead you to this jewel in the rough along the Estrella River delta, 9 kilometers (5 miles) north of Cahuita. Luis and Judy Arroyo have built this lodge and bird-watching sanctuary from the rubble of the 1991 earthquake. More than 250 species of birds have been spotted on the property, many with the help of the telescope on the wide second-floor deck. The spacious guest rooms feature white walls, blue tile floors, and fresh flowers. Buttercup, the resident three-toed sloth, oversees the proceedings from her spot on the couch of the airy sitting room–library. *Apdo. 569-7300, Limón, no phone, fax 798–0374. 5 rooms with bath. Facilities: breakfast room, weight room. $$*

★ **Magellan Inn.** This new group of bungalows near the end of the first entrance road into town is Cahuita's most elegant choice of accommodations by a long shot. The white-walled rooms feature original artwork, custom-made wooden furniture, wall-to-wall carpets, and tiled terraces with wicker chairs and tables. Jazz and classical music plays in the open-air bar, which is available to hotel customers only. The only drawback: The "king-size" beds that management touts are really two twin beds pushed together. *Apdo. 1132, Limón, no phone, fax 758–0652. 6 rooms with bath. Facilities: bar, outdoor pool. DC, MC, V. $$*

★ **Seaside Jenny.** The eponymous owner retains her Canadian lilt despite 16 years in Cahuita. Book here if proximity to the sea is what you crave. Located near the main part of town, the modern two-story structure is just 9 meters (10 yards) from the very audible water's edge. Upstairs cabins are $5 more but worth it for their sea views, balconies, and extra light; the ones downstairs are rather dingy. There are more beds in some—a good pointer for groups to keep in mind. Fans keep the rooms cool, and hammocks strung on the terraces catch Caribbean breezes. Furnishings are traditional. No mosquito nets here because you don't find the pests so close to the sea. *Tel. 758–1515, ext. 256. 7 rooms with bath. No credit cards. $*

Guayabo **Albergue La Calzada.** Young eucalyptus trees surround this bucolic
Lodging bird-watchers' lodge 365 meters (400 yards) before the national monument. The bedrooms are in a pondside cabin with views of the wooded hills and distant Caribbean. Best views are from upstairs, but these rooms, although cheaper, share a bath and have drafty corrugated iron roofs, noisy when it rains. Also noisy are the unfriendly geese outside. All rooms have firm wooden beds, paneling, flimsy curtains, and bedside lamps. *Apdo. 260, 7150 Turrialba, tel. 556–0465. 4 rooms without bath. Facilities: restaurant, bar. V. $$$*

Limón **Springfield.** Springfield is on the left of the road to Portete, opposite
Dining the hospital. Protected from the street by a leafy conservatory, this Caribbean kitchen produces tasty rice and bean dishes. Decor consists of wood paneling, red tablecloths, and a white tile floor. Out back is a huge dance floor that creaks to the beat of soca, salsa, and reggae on weekends. *Ctra. Portete, no phone. No reservations. MC, V. $–$$*

Lodging **Hotel Maribu Caribe.** Perched on a cliff overlooking the Caribbean,
★ between Limón and Portete, these white, conical thatched huts have great views, air-conditioning, and hot water. The gardens are landscaped with lawns, shrubs, palm trees, and a large, kidney-shaped pool. The poolside bar does away with the need for any added exertion. *Ctra. Portete, Limón, tel. 758–3541. 52 rooms with bath. Facilities: restaurant, snack bar, bar, pool, parking, armed security guard. MC, V. $$$*

Hotel Acón. This modern four-story building is smack in the center of town. It has bare but comfortable, air-conditioned bedrooms. Some are disturbed by the large and popular second-floor discotheque, so ask for a quiet room or head elsewhere. The restaurant receives good marks. *Calle 3 at Ave. 3, Limón, tel. 758–1010. 39 rooms with bath. Facilities: restaurant. No credit cards. $$*

Hotel Park. An interesting conglomeration of budget travelers assemble at the old lady of Limón's hotels. Situated downtown, one block north and one west from Parque Vargas, the bedrooms here are basic—no air-conditioning—but perfectly habitable for a night. Six rooms have a view of the bay, so ask on arrival; they cost marginally more. *Ave. 3 between Calles 1 and 2, Limón, tel. 758–3476. 24 rooms with bath. Facilities: restaurant. No credit cards. $*

Puerto Viejo de Limón *Dining*	**El Caribe.** Co-owned with the Stanfords disco downstairs, this breezy veranda has a shady promontory setting, affording an excellent vantage point from which to study surfing conditions. Charlie's kitchen turns out goodies like traditional rice and beans, *camarones* (shrimp), and *langosta* (lobster), all served with onions, garlic, vegetables, and Caribbean salad. If you don't feel up to a full meal, come here any time to sip a soft drink and munch chips. *No phone. No reservations. No credit cards. Lunch and dinner only. $$*

Dining and Lodging ★ **El Pizote.** Set back to the right of the track that runs into town, El Pizote observes local architectural mores while offering more than most in the way of amenities. Rooms feature polished wood paneling, reading lamps, mirrors, mats, firm beds, and fans. Some share a bathroom; others in individual huts have their own. A two-room bungalow accommodates six people. The restaurant serves breakfast, dinner, and drinks all day. Guanabana and papaya grow on the grounds; hiking trails lead off into the jungle. Children under 8 aren't welcome. *Apdo. 230, 2200 Coronado, San José, tel. and fax 229–1428. 8 rooms with shared bath, 7 rooms with bath. Facilities: restaurant, bar, volleyball. MC, V. $$–$$$*

Lodging ★ **Escape Caribeño.** Five hundred meters (550 yards) east of El Caribe, in the midst of the jungle, are these clean detached huts with tasteful furniture and large fans. Each has a well-stocked fridge, very welcome after the trek to get here. The restaurant serves breakfast only, but this may change. Bring your own food if you wish to cook. The beach is a couple minutes' walk away through the palm trees. Book via the Hotel Maritza, which has a phone; ask for Petra or the Escape Caribeño. *Tel. (Maritza) 758–3844. 11 rooms with bath. Facilities: breakfast room, kitchen. MC, V. $$*

Cabinas Black Sands. Go left at Violeta's Pulperia (ask the bus to drop you here) just before reaching Puerto Viejo, and Black Sands is 365 meters (400 yards) away, signposted. This beachside cabina is of Bri-Bri Indian design—bamboo, laurel wood, thatch, and stilts— and is surrounded by tropical foliage. Its isolated position, a 20-minute walk from Puerto Viejo, ensures privacy and tranquillity. The same can't be said for the rooms, whose dividing walls don't quite reach the ceiling. A basic kitchen is shared by all guests; bring your own food. *Ken Kerst, Lista de Correos, Puerto Viejo de Limón, Talamanca, no phone. 3 double rooms with shared bath. Facilities: kitchen. No credit cards. $*

Puerto Viejo de Sarapiquí and Environs *Dining and Lodging* ★ **Rara Avis.** Rara Avis is tough to get to but very worthwhile. A number of research projects underway are studying sustainable uses for the rain forest. The Waterfall Lodge, named for the 55-meter (180-foot) waterfall nearby, contains hardwood-paneled corner rooms with chairs, firm beds, balconies, and hammocks. El Plástico Lodge used to be a prison and has coed bunk rooms and reductions for IYHF members, students, and scientists. All rates include transport from Horquetas, guides, and three meals daily. Management requires a two-night minimum stay. *Apdo. 8105, 1000 San José, tel. 253–0844. 7 rooms with bath, 6 rooms with shared bath. Facilities: dining room. AE, MC, V. $$$*

Selva Verde Lodge. Located 5 kilometers (3 miles) west of Puerto Viejo in Chilamate, this is an expanding rancho-style complex on the edge of a 202-hectare (500-acre) private reserve of tropical rain forest. It caters to retirees on natural-history tours. The new River Lodge stands on stilts over the Sarapiquí River. All the buildings have wide verandas strung with hammocks, and bedrooms come with polished wood paneling, fans, and mosquito blinds. Activities include fishing, horse riding, boat trips, and guided walks. The rates include three meals per day in the hotel restaurant. *Apdo. 55, Chilamate, Heredia, tel. 766–6077, fax 766–6011. 45 rooms with bath, 9 rooms without bath. Facilities: restaurant, library. MC, V. $$$*

★ **El Gavilan Lodge.** Gavilan is a few kilometers southeast of Puerto Viejo: Branch (signposted) off the road from Horquetas. Erstwhile hub of a fruit and cattle farm, the lodge has two stories fronted by verandas. The comfortable bedrooms have white walls, terra-cotta floors, fans, and decorative artesania. Some feature en suite flashy purple bathrooms. Manicured gardens run down to the river. Colorful tanagers and three types of toucan feast on the citrus fruit in the trees. The food enjoys a good reputation. Most people come here as part of a tour with pickup in San José. Activities include fishing, horseback jungle treks, and boat trips up the Sarapiquí River toward the San Juan River and the border with Nicaragua. *Apdo. 445, Zapote, San José, tel. 234–9507, fax 253–6556. 14 rooms with bath. Facilities: dining room, Jacuzzi. No credit cards. $$*

Rancho Leona. Twelve kilometers (8 miles) southwest of Puerto Viejo in the village of La Virgen, this rancho has small rustic dormitories designed for kayaking trips (*see* Sports, *above*). The restaurant has a varied menu with good pasta dishes and fruit juices. The restaurant and rooms were built to accommodate customers on kayaking tours, but owners Ken and Leona Upcraft have opened the restaurant to the public and say they'll lodge you if there's room. Activities include kayaking, horseback riding, hiking, and river swimming. The owners plan more basic cabins farther into the jungle but within hiking distance. *La Virgen, Heredia, tel. 761–1019. 3 bunk rooms with shared bath. Facilities: restaurant. No credit cards. $*

Punta Uva **Selvyn's.** This unassuming hotel-restaurant on the east side of the
Dining and main road is as basic as it comes, but Selvyn serves up some of the
Lodging meanest Caribbean-style red snapper you can find. Don't come here
★ if you're in a hurry, though: Sometimes it seems as if he has to catch the fish after you order it. The simple, wood-paneled guest rooms are a bit claustrophobic, but you won't be spending much time there, anyway—the beach is only about 90 meters (100 yards) away. *Punta Uva, Talamanca, no phone. 8 rooms with shared bath. Facilities: restaurant. No credit cards. $*

Lodging **Villas del Caribe.** Undoubtedly the most elegant place in Costa Rica east of San José, this villa complex is right on the beach north of Punta Uva. Each multiroom villa has a blue-tile-lined kitchen with stove and refrigerator, a small sitting room with low-slung couches, a plant-filled bathroom, and a patio with sea view. Upstairs are one or two spacious bedrooms with a wooden deck and a view of the Caribbean. *Apdo. 8080–1000, San José, tel. 233–2200, fax 221–2801. 12 villas with bath. Facilities: restaurant. AE, DC, MC, V. $$$$*

Playa Chiquita Lodge. These wooden cabinas are tastefully furnished and set in thick jungle 180 meters (200 yards) back from the beautiful Chiquita beach, near Punta Uva. It is popular with birdwatchers who swap sightings in the evening. *Tel. 223–7479. 12 rooms with bath. Facilities: bar, restaurant. No credit cards. $$*

Miraflores Lodge. It's not too difficult to tell that this was a flower farm before the hotel was built four years ago: The collection of bromeliads and heliconias and the intricate landscaping are a dead giveaway. The buildings, designed in the indigenous style, with peaked thatched roofs and cane walls, make you feel as if you're off the tourist trail. The proprietor sells local artwork in an attempt to infuse some tourism money directly into the local economy. *Apdo. 7272–1000, San José, tel. 233–5217, fax 233–5420. 3 rooms with* *bath, 6 with shared bath. Facilities: breakfast room. No credit cards. $–$$*

Tortuguero
Dining and Lodging

Tortuga Lodge. Costa Rica Expeditions owns this thatched riverside lodge, renowned for its tarpon and snook fishing. The national record tarpon, weighing 182 pounds, was caught here in 1987. The bedrooms are comfortable and have fans, mosquito blinds, and hot water. A landscaped garden contains lawns, orchids, and other plants. It is situated across the river from the airstrip, 2 kilometers (1¼ miles) from the village. Most guests come as a part of tours. *Tel. 257–0766 and 710–6861, fax 257–1665. 25 rooms with bath. Facilities: dining room. AE, MC, V. $$$*

Mawamba Lodge. This is a relatively new lodge, 1 kilometer (⅗ mile) north of the village on the ocean side of the canal. Once whisked from Port Hamburgo in a fast launch (2½ hours), guests stay in comfortable rustic cabinas with fans and dine in the spacious dining room. Activities include tours of the jungle, canals, and turtle-laying beaches. *Tel. 223–2421. 36 rooms with bath. Facilities: dining room. MC, V. $$–$$$*

El Manatí. The friendly owners, Fernando and Lilia Figuls, followed the rough-hewn wood and cane indigenous architectural style when they carved this comfortable lodge out of the jungle across the river from the north edge of the village. The sparkling-clean wood-paneled rooms have firm beds, mosquito screens, and fans. The terraces look across a narrow lawn to the river. Chestnut-mandibled toucans, poison arrow frogs, and three types of monkey hang out in the jungle that looms behind the rooms. *Tel. 288–1828. Facilities: dining room. No credit cards. $$*

Tatané. A five-minute boat ride away from the village, on the canal to Barra del Colorado, this is the best budget option around these parts. The rustic A-frame cabinas are comfortable and clean enough. The owner, a turtle guide, takes guests to and from the town and on tours. *No phone. 6 rooms with shared bath. Facilities: dining room. No credit cards. $*

Tuís
Dining and Lodging

Rancho Naturalista. Southeast of Turrialba, 2½ kilometers (1½ miles) up a dirt track from the village of Tuís, this 51-hectare (125-acre) private reserve offers guided horseback and bird-watching tours. Three hundred species of birds, several of Morpho butterfly, and thousands of moth species live nearby. The two-story lodge is rustically decorated throughout. Good home cooking is served in the dining room. *Dept. 1425, Box 025216, Miami, FL 33102, tel. 267–7138. 5 rooms with bath, 3 with shared bath. Facilities: dining room. No credit cards. $$$*

Turrialba
Dining and Lodging
★

Turrialtico. Eight kilometers (5 miles) out of town on the Limón road, a hedged drive winds its way up to this dramatically positioned open-sided hotel/restaurant. The new second-floor rooms, handsomely designed with Guatemalan spreads on the firm beds and wood floors, could be the country's best bargain. Try to get a room on the west side for a dazzling view toward Turrialba and, if you're in luck, Irazú volcano. Although the restaurant's menu isn't extensive, the cooking is worthy: *Casado* (rice, beans, salad, and meat or fish) is a safe bet. A possible minus is that the place is a stopover for tour/rafting buses: About three per week come here to eat. *Ctra. Limón 8 km, Apdo. 121, Turrialba, tel. 556–1111. 12 rooms with bath. Facilities: restaurant, bar. No credit cards. $*

Lodging

Wagelia. To the left of the road in from Paraíso, this bungalow has bedrooms that look onto a tropical courtyard. Small rooms feature terra-cotta floors, white walls, firm wooden beds, brown patterned bedspreads, and bedside lamps; five have air-conditioning, for which you pay extra. The bright modern restaurant serves local fare at reasonable prices. *Apdo. 99, Turrialba, tel. 556–1566, fax 556– 1596. 18 rooms with bath. Facilities: restaurant, bar, TV room, parking. AE, MC, V. $$$*

Arts and Nightlife

The Arts May Day is celebrated in Limón with cricket matches, quadrille dances, and domino matches. During the week of October 12, Limón Carnival features street dances, concerts, and a spectacular New Orleans–style parade finale.

Nightlife Limón is quite lively after dark—popular dance floors are at the **Hotel Acón** and **Springfield** restaurant (*see* Dining and Lodging, *above*). In Cahuita most people gravitate toward the salsa/soca/reggae sounds of **Salón Vaz** on the main street, and in Puerto Viejo, **Stanford's** disco is the main event.

The Northwest

Costa Rica's Wild West—the country's driest region, with about 65 inches of rainfall per year—is strewn with cattle ranches, but not limited to them. Six semiactive volcanoes, large areas of wet and dry forest, limestone caverns, several large lakes, and mile upon mile of beaches lend an enlivening diversity to the scenery.

Guanacaste, Costa Rica's westernmost province, at the border of Nicaragua and the Pacific Ocean, derives its name from the broad ear-pod trees that give sporadic shade to lounging white Brahman cattle. It formed an independent province of Spain's colonial empire until 1787, when it was ceded to Nicaragua. In 1814, in order to provide Costa Rica with sufficient people for representation in the Cortes in Guatemala, Spain's colonial parliament, it became part of Costa Rica. After independence in 1821, both countries claimed Guanacaste and Guanacastecos were themselves divided: Liberia wished to return to Nicaragua while Nicoya favored Costa Rica. Nicoya got its way, helped by the fact that at the time the vote was taken, Nicaragua was engaged in a civil war.

In appearance, Guanacastecos resemble their darker Nicaraguan neighbors more than they do the *Cartagos*, as they call the Central Valley dwellers, whose perceived sense of cultural and racial superiority they somewhat resent. These descendants of Chorotegas and early Spanish settlers started many of the traditions that are now referred to as Costa Rican, and a strong folkloric character pervades the region. Look for a prevalence of traditional costumes, folk dancing, music, and recipes handed down from colonial times.

Because of the reliable climate, made drier still by the extensive deforestation, the beaches of the Northwest are popular during the rainy season. Development is so far mostly very low-key, but the area is being targeted for huge amounts of investment. Large luxury resort and condominium projects are currently underway in Tambor and Flamingo. Thousands of homes, hotel rooms, and tourism facilities are planned for Papagayo, but environmentalists oppose the massive development.

Important Addresses and Numbers

Tourist Information The **tourist office** in San José has information covering the Northwest (*see* Important Addresses and Numbers in San José and the

Central Valley, *above*). In Liberia, the **Casa de Cultura** (3 blocks from Central Plaza) has local tourist information. It is open Monday–Saturday 8–4.

Emergencies **Police** (tel. 117 in towns or 127 in rural areas); **Traffic Police** (tel. 227–8030); **Fire** (tel. 118); **Ambulance** (tel. 221–5818).

Arriving and Departing by Plane

Sansa and **Travelair** fly to Liberia, Tamarindo, Carrillo, and Nosara (*see* Getting Around in Staying in Costa Rica, *above*, for details).

Arriving and Departing by Car and Bus

By Car Road access to the Northwest is by way of the paved two-lane Interamerican Highway, which starts from the top of Paseo Colón in San José.

By Bus Bus service to the Northwest from San José includes the following: to **Monteverde,** departures from Calle 14 between Avenidas 9 and 11 (tel. 222–3854) Monday–Thursday at 2:30 PM and Saturday at 6:30 AM (3½-hour trip); to **Puntarenas** from Calle 12 between Avenidas 7 and 9 (tel. 222–0064) daily every 40 minutes between 5 AM and 7 PM (two-hour trip); to **Liberia** from Calle 14 between Avenidas 1 and 3 (tel. 222–1650) daily every two hours between 7 AM and 8 PM (four-hour trip); to **Arenal volcano** (Fortuna) from Calle 16 between Avenidas 1 and 3 (tel. 232–5660) daily at 6:15 AM, 8:40 AM, and 11:30 AM, returning at 2:45 PM (4½-hour trip); and to **Tamarindo** from Calle 14 between Avenidas 3 and 5 (tel. 222–2750) daily at 3:30 PM (5½-hour trip).

Getting Around

By Car Paved roads run to the Nicaraguan border, to Fortuna from San José, and down the spine of the Nicoya Peninsula as far as Carmona. Many roads in the region are unpaved and badly rutted. Most are passable by car, but if in doubt ask at the tourist office in San José.

By Bus Bus service within the area includes the following: to **Garza, Guiones,** and **Nosara** from Nicoya bus station daily at 1 PM; to **Samara** and **Carrillo** from Nicoya weekdays at 3 PM and weekends at 8 AM; to **Tilarán** from Monteverde daily at 7 AM (three-hour trip); to **Flamingo** and **Brasilito** from Santa Cruz daily at 6:30 AM and 3 PM; to **Tamarindo** from Santa Cruz daily at 8 PM, returning at 6:45 AM; to **Montezuma** from Paquera daily at 8 AM and 5 PM, returning at 5:30 AM and 2 PM. The best place to check schedules is the tourist office in San José.

By Boat The Puntarenas–Playa Naranjo car ferry takes 1½ hours and departs daily at 7 AM, 1:30 PM, and 4 PM, returning at 5:15 AM, noon, 3 PM, and 6 PM. The 1½-hour Puntarenas–Paquera passenger ferry departs daily at 6 AM and 3 PM, returning at 8 AM and 5 PM, and links with buses to Montezuma. The Tempisque car ferry crosses continuously and takes 20 minutes; lines can get very long in the dry season.

Guided Tours

Orientation **Swiss Travel** (tel. 231–4055) has tours to Arenal out of San José, as
Tours well as to Monteverde. **Costa Rica Sun Tours** (tel. 255–3518) will take you to the Arenal Observatory, perhaps combined with a trip to Monteverde. **Costa Rica Expeditions** (tel. 257–0766) offers eight- to 14-day tours around the whole country, including the Northwest.

Special-Interest Tours **Tikal Ecoadventures** (tel. 223–2811) runs highly informative week-long tours that take in Carara (*see* Exploring the Southwest, *below*), Manuel Antonio, the Lomas Barbudal Reserve, Playa Grande, Santa Rosa, and Arenal. **Geotur** (tel. 234–1867) operates a three-day horseback exploratory tour of the dry forests around Los Inocentes Lodge, where participants stay. The excellent **Horizontes** (tel. 222–2022) specializes in more independent tours with as few as eight people, including transport by four-wheel drive, naturalist guides, and guest lectures.

Day Trips Day trips to the idyllic Tortuga Island in the Gulf of Nicoya are very popular, and **Calypso Tours** (tel. 233–3617) has been doing them the longest. Monteverde can be included in the package. The **Burío Inn** (*see* Dining and Lodging, *below*) in Fortuna offers a wide range of excursions including visits to Caño Negro National Wildlife Refuge, Venado Caverns, Fortuna River waterfall by horseback, and the lower slopes of Arenal volcano. **Guanacaste Tours** (tel. 666–0306) is recommended for day trips from within the Northwest to Santa Rosa, Rincón de la Vieja, Palo Verde, Playa Ostional and Playa Grande by night (to see turtles), and Arenal; it picks up tour participants from large hotels in the area.

Exploring the Northwest

Tour 1 includes the port town of Puntarenas, the cloud-forest reserve and peaceful Quaker community at Monteverde, and Lake Arenal and the still active Arenal volcano. With minimal backtracking, this could be combined with Tour 2, which explores the northern attractions of Rincón de la Vieja and Santa Rosa. Tour 3 is a tour of the Nicoya Peninsula, which could be followed in either direction.

Highlights for First-time Visitors **Arenal volcano** (*see* Tour 1)
Barra Honda National Park (*see* Tour 3)
Cabo Blanco Strict Nature Reserve (*see* Tour 3)
Monteverde (*see* Tour 1)
Ostional (*see* Tour 3)
Rincón de la Vieja volcano (*see* Tour 2)
Santa Rosa National Park (*see* Tour 2)

Tour 1: Puntarenas, Monteverde, and Arenal *Numbers in the margin correspond to points of interest on the Northwest map.*

To reach Monteverde from San José, follow signs from Paseo Colón to the airport and then follow signs to San Ramón. The scenery along this section of the Interamerican Highway is dominated by the line of Barva, Poás, and Viejo volcanoes to the north. Passing lanes on the uphill stretches reduce the slowing effect of the often heavy traffic. Past San Ramón the highway begins its curving descent to sea level.

Five kilometers (3 miles) beyond Esparza, a popular truck stop, is ❶ the turn to **Puntarenas**. As its name implies, this erstwhile coffee-shipping port is situated on a narrow spit of sand protruding into the Gulf of Nicoya, with splendid views across to the peninsula. Most tourists stop here only on the way to the Nicoya Peninsula (by ferry). The boardwalk is pleasant, but this downtrodden town suffers from rising crime and polluted water and is not worth a special trip. Its grid-plan streets abound in restaurants and markets, and the southern palm-lined promenade is popular with day-trippers from San José, although the Ministry of Health warns against swimming here. In summer the series of theater, music, and dance shows at the Casa de la Cultura can be fun. The murky estuary to the north

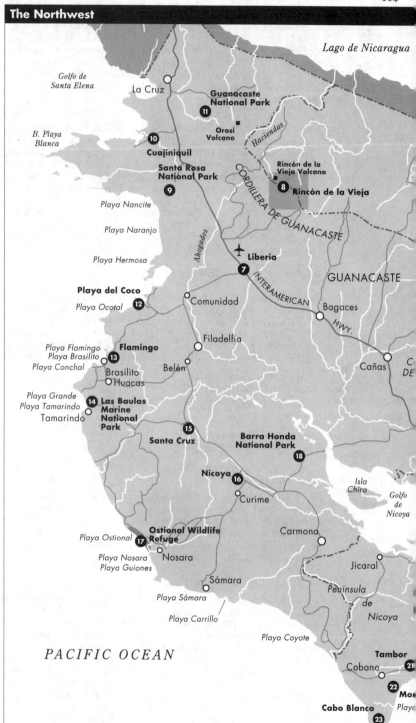

Lago de Nicaragua

Golfo de Santa Elena

La Cruz

Guanacaste National Park

11

Orosi Volcano

Haciendas

B. Playa Blanca

10

Cuajiniquil

Santa Rosa National Park

9

Rincón de la Vieja Volcano

8 **Rincón de la Vieja**

CORDILLERA DE GUANACASTE

Playa Nancite

Playa Naranjo

Playa Hermosa

Abogados

Liberia

7

INTERAMERICAN

GUANACASTE

Playa del Coco

Playa Ocotal **12**

Comunidad

Bagaces

HWY.

Filadelfia

Playa Flamingo
Playa Brasilito
Playa Conchal

Flamingo

13

Belén

Cañas

C
DE

Brasilito

Huacas

Playa Grande
Playa Tamarindo

14 **Las Baulas Marine National Park**

Tamarindo

15

Santa Cruz

Barra Honda National Park

18

Isla Chira

Golfo de Nicoya

Nicoya **16**

Curime

Carmona

Ostional Wildlife Refuge

Playa Ostional **17**

Nosara

Playa Nosara
Playa Guiones

Sámara

Jicaral

Península de Nicoya

Playa Sámara

Playa Carrillo

Playa Coyote

PACIFIC OCEAN

Tambor

21

Cobano

22

Mo

Cabo Blanco

Playa

23

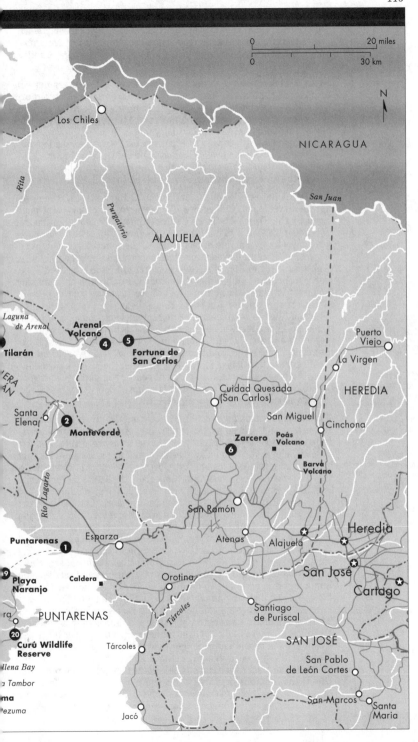

is fringed with mangroves; at its western end pelicans cast a watchful eye from the treetops over the Nicoya ferry, whose early morning departure provides the only sound reason to stay overnight. A modern harbor has been built at Caldera, 10 kilometers (6 miles) south.

With the Tilarán range rising steeply to the east, the Interamerican Highway heads northwest from the Puntarenas junction toward Guanacaste province. High daytime temperatures, little rainfall, and a very long dry season combine to make these northwestern lowlands a distinctive zone of tropical dry forest. Much of the forest cover has long since given way to expansive cattle ranches shaded only intermittently by the broad Guanacaste tree. In February the blossoms of the *corteza amarilla* color the landscape yellow, and in March the flowers of the carob tree add red to the palette.

Thirty kilometers (19 miles) farther on, at Río Lagarto, is the turn **❷** for **Monteverde,** 10,522 hectares (26,000 acres) of cloud forest managed by the **Tropical Science Center** (Apdo. 676–2050, San Pedro, tel. 240–6696) as a private nature reserve. Monteverde, in close proximity to several fine hotels, is one of the country's best-kept reserves, with well-marked trails, lush vegetation, and a cool climate. The second leg of the trip, a 30-kilometer (19-mile) track to the reserve, is unpaved and snakes dramatically up through hilly farming country; it takes 1½ hours to negotiate it, faster by four-wheel drive. At the junction for Santa Elena, bear right for the reserve. The Monteverde settlement has no real nucleus; houses and hotels flank a 5-kilometer (3-mile) road at intervals until you arrive at the reserve's entrance. Its first residents were a handful of Costa Rican families, fleeing the rough-and-ready life of nearby gold-mining fields during the 1940s. They were joined in the 1950s by Quakers from Alabama who came in search of peace, tranquillity, and good grazing, but the cloud forest that lay above their dairy farms was soon to attract the attention of ecologists.

The collision of moist winds with the continental divide here creates a constant mist whose particles provide nutrients for plants growing at the upper layers of the forest. Giant trees are enshrouded in a cascade of orchids, bromeliads, mosses, and ferns. In those patches where sunlight is able to penetrate, brilliantly colored flowers flourish. The sheer size of everything, especially the leaves, is very striking. No less astounding is the variety: 2,500 plant species, 400 species of birds, 500 types of butterflies, and more than 100 different mammals have so far been catalogued at Monteverde. A damp and exotic mixture of shades, smells, and sounds, the cloud forest is also famous for its population of resplendent quetzals who can be spotted feeding on the *aguacatillo* (like an avocado) trees; best viewing times are early mornings from January until September, especially in April and May during mating season. Other inhabitants include hummingbirds and multicolored frogs. For those who don't have a lucky eye, a short-stay aquarium is located in the field station; captives here stay only a week before being rereleased into the wild. The reserve limits visitors to 100 people at a time, so get there early and allow a generous slice of time for leisurely hiking in order to see the forest's flora and fauna; longer hikes are made possible by some strategically placed overnight refuges along the way. At the entrance to the reserve you can buy self-guide pamphlets and rent gum boots, and a map is provided when you pay the entrance fee. *Tel. 645–5122. Admission to reserve: $8; guides: $15 per person; refuges: 545 colones per night; boot rentals: 100 colones. Open 7–4.*

On your way down you can visit the **Hummingbird Gallery** (admission free; open daily 9:30–5), located near the reserve entrance. Here you'll find books, gifts, and a display of stunning photos by Michael and Patricia Fogden. Farther down on the right is the **Cheese Factory** (admission free; open Mon.–Sat. 7:30–4, Sun. 7:30–12:30). Watch the art of cheese making through a window in the sales room—you'll surely be lured into buying some.

Several conservation areas have sprung up nearby and make attractive day trips for reserve visitors. The **Santa Elena Reserve** (nominal fee, open daily 7–4), a 900-acre forest 5 kilometers (3 miles) north of the town of Santa Elena, just west of Monteverde, has a series of trails that can be walked alone or with a guide. Boot rental is available at the entrance.

The **Butterfly Garden** (admission $5; open daily 9:30–4), near the Pension Monteverde Inn, has hundreds of tropical butterflies on display in three enclosed botanical gardens from which there are stunning views of the Gulf of Nicoya. A guided tour helps visitors understand the stages of a butterfly's life. The private **bird farm** (nominal fee, open daily 9–4) next door has several trails through secondary forest. More than 90 bird species have been sighted here, from the crowned motmot to the resplendent quetzal. The Monteverde Conservation League's **Bajo del Tigre** trail (follow signs along the highway on the way to Monteverde) makes for a pleasant, 1.6-kilometer (1-mile) hike through secondary forest.

Time Out   **Stella's** bakery, located halfway between Santa Elena and Monteverde, serves everything from chocolate brownies to hearty breakfasts in a warm, wood-paneled room decorated with Stella's oil painting and her daughter Meg's stained-glass windows. You can also sip coffee on the backyard patio.

If your bones can take it, a very rough track leads from Santa Elena to Tilarán via Cabeceras, doing away with the need to return to the Interamerican Highway. You may well need four-wheel drive—inquire as to the present condition of the road—but the views of Nicoya Peninsula and Lake Arenal and Arenal volcano reward those willing to bump around a bit. Consider also the fact that you don't really save much time—it takes about 2½ hours as opposed to the three required via Lagarto and Cañas on the highway.

❸ The quiet whitewashed town of **Tilarán,** on the west side of Lake Arenal, is used as a base by bronzed windsurfers. If you took away the volcanoes, you might mistake the surrounding countryside of green, rolling hills for the English Lake District. The lake is popular for water sports and fishing for *guapote* (rainbow bass).

❹ For those who have never seen an active volcano, **Arenal volcano** makes a spectacular first—its perfect conical profile dominates the southern end of Lake Arenal. To get to the base of the volcano, take the road south (though slated for paving in the near future, it is currently a rough approach, and the countless twists and turns make for a rather drawn-out journey) from the town of Arenal. Shortly before the dam at the southern end is the turn to Arenal Lodge (*see* Dining and Lodging, *below*). Next you come to the right turn to the Smithsonian Institution's Observatory. The track provides access to the base of the volcano, but you should attempt exploration only with a guide, either from the observatory or from the town of
❺ **Fortuna de San Carlos,** 17 kilometers (11 miles) beyond the dam.

Time Out **Tabacon Resort,** 12 kilometers (7 miles) northwest of La Fortuna on the highway to Arenal, is a restaurant and spa with bubbling thermal waters, waterfalls, a Jacuzzi, and a poolside bar—with great views of the volcano.

Arenal lay dormant until 1968. On July 29 of that year an earthquake shook the area, and 12 hours later Arenal blew. The town of Pueblo Nuevo to the west bore the brunt of the shock waves, poisonous gases, and falling rocks; 78 people died in all. Since then Arenal has been in a constant state of activity. Night is the best time for observing it, when you can clearly see rocks spewing skyward and red-hot molten lava enveloping the top of the cone. Eruptions, accompanied by thunderous sounds, are sometimes as frequent as one per hour. Phases of inactivity do occur, however, so it is wise to check just before you go to judge whether your trip will be worthwhile. Hiking is possible on the volcano's lower slopes, but definitely not higher up; in 1988 two people were killed when they attempted to climb it. Ask at the observatory or the Burío Inn in Fortuna (*see* Dining and Lodging, *below*).

From Fortuna to San José takes three hours by car, via Ciudad Quesada and Zarcero. The road initially runs through flat fertile farmland before climbing to **Ciudad Quesada.** Looking back, you'll take in excellent views of Arenal rising from the surrounding plain.

❻ Climbing farther, you come to **Zarcero,** set just below a steep ridge and famous for the topiary in its main square: The hedges here have been clipped into everything from elephants to motorcycle-riding monkeys.

Time Out **Super Dos,** on the main road opposite the church in Zarcero, is a tiny café-store where you can get a coffee and *empanada de piña* (pineapple pie) while you mull over buying some of the excellent local peach preserves.

From Zarcero to San José takes around an hour.

Tour 2: Capital of Guanacaste province, **Liberia** is a low-rise, grid-plan, cat-
Northern tle-market town, with a huge central square dominated by a hideous
Guanacaste modern church. It is the gateway to a northern route that
❼ encompasses Rincón de la Vieja volcano, several spectacular and biologically important national parks, and a turtle-nesting site on the Pacific coast. There isn't a lot to see or do here, but if you do have the time, visit the museum and obtain tourist information at the **Casa de Cultura** (tel. 666–1606; open Mon.–Sat. 8–4), three blocks south of Central Park.

❽ The composite mass of **Rincón de la Vieja,** often enveloped in a mixture of sulfurous gases and cloud, dominates the scenery to the right of the Interamerican Highway as you head north (*see* Chapter 3, National Parks and Wildlife Reserves). Some compare this national park's geysers, mud pots, and hot springs to those of Yellowstone National Park in the United States. Access to the park—14,084 protected hectares (34,787 acres) in all, much of it dry forest that has been regenerated since the park's inception in 1973—is via 26 kilometers (16 miles) of unpaved road. The road begins 6 kilometers (4 miles) north of Liberia off the Interamerican Highway (for Albergue Guachipelín) or 25 kilometers (15 miles) along the Colonia Blanca route northeast from Liberia, which follows the course of the Río Liberia to the Santa María park headquarters. Both tracks are veritable bone shakers. Nonetheless, the wildlife here is tremendously diverse: 200 species of birds, including keel-billed toucans and blue-crowned motmots, plus mammals such as brocket deer, tapirs, coatis, jaguars, sloths, armadillos, and raccoons. Needless to say, hiking here is fantastic, but it's wise to do some planning to know where to head. Some information is available at the Park Headquarters by the entrance gate, but you are advised to head to Rincón de la Vieja Mountain Lodge (*see* Dining and Lodging, *below*), which has guides available. *Admission: 200 colones. Open daily 8–4.*

The volcano complex has two peaks: **Santa María** (1,916 meters/ 6,284 feet) and **Rincón de la Vieja** (1,898 meters/6,225 feet) to the northeast. The latter is vegetationless and has two craters. Rincón de la Vieja is thought unlikely to erupt violently due to the profusion of fumaroles through which it can constantly let off steam. The last violent eruptions were between 1966 and 1970. If you want to explore the slopes of the volcano, it is advisable to go with a guide; the abundant hot springs and geysers have given unsuspecting visitors some very nasty burns in the past. **Las Hornillas** ("the kitchen stoves"), to the south of the volcano, is a 50-hectare (124-acre) medley of mud cones, hot-water pools, bubbling mud pots, and vent holes, most active during the rainy season. To the east, **Los Azufrales** are hot sulfur springs in which you can bathe; be careful not to get sulfur in your eyes, though. The Rincón de la Vieja Mountain Lodge (*see* Dining and Lodging, *below*) has guides, but phone ahead to check availability.

The Interamerican Highway north is mostly arrow straight, dipping and rising every now and then in gentle undulations. West of the highway, 25 kilometers (16 miles) north at Km 269, is **Santa Rosa National Park** (*see* Chapter 3, National Parks and Wildlife Reserves). Campers enjoy the park's rugged terrain and isolated feel. The sparseness of vegetation in this arid zone makes it easier to see animals. From the entrance gate where you pay the nominal fee, 7 kilometers (4½ miles) of paved road leads to the park headquarters. A campsite, overhung by giant strangler figs, is located here, and provides washing facilities and picnic tables. Be careful of snakes.

Santa Rosa was established in 1971 to protect La Casona hacienda, scene of the famous 1856 battle in which a ragged force of ill-equipped Costa Ricans routed the superior army of William Walker. A U.S. filibuster from Tennessee, Walker had established himself as chief of staff of the Nicaragua army as part of his Manifest Destiny– influenced scheme to create a slave empire in the region. In 1857, the hostilities having continued onto Nicaraguan soil, Juan Santamaría, a drummer boy from Alajuela, threw burning fagots into the building where Walker and his henchmen were gathered, so ending the war, and thereby winning undying national fame for his self-sacrificing act. The rambling colonial-style farmstead of La Casona stands as a monument to this national triumph and contains an interesting museum (open daily 8–4:30) with maps, weapons, uniforms, and furniture. The start of a short explanatory nature trail is visible just out front.

For ecologists, Santa Rosa has a more important role in protecting and regenerating 49,500 hectares (122,300 acres) of premontane moist, basal belt transition, and deciduous tropical dry forests. The central administrative area is a hive of scientific activity. Much of their research here has been into forest propagation, the fruits of which are evident in former cattle pastures where windblown seeds have been allowed to establish themselves. Bush fires are a constant hazard in the dry season, making firebreaks a necessity. Typical dry forest vegetation includes oak, wild cherry, mahogany, calabash, bull-horn acacia, hibiscus, and gumbo limbo, with its distinctive reddish-brown bark, which is perceived as similar to Indian skin. Because of the less luxuriant foliage, the park is a good one for viewing wildlife, especially if you station yourself next to water holes during the dry season. Inhabitants include spider, white-faced, and howler monkeys, deer, armadillos, coyotes, tapirs, coatis, and ocelots. Ocelots, commonly known as manigordos or fatpaws on account of their large feet, are striped wildcats that have been brought back from the brink of extinction by the park's conservation methods. These wildlands also define the southernmost distribution of many North American species such as the Virginia opossum and cantil moccasin.

Thirteen kilometers (8 miles) west of the administrative area—a two- to three-hour hike or one hour by four-wheel drive—is the white-sand **Playa Naranjo,** popular for beachcombing due to its pretty shells and for surfing because of its near-perfect break. The campsite here has washing facilities, but bring your own water. Make sure to catch the lookout at the northern tip of the beach with views over the entire park. Turtle *arribadas*—the phenomenon of turtles arriving on a beach to nest—do take place on Naranjo, but the big ones occur at a point reached via a two-hour walk north on Nancite (also accessible by four-wheel drive).

It is estimated that 200,000 of the 500,000 turtles that nest each year in Costa Rica choose **Nancite.** Backed by dense hibiscus and button mangroves, the gray-sand beach is penned in by steep, tawny, brush-covered hills. Previously a difficult point to get to, it is now the only totally protected Olive Ridley turtle arribada in the world. The busy time is August to December, peaking September and October. Olive Ridleys are the smallest of the sea turtles (average carapace, or hardback shell, is 55–75 centimeters [21–29 inches]) and the least shy. The majority arrive at night, plowing the sand as they move up the beach and sniffing for the high-tide line, beyond which they use their hind flippers to dig holes in which they will lay their eggs. They spend an average of one hour on the beach before scurrying back to the sea. Hatching also takes place at night. The phototropic baby turtles magically know to head for the sea, vital for their continued survival, since the brightest part of any beach is over the ocean. Many of the nests are churned up during subsequent arribadas, and predators such as *pizotes* (coatis), ghost crabs, raccoons, and coyotes lie in wait; hence just 0.2% of eggs reach the sea as young turtles. Between Naranjo and Nancite, another campground at Estero Real is available with tables only. Permits are needed to stay at Nancite; ask at the headquarters. Throughout the park it is wise to carry your own water since water holes are none too clean. *Park admission: 200 colones. Camping: 300 colones. Open daily 7–5.*

Ten kilometers (6 miles) farther north on the Interamerican is the left turn to **Cuajiniquil,** famous for its waterfalls, and the so-called Sección Murciélago. If you have time and a four-wheel-drive vehicle, Cuajiniquil has lovely views. Murciélago hacienda was expropriated from the Somoza family by the Costa Rican government in 1978, "in order to extend the Santa Rosa National Park," so the executive decree ran, although the real reason was political. The Bay of Santa Elena is renowned for its calm waters, which is why it is now threatened by tourist development. Playa Blanca in the extreme west has smooth white sand, as its name implies. The rough track there passes through a valley of uneven width, caused, according to geologists, by the diverse granulation of the sediments formerly depos-

ited here. To the south rise the rocky Santa Elena hills (711 meters/
2,332 feet), bare except for a few chigua and nancite shrubs.

Time Out **Restaurant Cuajiniquil,** on the way to the ranger station, is a reliable
place for a fish lunch and cooling beer.

⓫ To the east of the Interamerican Highway is **Guanacaste National
Park,** created in 1989 to preserve rain forests around Cacao and
Orosi volcanoes, which are seasonally inhabited by migrants from
Santa Rosa. Much of the park's territory is cattle pasture, which it is
hoped will regenerate into forest. Three biological stations within
the park have places for visitors to stay. Mengo Biological Station
lies on the slopes of Cacao volcano at an altitude of 1,100 meters
(3,609 feet); accommodation is in rustic wooden dormitories with
bedding provided, but bring a towel. From here a trail leads up Cacao volcano (1,659 meters/5,443 feet), another north to the modern
Maritza Station, a three-hour hike away at the base of Orosi (1,487
meters/4,877 feet), with more lodging available. You can also reach
Maritza by four-wheel drive. From here you can trek two hours to
Llano de los Indios, a cattle pasture dotted with volcanic petro-
glyphs. Farther north and a little east is Pitilla Station, slightly
more rustic and with views of the coast and Lake Nicaragua despite
its lower elevation. *Tel. 692–5598 at Santa Rosa for information
and/or reservations.*

Tour 3: *Nicoya,* which comes from the indigenous Necocyauh language,
The Nicoya means "land with water on both sides." Two of the three ways of get-
Peninsula ting to the peninsula thus require boarding a boat. This trip to the
beaches and wildlife refuges of the peninsula can be made via the
Gulf of Nicoya or the Tempisque River, both of which afford lovely
sunset views, or by the overland route, with views of lush vegetation in the rainy season or parched fields in the dry season. If you are
heading specifically for the south, it makes most sense to catch the
ferry from Puntarenas (*see* Getting Around, *above*) to Playa
Naranjo. The other options are the Tempisque ferry, the fastest
route from San José to Nicoya, and the highway running southwest
from Liberia. Our tour starts with the Tempisque basin and then
works its way south from Liberia more or less down the spine of the
peninsula.

On the Interamerican Highway headed southward from Liberia,
make a right at the gas station in Bagaces, 15 kilometers (9 miles)
north of Cañas, which will lead you after 15 kilometers to the Lomas
Barbudal Reserve and after 35 kilometers the adjacent **Palo Verde
National Park,** refuges for migratory waterfowl (*see* Chapter 3, National Parks and Wildlife Reserves). Bordered in the west by the meandering Río Tempisque, the territories extend over 9,466 hectares
(23,381 acres) of mainly flat terrain. Migrant herons, egrets, ducks,
and grebes pause here to rest up on the Tempisque's abandoned oxbow lakes and lagoons. You can camp in the park, and sometimes
lodging and meals are available on request. Lodging is also available
at the Organization for Tropical Research station (tel. 240–6696).
Tel. 671–1062. Admission: 200 colones. Open daily 8–4.

The highway from Liberia to Nicoya starts opposite the Hotel
Bramadero on the Carretera Interamericana. It runs in straight
sweeps through cattle country sporadically shaded by guanacaste
and tabebuia trees. Just past the village of Comunidad is the turn to
⓬ **Playa del Coco,** Hermosa, and Ocotal (*see* Beaches, *below*). Playa del
Coco is for those who want noise, discos, and bustle. Hermosa has a
village atmosphere, and Ocotal is isolated.

Five kilometers (3 miles) past the town of Filadelfia is the turn to the surfing hot spot of Tamarindo, the turtle haven of Playa Grande, and **13** ritzy **Flamingo,** paved as far as the Huacas junction. At this crossroads, branch right for Flamingo, left for Tamarindo and Playa Grande. The Flamingo road brushes the coast at Brasilito, a small fishing village with a fair amount of activity around the central **14** green. Just north of Tamarindo, the **Las Baulas Marine National Park** protects Playa Grande, an important nesting site of the leatherback sea turtle (*see* Chapter 3, National Parks and Wildlife Reserves).

Continuing south, sixteen kilometers (10 miles) south of the Belén **15** junction is the National Folklore City of **Santa Cruz,** dedicated to preserving Guanacaste's rich traditions and customs. Music and dance programs are still held in town despite a recent fire, which destroyed much of the town's center and the popular Casa de la Cultura.

Time Out **Coope-Tortillas** has enjoyed resounding success as a country restaurant and tortilla bakery founded to help create jobs for local women. Watch tortillas bake the old-fashioned way—on thick, round plates on an open fire—and have a hearty, family-style meal at a picnic table in this former electricity-generating plant. *Open daily 5 AM– 7 PM.*

Between Santa Cruz and Nicoya, near the town of Santa Barbara, is the village of Guaitil. Artists here have rescued a vanishing tradition by producing clay pottery in the manner of pre-Columbian Chorotegans. You can visit the workshop (open 6 AM–9 PM) and select designs of your choice. The hand-wrought pots, jars, dishes, and urns are painted with natural earth-based pigments before being fired in a stone kiln and polished with a natural glaze. You'll also see pots for sale outside private houses, often slightly cheaper.

16 **Nicoya,** although often referred to as Guanacaste's colonial capital, is mainly modern. This is a typical small town, not really worth visiting unless you want a taste of everyday life. Its only colonial landmark is the recently restored, whitewashed San Blas church in the central square. It was built in the 16th century and contains a museum of silver, bronze, and copper objects dating back to pre-Columbian times. The Chorotegan chief Nicoya greeted the Spanish conquistadors upon their arrival here in 1523, and many of his people were converted to Catholicism. Great emphasis is currently being placed on reviving the culture and traditions of the Chorotegans.

A road leads southwest from Nicoya via Curime to Sámara, Nosara, **17** and **Ostional.** It is paved for the first 10 kilometers (6 miles) only, and the unpaved section is slow. The trip takes an hour to Sámara, 1½ hours to Nosara. Apart from sun and sand (*see* Beaches, *below*), the main reason for this trip is to visit the **Ostional Wildlife Refuge,** with its wonderful opportunities for turtle-watching. During the rainy season you will probably need four-wheel drive to ford the river just north of Nosara. A track then leads through shrubs to the reserve, which protects Costa Rica's other major breeding ground for Olive Ridley turtles (*see* Tour 2: Nancite, *above*). Local people run the reserve on a cooperative basis. During the first 36 hours of the arribadas they harvest the eggs—eggs laid during this time would as likely as not be destroyed by subsequent waves of mother turtles. The eggs, believed by some to be powerful aphrodisiacs, are sold to be eaten raw in bars. Thereafter members of the cooperative take turns to guard the beach from poachers, but they are happy to let visitors view the turtles.

⓲ **Barra Honda National Park** covers 2,300 hectares (5,681 acres) north of the road that runs between the Nicoya–Carmona highway and Tempisque ferry (*see* Chapter 3, National Parks and Wildlife Reserves). The limestone ridge that rises from the surrounding savanna was once thought to be a volcano but was later found to contain an intricate network of caves, formed as a result of erosion once the ridge had emerged from beneath the sea. Some remain unexplored, and surprisingly abundant animal life exists in the caves, including bats, birds, blind fish and salamanders, snails, and rats. In the dry season, with a week's notice rangers will take you down a 15-meter (50-foot) steel ladder to the **Terciopelo cave,** which shelters unusual formations shaped like fried eggs, popcorn, shark's teeth, and sonorous columns collectively known as the organ. Travel companies no longer take tourists or speleologists deeper underground, but local groups reportedly have organized tours into the caves. Check with park guards to verify safety standards before taking a trip, and don't attempt to visit the caves on your own unless accompanied by a park guard. Those with vertigo, asthma, or claustrophobia are advised not to attempt these explorations. Barra Honda peak (330 meters/1,082 feet) can be climbed from the northwest; follow in sequence the Ojoche, Trampa, and Terciopelo trails (the southern wall is almost vertical). From the summit plateau there are fantastic views over the islet-studded Gulf of Nicoya; the plateau surface is dotted with small orifices and whimsically eroded white rocks, and some of the ground feels dangerously hollow. Surface wildlife includes howler monkeys, skunks, coatis, parakeets, and iguanas. The relatively open dry deciduous forest vegetation means that viewing the fauna is not all that difficult. The park has camping facilities. *Tel. 671–1062. Admission: 200 colones. Open 8–4.*

The highway south is paved as far as Carmona. Beyond Carmona, remain on the coastal route and you will arrive after 17 kilometers ⓳ (11 miles) at **Playa Naranjo,** linked by ferry to Puntarenas (*see* Getting Around, *above*). From here on out, the road to the southern tip of the peninsula is gravel, and it winds up and down and around various bays. Much of the countryside is still wild and wooded, although some has been turned into fruit farms or cattle pasture. Paquera, 45 minutes away, is the next place with shops and bars, also linked to Puntarenas by a ferry for foot passengers only. Seven kilometers ⓴ (4½ miles) south is the private **Curú Wildlife Refuge,** where you'll find hordes of phantom crabs on the beach, howler and white-faced monkeys readily visible in the banana trees, and plenty of bird-watching opportunities. Some very basic accommodation, originally designed for students and researchers, is available by the beach; call ahead if you're interested. *Tel. 661–2392. Admission: $5. Lodging: $25 per person, including 3 meals per day and admission.*

㉑ The next village that you reach is **Tambor,** a sleepy place nestled in the back of the large half-moon Ballena Bay. You can hike from here around the Piedra Amarilla point to Tango Mar resort; it's about an 8-kilometer (5-mile) trek. The trees nearby resound with the throaty utterings of male howler monkeys, and a new marina is being built at the southern end of the beach.

Time Out   **Restaurant La Bahía** at the wharf has good seafood and fine views.

As you continue past the turn to Tango Mar resort, Cobano is the next real village, a motley collection of wooden bungalows straddling a dusty crossroads. Turn left for Montezuma and Cabo Blanco, and mind that the final hill down to Montezuma is extremely steep and shouldn't be attempted in an ordinary car if the hill is wet.

㉒ **Montezuma** is beautifully positioned next to a sandy bay, hemmed in by a precipitous, wooded bank. Young foreigners in sandals and ethnic clothing seem to make this their first destination after touching down in San José, and if you don't mind entering the odd conversation on such *Mother Jones*–related subjects as yogurt and cheap deals, it is an entertaining place to be. The bars are full and resound with endearingly out-of-date music from the '60s to the early '80s. Just over a bridge 270 meters (900 feet) south, a path leads upstream to a 30-meter (100-foot) waterfall, a good swimming spot but overcrowded at times.

Fording two streams en route, the rough track leads from Montezuma to **Cabo Blanco** (about a one-hour walk), named by conquistadors on account of the white earth and cliffs. The **Cabo Blanco Strict Nature Reserve,** 1,172 hectares (2,895 acres) in all, was created by the pioneering efforts of the Wessbergs, who arrived during the 1950s to live near Montezuma. As a strict reserve, no tourist facilities exist, although rangers will act as guides to visitors who turn up. Trails run along the coast and onto the mountainous central crest. The reserve receives more rainfall than other parts of the peninsula, and hence the vegetation is properly described as tropical moist forest; there are more evergreen species here than in Santa Rosa, and it is generally lusher. The most abundant trees are strawberry, apamate, brazilwood, cow tree, capulen, pochote, and sapodilla. Sapodillas produce a white latex used to make gum; you will often see *V*-shape scars where they have been cut to allow the latex to run into containers placed at the base. The wildlife is quite diverse, notwithstanding the comparatively diminutive size of the reserve. Wessberg catalogued a full array of animals here: porcupine, hog-nosed skunk, spotted skunk, gray fox, anteater, cougar, and jaguar. Resident bird species include coastal pelicans, white-throated magpies, toucans, cattle egrets, green herons, parrots, and turquoise-browed motmots. Off the tip of the cape is the 700-square-meter (7,511-square-foot) **Isla Cabo Blanco,** with pelicans, frigate birds, brown boobies, and an abandoned lighthouse. *Admission: 200 colones. Open daily 8–4.*

What to See and Do with Children

Beaches provide the best entertainment for youngsters in the Northwest, although care should be taken because of riptides (*see* Beaches, *below*). The safest beaches for swimming are probably **Playa Ocotal** and **Playa Hermosa,** on either side of Playa del Coco.

In Monteverde, schoolchildren have raised the money to buy 6,885 hectares (17,000 acres) of rain forest behind the main reserve, and the resultant **Children's Rain Forest League** (tel. 645–5003) plans to host educational programs, among other activities. The office is opposite the gas station in Monteverde.

Off the Beaten Track

The 9,963-hectare (24,600-acre) **Caño Negro Wildlife Refuge** (tel. 460–1301) in the far north is miles off most people's itineraries, but the vast Lake Caño Negro makes this an excellent place for watching waterfowl like the roseate spoonbill, jabiru stork, and anhinga, as well as for observing a host of resident exotic animals (*see* Chapter 3, National Parks and Wildlife Reserves). In the dry season you can rent horses; in the rainy season you are better off renting a boat for exploration of the area. Camp or stay in basic lodging for around $8, including meals. Approach via Upala—a bus from there takes 45 minutes—or take Esteban Cruz's popular tour down the Río Frío (tel. 471-1032). The tour starts in Los Chiles, about a 90-minute drive from La Fortuna, near Arenal volcano. Sunset Tours (tel. 479-9099) in La Fortuna also runs day-long tours down the Río Frío to Caño Negro.

There is talk of converting the former **Isla San Lucas penal colony** in the Gulf of Nicoya into a holiday playground. It may be worth getting here before the bulldozers move in, in order to see what island prison life was really like. There are no tours to San Lucas, but you can try to charter a boat from the Pacific port of Puntarenas.

Shopping

Arts and Crafts In Monteverde, **CASEM,** the artisans' cooperative (open Mon.–Sat. 8–5, Sun. 10–4), is next door to El Bosque and sells locally made handicrafts. The **Hummingbird Gallery** near the reserve entrance sells prints, slides, and T-shirts. In Guaitil and San Vicente, close to Santa Cruz, you can buy Chorotegan pottery made as it was in pre-Columbian times.

Local Foods **La Fábrica de Queso** (The Cheese Factory) in Monteverde allows you to observe cheese making and buy the results. Zarcero is famous for its fruit preserves and white cheese, both of which are for sale along its main street.

Sports

Bicycling You can rent mountain bikes opposite El Jardín restaurant in La Fortuna for strenuous excursions.

Boating and Water Sports **Condovac Hotel** (tel. 670-0283) on Playa Hermosa rents canoes, kayaks, and catamarans for 3,500–9,000 colones.

Fishing Lake Arenal provides the best freshwater fishing in Costa Rica, with *guapote* (rainbow bass) aplenty, although it is difficult to fish from the shore. **Arenal Lodge** and **Burío Inn** (*see* Dining and Lodging, *below*) have boats and guides. Good sea sportfishing is common along the coast, especially at Flamingo, Tamarindo, Ocotal, Garza, and Guanamar; it can usually be arranged through your hotel.

Horseback Riding In Monteverde, **Meg's Stable** (tel. 645-5052), opposite the Cheese Factory, rents horses.

Scuba Diving and Snorkeling Scuba diving is offered at **Hotel Ocotal** (*see* Dining and Lodging, *below*) for about $90 daily per person; the hotel also rents snorkeling gear. Snorkeling gear is also available for rent at Tamarindo, Hermosa, Carrillo, and Flamingo beaches.

Surfing Boca Barranca near Puntarenas has one of the world's longest lefts, but the water is dirty from the nearby river. Tamarindo is a good base for the five reef breaks, three river mouths, a couple of point breaks, and the superb 5-kilometer (3-mile) Playa Grande beach break nearby. Inquire at the reception desk of the **Hotel Tamarindo Diriá** (*see* Dining and Lodging, *below*); staff members can give the latest surf report. Sámara and Nosara both have decent beach breaks. Roja Bruja in the Santa Rosa National Park, accessible by car only in summer, has a right river mouth. In all of these spots you should be on your guard against riptides.

Windsurfing Experts are promoting Lake Arenal as a world-class windsurfing site comparable to the Columbia River Gorge in Oregon, due to its usually strong winds during the dry season, between December and April. Rent boards through your hotel or **Tilawa Viento Surf** (tel. 695–5008) in Tilarán. Coastal windsurfing hasn't yet caught on, but it is sure to do so.

Beaches

The Northwest coast features shrubby dry forest vegetation in contrast to the tropical beach backdrops that you find farther south. The great advantage is the climate, which is far more reliable (drier) during the rainy season. Swimmers should be careful of riptides, which are quite prevalent (*see* Beaches in The Southwest, *below*, for how to deal with them). What follows is a brief appraisal of selected beaches from north to south. Near Coco, which is rather dirty, both the beaches of Ocotal (in a very pretty cove with snorkeling potential and good views) and of Hermosa (a curving white-sand beach hemmed in by rocky outcrops) are recommended strands. Pan de Azucar offers pretty good for snorkeling and is deserted, but it's rather stony in the rainy season. Flamingo is the nearest thing to a built-up resort; despite a few condos it is still low-key, and the beach is white and handsome. Brasilito allows you to observe the goings-on of fishing-village life. Conchal is famous for its tiny shells. Grande, a restricted-access turtle-nesting beach a 30-minute walk north, is safest for swimming, but nearby Tamarindo has a long white strand backed by good bars. Nosara has a long beach that is overlooked from on high by the apartments of foreign retirees but is backed by dense jungle where you might see wildlife. Guiones has a coral reef suitable for snorkeling. Carrillo is on a very picturesque and deserted half-moon bay. Montezuma has several colorful, shell-strewn beaches, some of them long and some short.

Dining and Lodging

Dining Guanacaste's traditional foods derive from dishes prepared by pre-Columbian Chorotegans. Typical dishes include the *frito guana-casteco* (similar to *gallo pinto*), *pedre* (a mixture of carob beans, pork, chicken, onions, sweet peppers, salt, and mint), *sopa de albondigas* (meatball soup with chopped eggs and spices), and *arroz de maíz* (not actually rice but ricelike corn). The Northwest also produces the country's best steak. Most of the places we list serve international as well as local dishes, so you can take your pick.

Highly recommended restaurants are indicated by a star ★. For ratings, *see* Dining and Lodging in Staying in Costa Rica, *above.*

Lodging The Northwest has a good mix of quality hotels, nature lodges, and more basic *cabinas* (cottages). It is wise to book ahead during the dry season, especially for weekends, when Ticos can fill beach hotels, especially, to bursting.

Highly recommended hotels are indicated by a star ★. For ratings, *see* Dining and Lodging in Staying in Costa Rica, *above.*

Arenal
Dining and Lodging
Mirador Los Lagos. These hillside cabinas have large clean bedrooms and good food, and a sweeping vista across the lake to the distant Arenal volcano is an added attraction. Watch out for the hotel's sign about 6 kilometers (4 miles) northwest of Arenal town. *Ctra. a Arenal Kms. 41 y 42, tel. 695–5169. 11 rooms with bath. Facilities: restaurant, bar. V. $$*

Brasilito **El Camerón Dorado.** This bar-restaurant derives much of its appeal
Dining from the shady setting on Brasilito's beautiful beach, and no less
from the small vessel fishing fleet anchored offshore that assures
you of the freshness of seafood available. Due to the spectacular sun-
sets, it's a popular place for an early evening drink. *200 meters (656
feet) north of Brasilito Plaza, tel. 654–4028. No reservations. DC,
MC, V. $*

Lodging **Cabinas Conchal.** New cabinas, set a few yards back from the remarkable shell-strewn cove, are quite basic but clean. Bedrooms
contain heavy wooden beds, and some furnish extra bunks for
groups or families. *Apdo. 185, 5150 Santa Cruz, Guanacaste, no
phone. 8 rooms with bath. No facilities. No credit cards. $*

Carrillo **Hotel La Guanamar.** Beautifully positioned above the southern end
Dining and of Playa Carrillo, this used to be a private fishing club, and as a hotel
Lodging it continues its tradition as a sportfishing mecca. It occupies several
★ levels, connected by wooden terraces and steps, thus bringing to
mind a luxury cruiser. The white bedrooms contain elaborate head-
boards, patterned bed covers, olive-green carpets, and amazing
views. *Apdo. 7–1880, 1000 San José, tel. 239–2000, fax 293–4839. 41
rooms with bath. Facilities: restaurant, bar, pool, airstrip, parking. DC, MC, V. $$$$*

Coco **Mariscos La Guajira.** West along the beach is this open-sided or-
Dining ange-painted restaurant, fronted by round, palm-thatch shades.
Try ceviche (raw seafood salad, marinated in lime juice and chilis)
for starters. As main courses, *dorado* (fish) served with salad and
fried bananas, *camarones* (shrimp in garlic and butter served with
fries and salad), and *langosta al ajillo* (lobster in garlic) are all recommended. The informal, beachy decor consists of wooden tables,
cement floor, and potted plants. *Tel. 670–0107. No reservations.
MC, V. $*

Lodging **Cabinas Chale.** Turn right 455 meters (500 yards) down a dirt road
just as you come into town. Families from San José invade these
modern cabinas on weekends; if you can't stand the sight of children,
steer clear. The bedrooms are bright and large, containing up to five
beds, a fridge, table and chairs, tile floor, and overhead fans. They
are spotlessly clean and have modern bathrooms. The location is remote and quiet: Take a 45-meter (50-yard) stroll to the beach
straight ahead, and walk west another 455 meters (500 yards) to
Coco proper. The other bonus is the large, chlorinated pool. *Playa
del Coco, Guanacaste, tel. 670–0036, fax 670–0303. 16 rooms with
bath, 5 bungalows. Facilities: pool, badminton/basketball court, secure parking. V. $*

★ **Hotel Anexo Luna Tica.** This new two-story wooden structure is on
the street that runs parallel to the beach, west of the soccer pitch.
Don't confuse it with the dingy cabins of the same name on the opposite side of the street, closest to the sea. The bedrooms—all connected by a single veranda—have red wood floors, polished
paneling, firm beds, overhead fans, and decorative photos. Those
upstairs have more light, although none look out on the sea. *Apdo.
67, Liberia, tel. 670–0279, fax 670–0392. 18 rooms with bath. No
credit cards. $*

Flamingo **Marie's Restaurant.** Sadly, the pool and garden attached to this res-
Dining taurant have been filled in, but the friendly owner and fresh food
★ make it worth a visit. Shortly after the road bends to the north end
of Flamingo, look for Marie's small veranda furnished with sliced
tree-trunk tables, and settle back for a rewarding meal of generous
helpings of fresh seafood at very reasonable rates. The house spe-

cialty is *plato de mariscos* (shrimp, lobster, and oysters served with garlic butter, potatoes, and salad), but be sure to save room for pudding—the *tres leches*, similar to treacle sponge, topped with the cream of three different milks, is superb. *Tel. 654–4136. No reservations. AE, MC, V. Closed Sept. 19–Oct. 6. $$*

Tio's Sports Bar and Restaurant. This thatched-roof hangout is a favorite among locals, who gather on weekends to eat Mexican food, tee off from the driving range, watch cable TV, use the tennis court, or play baseball. The rustic dining room with plastic lawn furniture and floral-print tablecloths is a fun, relaxed place. *Playa Flamingo, tel. 654–4236. No reservations. No credit cards. Closed Oct., Tues. Dec.–Apr., and weekdays May–Nov. $$*

Dining and Lodging   **Flamingo Beach Hotel.** Holiday Inn purchased this luxury resort and is undertaking major renovations aimed at turning it into a five-star hotel. There were start-up problems at press time, but the room and kitchen-equipped condominiums were filled to capacity. *Apdo. 692, Alajuela 4050, tel. 654–4010, fax 654–4060. 120 rooms with bath, 23 condominiums. Facilities: 2 restaurants, bar, 3 pools, tennis court, parking. AE, DC, MC, V. $$$$*

Mariner Inn. Near the marina, this white, two-story building with an unsightly, purple-tile bar is the most inexpensive hotel in Flamingo. Rooms are tiny, but they have air-conditioning, ceiling fans, and firm beds. *Apdo. 65, Santa Cruz, tel. 654–4081, fax 654–4024. 11 rooms with bath, 1 suite. Facilities: restaurant, bar, pool, parking. AE. $$*

Fortuna de San Carlos Dining   **La Vaca Muca.** It isn't a posh place, but the food is good (the cook, Emilce Vargas, used to be chef at the Arenal Lodge) and you get more than you pay for. Just 1 kilometer (⅗ mile) west of town, this restaurant is draped with foliage outside and has turquoise paneling and bamboo inside. *Tel. 479–9186. No reservations. MC, V. $–$$*

El Jardín. Opposite the gas station, this friendly diner serves respectable fish dishes. Try guapote if it's on the menu, but it's very bony, so ask if they'll fillet it. The extensive menu also includes chicken legs, pork chops, liver, tongue, and more. The *refrescos naturales* (fruit juices) are especially good here. *Tel. 479–9072. No reservations. MC, V. $*

Dining and Lodging
★   **Arenal Lodge.** This modern white bungalow is surrounded by macadamia trees and rain forest, high above Lake Arenal dam and midway between Arenal and Fortuna. Four-wheel drive is needed to negotiate the steep 2-kilometer (1¼-mile) drive, but the hotel will ferry you from the bottom for a small fee. The bedroom suites, some in a newer annex, are all pleasantly furnished, and there are also cheaper, smaller, and darker rooms that don't look out at the volcano. The lodge's perks include an extensive library, a small snooker table, and manicured gardens. Activities include angling and hiking. *Apdo. 1139, 1250 Escazú, tel. 289–6588, fax 289–6798. 6 rooms with bath, 9 suites. Facilities: dining room, snooker table, library, parking. AE, MC, V. $$$*

Las Cabañitas Resort. One of the few resorts in the area with a swimming pool, this group of red-roofed cabinas set on landscaped grounds several blocks outside of town has terraces that face the volcano and rocking chairs from which to enjoy the view. The wood-paneled cabins have solid wood furnishings and quilted bedspreads. The hotel can arrange tours and car rentals. *Apdo. 5–4417, La Fortuna, San Carlos, tel. and fax 479–9091. 25 cabins with bath. Facilities: restaurant, bar, room service, catering, pool, car rental, gift shop, parking. AE, MC, V. $$$*

Arenal Observatory. Three kilometers (2 miles) east of the dam on

Lake Arenal, you'll discover a 9-kilometer (5½-mile) dirt track that leads to the observatory, the closest lodge to Arenal's base. On the way, you cross three large rivers whose bridges are regularly washed away, restricting access to those with four-wheel drive. Built in 1987 for researchers, the lodge is rustic but comfortable; some bedrooms are dorms, some are doubles. The dining room has great views in both directions and serves hearty food that is included in the price of the room. *Tel. and fax 695–5033. (Reservations also can be made through Sun Tours, tel. 255–3518. AE, MC, V.) 10 rooms with bath, 1 cabin with fireplace. Facilities: dining room. AE, MC, V. $$*

Lodging
★
Burío Inn. Peter Gorinsky created the Arenal Lodge, but he grew tired of its inaccessibility and started this inn in Fortuna itself. The rates here are lower and the accommodations comfortable. Bedrooms have firm beds, sloping polished wood ceilings, framed textiles, and modern bathrooms with hot showers. Continental breakfast is served in the common room, surrounded by fishing rods and natural-history books. Available activities include nocturnal trips to the lower slopes of the volcano, horseback riding, and fishing. *Apdo. 1234, 1250, Escazú, tel. and fax 228–6623. 8 rooms with bath, dormitory with bath. Facilities: breakfast room, fishing tackle hire, tours. MC, V. $–$$*

Hotel San Bosco. The owners have added a two-story hotel covered in blue-tile mosaics to complement the string of small, inexpensive cabinas. Two kitchen-equipped cabinas (which sleep eight or 12) are a good deal for families. The spotlessly clean, white-walled rooms have polished wood furniture and firm beds and are linked by a long veranda lined with benches and potted plants. *200 meters (220 yards) north of La Fortuna's gas station, tel. 479–9050, fax 479–9109. 16 rooms, 11 cabinas. Facilities: garden, parking. V. $–$$*

Garza
Dining and
Lodging
Hotel Villagio La Guaria Morada. Don't be confused by the rustic thatch: This is a luxury complex whose elegant white bedrooms form an arc around a landscaped tropical garden. Activities include deep-sea fishing, waterskiing, horseback riding, scuba diving (bring your own gear), croquet, and volleyball. *Apdo. 860, 1007 Centro Colón, San José, tel. 233–2476, fax 222–4073. 30 rooms with bath. Facilities: restaurant, bar, casino, disco, pool, parking. MC, V. $$$$*

Hermosa
Dining and
Lodging
El Velero Hotel. This elegant, two-story beachfront hotel has large, white rooms with arched doorways. Instead of giving the rooms ocean views, the Canadian owners built the restaurant, pool, and bar on the beach side for a delightful dining experience. Sample the jumbo shrimp with rice and vegetables. *Playa Hermosa, Guanacaste, tel. and fax 670–0310. 13 rooms with bath. Facilities: restaurant, bar, pool, parking. AE, MC, V. $$$*

Hotel Cabinas Playa Hermosa. Monkeys and birds frolic outside these peaceful white cabinas (sleep five) on the far end of one of Costa Rica's relatively undeveloped beaches. The restaurant serves pasta, steak, and seafood; try the lobster or surf and turf, a hearty fare. A fishing boat is available for rent. *Apdo. 112, Liberia, Guanacaste, tel. and fax 670–0136. 20 cabinas with bath. Facilities: restaurant, parking. No credit cards. $$*

Dining
Aqua Sport. This beachfront complex has a gift shop and water-sports equipment rentals, but the main draw is a casual open-air restaurant decorated with tree trunks and so engulfed in greenery that it is practically hidden from view. The seafood platter of lobster, shrimp, calamari, and oysters is highly recommended. *Apdo. 100–5019, Playa del Coco, tel. 670–0450. Reservations accepted. AE, MC, V. $–$$*

Liberia **Pókopí.** In Costa Rica's cattle capital, Pókopí eclipses rival steak
Dining houses, the drab decor being its only real deficiency. The meat
comes from a nearby export warehouse: Chateaubriand con salsa
Barnesa (with béarnaise sauce, fresh vegetables, and a stuffed tomato) imparts the meaning of export quality. And it isn't all beef:
Filet a la Golberg translates to dorado covered in a white sauce with
mushrooms, onions, green pepper, and white wine. To find the
place, drive or walk 455 meters (500 yards) down the Nicoya road;
it's on the right, 65 meters (75 yards) west of the *bomba* (gas sta-
tion). *Tel. 666-1036. AE, DC, MC, V. $$*

Lodging **Hotel La Siesta.** The advantage of this modern hotel, though slightly
pricier than the Bramadero, is the quiet location three blocks south
of the central plaza. The rooms are smaller than the Bramadero's but
surround a verdant patio with a small pool. Narrow, firm beds;
white walls; and functional bathrooms beginning to show signs of
age characterize the pickings. All accommodations are air-condi-
tioned, but the upstairs rooms are slightly larger and quieter. *Apdo.
15, 5000 Liberia, tel. 666-0678, fax 666-2532. 24 rooms with bath.
Facilities: bar, restaurant, pool, locked parking lot. AE, MC, V. $$*
Hotel Bramadero. Set back from the Interamerican Highway, oppo-
site the turn to Nicoya, this modern hotel gives solid value. An interior spruce-up wouldn't be a bad idea, but bedrooms are clean and
have chunky wood doors, white walls, firm wooden beds, tiles,
dressers, and mirrors. You pay extra for air-conditioning, but the
unequipped units have good overhead fans. Most rooms look onto a
cloister, with rocking chairs and a pool that's illuminated by colored
bulbs at night. For utmost tranquillity ask for a room at the rear,
though the highway traffic out front is never oppressively noisy. An
open-air bar-restaurant fronts the hotel but the food is undistin-
guished. *Apdo. 70, Liberia, tel. 666-0371, fax 666-0203. 20 rooms
with bath. Facilities: restaurant, bar, pool, guard for parking. MC,
V. $-$$*

Monteverde **El Bosque.** Convenient to the Bajo Tigre nature trail and Meg's rid-
Dining ing stable, El Bosque is one of the few independent restaurants
here. It is a popular shady diner with a veranda; the paneled dining
room has a tile floor and wood tables. *Casados* (rice, beans, salad,
and meat or fish) are good but the service can be rather offhand. *Tel.
645-5158. No credit cards. Closed Oct. $*

Dining and **El Sapo Dorado.** Having started its life as a nightclub, El Sapo
Lodging Dorado (The Golden Toad) became a popular restaurant and gradu-
★ ated into a very pleasant hotel. Geovanny's family arrived here to
farm 10 years before the Quakers did, and he and his wife, Hannah,
have recently built secluded hillside cabins with polished paneling,
tables, open fires, and rocking chairs. The restaurant is renowned
for its pasta, pizza, vegetarian dishes, and fresh sailfish from
Puntarenas; the dance floor is still put to use with live music on
weekends; and the 6-kilometer (4-mile) distance from the park entrance isn't a problem if you enjoy hiking or have a car. *Apdo. 09-
5655, Monteverde, tel. and fax 645-5010. 10 rooms with bath. Facilities: restaurant, bar, parking, garden, massage. No credit cards.
$$$*

★ **Hotel Belmar.** Built into the hillside, Hotel Belmar resembles two
tall Swiss chalets and commands extensive views of the Gulf of
Nicoya and the hilly peninsula. The amiable Chilean owners have de-
signed both elegant and rustic rooms, paneled with polished wood;
duvets cover the beds, and most rooms have balconies. In the dining
room, you can count on adventurous and delicious *platos del día* (dai-
ly specials). *Monteverde, Puntarenas, tel. 645-5201, fax 645-5135.*

34 rooms with bath. Facilities: restaurant, bar, basketball, garden, parking. No credit cards. $$–$$$

★ **Fonda Vela.** The most innovatively designed of Monteverde's hotels is also one of the closest to the reserve entrance. Owned by the Smith brothers, whose family were among the first American arrivals in the 1950s, these steep-roof chalets contain large bedrooms with white stucco walls, wooden floors, and huge windows. Some have markedly better views of the wooded grounds, so specify when booking. Local and international recipes, prepared with flair, are served in the dining room or on the veranda. Activities include horseback riding and nature walks. *Apdo. 07–0060–1000, San José, tel. 645–5125, fax 645–5119. 28 rooms with bath. Facilities: restaurant, bar, parking, garden, horse rental. AE, DC, MC, V. $$*

Pensión Monteverde Inn. The cheapest inn in Monteverde is quite far—about 5 kilometers (3 miles)—from the park entrance. The bedrooms are basic, but they have stunning views of the Gulf of Nicoya and contain hardwood floors, firm beds, and powerful, hot showers. Home cooking is served by the chatty David Savage and family. Their dog, Bambi, warms up to guests soon enough. *Apdo. 10165, San José, tel. 645–5156. 8 rooms with bath, 2 rooms without bath. Facilities: dining room, parking. No credit cards. $*

Montezuma
Dining and
Lodging
★ **El Sano Banano.** This unpretentious vegetarian restaurant and bungalow colony on the right of the road as you enter Montezuma serves creative dishes and is a good place to acquaint yourself with the town's vaguely hippie atmosphere. Try the *sopa nutriva* or the eggplant parmesan with mashed potatoes. The owners have built several cabins and some funky new domed bungalows (sleep four) in the woods near the beach, about a 10-minute walk from town. Some bungalows have kitchen facilities. *Tel. 661–1122, ext. 272. No reservations. 6 rooms with bath, 6 bungalows. Facilities: restaurant. AE, DC, MC, V. $$*

Lodging **Cabinas Mar y Cielo.** The advantage of this property over the Hotel Moctezuma is the quieter location—still on the beach, but farther away from the boisterous bars. Decor and prices are very much alike in both establishments, and they are similarly popular as well: Book ahead. *Montezuma, tel. 661–1122, ext. 261. 6 rooms with bath. Facilities: restaurant, bar. No credit cards. $*

★ **Hotel Moctezuma.** The large rooms in this beachside hotel have varnished paneling, firm beds, large fans, and clean bathrooms. The best ones open onto a wide veranda over the beach. *Montezuma, tel. 661–1122, ext. 258. 15 rooms with bath, 6 rooms without bath. Facilities: restaurant, bar. V. $*

Nicoya **Hotel Jenny.** If you do need to stay in Nicoya, this hotel—a little
Lodging sterile, but adequate—is just south of the main square. It has white walls, wooden beds, tile floors, air-conditioning, TVs, and reasonable rates. *Tel. 668–5050, fax 668–6471. 24 rooms with bath. Facilities: guarded parking. V. $*

Nosara **Hotel Playas de Nosara.** This bungalow hotel is perched high on a
Dining and promontory overlooking rain forest and palm-fringed crescents.
Lodging Bedrooms have balconies, terra-cotta floors, white walls, and tapestry wall hangings, but they're actually rather plain and uninspired compared with the magnificent setting. Look for the hotel's sign 2 kilometers (1¼ miles) south of Nosara. *Apdo. 4, Bocas de Nosara, Nicoya, tel. and fax 480–0495. 22 rooms with bath. Facilities: restaurant, bar, parking. No credit cards. $$$*

★ **Hotel Chorotega.** Located in the town itself, just south of the airstrip, this wooden hotel is pleasant and cheap. The nicest bedrooms are upstairs, off a narrow veranda, and have untreated wood paneling, firm beds, and good fans. Shared bathrooms are clean. If you ask, the owners will usually drive you to Ostional to observe the turtles; negotiate an appropriate fee beforehand. *Nosara, tel. 680–0836. 2 rooms with bath, 6 rooms without bath. Facilities: restaurant, bar. No credit cards. $*

Ocotal
Dining and
Lodging
★

Hotel Ocotal. Three kilometers (2 miles) west of Coco down a dirt track, this luxury hotel is situated above the secluded Ocotal bay. Apart from the sportfishing fleet, exceptional views are its main asset. From the upper rooms you look north to the Santa Elena Peninsula and northwest to Rincón de la Vieja. These rooms have blue carpets, patterned bedspreads, white walls, watercolors, overhead fans, TVs, and huge French windows. Units down the hill are bigger and triangular in shape with polished wood floors, but they afford less expansive views. The pool is large and attractively landscaped into the hillside; the dining room and other public areas have a captain's bridge position, and huge windows allow you to take full advantage of the panorama. *Apdo. 1, Playa del Coco, Guanacaste, tel. 670–0323, fax 670–0083. 34 rooms with bath, 3 suites, 6 bungalows. Facilities: restaurant, bar, pool, floodlighted tennis court, secure parking, horseback riding, independent dive shop. AE, DC, MC, V. $$$*

Pan de Azucar
Dining and
Lodging
★

Hotel Sugar Beach. Reached via a dirt track 8 kilometers (5 miles) north of Flamingo, this newly remodeled and expanded hotel overlooks a small, curving white-sand beach. Four small but well-furnished bedrooms occupy sections of a raised circular hut; they have hardwood floors, fans, and oil paintings. The six posher rooms—set slightly farther back—all face the sea and have air-conditioning. Behind these, the new owners have built 16 new rooms with similar amenities. You'll find the islet-scattered bay very pretty; in the rainy season, however, much of the "sugar" is washed away to expose a rocky shoreline, but sandy spots remain for swimming. The islets, in fact, are cunningly positioned to blot the Flamingo condos from view. Wildlife abounds, most noticeably howler monkeys and iguanas, and excellent snorkeling is to be had at either edge of the bay. The open-sided rotunda restaurant should not disappoint, especially if you choose seafood. *Apdo. 90, Santa Cruz, Guanacaste, tel. 670–4242, fax 670–4239. 26 rooms with bath. Facilities: restaurant, bar, parking. AE, MC, V. $$$*

Portrero
Dining and
Lodging

Bahía Portrero Beach and Fishing Resort. Under new Canadian ownership, this squat, white bungalow was undergoing major renovations at press time. Fishing and water sports are the major activities. The beach is ideal for young children because the sea is shallow and safe, and the long, practically deserted strand is relaxing for all. *Apdo. 45, Santa Cruz, Guanacaste, tel. and fax 654–4183. 14 rooms with bath. Facilities: restaurant, bar, pool, parking. AE, MC, V. $$$*

Puntarenas
Dining

La Caravelle. The red-patterned tablecloths and dark-blue walls adorned with antique musical instruments create a chic ambience in this unexpectedly classy French restaurant opposite the sea. The cooking concentrates on sauces: Try the *corvina al gratin con hongos* (sea bass with a white wine sauce) or *mignon con salsa Oporto y hongos* (filet mignon with port and mushroom sauce). If you want to accompany this with claret, prepare to dig deep into your pocket. *Paseo de los Turistas, tel. 661–2262. Reservations advised. MC, V. Closed Mon.–Tues. $$*

Dining and
Lodging

Hotel Porto Bello. Located 2 kilometers (1¼ miles) from downtown, one block north of the main road, Porto Bello's main asset is its thickly planted garden next to the wide estuary. Bedrooms are housed in white stucco bungalow units with tile floors, zanily patterned bedspreads, air-conditioning, TVs, and verandas. *Apdo. 108, Puntarenas, tel. 661–1322, fax 661–0036. 35 rooms with bath. Facilities: restaurant, bar, garden, pool, parking. AE, MC, V. $$*

Lodging **Hotel Tioga.** The blue-and-white courtyard in this central hotel has
★ the look of an ocean liner. Bedrooms, the best of which are upstairs overlooking the gulf, have air-conditioning, tile floors, quilted pink bedspreads, floral pastel curtains, and functional 1970s furniture. A tiny pool in the courtyard sports an islet with a palm tree. *Apdo. 96, Paseo de los Turistas, Puntarenas, tel. 661–0271, fax 661–0127. 46 rooms with bath. Facilities: cafeteria, bar, pool, safe parking. AE, MC, V. $$*

Hotel Cayuga. Have a look at a few rooms in this modern building because they vary a lot. While no more than functional, the best ones are clean and offer a good value, plus the management is friendly. *Apdo. 306, Calle 4 between Avenidas Central and 1, Puntarenas, tel. 661–0344, fax 661–1280. 31 rooms with bath. Facilities: restaurant. AE, MC, V. $*

Rincón de la **Rincón de la Vieja Mountain Lodge.** Resting on the slopes of Rincón
Vieja de la Vieja, this is an ideal base for exploring the volcano. The lodge
Dining and and cabins are paneled, and beds are in small, comfy bunk dormito-
Lodging ries; if you come midweek in low season you probably will get a room
★ to yourself. The sitting room has a terra-cotta floor, varnished paneling, maps of the surroundings, a scientific library, and cases of butterflies and some fairly hairy, hair-raising insects. A large upstairs veranda has sofas and chairs. The food is good: meat, fish, and vegetarian entrées, with much of the produce being homegrown. The owner Alvaro's affable staff can take you to explore the volcano on foot or horseback. Don't imagine that guides are just for sissies; tourists have been badly burned here. *Apdo. 114, 5000 Liberia, tel. 225–1073, fax 234–1676. 22 dormitories with bath, 3 with shared bath; capacity: 45. Facilities: dining room, pool, parking. MC, V. $$*

Tamarindo **Hotel Tamarindo Diriá.** A shady tropical garden next to the beach
Dining and does away with the need to stray far from the bounds of Tamarindo's
Lodging poshest hotel. The modern three-story building has new owners who have remodeled and filled the previously dark rooms with striking white-painted furnishings with aqua trim and matching ceilings. It's a bit much, but each has a spacious balcony looking onto tree tops. The thatched rotunda bar and restaurant overlook a large rectangular pool. *Apdo. 676–1000, San José, tel. 289–8616, fax 289–8727. 70 rooms with bath. Facilities: restaurant, bar, pool, tennis, secure parking. AE, DC, MC, V. $$$$*

El Jardín del Edén. This resort is smaller and a better value than the Diriá, the only disadvantage being that it's a short walk from the beach. The three-tiered, mauve hotel, set among lush gardens (hence the name Garden of Eden) on a hill, has rooms with green interiors and elegantly styled bathrooms. All rooms have ocean views, air-conditioning, refrigerators, and fans. Two pools, a Jacuzzi, and a thatched-roof restaurant that serves French and Italian food are set amid the landscaped grounds. Fishing packages are available. *Apdo. 1094–2050, San Pedro, tel. and fax 220–2096. 18 rooms with bath, 2 apartments. Facilities: restaurant, 2 bars, 2 pools, Jacuzzi, parking. AE, MC, V. $$$*

★ **El Milagro.** One of Tamarindo's more innovative hotels started off as a restaurant run by a young English-speaking Dutch couple. Robert Boasson, the chef, mastered his art in Switzerland and Amsterdam before coming to Costa Rica. The couple recently built individual tile-roofed cabins with wood ceilings, firm beds, large fans, and terraces. Views of the small pool can be enjoyed with candlelight dinners in the open-air restaurant. The menu is short but refined; if you feel like a very worthwhile splurge, order the platter of three fish with four sauces. *Playa Tamarindo, Guanacaste, tel. and fax 654–4240. 31 rooms with bath. Facilities: restaurant, bar, pool. AE, V.* $$

★ **Cabinas Zullymar.** At the southern end of town, these clean and varied cabinas are a good bargain. Bedrooms have clean white walls, sloping wood ceilings, and large modern bathrooms; air-conditioning and a fridge come for a price. Pre-Columbian–style statues adorn the garden. Across the road on the beach, the restaurant serves inexpensive maritime food in a colorful setting marked by white wooden chairs, pink and green tablecloths, and abundant potted plants. A pool is planned. *Apdo. 68, Santa Cruz, Guanacaste, tel. 226–4732. 27 rooms with bath. Facilities: restaurant, bar, parking. No credit cards.* $

Tambor
Dining and
Lodging
★

Hotel Playa Tambor. This huge luxury hotel on the beach, once the rustic La Hacienda lodge and working farm, drew fire from environmentalists, who argued that its sheer size is detrimental to the zone. Opened in late 1992, the resort has hundreds of posh rooms equipped with cable TV, minibars, and air-conditioning; all have balconies, some with sea views. Activities include a variety of nightly shows, horseback riding, and water sports. Rooms are sold as a package only, with meals and beverages included. *Tel. 661–1915, fax 661–2069. 402 rooms with bath. Facilities: 3 restaurants, theater, disco, garden, pool, parking. AE, DC, MC, V.* $$$$

★ **Tango Mar.** Located 2 kilometers (1¼ miles) west of Tambor, this is one of Costa Rica's finest resort hotels. Choose between rustic palm-thatch cabins on stilts or rooms in the main hotel. The former are much more interesting; some have fully equipped kitchens, and all are paneled and come with features such as clock radios, fans, and hot showers. Those in the main hotel are luxurious by conventional standards but largely uninspired, and all have balconies and excellent sea views. The restaurant serves international cuisine. In the shady grounds is a small spring-fed pool that is sculpted from rock, and an immaculate nine-hole golf course. *Apdo. 3877, 1000 San José, tel. and fax 661–2798. 6 villas with bath, 18 rooms with bath. Facilities: restaurant, bar, pool, golf course, sailboats, surfboards, fishing, waterskiing, motorbikes. AE, MC, V.* $$$$

Lodging
★

Hotel Dos Lagartos. This small hotel with friendly young management is surrounded by trees and sits 45 meters (50 yards) back from Tambor beach. The bedrooms have tile and wood floors, tartan sheets, and large windows to take in the view. The dining room was closed at press time but may reopen soon. If you are on a budget, you will be very happy to have found this place. *Tambor de Puntarenas, tel. 661–1122, ext. 236. 4 rooms with bath, 16 rooms without bath. No credit cards.* $

The Arts and Nightlife

The Arts   Santa Cruz celebrates its patron-saint day from January 15 onward with marimba music, folk dances, and Tico-style bullfights. On July 16 you can see a colorful regatta and carnival in Puntarenas in honor of its patron saint. The annexation of Guanacaste is celebrated on July 25 with folk dances, bullfights, and rodeos in Liberia. The festival of La Yeguita in Nicoya on December 12 features a solemn procession, dancing, fireworks, and bullfights.

Nightlife,   There are dance floors at El Sapo Dorado hotel and at La Cascada
Bars, Discos restaurant, both in Monteverde, and discos behind the Pokopí in Liberia (*see* Dining and Lodging, *above*) and on the seafront at Playa del Coco; all are lively on weekends. In Tamarindo, people head to the Restaurant Zullymar and Fiesta del Mar bars for evening drinks. After dark in Montezuma centers on Hotel Moctezuma and Chico's bar.

Cabaret   Fiesta Brava will appeal to the John Wayne in you. Hollering, whooping cowboys accompany visitors on the last stretch as they arrive at the working ranch and 1824 adobe farmhouse. Music, lasso shows, bullriding, dancing, and a Guanacaste specialty dinner all follow. Contact the Hacienda La Cueva via travel agencies or direct (tel. 666–0450).

The Southwest

Travelers to the southwest portion of Costa Rica—a lush, tropical coastal plain overlooked by the highest mountain chain in the country, the Cordillera de Talamanca—should thank the national park system for preserving some of the most breathtaking natural areas in the country. Carara and Manuel Antonio national parks to the north of this region are protected areas of indigenous forest. A transition zone between the dry north and humid south, Carara's buttressed estave trees and scarlet macaws occupying its riverside gallery rain forest vie for attention with a giant lagoon full of waterfowl and wallowing crocodiles. Manuel Antonio, synonymous for many people with tropical paradise, protects an indented stretch of coastal rain forest that serves as a backdrop for a series of idyllic white sandy beaches. Visitors to Chirripó and La Amistad national parks can climb Costa Rica's highest mountain, explore remote wilderness, and experience the gamut of habitats from tropical rain forest to glacial lakes. On the Osa Peninsula, the creation of Corcovado National Park has put something of a halt to the furious logging, gold mining, and overall destruction of this rain forest. This is the wettest national park in Costa Rica. Partially coastal, it contains a wide range of habitats including large areas of swamp, *jolillo*, montane, and cloud forest, the last notable for oak trees.

Some parts of the Southwest have not fared so well. The coastal plain running from Tárcoles to Canoas on the Panama frontier is what attracted United Fruit in the 1930s when it was looking for alternative sites for its blight-stricken banana crops in Limón. From 1938 until 1985, when the company pulled out, bananas dominated the scenery, especially around Golfito, which was made into a banana shipping capital. In its wake, United Fruit has left a very depressed economic situation and soil now only suitable for growing rather ugly and monotonous African palms.

None of the above is meant to deter you, nor should it. The Southwest contains the most dramatic and diverse scenery and wildlife in Costa Rica, as well as some of its prettiest beaches. Anglers can fish the renowned Pacific rivermouths, rafters can take on the ferocious Río General, trekkers can climb Chirripó, and bird-watchers are almost guaranteed, with perseverance, to glimpse the resplendent quetzal.

Important Addresses and Numbers

Tourist   The tourist office in San José has information on the Southwest (*see*
Information Important Addresses and Numbers in San José and the Central Val-

ley, *above*). **La Buena Nota** (tel. 777–0345), on the left just after the bridge entering Quepos, is a crafts shop–cum–informal local information center.

Emergencies **Police** (tel. 117 in towns or 127 in rural areas); **Traffic Police** (tel. 227–8030); **Fire** (tel. 118); **Ambulance** (tel. 221–5818).

Arriving and Departing by Plane

Sansa (tel. 233–5330) flies to Quepos, Golfito, Palmar Sur, and Coto 47. **Travelair** (tel. 220–3054) flies to Quepos, Golfito, Palmar Sur, and Puerto Jiménez (*see* Getting Around in Staying in Costa Rica, *above*, for details).

Arriving and Departing by Car and Bus

By Car The Pan-American and San José–Orotina highways are the main access roads to the region; both are paved.

By Bus Buses from San José to **Jacó** leave Calle 16 between Avenidas 1 and 3 (Coca-Cola Bus Station, tel. 232–1829) daily at 7:15 AM and 3:30 PM, returning at 5 AM and 3 PM (2½-hour trip); to **Manuel Antonio** from the Coca-Cola Station (tel. 223–5567) daily at 6 AM, noon, and 6 PM (3½-hour trip), returning at 6 AM, noon, and 5 PM; to **San Isidro** daily from the Coca-Cola Station (tel. 222–2422) hourly between 5:30 AM and 5 PM (three-hour trip, returning at the same times); and to **Golfito** from Avenida 18 between Calles 2 and 4 (tel. 221–4214) daily at 7 AM, 11 AM, and 3 PM (eight-hour trip), returning at 5 AM and 1 PM.

Getting Around

By Car The Interamerican Highway is paved with two lanes all the way to Panama. Be careful in the foggy and icy conditions atop the Cerro de la Muerte. To Quepos, the road is paved only as far as Parrita, although at press time crews were rebuilding the muddy road between the two towns; from Parrita, a gravel road runs down the coast as far as Dominical, linked by paved road with San Isidro.

By Bus Buses leave Puntarenas for Quepos daily at 5 AM and 2:30 PM (three hours). Buses leave daily at 7 AM and 1:30 PM from Centro Comercial El Valle in San Isidro for Dominical and Quepos, and at 5:30 AM and noon for Puerto Jiménez (five-hour trip); the latter can drop you at La Palma (for Corcovado); the alternative for reaching Corcovado is to catch the daily 5 AM bus from Puerto Jiménez. The adventurous may wish to inquire locally about trucks leaving Puerto Jiménez for Carate.

By Boat The Golfito/Puerto Jiménez ferry leaves the Golfito *muelle* (dock) daily at 11:30 AM and returns at 6 AM. Private boats are also available for hire.

Guided Tours

Excursions **Geotur's** (tel. 234–1867) excellent Carara day tour includes a swim stop at Jacó beach. **Jungle Trails'** (tel. 255–3486) day tour to Carara allows visitors to plant an endangered tree to expand the buffer zone.

Special-
Interest and
Walking Tours **Jungle Trails** (tel. 255–3486) offers a four-day hiking trip to climb Chirripó and a five-day camping trip to Corcovado. **Costa Rica Expeditions** (tel. 257–0766) organizes a range of package options from camping to hotel-based trips. **Costa Rica Sun Tours** (tel. 255–2011) arranges visits to the remote Tiskita Jungle Lodge (*see* Dining and

Lodging, *below*) in the far southwest at around $400 for four days and three nights. The same company is recommended for trips to Manuel Antonio.

Cruises **Okeanos Aggressor** (tel. 800/348–2628 in the U.S.) and **Swiss Travel** (tel. 231–4055) arrange 10- to 12-day cruise trips to explore the remote Coco Island, which lies 592 kilometers (370 miles) offshore and is the largest uninhabited island in the world.

Exploring the Southwest

Tour 1 takes in Carara National Park, the surfing resort town of Jacó, and the seaside rain forest of Manuel Antonio. Tour 2 moves south along the Interamerican Highway and includes Cerro de la Muerte, San Isidro, Chirripó, La Amistad, San Vito, Golfito, and Corcovado. To link the two, you can drive the 70 kilometers (44 miles) from Quepos to San Isidro via Dominical in around two hours.

Highlights for **Carara National Park** (*see* Tour 1)
First-time **Cerro Chirripó** (*see* Tour 2)
Visitors **Corcovado National Park** (*see* Tour 2)
Manuel Antonio National Park (*see* Tour 1)
Quetzals, San Gerardo de Dota (*see* Tour 2)
Wilson Botanical Garden (*see* Tour 2)

Tour 1: *Numbers in the margin correspond to points of interest on the*
Carara, Jacó, *Southwest map.*
and Manuel
Antonio There are two ways of getting to the coast southwest of San José, where you'll find some of the finest beaches in Costa Rica. One is to leave via Paseo Colón, turn right along the airport highway as far as the turn to Atenas, and then go past Orotina to Carara and the coast. This is the best route if you are aiming for Carara or Jacó, or if time is short. The alternative is to turn left at the top of Paseo Colón and take the Escazú highway via Ciudad Colón to Santiago de Puriscal. This route takes in more dramatic scenery as it passes through rolling countryside planted with coffee, orange trees, and sugarcane on the way to higher pastures sprinkled with oak and pine, backdropped by a jagged outline of lofty mountains. Although shorter in distance, it takes rather longer because the road between Santiago de Puriscal and Parrita is unpaved.

Taking the first course, once past Orotina, you'll find the road to Carara enters flatter, hotter, and more humid countryside, much of it rice paddies. Follow a series of necessary turns (signposted) if you are to remain on the Quepos road. **Carara National Park** (*see* Chapter 3, National Parks and Wildlife Reserves), which protects a transition zone between the drier north and the more humid south, provides an enjoyable hike for those who start out early in the morning to see the animals and makes a nice day trip in combination with the beaches, some just minutes away. The ranger station appears shortly after the bridge over the Tárcoles. Waterfowl, waders, amphibians, and reptiles live in the marshes. A horseshoe lagoon, which was abandoned as an oxbow lake by the meandering Tárcoles and is now almost entirely covered with water hyacinth, hosts exotic birds such as the *jacana spinosa* as well as large crocodiles. Artificial nests have been built deep in the forest to protect the endangered scarlet macaw, which is under constant threat from poachers who take chicks to sell in the illegal international pet trade. Much of the 4,704-hectare (11,614-acre) reserve is covered in primary forest, growing on quite steep slopes. The trees here, laden with vines and epiphytes, are immense—the smooth-bark cow tree reaches 45 me-

The Southwest

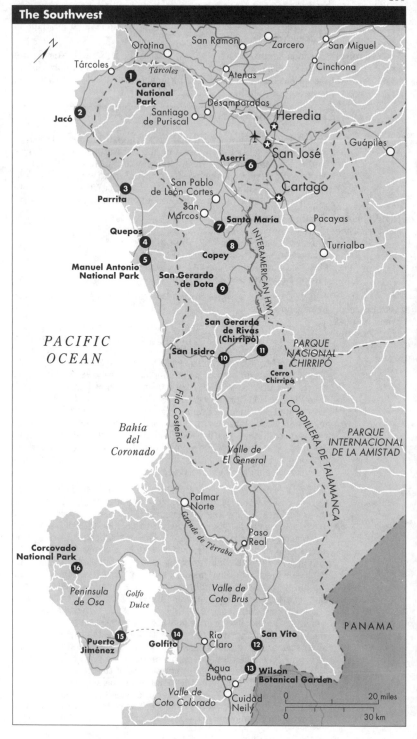

ters (150 feet) in height. Carara makes a worthwhile stop because the relatively less dense undergrowth means that wildlife is easier to see here than in many other places. You might also see spectacled owls, boat-billed herons, blue-crowned motmots, scarlet macaws, roseate spoonbills, crocodiles, iguanas, sloths, coatis, and white-faced monkeys. Jaguars, although they do live here, are hardly ever seen. Important archaeological discoveries have also been made here, in particular the Lomas Carara pre-Columbian cemetery, which covers 6 hectares (15 acres). *Admission: 200 colones. Open daily 8–4.*

South of Carara the highway brushes the coast at the small village of Tárcoles, and 15 kilometers (9 miles) farther on it arrives at **Jacó.** The relative proximity to San José coupled with the attractiveness of its wide sandy bay, hemmed in by rocky forested outcrops, has contributed to Jacó's popularity as a resort. Around 30 well-dispersed hotels have been built here, but they are largely hidden behind palms, and you'll still receive the impression of a relatively quiet and undeveloped place during low season. High season is bustling. But if you do want fun in the sun and something vaguely resembling nightlife, this is the closest you'll come outside the capital. The surfing is also quite good, although riptides make the sea hazardous and the beach is somewhat dirty. The *núcleo turístico* for day visitors consists of locked closets, bathrooms, and showers.

The road south hugs the steep contours of Jacó's bay until you reach Pochotal, where it slants inland through paddy fields and a few lingering banana plants. Three kilometers (2 miles) from Jacó is the turn to Playa Hermosa, famed for its strong break and hence the venue of an annual surfing contest. Playa Esterillos Oeste, 22 kilometers (14 miles) from Jacó, is another surfers' haunt as well as a quieter beach alternative to Jacó. Another 22 kilometers (13.75 miles) on, the first African palms herald your imminent arrival in **Parrita,** a dusty town of painted wooden bungalows. Just to the south of town is a right turn to Playa Palo Seco, an endless beach backed by palms and mangrove swamps. The surfing here can be very good and the swimming is safe. The 25 kilometers (15 miles) between Parrita and Quepos is mainly unpaved and very dusty, but smooth enough. It runs through a rather monotonous plantation of tall African palms, first planted in 1945 by banana companies who were losing their crops to Panama disease. The extracted oil is used for margarine, cooking oil, scent, and soap.

Quepos is the largest town in the area, with around 12,000 inhabitants. Juan Vásquez de Coronado, the first Spanish conquistador to arrive here in 1563, encountered the Quepos Indians, an offshoot tribe of the Borucas, who lived by a combination of farming and fishing. Clashes, displacement, and intermarriage served to drastically deplete the indigenous population, for whom colonies were only established at the end of the 19th century. Like Golfito, Quepos was once a major banana port but saw its fortunes dwindle along with those of the banana company, United Fruit. Only recently has revenue from tourism and African palms begun to remove some of the shabbiness that had set in. The town has some good budget hotels, but for beaches you should ride on to Manuel Antonio.

Manuel Antonio National Park begins 5 kilometers (3 miles) south of Quepos (*see* Chapter 3, National Parks and Wildlife Reserves). This park, while touted as a paradise, is lovely but overcrowded. For peace, quiet, and animal life, stick to the less-traveled parks. The road between is growing increasingly crowded by hotels, none of which are very cheap and some of which fit into the super-deluxe category. Environmentalists are pushing to halt the unbridled development on Costa Rica's most beautiful stretch of coast, which was terribly battered by tropical storm Gert in September 1993. The cheapest accommodation is located near the end of the road at the park entrance. To enter the park, you need to wade through a narrow estuary, at times waist-deep. At the ranger station on the far side you can pick up a map.

The park is small. just 682 hectares (1,685 acres). It protects a remarkable stretch of coast comprising three idyllic white-sand horseshoe beaches, divided by some primary forest, though much of it was knocked down by the storm. Bully, black locust, cow, and silk cotton trees all grow in the area. Mangrove swamps, marshland, and open water lagoons contribute further to the park's biodiversity. Shier squirrel monkeys, which are known to exist only here and on the Osa Peninsula and are thought to be in danger of extinction, are occasionally visible. From the beach you might glimpse two- and three-toed sloths, raccoons, coatis, and white-faced monkeys. Be careful of the *manzanillo* tree (indicated by warning signs), whose leaves, bark, and fruit—which resemble apples but aren't—secrete a toxic gooey substance that irritates the skin.

Plan for sunbathing, swimming, snorkeling, hiking, and a respite at the picnic area; a full day is advisable. The first beach after the ranger station, South Espadilla, is the longest and least crowded, as riptides make it treacherous for swimmers. At its southern end is a *tombolo* (isthmus formed from sedimentation and accumulated debris) leading to a steep forested path to Cathedral Point. Visible east of here is the precipitous vegetation-crowned Mogote Island, one of the park's 12 islands and site of pre-Columbian Quepo Indian burials. East of the tombolo is Manuel Antonio, a small, sandy, and relatively safe beach. At low tide you can see an obsolete Quepo turtle trap near the rocks on the right—turtles would become stranded as the tide receded in a pool formed by a semicircular rock. Walking farther east you arrive at the slightly rockier Playas Puerto Escondido, with a dramatic blowhole, and Playita. *Admission: 200 colones. Open daily 8–4.*

Tour 2: South Along the Interamerican Highway Southbound along the Interamerican Highway you can opt for the scenic but slightly more circuitous route via Aserrí or travel via the divided highway to Cartago. If you choose the former, follow signs
❻ to Desamparados and Aserrí. The road snakes uphill, leaving San José sprawled below. **Aserrí** has attractive colonial architecture and a pretty central plaza. The jagged Cerros de Escazú rise to the right of the road.

Time Out Two kilometers (1¼ miles) beyond Aserrí on the right is the entrance to **Mirador Ram Luna,** a good bar-restaurant with panoramic views of the capital; they're especially spectacular at night. Even if it isn't mealtime, you owe it to yourself to have a quick drink on the terrace here.

❼ Meandering through orderly coffee plantations, which lend a neat landscaped look, the road passes through the peaceful mountain villages of San Pablo, San Marcos, and **Santa María.** Although San Gerardo de Dota is a more interesting trip, stop here for a bit of history. Santa María's wooden, primary-colored bungalows nestle in a bowl surrounded by steep hills. José Figueres (leader of the 1948 revolution and later president) lived on a farm nearby, and the 1948 Civil War had its roots here. The central plaza is dominated by a rococo sculpture dedicated to the townspeople for the part they played

So, you're getting away from it all.

Just make sure you can get back.

AT&T Access Numbers
Dial the number of the country you're in to reach AT&T.

ANGUILLA	1-800-872-2881	**COLOMBIA**	**980-11-0010**	JAMAICA††	0-800-872-2881
ANTIGUA (Public Card Phones)	#1	*COSTA RICA	114	MEXICO◊◊◊	95-800-462-4240
ARGENTINA♦	001-800-200-1111	**CURACAO**	**001-800-872-2881**	MONTSERRAT†	1-800-872-2881
BAHAMAS	**1-800-872-2881**	DOMINICA	1-800-872-2881	**NICARAGUA**	**174**
BELIZE♦	555	DOMINICAN REP.††	1-800-872-2881	PANAMA	109
BERMUDA†	1-800-872-2881	ECUADOR†	119	PARAGUAY†	0081-800
*BOLIVIA	0-800-1112	*EL SALVADOR	190	PERU†	191
BONAIRE	**001-800-872-2881**	GRENADA†	1-800-872-2881	ST. KITTS/NEVIS	1-800-872-2881
BRAZIL	**000-8010**	*GUATEMALA	190	**ST. MAARTEN**	**001-800-872-2881**
BRITISH V.I.	1-800-872-2881	*GUYANA††	**165**	**SURINAME**	**156**
CAYMAN ISLANDS	1-800-872-2881	HAITI†	001-800-972-2883	URUGUAY	00-0410
CHILE	**00◊-0312**	HONDURAS†	123	*VENEZUELA	80-011-120

Countries in bold face permit country-to-country calling in addition to calls to the U.S. **World Connect**℠ prices consist of **USADirect**® rates plus an additional charge based on the country you are calling. Collect calling available to the U.S. only. *Public phones require deposit of coin or phone card. †May not be available from every phone. ††Collect calling only. ♦Not available from public phones. ◊Await second dial tone. ◊◊When calling from public phones, use phones marked "Ladatel." ©1994 AT&T.

Here's a travel tip that will make it easy to call back to the States. Dial the access number for the country you're visiting and connect right to AT&T. It's the quick way to get English-speaking AT&T operators and can minimize hotel telephone surcharges.

If all the countries you're visiting aren't listed above, call **1 800 241-5555** for a free wallet card with all AT&T access numbers. Easy international calling from AT&T. **TrueWorld Connections.**

AT&T

American Express offers Travelers Cheques built for two.

Cheques *for Two*℠ from American Express are the Travelers Cheques that allow either of you to use them because both of you have signed them. And only one of you needs to be present to purchase them.

Cheques *for Two* are accepted anywhere regular American Express Travelers Cheques are, which is just about everywhere. So stop by your bank, AAA* or any American Express Travel Service Office and ask for Cheques *for Two*.

in the preservation of democracy. From Santa María a rough track winds up the Pirris Valley through coffee fields, fruit trees, and forests to the tiny village of **Copey**, 9 kilometers (6 miles) away. This is a wild and relatively untouched area, superb for walking, bird-watching, and trout fishing. The Interamerican Highway is 7 kilometers (4 miles) uphill from Copey.

The southbound Interamerican Highway climbs through ever more temperate vegetation; eucalyptus gives way to hardier cypress and then to a stunted blend of shrubs, grasses, and herbaceous plants of Andean origin, generically known as *páramos*. This is the highest road in southern Central America; fog and slippery conditions are a perennial problem, and you may find your windshield misting over because of the dramatic change in temperature.

At the 80 Km marker, a right turn leads to **San Gerardo de Dota,** 9 kilometers (6 miles) down a twisting track that descends abruptly into the Savegre Valley. This damp, epiphyte-laden forest of giant ceiba trees, now broken up by bare, stump-strewn patches, is renowned for its high count of resplendent quetzals, for many the most beautiful bird in the New World. Males are the more spectacular, with metallic green feathers, bright crimson stomachs, helmetlike crests, and long tail streamers with violet-blue highlights that are especially dramatic in flight. Look for fruit trees from the laurel family called *aguacatillos*. This species, similar to the avocado tree, is sometimes found growing by the roadside and is where quetzals commonly feed. Ask a local if you need guidance. Morning and evening are the best times to spot the birds.

Continuing along the highway over the 3,476-meter (11,400-foot) Cerro de la Muerte, there are places, if clear, from where you can see both oceans. Beginning the descent to San Isidro, Chirripó—at 3,819 meters (12,500 feet) the highest mountain in the country—is visible on your left, revealing its tawny-violet, almost vegetationless profile. In terms of size, however, Mt. Chirripó looks more impressive from down in San Isidro.

The second-largest town in the province of San José, **San Isidro** is a bustling market town with colorful, modern grid-plan streets. The large central square is the hub of the town's activity, and a couple of blocks south of here is the market. **Chirripó National Park** is nearby, and the market is a good place to stock up on provisions if you're heading for the summit (*see* Chapter 3, National Parks and Wildlife Reserves).

Time Out The **Hotel-Restaurante Chirripó terrace bar** in San Isidro is good for its omelets and people-watching.

Chirripó's gateway is **San Gerardo de Rivas,** 15 kilometers (9 miles) northwest of San Isidro. It is home to the ranger station and a bunkhouse (*see* Dining and Lodging, *below*). If you are planning to make the tough one- to two-day ascent of Cerro Chirripó (3,819 meters/ 12,500 feet) you need to register and pay at the ranger station. Basic maps are available here, but try to buy a large-scale topographical map in San José. Carry plenty of water and warm, waterproof clothing. The most popular trail to the summit is the so-called Thermometer, along which climbers measure whether they have it in them to make the complete ascent. Leave early on the first day, between 4 and 5 AM, in order to complete the 11-hour hike to the overnight huts in daylight. Walk uphill from San Gerardo, and fork right to the sign marked "Sendero al Cerro Chirripó." From here, keep the forest to your right until you hit the trail proper, which winds through cloud forest before reaching the bleak páramos. Signs every 2 kilometers (1¼ miles) indicate your altitude and distance from the summit; the overnight huts are 4 kilometers (2½ miles) short of the summit. The lakes (or tarns), cirques, moraines, and rounded rock forms near the top are evidence of Pleistocene and Wisconsin glaciation. *Admission: 200 colones. Open 7–4.*

As you go south, with the Interamerican Highway descending into the Valle de El General, squat, silvery-green pineapple plants blanket the gentle contours. The road is fast and the scenery spectacular, with the jagged gray-blue profile of the 3,354-meter (11,000-foot) Cordillera de Talamanca forming a lofty backdrop to the east while the 915-meter (3,000-foot) Fila Costeña attempts a vague symmetry to the west.

After Paso Real you can either stay with the Interamerican as it follows the snaking Río Grande de Térraba toward Palmar Norte and Golfito or turn left across the river to San Vito. The latter detour is highly recommended if you have time.

A bridge over the Térraba is being built, a timesaving godsend for locals but a pity for tourists, because the pulley ferry was rather restful. The San Vito road climbs along a spur ridge south of the **Coto Brus Valley.** North of the Coto Brus is the vast mountainous **Parque Internacional de La Amistad,** which, contiguous with the Chirripó Park, forms the largest and most diverse protected area in Costa Rica (*see* Off the Beaten Track, *below*).

⑫ San Vito is a charming small town that lies at an altitude of 960 meters (3,150 feet), close to the Panama border. It owes its foundation in 1952 to a government scheme whereby 200 Italian families were given grants to convert the rain forest into coffee, fruit, and cattle farms. After much initial hardship and wrangling over the size of the agreed grant, a relatively large modern town with around 40,000 inhabitants has resulted.

⑬ Six kilometers (4 miles) south on the Ciudad Neily road is the **Wilson Botanical Garden.** These 12 hillside hectares (30 acres) were converted from a coffee plantation in 1963 by U.S. landscapers Robert and Catherine Wilson, who planted a huge collection of tropical species (around 2,000), in particular palms, orchids, aroids, ferns, bromeliads, heliconias, and marantas, all linked by a series of neat grass paths. The garden and adjoining premontane forest were transferred to the Organization for Tropical Studies in 1973 and in 1983 became part of the Amistad reserve. It functions mainly as a research and teaching center, but visitors are welcome (*see also* Dining and Lodging, *below*). Helpful booklets provide you with a self-guided tour. *Admission: $16, including lunch. Open daily 7:30–5.*

Beyond Agua Buena, the 19 kilometers (12 miles) to Ciudad Neily are unpaved, twisty, and spectacular, with views over the Coto Colorado plain to the Osa Peninsula. South along the Interamerican you come to the frontier town of Paso Canoas, where vacuum cleaners and other electrical items that are heavily taxed in Costa Rica swiftly change hands. The highway north leads to Río Claro and the turn to Golfito.

Once thriving, this area was devastated when United Fruit pulled out in 1985 due to labor disputes, rising export taxes, and a diminishing Pacific banana market. The company had arrived in 1938 to **⑭** supplement its diseased plantations in Limón, and **Golfito** became the center of activity, with a dock that could handle 4,000 bananas per hour and elegant housing for its plantation managers. Pesticides used on the bananas have made other types of agriculture almost impossible, and the unsightly African palms have proved to be about the only crop that will grow. In order to inject new life into Golfito, the government declared the town a duty-free port in 1990; visitors need to arrive and register at least 24 hours in advance to take advantage of this.

Golfito is beautifully situated overlooking a small gulf (hence its name) and hemmed in by a steep bank of forest. At the northwestern end is the so-called American zone, full of elegant stilted wooden houses where the expatriate managers lived, courtesy of United Fruit. With a golf course nearby, life here must have been just about bearable.

⓯ A ferry as well as private boats leave from the harbor to cross Golfo Dulce to **Puerto Jiménez,** a one-horse town on the Osa Peninsula. The headquarters of the Corcovado National Park (tel. 735–5036) are at the southern end of town, opposite the Texaco gas station. This is where you obtain permission to enter the park and can ask about travel routes and present conditions. You can also arrange meals and lodging at the various ranger stations, but check the arrangements carefully.

Time Out   **La Carolina soda** on Puerto Jiménez's main drag is a good central place for a casado and a drink.

⓰ Comprising 43,740 hectares (108,000 acres), **Corcovado National Park** is one of the largest parks in the system (*see* Chapter 3, National Parks and Wildlife Reserves). It was created in 1975 to ward off the threat that increased logging, colonization, and gold mining posed to the area. Land owned by the U.S. company Osa Forest Products was expropriated by the government in 1970. Mechanized gold mining is very damaging to rivers and still goes on outside the park boundary; you can see this at Coopeunioro on the Rincón River near Los Patos station. Individual *oreros* (panners) caused silting problems and so were forcibly evicted in 1986; many still breach the regulations. Rife unemployment, exacerbated by United Fruit's departure, puts pressure on all these problems.

Corcovado provides hardy travelers with an experience of what it's really like to be in the middle of the jungle. With an annual rainfall of 200 inches, much of the territory is virgin tropical rain forest. Cleared areas are now growing back. The topography is mainly rugged and steep, rising to 745 meters (2,444 feet). Habitats include montane forest, cloud forest, alluvial plains forest, mangrove, marshes, and swamps. Walking has great bird-watching potential; 285 species have been catalogued. Tapirs, jaguars, and squirrel monkeys also live here, but more discreetly. The tall forest abruptly meets the beaches; sperm whales are sometimes sighted offshore. The Cuban exiles reputedly took advantage of this area's isolation to prepare for the Bay of Pigs, and the Sandinistas did similarly prior to the overthrow of Somoza.

Visiting Corcovado independently is best done in groups of three or more, and it requires preparation. Potential hazards range from heat-related health problems to snakes. Bring binoculars, camping equipment, rain gear, high boots, long socks, snakebite and first-aid kit, insect repellent, water-purifying tablets, food, and water. One of the routes recommended by the rangers is as follows: Take the 5:30 AM bus from Puerto Jiménez to La Palma. Take a taxi to the trailhead at Los Patos; if you reach the mining cooperative you've gone 180 meters (200 yards) beyond the correct turn (visiting this mining community offers a lesson in the havoc gold mining can cause to a river, incidentally). Walk eight to 10 hours to Sirena station near the coast, then on past Playa Madrigal to La Leona station campsite (parts of this hike can be done only at low tide). Around Sirena, some interesting shorter trails are marked by silver tags. You then have a day-long hike back to Puerto Jiménez, or you can arrange for a pickup from Playa Carate, a 30- to 40-minute walk south of La Leona. Check on the tides in order to cross rivers; ask about this in La Leona and La Sirena. The other way of getting to Corcovado is by boat from one of Osa Peninsula's nature lodges (see Dining and Lodging, below).

Playa Zancudo can also be reached by boat from Golfito, or by road in two hours. Zancudo is a village of wooden houses in a palm grove behind an endless beach. It has an insular feel due to its isolation. Local fishermen will take you on boat tours of the mangrove river network, where you might see crocodiles.

What to See and Do with Children

The best beaches for children in the southwest are the second two beaches that you come to in Manuel Antonio National Park, Manuel Antonio and Puerto Escondido, and **Playa Gallardo,** just west of Golfito. Elsewhere, the strong currents and large waves make swimming for children very dangerous.

Off the Beaten Track

La Amistad National Park—at 198,450 hectares (490,000 acres), by far the largest park in the system—can be reached from San Vito. The park administration is at Las Tablas, 40 kilometers (25 miles) northwest. Within the park's terrain, ranging from 213 meters (700 feet) to 3,537 meters (11,600 feet), reside two-thirds of the country's vertebrate species and half the country's bird species. Before you go, ask for the latest information from the National Parks Service in San José (Calle 25 between Avenidas 8 and 10, tel. 257–0922).

The peaceful Indian village of **Boruca** rests amid communally farmed hill country above the Paseo Real–Palmar Norte stretch of the Interamerican Highway. The Indians weave naturally dyed cotton garments and carve balsa-wood masks (see The Arts and Nightlife, below).

There is a back route to or from Golfito via the rough track that leads past the airport through the **Golfito Wildlife Refuge** before emerging on the Interamerican Highway at Briceño. The track is steep in parts and very rutted, but you should be able to manage it by car. A dense evergreen forest of lofty yellow saman, manwood, and silk cotton trees shelters collared peccaries, raccoons, coatis, and blue morpho butterflies.

Caño Island lies 19 kilometers (12 miles) off the Osa Peninsula. Most of its 299 hectares (740 acres) are covered in evergreen forest containing fig, locust, and rubber trees. Coastal Indians used it as a burial ground, and the numerous bits and pieces unearthed here have prompted archaeologists to speculate about pre-Columbian long-distance maritime trade. The surrounding coral reefs are superb for diving and snorkeling. Lodges that we list on the Osa offer day trips to Caño. Alternatively, you can arrange an independent trip with the Corcovado National Park.

Shopping

Markets are lively in San Isidro de El General, Quepos, and Golfito, where you can pick up fruit, coffee, and leather goods.

Sports

Fishing The Pacific river mouths provide the best shore fishing in the country. Snook and *corvina* (sea bass) are abundant, and snapper mill around the rocks. Hair and plastic-tailed jigs are favored baits—ask in one of the fishing shops what people are currently using. Popular river mouths are the Parrita and Tulin rivers, between Jacó and Quepos, and the Naranja and Savegre, south of Quepos. Good sportfishing is available from Quepos with **Costa Rican Dreams** (tel. 239–3387) and **Sportsfishing Costa Rica** (tel. 257–3553 or 800/862–1003). Farther south, **Río Sierpe Lodge** (tel. 220–1712) has sportfishing boats.

Scuba Diving and Snorkeling Contact **El Caballito del Mar** (tel. 232–7722), near Drake's Bay on the northwest coast of the Osa Peninsula. Another option is **Leomar** (tel. 775–0230) in Golfito. Snorkeling equipment can be rented at several shops in Jacó, Manuel Antonio, and Drake's Bay.

Surfing Jacó has a decent beach break, but a better one can be found at Hermosa, 5 kilometers (3 miles) south. Escondida has a left and right reef accessible by boat from Jacó. **Jacó Beach Surf Shop** (tel. 664–3036) rents boards and sells wax. Pavones, two hours' drive south of Golfito, has a classic left point, so long that you can take a proverbial nap on it. Note that Sansa airlines now refuses to carry boards.

Walking Serious hikers can climb Chirripó or explore the Corcovado, La Amistad, and Golfito national parks (*see* Tour 2 and Off the Beaten Track, *above*). Manuel Antonio, Copey, and San Gerardo de Dota offer somewhat gentler expeditions.

White-water Rafting General River trips run from San Isidro to El Brujo—you camp en route—where the scenery is spectacular and the rapids are thrilling (*see* Sports in The Atlantic Lowlands, *above*, for rafting companies).

Beaches

The varied beaches of the Southwest are some of the best in the country (*see* Exploring, *above*, for individual beach descriptions). All are backed by lush tropical vegetation and have smooth white sand and large breakers (*see* Sports, *above*, for surfing information). Unfortunately, riptides are as dangerous here as anywhere else in Costa Rica—Jacó and Espadilla at Manuel Antonio are especially notorious. Riptides are characterized by a strong current running parallel to the shore at about waist depth and then out to sea for a hundred yards or so. The important thing to remember if you feel yourself being caught is not to struggle against it, but let it take you out to where its power dissipates beyond the breakers. Having conserved your strength, you should then be able to swim diagonally back to shore away from where the current has just brought you—i.e., still farther away from your original starting position.

Dining and Lodging

Dining With the possible exception of Manuel Antonio, the Southwest is not renowned for its gourmet cooking, but acceptable places to eat can be found throughout the area. Fruits of the region include pineapple and *mamón chino*, whose red spiky shells contain a succulent white fruit tasting like something between a lychee and a grape. Dress is casual in restaurants listed.

Highly recommended restaurants are indicated by a star ★. For ratings, *see* Dining and Lodging in Staying in Costa Rica, *above*.

Lodging Jacó and Manuel Antonio aside, most places to stay in the region are *cabinas* (cottages) or nature lodges, which offer varying degrees of comfort. Most of the latter are difficult to reach but spectacularly situated.

Highly recommended hotels are indicated by a star ★. For ratings, *see* Dining and Lodging in Staying in Costa Rica, *above*.

Dominical
Dining and
Lodging

Cabinas Punta Dominical. Perched on a point in the jungle overlooking rocky Dominicalito Beach, at the southern end of Dominical Beach, these tranquil cabins with ceiling fans are designed to complement their fine views. Each unit sleeps four people. The large airy restaurant-bar serves good food. *Apdo. 196, San Isidro de El General, tel. and fax 771–1903. 4 cabins with bath. Facilities: restaurant/bar. AE, MC, V. $$*

Golfito
Dining
★

Jardín Cervecero Alamedas. Installed in a former banana administrator's house in the American zone, Alamedas's combination of green-and-red tablecloths and white chairs hints at Italian patriotism. It is open-sided apart from a white trellis, allowing free passage of any transitory breeze. The fried rice, fish, and pasta dishes, served by a friendly staff, make this the pick of Golfito's restaurants. *100 meters (328 feet) south of airstrip, tel. 775–0126. No reservations. AE, DC, MC, V. $–$$*

Dining and
Lodging

Hotel Las Gaviotas. Just south of town on the water's edge, this hotel has wonderful views over the inner gulf. Bedrooms lead off a terrace overlooking the sea and have terra-cotta tile floors, white walls, firm beds, fans, air-conditioning, and patterned quilted bedspreads. Outside each room is a small veranda with chairs. The restaurant looks onto the pool, which has a terrace that is barely divided from the sea. *Playa Tortuga, Golfito, tel. 775–0062, fax 775–0544. 18 rooms with bath, 3 suites with kitchen areas. Facilities: restaurant, bar, pool, parking. MC, V. $$*

Lodging

Costa Sur. Slightly cheaper than Las Gaviotas and extremely convenient to the airstrip, Costa Sur is a white colonial-style hotel with rooms encircling a courtyard. The pristine bedrooms feature white tile floors, fans, and sloping wood ceilings. *50 meters (165 feet) south of airport, Golfito, tel. 775–0871. 24 rooms with bath. Facilities: bar, restaurant. MC, V. $–$$*

Jacó
Dining and
Lodging
★

Hotel Cocal. The cloistered bedrooms here are slightly pricier than those at El Jardín. However, they are newer, though still rustic in style, and surround a slicker, greener courtyard and two pools. Staying here is especially worthwhile if you manage to secure one of the three rooms facing the sea. The new U.S. owners are planning to add 16 rooms. The magnificent position of the upstairs restaurant only improves an already satisfying dining experience. *Playa de Jacó, tel. 664–3067, fax 643–3082. 29 rooms with bath. Facilities: restaurant, bar, pool, secure parking. AE, MC, V. $$–$$$*
El Jardín. The bedrooms of this small hotel, at the north end of the beach, are set in a cloister surrounding the pool. Their sloping paneled ceilings, red cement floors, white stucco walls, and dark furniture are easy to live with. The popular French restaurant is open-sided to take advantage of the sea breezes; it contains chunky wood furniture, a high thatched ceiling, heavy beams, and plants. To go with the fresh seafood you can select from an extensive list of

sauces—the menu suggests conventional combinations. Meat dishes include fillets and brochettes, again with an intriguing array of accompaniments. You can sip cocktails while you mull over your choice. It's quite costly but worth it. *Playa Jacó, tel. and fax 680–3050. 7 rooms with bath. Facilities: restaurant, bar. Dinner reservations recommended. Dress: casual. MC, V. Restaurant closed July–Oct., lunch, and Wed. $$*

Lodging **Hotel Jacó Beach.** If amenities are what you're after, this vast complex has them all. The modern building has seen better days, but it's next to the beach and contains comfortable, clean bedrooms, countless sporting facilities, and a disco. This hotel is chiefly the preserve of Canadian package tourists. New kitchen-equipped villas are an attractive option for families. *Apdo. 962, 1000 San José, tel. 220–1441. 130 rooms with bath, 29 villas. Facilities: restaurant, bar, tennis, pool, parking, surfboards, bicycles. AE, MC, V. $$$*

★ **Villas Miramar.** The 10 colonial-style white bungalows here surround Jacó's most attractive garden and pool. Each contains a double bedroom, bathroom, fully equipped large kitchen, and dining area. Decor is minimalist and seasideish: white walls, tile floor, and wooden beds. The unobtrusive but friendly owners are a further attribute. *Apdo. 124, Playa de Jacó, tel. 643–3003, fax 643–3617. 10 bungalows with bath and kitchen. Facilities: pool, garden, parking. MC, V. $$*

Tangeri Chalets. If there are several of you, Tangeri's eccentrically designed bungalows, which sleep six, offer good value. No longer in the first flush of youth, they are nonetheless clean enough and comfortable. The best part is the veranda dining patio; bedrooms are rather dark but perfectly okay. The beachside garden contains shady palms and two pools, seemingly the norm around here. Posh, new, air-conditioned, and comfortable bedrooms, without kitchens, go for the same price as whole bungalows. *Apdo. 622, 4050 Alajuela, tel. and fax 643–3636. 10 bungalows, 14 rooms with bath. Facilities: restaurant, pool, garden, basketball court, secure parking. AE, V. $–$$*

El Bohio. This is where boisterous young budget-minded itinerants stay. Most bedrooms are simple and rather dark, but adequate. More expensive, newer, larger units with kitchens are available, but frankly, if you're after this type of thing, you get far better value at Villas Miramar. El Bohio is well placed right on the beach; cabins surround an unkempt garden with a pool and a thatched bar. *Playa de Jacó, tel. 643–3017. 7 rooms with bath, 8 bungalows. Facilities: pool, bar, parking. No credit cards. $*

Las Tablas (Coto Brus) **La Amistad Lodge.** This remote, Swiss-style lodge, fashioned of shiny cristobal wood in the tiny border town of Las Mellizas, where blue mountains run crookedly into Panama, was once a private family home. Located on a 1,215-hectare (3,000-acre) farm in the Las Tablas reserve, bordering La Amistad National Park, it is a good base for venturing off into Costa Rica's least-explored territory. Walk the trails with a guide or relax beside a huge fieldstone fireplace in a second-floor salon. Rooms are sparsely but comfortably furnished, with firm beds. Packages include meals, tours, and round-trip land transportation from San José. *Apdo. 774–1000, San José; reservations c/o Tropical Rainbow Tours, tel. 233–8228, fax 255–4636. Facilities: restaurant, bar, parking. MC, V. $$$$*

Dining and Lodging

Manuel Antonio **Barba Roja.** With a reputation as lofty as its setting, Barba Roja's chief drawing cards are its sweeping view over the Manuel Antonio shoreline and its chic clientele. The partly open dining room is furnished with dark hardwoods; local landscapes hang on the walls.

Dining ★

Food takes a very close second to atmosphere; opt for one of the daily specials on the board. In recognition of the devastating effect that heat has on appetites, excellent sandwiches are served at lunchtime. Breakfasting here is also popular, not least because of the delicious whole-wheat toast. *Ctra. Quepos–Manuel Antonio, tel. 777–0331. Dinner reservations advised. V. Closed Mon. $$–$$$*

Dining and Lodging ★ **Hotel La Mariposa.** High on a promontory, Manuel Antonio's classiest hotel has even better views than its neighbor, Barba Roja: Here you can admire the inland hills as well as the shoreline. The main building is a white Spanish-style villa with an open dining room sporting pink and purple wicker furniture. The split-level units nestle into the steep garden and feature sitting rooms, balcony bedrooms, and conservatory bathrooms alive with plants. Outside each you'll find a veranda, hammock, and more plants. *Ctra. Quepos–Manuel Antonio, San José, tel. 777–0355, fax 777–0050. 10 villas with bath. Facilities: restaurant, bar, pool, parking. No credit cards. $$$$*

Hotel Plinio. This large wooden cabin, draped with jungle foliage, lies to the north of the Quepos–Manuel Antonio road, just outside Quepos. The bedrooms are set beneath a high, cool, thatched roof and have firm beds, wood floors, and varnished paneling. They're linked by a wide, covered balcony, with armchairs and large maps of the country. The jungle cabin with kitchen is more secluded and cheaper, if there are four or more of you (sleeps six). All prices include breakfast served in the popular restaurant, renowned for its home-baked German bread and spinach lasagna. *Apdo. 71, Quepos, tel. 777–0055, fax 777–0558. 13 rooms with bath, 6 suites, 1 cabin with bath. Facilities: restaurant, bar, pool. AE, MC, V. $$$*

Hotel Vela Bar. Ninety meters (100 yards) back from the first Manuel Antonio beach, the bedrooms here have white stucco walls, terracotta floors, wooden beds, fans, and framed tapestries. The apartments (sleep four) are a good value for groups. No views to speak of here—the hotel is neatly tucked away in the trees. A rustic rotunda restaurant remains popular as a vegetarian hangout, but also serves entrees like *pollo en salsa* (chicken in white sauce) and *plato típico* (rice, beans, salad, and meat of your choice). It is rather expensive for what you get, but prices are certainly not prohibitive. *Apdo. 13, Quepos, tel. 777–0413, fax 777–1071. 7 rooms with bath, 2 bungalows. Facilities: restaurant, bar, parking. AE, DC, MC, V. $–$$*

Lodging ★ **Villas Nicolas and Villas El Parque.** The more elevated of these tiered apartments—Mediterranean white with barrel-tile roofs—have wonderful views over the Pacific. Those at the bottom look out at the jungle. Half the units have well-equipped kitchens; all have terra-cotta and hardwood floors, modern printed textile furnishings, and seaward balconies. Some interconnect to form larger units. Waterfalls unite separate two- and three-tier pools. It's a tasteful, chic, and friendly place. *Apdo. 236, Quepos, tel. 770–481. 54 rooms with bath. Facilities: restaurant, pool, parking. AE, MC, V. $$–$$$*

Osa Peninsula *Dining and Lodging* **Drake Bay Wilderness Camp.** Situated on the Osa's northwest coast, close to where Sir Francis Drake landed some 400 years ago, this operation caters to fishermen, divers, bird-watchers, photographers, and biologists. The rustic cabins, which are set on the beach, have fans and hot water. The owners keep horses and equipment for fishing, diving, and snorkeling. Full board is compulsory. The owners will pick you up in San José or Quepos for a fee. *Apdo. 98–8150, Palmar Norte, Osa Peninsula, tel. and fax 771–2436. 20 cabins with bath, 4 tent cabins with shared bath. Facilities: dining room, sporting equipment for hire. MC, V. $$–$$$*

★ **Marenco Biological Station.** Eleven kilometers (7 miles) southwest of Drake, this is a private 500-hectare (1,235-acre) reserve, accessible only by boat from Dominical or Sierpe River, or by plane direct from San José. It functions as a research station, so you may be treated to an evening talk by a visiting expert. The wood and bamboo cabins are set into the hillside on stilts, with superb views of the Pacific and coastline opposite. They have polished paneling, leather rocking chairs, and balconies. The nearby Isla del Caño, donning a necklace of coral reef, makes for a perfect diving-snorkeling day trip. Other activities here include hiking, swimming, birding, and trips into Corcovado. *Apdo. 4025, 1000 San José, tel. 221–1594, fax 255–1340. 25 rooms with bath. Facilities: dining room. AE, MC, V. $$–$$$*

Bosque del Cabo. Sixteen kilometers (10 miles) south of Puerto Jiménez, these double-occupancy thatched bungalows are situated on a 40-hectare (100-acre) private reserve, half of it wooded. The area is visited by scarlet macaws and a host of other rare tropical creatures. Activities include horseback riding, sportfishing, surfing, and trips to Corcovado. *Tel. 222–4547, fax 735–5073. 6 rooms with bath. Facilities: dining room. No credit cards. $$*

Lodging **Cabinas Manglares.** Although fairly basic, this white, quasi-colonial group of cabinas is the most comfortable accommodation in Puerto Jiménez itself. The cabinas have cement floors, white walls decorated with artesania, fans, tables, and comfy wooden beds. A 10-minute walk will get you here from where the *lancha* (ferry) drops you, 150 meters (500 feet) west of the airport. *Tel. 735–5002, fax 735–5121. 9 rooms with bath. Facilities: restaurant, bar. MC, V. $$*

Parrita **Apartotel La Isla.** Situated between the sea and a mangrove river,
Lodging this hotel has a main building as well as modern white cabinas that
★ sleep six but are still good value for four. They're set well apart from each other, and since no other hotels exist in the vicinity, the beach is virtually deserted. Each cabina has tile floors, fans, a kitchen, two bedrooms, and rustic wooden furniture; you can cook either in your own kitchen or on the central barbecue. Activities include surfing, canoeing, and horseback riding. *Playa Palo Seco, Parrita, tel. 777–9016, fax 233–5384. 16 rooms with bath, 16 bungalows. Facilities: restaurant, bar, tennis, pool, Jacuzzi. AE, MC, V. $$–$$$*

Quepos **Hotel Quepos.** The only difference between this hotel and the
Lodging Ceciliano is that the rooms at Quepos have hardwood floors. It's located in front of the soccer pitch. *Apdo. 79, Quepos, tel. 777–0274. 13 rooms with bath. Facilities: TV lounge, safe parking. No credit cards. $*

San Gerardo **Cabinas Chacon.** Nearly 30 years ago, Efrain Chacon and his broth-
de Dota er bushwhacked their way through the mountains to homestead in
Dining and San Gerardo. With hard work and business acumen, they built a suc-
Lodging cessful dairy farm. Now a hotelier and staunch conservationist,
★ Efrain aids researchers and takes visitors on tours of his extensive farm. The tours provide a wealth of information on natural and polit-

ical history and nearly always include a quetzal-spotting. The cabins are comfortable and clean, and the main house has a bar with a fireplace and a veranda. Meals are included. Efrain will pick up guests from anywhere in the country for a fee. *Apdo. 482, Cartago, tel. and fax 771–1732. 14 cabins with bath. Facilities: restaurant, bar, parking. V. $$*

El Quetzal. If you have yet to spy this iridescent bird, these remote concrete cabins should afford you ample opportunities, being near to fruit trees where quetzals feed and roost. The cabins, one with a fireplace and the other with a wood stove, house between six and eight people, though you pay per person, and the fee includes three meals. A bare concrete floor and metal furniture offer little in the way of creature comforts, but there are a veranda with hammocks overlooking a stream, friendly owners, and creditable food. Look for the sign on the left, 4 kilometers (2½ miles) before the town. *San Gerardo de Dota, tel. 771–2376. 2 cabins with bath. Facilities: full board, parking. No credit cards. $*

Dining   **Los Lagos.** Across the street from his niece's cabins at El Quetzal, Ulises Monge has opened a restaurant with a limited menu built around freshly caught trout (try it fried or broiled, accompanied by rice and vegetables). The blue, family-style dining room has large windows that overlook a fountain filled with—you guessed it—live trout. Buy tart local apples and peaches grown on the Monges's farm. *No phone. No credit cards. $*

San Gerardo   **Posada del Descanso.** 100 meters (330 feet) beyond the ranger sta-
de Rivas   tion, Francisco Elizondo's bunkhouse is the best lodging option in
Dining and   San Gerardo. Guests sleep in bunk dorms or double-bed *cabinas*.
Lodging   The rate includes three meals daily served on the veranda. *San Gerardo de Rivas, tel. 771–0433, ext. 106 (leave a message arranging to call back). 3 bunk dorms with shared bath, 4 cabinas with bath. No credit cards. $*

San Isidro de   **Hotel del Sur.** This is a white, motel-style building with a red barrel-
El General   tile roof, 6 kilometers (4 miles) south of town. Although in need of
Dining and   refurbishing when inspected, it is the most comfortable option here,
Lodging   and considering the amenities, it's a good value. Bedrooms have plain carpets, white walls, black wood furniture, patterned bedspreads, and springy beds; those overlooking the verdant courtyard with a fountain are nicest. Bungalows farther back offer escape from the drone of the highway. *Apdo. 4–8000 San Isidro, P.Z., tel. 771–3033, fax 771–0410. 53 rooms with bath, 12 bungalows. Facilities: restaurant, bar, parking, pool, tennis, basketball, ping-pong, pool table. DC, MC, V. $$*

Hotel-Restaurante Chirripó. People-watching and honest tasty fare are the attractions of this veranda restaurant on the main square. Menu highlights include the generous *torta Española* (Spanish omelet with ham, mushrooms, and fried potatoes). The modern but sterile bedrooms are inferior to the Iguazú's, although some have views of Chirripó. *San Isidro, P.Z., tel. 771–0529. 24 rooms with bath, 17 rooms without bath. Facilities: restaurant, bar, parking. V. $*

Lodging   **Hotel Iguazú.** You'll find the newest and most economical in-town ho-
★   tel a couple of blocks north of the main square, opposite the Banco Nacional. The large bright bedrooms are spotless and have tile floors, firm beds, tables, and TVs. Ask for a west-facing window overlooking Chirripó. *San Isidro, P.Z., tel. 771–2571. 21 rooms with bath. No facilities. No credit cards. $*

San Vito
Dining and
Lodging
★
Wilson Botanical Garden. Accommodations here used to be restricted to spartan dormitories with bunk beds and tiny windows, facilities catering mainly to scientists on long stays. Thanks to some recent renovations, however, the original rooms are lighter and more pleasant, and an additional three cabins have been built. Rates are high for what you get, but staying overnight is the easiest way to see the garden at dusk and dawn, a highly recommended experience. *OTS Apdo. 676, 2050 San Pedro, tel. 240–6696. 2 rooms with bath, 7 rooms without bath, 3 cabins with bath. Facilities: restaurant, garden, parking. V. $$*

Hotel El Ceibo. El Ceibo's owner, Antonio, arrived here from Italy at age 2, and he'll readily chat about early San Vito life over the bar. His modern bedrooms are pleasant and clean—rubber mattresses are their only drawback—and the bathrooms have powerful, hot showers. Those upstairs off a white-painted veranda are nicest. The airy restaurant features a sloping wood ceiling, arched windows, wine trolley, and solidly good fare. Nearby are a bar, stools, TV, and sofas. *San Vito, tel. and fax 773–3025. 38 rooms with bath. Facilities: restaurant, bar, parking. MC, V. $*

Lodging
Cabinas Las Mirlas. These wooden cabins are set on stilts overlooking a creek and a wooded park. They have hardwood and tile floors, white walls, and hot-water showers. More basic than El Ceibo, they're also around half the price. Take the road that circles the Parque Educativo Aprenabrus and look for the sign on the left after 365 meters (400 yards). *San Vito, tel. 773–3054. 9 cabins with bath. Facilities: parking. No credit cards. $*

Tarcoles
Dining and
Lodging
★
Villa Caletas. Set atop a cliff, these striking white villas with black trim seem remote, but they are only minutes from Jacó and Carara National Park. Guest rooms are decorated in the French style, with fine antique wood furniture, black iron bedframes, and sweeping draperies. The villas built along the slopes all have astounding views of both rolling mountains and the ocean. An open-air restaurant serves international cuisine. A cleverly designed pool appears to blend into the horizon. *Apdo. 12358–1000, San José, tel. 257–3653, fax 222–2059. 8 rooms with bath, 14 villas, 1 suite. Facilities: restaurant, bar, pool, garden, parking. AE, MC, V. $$$$*

Tiskita
Dining and
Lodging
★
Tiskita Jungle Lodge. South of Golfito by 2½ hours (15 minutes by plane), Peter Aspinall has planted 100 different fruit trees from all over the world as a kind of research exercise into alternative exports for Costa Rica. For guests he has built wooden cabins on stilts, surrounded by screens and lush vegetation and equipped with rustic furniture and open bathrooms from which you can observe wildlife. Surfers are drawn here by the country's longest left-hand break, measuring 1,500 meters (4,920 feet); bring your own board. Trails allow you to safely explore the jungle and the veritable melange of wildlife lured by the fruit trees' fine pickings. Other activities include snorkeling (equipment available), swimming, and beachcombing. *C/o Costa Rica Sun Tours, Apdo. 1195, 1250 Escazu, tel. 255–2011, fax 255–3529. 12 cabins with bath. Facilities: dining room. AE, DC, MC, V. Closed Sept.–Oct. $$–$$$*

Trinidad
Dining and
Lodging
Albergue de Montaña Tapantí. These detached wooden cabins lie just outside the bounds of the Tapantí Reserve, but it's still a six-hour hike from the ranger station. They have wood floors, patterned bedspreads, and modern gray sofas. The views, cozy restaurant-bar, and good food make this a sensible halt on the route south, and a promising base from which to fish, bird-watch, and explore the surrounding countryside. You'll find it on the west side of the Interamerican Highway, 1 kilometer (⅝ mile) south of Trinidad.

Ctra. Inter Americana, Trinidad, tel. 233–0133, fax 222–0436. 6 cabins with bath, 4 rooms with bath. Facilities: restaurant, bar, parking, horseback riding, mountain biking. No credit cards. $$

Zancudo **Cabinas Sol y Mar.** A 20-minute walk south of where the boat drops
Dining and you, these beachside cabins are easily the nicest place to stay in
Lodging Zancudo. The owners have designed and built structures that look
★ like polyhedral space modules, furnished Oriental-style with ele-
gant charcoal clay tiles, wooden beds, and white canvas sofas.
Transportation can be arranged from the dock if you call ahead.
*Apdo. 87, Golfito, tel. 775–0353. 4 cabins with bath. Facilities: res-
taurant, bar. No credit cards. $$*

The Arts and Nightlife

The Arts The Fiesta de los Diablitos in Boruca, December 30–January 1, re-
enacts the struggle between the Indians (*diablitos*, or "little devils")
and the Spanish conquistadores (a bull made of sacks); on New
Year's Day the bull is symbolically killed and burned. On May 15,
San Isidros countrywide, including San Isidro de El General, honor
the patron saint of farmers with a blessing of animals and crops, and
fun fairs.

Nightlife Jacó is a lively town after dark—popular bar-discotheques include
La Central on the beach opposite Tienda La Flor, and **Upe** (tel. 643–
3002), on the road to the airport. The **Arco Iris Disco** (tel. 777–0449)
in Quepos and the disco at the seaside restaurant **Mar y Sombra** (tel.
777–0468) in Manuel Antonio are popular evening hangouts.

5 Guatemala

By David
Dudenhoefer

David
Dudenhoefer
is an
environmental
and travel
writer based
in Central
America and
the author of
The Panama
Traveler
(Windham
Bay Press).

Guatemala has been captivating visitors for centuries. From the time of conquistador Pedro Alvarado, who stopped between battles to marvel at the beauty of Lake Atitlán, to that of Aldous Huxley, who waxed poetic on the same lake's shores centuries later, this intricate jewel of a country has inspired its share of foreigners. While its physical beauty is impressive, it is its incredible diversity that makes Guatemala such an intriguing country to visit. In a matter of days one can stroll the cobblestone streets of an ancient colonial capital, barter with Indians who still speak the tongues of and worship the gods of the ancient Mayas, and explore the exotic web of life that constitutes the tropical rain forest.

Perched at the top of the Central American isthmus and anchored below the Yucatán Peninsula, Guatemala is divided politically into a number of departments or states, and divided topographically into a number of distinct regions: the Pacific Lowlands, the Western Highlands, the Verapaces, the desert of Zacapa, the Caribbean Lowlands, and the jungle region of El Petén. With a territory of 108,900 square kilometers (42,042 square miles), Guatemala is slightly larger than Ohio and is home to more than 9 million people. Within this relatively small and sparsely populated area you can find palm-lined beaches, luxuriant cloud forests, 37 volcanoes (several of which are active), rugged mountain ranges, tumultuous boulder-strewn rivers, a scrubby desert valley, and expansive stretches of rain forest that are home to spider monkeys, toucans, iguanas, and massive mahogany trees draped with mosses, ferns, vines, bromeliads, and rare orchids.

As dramatic as the varied landscapes that this country offers may be, its multifaceted human panorama is equally intriguing. Half of Guatemala's population is indigenous, and though the country's Indians have adopted at least some of the European customs forced upon their ancestors as long as five centuries ago, they remain some of the most dedicated protectors of indigenous culture in the Americas. All of Guatemala's Indians are Mayan, but at least 22 different ethnicities, differentiated by language, exist within that group. The other half of Guatemala's population is divided among Ladinos, the descendants of Europeans and Indians; Garifunas, a handful of African immigrants who live on the Caribbean coast; and the European minority, predominantly Hispanic, which has maintained its imported bloodline and colonial lease on power. This diversity creates a kind of multithreaded human tapestry, which makes Guatemala even more colorful than the Indian weavers' most intricate patterns suggest.

Guatemala's modern history has been largely the story of a struggle for land and political equality in the face of military rule. In 1944 Jorge Ubico, the last of the old-time strongmen, was deposed in a peaceful revolution. Elected in his place was schoolteacher Juan José Arévalo, who promised to modernize the country through education and agrarian reform. Arévalo was succeeded by Jacobo Arbenz, who accelerated land reform by daring to expropriate a small part of the vast holdings of the U.S.-owned United Fruit Company.

In 1954 the U.S. government, worried about what it perceived as Communist influences in the Arbenz administration, sponsored a successful coup that ousted the democratically elected president. The coup effectively closed the door on political participation for the majority for the next 29 years as one military or right-wing government after another staged fraudulent elections.

In 1961 dissident army officers attempted a coup in response to government corruption. Although the revolt was put down, it set the stage for a prolonged guerrilla war. By the late 1970s the guerrillas had begun to tap into long-held grievances of Guatemala's disenfranchised, landless peasants, most of them Indians. In response to the guerrillas' growing popularity, the government unleashed a violent campaign of genocidal intensity. In the 33 years since the start of the insurgency, as many as 120,000 people have been lost in massacres of entire villages and isolated disappearances on city streets. Thousands fled across the border to Mexico, where they remain refugees.

In 1983, having diminished the threat of a guerrilla victory and burdened by a troubled economy, the military allowed elections to be held. Despite the trappings of an electoral system, however, Guatemala's political situation remains at an uneasy status quo. Elections are marked by abstentionism of up to 85%, guerrillas continue to operate in isolated mountain villages and jungle regions, and state-sponsored extrajudicial killings continue sporadically. At press time (spring 1994) the government and leftist guerrillas were involved in intense peace negotiations under the moderation of the United Nations; the talks could produce a ceasefire in 1995. Currently, though, the country has a strong military presence that may unnerve visitors at first but poses no threat to them.

The presence of violent bandits, however, is a growing problem, especially along highways after dark or along footpaths to the more remote tourist sights. The need for proper precautions, however, should not dissuade visitors from experiencing a country that, perhaps better than any other, represents the beauty and diversity that is the New World.

Before You Go

Government Tourist Offices

In the United States INGUAT (299 Alhambra Circle, Suite 510, Coral Gables, FL 33134, tel. 800/742–4529; fax 305/442–1013).

In Canada SACA (72 McGill St., Toronto, Ont., M5B–1H2, tel. 416/348–8597).

In the United Kingdom Guatemalan Embassy (13 Fawcett St., London SW10 9HN, tel. 071/351–3042).

When to Go

Most travelers visit Guatemala during the summer (June–Aug.) and winter (Jan.–Apr.) high seasons. The busiest time of year is around Holy Week, from Palm Sunday to Easter Sunday, when hotels in Antigua, Panajachel, and Chichicastenango book up months ahead of time. The rainy season runs from May to November, with a few dry spells in July and August. A typical rainy-season day is sunny in the morning, cloudy at midday, and pouring through the afternoon and evening. Though occasional cold fronts roll south every winter, Guatemala's climate depends more on altitude than season. While the coasts and El Petén are hot and humid, the mountains are drier, with warm days and cool nights. The higher you go, the colder it gets. The following are the average daily maximum and minimum temperatures for Guatemala City.

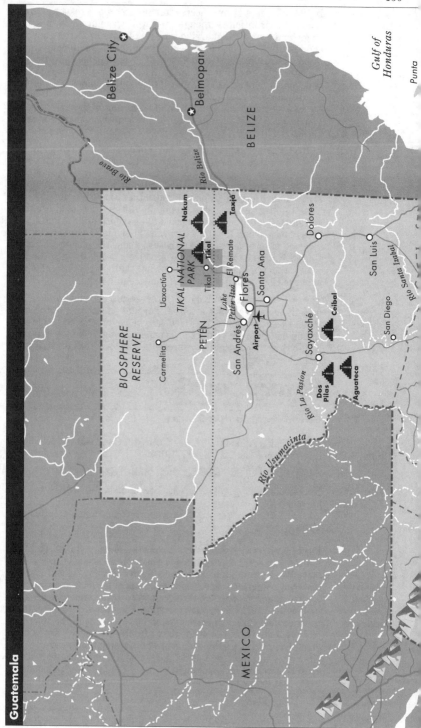

Guatemala

Jan.	73F	23C	May	84F	29C	Sept.	79F	26C
	52	11		60	16		60	16
Feb.	77F	25C	June	81F	27C	Oct.	76F	24C
	54	12		61	16		60	16
Mar.	81F	27C	July	78F	26C	Nov.	74F	24C
	57	14		60	16		57	14
Apr.	82F	28C	Aug.	79F	26C	Dec.	72F	22C
	58	14		60	16		55	13

Festivals and Seasonal Events

February: Antigua's biennial cultural festival (1995, 1997, 1999) sponsors a variety of artistic events held in the city's ruins and ancient buildings.

April: During Holy Week in Antigua, residents create colorful religious processions and reenactments of Christ's last days in Jerusalem.

September 15: Independence Day is celebrated with traditional music, dances, and costumes throughout the country.

November 1: On All Saints' Day you'll find huge kites flying from the cemetery of Santiago Sacatepequez, near Guatemala City.

December: Antigua hosts a series of processions in its streets during the weeks preceding Christmas.

Guatemalan Currency

The quetzal, named after Guatemala's national bird, is divided into 100 centavos. There are 1-, 5-, 10-, and 25-centavo coins. Bills come in denominations of ½, 1, 5, 10, 20, 50, and 100 quetzals. At press time (spring 1994) the quetzal was worth about 17¢—5.6 quetzals to a U.S. dollar. Traveler's checks and cash can be exchanged in banks and at most hotels (which give a lower rate than the banks), and cash can be changed on the street in the area around the Central Post Office for slightly more than the official rate, but it's illegal and you run the risk of being shortchanged. Unless otherwise stated, prices in this chapter will be quoted in U.S. dollar amounts.

What It Will Cost

Guatemala can be remarkably inexpensive, especially in the highlands. It is the least expensive country in this book, but as in Belize and Costa Rica, the first-class hotels have prices approaching those in developed countries. Trips into remote parts of the jungle or specialty travel like river rafting and deep-sea fishing are also relatively expensive.

Taxes Guatemalan stores, restaurants, and hotels charge a 7% value added tax, while most hotels and some tourist restaurants charge an added 10% tourist tax. When departing from Guatemala by air, tourists must pay a $10 (56-quetzal) exit tax.

Sample Costs Cup of coffee, 3 quetzals; bottle of beer, 5 quetzals; ½-kilometer taxi ride, 25 quetzals.

Passports and Visas

British, U.S., and Canadian citizens need a valid passport and a visa or tourist card to enter Guatemala. The best way to travel is with a tourist card, which can be purchased for $5 from the airline when departing your country or from immigration officials at the airport in Guatemala, though it's easier to pick one up at the airport of embarkation. A multiple-entry visa is needed if you arrive by land, and can be obtained from the Guatemalan consulate in your country. The tourist card allows you to stay longer. If you want to extend or replace a lost tourist card or visa, contact the Immigration Office (41 Calle 17–36, Zona 8, tel. 714–670) in Guatemala City.

U.S. Citizens For more information, contact the Guatemalan Consulate (2220 R St., NW, Washington DC 20008, tel. 202/745–4952). Other consulates are located in New York, Miami, Houston, San Diego, and Los Angeles.

Canadian For more information, contact the Guatemalan Consulate (1140 **Citizens** Maisonneuve O., Suite 1040, Montreal, Que. 113AIM8, tel. 514/228–7327).

British For more information, contact the Guatemalan Embassy (13 **Citizens** Fawcett St., London SSW10, tel. 351–3042).

Security

Although you are probably safer in Guatemala than in the average U.S. city, crime there is on the upswing.

In early spring of 1994 several women from the United States were attacked as part of a country-wide hysteria fueled by rumors that foreigners were stealing children to sell their organs. The U.S. State Department issued a travel advisory calling for extreme caution for visitors to Guatemala. It is still probably not a good idea for travelers to spend time with children in small villages when they are not accompanied by their parents.

The U.S. State Department's Bureau of Consular Affairs singles out pickpocketing and armed car theft as two major areas of concern. Keep a tight grip on your bags when in crowded areas such as open-air markets, particularly in Chichicastenango. A common ploy used by highway robbers is to construct a roadblock, such as logs strewn across the road, and then hide; when the unsuspecting motorist gets out of the car to remove the obstruction, he or she is assaulted. If you come upon an unmanned roadblock, don't stop; turn around. If you are stopped by thieves with guns, remain calm: Those who offer no resistance are usually not hurt. Visitors should also avoid intercity road travel after sunset and hire taxicabs only from stands located at the airport, major hotels, and main intersections. For the latest information on security conditions in the country and advice on the safest routes for traveling to popular sites, call the Citizens' Emergency Center in Washington, DC (tel. 202/647–5225).

Theft remains a problem, especially in the capital. It's not as rough as New York or Miami, but Guatemala City has plenty of hungry people, so be careful with precious articles while strolling in Zone 1, and don't wander that area's streets after midnight. On the other hand, Zone 10 is probably the safest zone in the city. Areas that attract large numbers of tourists usually draw people who prey on them, and Guatemala is no exception to that rule. Antigua can be dangerous late at night, particularly at the Cerro de la Cruz park. Both Agua and Pacaya volcanoes have been plagued by robberies and occasional violence. Most people who ascend them encounter no problems, but climbing those two volcanoes is not recommended. It should only be done with a guide and a guard, or on Saturday, when there's a crowd.

Customs and Duties

On Arrival Tourists may enter Guatemala with a camera, up to six rolls of film, any clothes and devices needed while traveling, 500 milligrams of tobacco, 3 liters of wine or other alcoholic beverages, and 2 kilograms of candy. But unless you bring in a lot of merchandise, customs officers probably won't even check your luggage.

On Departure Tourists are allowed merchandise valued at no more than $450 per person duty-free, including 2 bottles of liquor and 1 carton of cigarettes. No fruit or vegetables may be brought out.

Language

Spanish is the official language, but it is the mother tongue of only about half the population. The country's Indians speak one of more than a dozen indigenous languages, and most speak Spanish as a second language. In the area around the Caribbean town of Livingston, most people speak Garifuna, which is a mad mixture of African and European languages.

Car Rentals

Five international rental-car companies (**Avis, Budget, Dollar, Hertz,** and **National**) and five local companies (**Ahorrent, Rental, Tabarini, Tally,** and **Tikal**) have offices in Guatemala City, and most have representatives at both the Guatemala City and Santa Elena airports. Cars and Jeeps can also be rented in Antigua and in Santa Elena, El Petén, where **Hertz** (tel. 500–207) has an office in the Camino Real Tikal. Car rental companies include **Avis** (12 Calle 2–73, Zona 9, tel. 316–990, 312–747); **Ahorrent** (Boulevard Liberación 4–83, Zona 9, tel. 320–544, 327–515); **Budget** (Avenida La Reforma 15–00, Zona 9, tel. 316–546, 322–591, 312–788, 367–669, 343–411); **Dollar Rent a Car** (Avenida Reforma 6–14, Zona 9, tel. 348–285–7); **Hertz** (7 Avenida 14–76, Zona 9, tel. 322–242, 347–421, 315–412, 315–374); **National Car Rental** (14 Calle 1–42, Zona 10, tel. 680–175, 683–057); **Rental** (11 Calle 2–18, Zona 9, tel. 341–416); **Tabarini** (2 Calle A 7–30, Zona 10, tel. 319–814, 322–161, 316–108); **Tally** (7 Avenida 14–60, Zona 1, tel. 514–113, 23–327); **Tikal** (2 Calle 6–56, Zona 10, tel. 324–721).

Further Reading

For travel literature, try Ronald Wright's *Time Among the Maya* or Aldous Huxley's *Beyond the Mexique Bay*, which describes his travels in 1934. Nobel laureate Miguel Angel Asturias is the country's most famous author, and his works are full of history and cultural insight, namely *Weekend in Guatemala* and *Men of Maize*. Michael Coe's *The Maya* is an authoritative book on the lost societies of the region's prehistory, as is Eric S. Thompson's *The Rise and Fall of the Maya Civilization*. For information about the flora and fauna, try John C. Kricher's *A Neotropical Companion*. And for historical and political information, try James Painter's *Guatemala: False Hope, False Freedom*, or Jean-Marie Simon's *Guatemala: Eternal Spring, Eternal Tyranny*, which includes excellent photographs.

Arriving and Departing

From North America, Canada, and the United Kingdom by Plane

Airports and Airlines The country has two international airports: **La Aurora** (tel. 326–084–7), at the edge of Guatemala City, and the smaller Flores airport near Flores, in El Petén, which is a stop for some flights between the capital and Mexico. The main airport, La Aurora, is served by the following airlines: **Aerovias** (tel. 319–663), **American** (tel. 347–379), **Aviateca** (tel. 81–479), **Continental** (tel. 353–341), **Copa** (tel. 316–903), **Iberia** (tel. 320–911), **KLM** (tel. 370–222–4), **Lacsa** (tel. 346–905), **Mexicana** (tel. 336–001), **United** (tel. 322–995), **Sasha** (tel. 352–671), **Sam** (tel. 323–242), **Taca** (tel. 322–360), **Tapsa** (tel. 314–860), and **Tikal Jets** (tel. 345–631). There are direct flights to Guatemala from the following U.S. cities: Los Angeles, Dallas, Houston, New York, Washington, and Miami. Though no direct flights are available from the United Kingdom or Canada, connections can be made through U.S. airports.

Flying Time to Guatemala City From Miami it is 2½ hours to Guatemala City; from Houston, 4½ hours; from New York, 5½ hours; from San Francisco, 7 hours; and from Chicago, 5½ hours.

From the United States by Car, Boat, and Bus

It is possible to enter Guatemala by land from Mexico, Belize, El Salvador, and Honduras.

By Car The Interamerican Highway connects the country with Mexico at La Mesilla and with El Salvador at San Cristobal Frontera, and it passes through most major cities. It's also possible to travel to El Salvador via the coastal highway, crossing at Ciudad Pedro de Alvarado or via CA8 to Valle Nuevo. Pacific routes to Mexico pass through Tecún Umán and El Carmen/Talismán. On the Caribbean side, a daily minibus service operates from Santa Elena, El Petén, to Belize City and Chetumal.

By Boat The "back-door" route via the Usumacinta River into Mexico heads out of Sayaxche, in El Petén, where boats leave for Benemerito, Mexico. The route requires several days of jungle travel and is best done with a tour group. You'll have to get your passport stamped in Flores. There are also two routes into Honduras, through Esquipulas, or El Florido, near the ruins of Copán. A boat leaves from Puerto Barrios to Punta Gorda, Belize, departing on Tuesdays and Fridays at 7:30 AM.

By Bus There is bus service from Guatemala City to both the Mexican and Honduran borders and direct service to San Salvador. For bus service to La Mesilla, on the Mexican border: **El Condor** (tel. 28–504, 19 Calle 2–01, Zona 1, G.C.). Departures at 4, 9, 10, and 11 AM. 7-hour trip. For service to Tecún Umán, on the Mexican border: **Fortaleza,** (tel. 517–994, 19 Calle 8–70, Zona 1, G.C.). Hourly departures from 1 AM to 7 PM. Trip takes 5 hours. For service to El Carmen/Talismán, on the Mexican border: **Galgos** (tel. 543–868, 7 Avenida 19–44, Zona 1, G.C.). Departures 5:30, 10 AM, and 1:30 and 4 PM. Trip takes 5 hours. For service to San Salvador: **Melva International** (tel. 310–874, 3 Avenida 1–38, Zona 9, G.C.). Hourly departures from 5:30 AM to 4:30 PM. Trip time: 5 hours. For service to Esquipulas, on the border of Honduras: **Rutas Orientales** (tel. 537–282, 19 Calle 8–18, Zona 1, G.C.). Hourly departures 4 AM to 6 PM. Trip time: 4 hours. For El

Florido, take the bus to Chiquimula at 7 and 10 AM or 12:30 PM and change there.

From the United Kingdom by Plane

Most routes from the United Kingdom to Guatemala go via the United States using the airlines listed above. **KLM** flies to Guatemala from Amsterdam via the Netherlands Antilles.

Staying in Guatemala

Getting Around

By Plane The only commercial domestic air service is the route between Guatemala City and Flores, which connects the capital to the jungle region of El Petén. Four airlines (**Aviateca,** tel. 81–415; **Aerovias,** tel. 319–663; **Tapsa,** tel. 314–860 and **Tikal Jets,** tel. 345–631) fly to Flores, with flights leaving Guatemala City around 7 AM and returning around 4 PM; round-trip airfare runs about $150.

By Train Though there is train service to both coasts, it is sporadic and excruciatingly slow and is not advisable unless you're a fanatical train buff. Guatemala is served by a national rail service—**Ferrocarriles de Guatemala** (9 Avenida, 18–03, Zona 1, G.C., tel. 2/830–30). Service is not extensive, but it does go to the Mexican border town of Tecunumán. Contact the main office, or go to the government tourist office, IGUAT, for time tables.

By Bus Buses are the most widely used form of public transportation, with service covering almost every place that has a road. Buses range from comfortable tour bus–style vehicles complete with attendants selling snacks, to rundown converted school buses carrying twice as many people as they were built to hold, plus animals. Most interurban buses leave Guatemala City from private terminals scattered around Zone 1 or from the big terminal in Zone 4. For information on bus companies and schedules, *see* Getting Around in each city or regional section.

By Car A valid driver's license in your home country is all that's needed to drive legally. Roads to larger towns and cities are generally paved; you'll mostly find dirt roads leading to small towns. Four-wheel drive is a necessity in many remote areas, especially at the height of the rainy season. Gas stations are also scarce off the main roads, so be sure to fill up before heading into rural areas. Also, don't count on finding repair shops outside the major towns.

Keep eyes peeled for children or animals entering the road and for branches in the middle of the road, a signal to drivers that there is a stopped car or accident around the next bend (but don't stop for unmanned roadblocks; *see* Security, *above*). *Alto* (stop) signs or *tumulos* (speed bumps) are often found near military checkpoints; sometimes you may have to stop and let officials check you out. *Frene con motor* (brake with motor) means a steep descent lies ahead.

Parking Breaking into cars is common in the capital, so it's best to park in a guarded lot and avoid leaving anything of value in the car. All expensive and most moderate hotels have protected parking areas.

Telephones

Local Calls Pay phones take 10-centavo coins, but they are difficult to find even in the capital and major cities and are virtually nonexistent in most of the country. Though more expensive, it's easier to make local calls from your hotel. **Guatel** is the government phone company, and any decent-size town has a Guatel office, most of which are open daily from 7 AM to midnight. You usually have to wait to submit the number to the cashier, and then wait again to be called and directed to a booth.

In-country Calls When calling other parts of Guatemala from the capital, dial 0 first. When calling the capital from other parts of Guatemala, dial 02 before a five- or six-digit number.

International Calls Direct phones to AT&T operators in the U.S. are in the airport and at the Guatel office in Guatemala City's Zone 1. At any other phone, dial 190 for an **AT&T** operator, 189 for **MCI**, 195 for **Sprint International**, 198 for a Canadian operator, 121 for all other countries *or* for Guatemalan operator assistance (Spanish), and 124 for information (Spanish). When calling from abroad, dial 502–2 before five- or six-digit numbers for Guatemala City and 502–9 before the six-digit numbers used in the rest of the country. Phone calls can be made and faxes sent inexpensively in Antigua at the Villa San Francisco (1 Avenida Sur 15); in Panajachel at the Grapevine (Calle Santander); and in Quetzaltenango at the Tecun Saloon (Pasaje Enriquez off the Central Park).

Mail

Travelers can receive mail addressed to Poste Restante Guatemala at the main post office (Correos Central, 7 Avenida, 12 Calle, Zona 1, G.C.). Letters to the United States take from one to two weeks, slightly longer to Canada and the United Kingdom. Postage is inexpensive; a letter to the United States costs 30 centavos, and it's 1 quetzal to the United Kingdom. If you want to ship packages, it's safer to use a major shipping service like **UPS** (tel. 312–421 in Guatemala City, tel. 323–147 in Antigua) or a smaller service like **Quick Shopping** (6 Calle Poniente 27, tel. 320–697 in Antigua). Avoid express-mail services common in the capital. If you have to get something somewhere fast, use **DHL** (tel. 323–023 in Guatemala City), which is expensive but efficient.

To receive mail, American Express cardholders or traveler's-check holders can use the **American Express** office (Avenida Reforma 9–00, Zone 9, G.C., tel. 311–311); you must show your card or check when you pick up your mail.

Tipping

Gratuity is not included in restaurant bills, and it is customary to tip 10%. Bellhops and maids expect tips only in the expensive hotels. Guards who show you around ruins and locals who help you find hotels or give you little tours should also be tipped. Indians will often charge a quetzal to let you take their photo, which may seem absurd, but these folks are poor.

Opening and Closing Times

Banks Most banks are open from 9 to 3:30, although the branch offices of the major banks stay open until 8.

Museums Museums are open from 9 to 5.

Shops Most shops are open from 9 to 6, with a lunch hour from 1 to 2.

Shopping

Guatemala offers the shopper a mind-boggling selection of traditional handicrafts. The work of local artisans and weavers is usually called *típica*, which roughly translates as "typical goods." It can be remarkably inexpensive, though the asking prices are sometimes rather high. Every tourist town has an overabundance of típica shops, but better deals can usually be found on the street. Bargaining is the modus operandi of street vendors and is also common in the markets and many shops. A piece of sound advice on bargaining: Be patient. And if you didn't remember to buy something in the highlands, don't despair, the market in Guatemala City's Zone 1 has a little bit of everything at prices as low as you'll find anywhere else.

Guatemala's markets provide a wonderful glimpse into the everyday lives of the population. Vendors lining a jumble of narrow, warren-like passages hawk fruit and vegetables, flowers, meat, nuts, candles, incense, toiletries, and gaudy U.S.-made T-shirts. Markets are held on the following days:

Mon.: Chimaltenango, Zunil
Tues.: Comalapa, Sololá
Wed.: Santiago Sacatepéquez, Santa Lucía Reforma
Thurs.: Nahualá, Todos Santos Cuchumatán, Chichicastenango, Nebaj, El Quiché
Fri.: Patzún, San Francisco El Alto
Sat.: Patzicía, Totonicapán
Sun.: Tecpán Guatemala, Chichicastenango, Momostenango, San Cristóbal Verapaz

Sports and Outdoor Activities

Bicycling The highlands have great potential for mountain biking, but the amount of traffic on the country's few good roads makes touring a slightly scary idea.

Bird-watching More species of birds reside in Guatemala than in the United States and Canada combined, and birding easily complements any archaeological tour or beach excursion. The best guidebooks for bird-watching are *Birds of Mexico*, best purchased before your trip, or *Birds of Tikal*, which is available in many Guatemalan bookstores.

Fishing The Pacific coast offers excellent deep-sea fishing, especially for billfish and mahimahi. The Caribbean coast makes for good snook fishing, and Lake Atitlán has been stocked with black bass. **Izabal Adventures** (tel. 340–323) and **Jaguar Tours** (tel. 340–421) arrange fishing trips.

Hiking Many highland villages can't be reached by car, so hiking is the only way to explore much of the country. Likewise, many archaeological sites in El Petén are best reached on foot, though lowland hiking is a much hotter and muddier affair than its highland equivalent. A number of volcanoes make excellent climbs, some of which can be combined into trips of several days. Traveling with an adventure-travel company is a good way to avoid getting lost or robbed (*see* Tour Companies, *below*).

River Trips Countless white-water rivers, most of which have never been run, traverse Guatemala, as well as slow-moving lowland rivers that have been navigated for millennia. To add to the adventure, most of the popular rivers flow through lush tropical forests that abound with wildlife. The Dulce River, which flows into the Caribbean, is beautiful and easy to explore in a day. The Polochic and the Oscuro are two beautiful rivers that flow into Lake Izabal. Trips can be arranged through **Izabal Adventures** (tel. 340–323). The lowland Pasión and Usumacinta rivers, important trade routes of the ancient Maya, are easily navigated and pass important ruins. The Candelaria River (season: Mar.–May) runs through virgin forest and a fascinating series of caves. White-water rivers are rated on a scale of I to VI. Class I signifies no rapids; Class II, small rapids; Class III, difficult rapids with waves; Class IV, very difficult or advanced; and Class V, violent hydrolics for experts only. Class VI rivers are unrunnable. White-water rivers in Guatemala include Motagua and Naranjo (Class II–III; year-round), Cahabón (Class III–IV; year-round), and Chiquibul (Class II–III). Trips arranged by **Maya Expeditions** (tel. 947–951) include visits to nearby archaeological sites.

Ruins   The heart of the ancient Mayan empire is now the Department of El Petén, much of which remains covered with luxuriant tropical rain forest. Only a fraction of the estimated 1,500 ruins scattered across El Petén have been excavated at all, and all of them remain surrounded, if not covered, by the jungle. Aside from Tikal, travel to the ruins usually involves boat trips, horseback riding, hiking, or driving a four-wheel-drive vehicle down muddy roads, all of which makes the trip there an adventure in its own right.

Spelunking   An awesome selection of caves await the subterranean adventurer. Actun Kan, in El Petén, at Santa Elena, is very accessible, and Naj Tunich, near Poptun, has underground lagoons and carbon frescoes painted by the ancient Maya. Lanquin, in Alta Verapaz, is a mind-boggling collection of chambers, and the Candelaria River, also in Verapaz, passes through a series of caverns that are only accessible by water a few months of the year. In Guatemala, many caves remain largely unexplored.

Tennis   Several of the most expensive hotels in Guatemala City have tennis courts, as do the Ramada in Antigua, Hotel Atitlán in Panajachel, and the Camino Real Tikal near Tikal.

Tour Companies

Most of the dozens of tour companies that operate out of Guatemala City go to four main destinations—Antigua, Lake Atitlán, Chichicastenango, and Tikal—but some also offer tours off the beaten track, including adventure and natural-history treks. **Izabal Adventures** (tel. 340–323) probably offers the widest variety of specialized adventure and ecotourism expeditions for independent travelers: These include tours to remote archaeological sites, the Atlantic zone, plus river and sportfishing trips. **Expedición Panamundo** (tel. 317–641) has an extensive and well-organized system of operations, including camping tours, where participants travel by bus, of the entire Mayan region (Guatemala, Belize, and Mexico). **Maya Expeditions** (tel. 947–951) is the country's premier white-water rafting outfitter. **Intertours** (tel. 315–421) goes to Copán and Rio Dulce and adds interesting excursions to the traditional highland circuit. **Jaguar Tours** (tel. 340–421) offers a variety of Petén trips. **ATC** (tel. 536–014) has trips down the Usumacinta River that continue into Mexico. **Viva Tours** (tel. 341–612) offers fishing and volcano expeditions. **Caribbean International** (tel. 500–145) specializes in journeys to El Petén, Caribbean, and Alta Verapaz. **Centro**

de Reservaciones (tel. 80–887) has short excursions to Copán Rio Dulce, and the Quetzal Reserve. **Turansa** (tel. 953–575) runs one-day tours to Mixco Viejo and the Pacific archaeological sites. **Tropical Tours** (tel. 345–893) concentrates on Alta Verapaz. **Maya Tours** (tel. 352–797) specializes in adventure and archaeological tours.

Dining

Though all the expensive hotels and most of the moderate ones have restaurants, you can almost always find better cuisine at nearby restaurants, often for less money. Guatemala has a surprising selection of high quality, reasonably priced restaurants. Guatemala City has the kind of dining variety that one might expect from a major city center, but Antigua and Panajachel also have a remarkable number of fine restaurants, most of which have international menus or specialize in the traditions of another country or region. A few restaurants, however, specialize in Guatemalan cuisine.

The basis of Guatemalan food is corn, which is usually eaten in the form of a tortilla—a thin pancake hot off the grill—or as a tamale or on the cob. Beans accompany most meals, either whole in a sauce or mashed and refried. In restaurants these two items often accompany grilled beef or chicken. Turkey is a popular fowl, and in rural areas it's common to see *venado* (venison) and *tepezcuintle* (a large rain-forest rodent) on the menu. (Travelers should be aware that tepezcuintle is an endangered species, and the more it's ordered, the more it will be hunted down.) The most popular fish in the finer restaurants is the delicious *robalo*, known as snook in the United States, where it is strictly a sport fish. Meats are often served in *caldos* (stews) or cooked in a spicy sauce.

Ratings Prices are per person and include first course, entrée, and dessert, plus tax and tip. Drinks are not included. Highly recommended restaurants are indicated by a star ★.

Category	Cost
$$$	over $12
$$	$5–$12
$	under $5

Lodging

The level of comfort and quality of facilities ranges from the luxurious suites of the Camino Real to the stark rooms, tiny beds, and cold showers of the ubiquitous budget hotels. Most of Guatemala City's Expensive and Very Expensive hotels and restaurants are found in the new city, whereas most Moderate and Inexpensive hotels and restaurants are in the old city. Rooms in remote highland villages are rustic to nonexistent. Though there are few official campgrounds, you can camp anywhere. If you do, don't leave possessions unguarded if you're near villages.

Ratings Prices are for a double room, including all taxes. Highly recommended lodgings are indicated by a star ★.

Category	Cost
$$$$	over $75
$$$	$40–$75
$$	$15–$40
$	under $15

Guatemala City

The capital is a big, busy, and not-too-pretty city, and it is hardly the reason one visits Guatemala. However, it is almost unavoidable, since most tourists arrive and depart here, and travel from one region of the country to the next usually means passing through. Though the city as a whole isn't terribly attractive, it has some of the country's best hotels and restaurants, several excellent museums, occasional cultural events, a healthy nightlife, and all the amenities of the modern world that you might miss while exploring the country's less-developed regions.

A sprawling metropolis divided into 21 zones, this city of more than 2.5 million is intimidating when one first examines the map. But travelers have few reasons to stray from four central zones—1, 4, 9, and 10—which makes Guatemala City, or Guate, as the locals call it, much easier to manage. The area where tourists spend the most time can be divided into two basic units: the old city, which is centered on Zona Uno (Zone 1); and the new city, to the south, which comprises Zonas Nueve y Diez (Zones 9 and 10) and stretches up into Zona Cuatro (Zone 4), a sort of transition area between the new and old.

Those monuments and historic buildings that have survived this century's earthquakes are found in the old city, which is for the most part a crowded, slightly gloomy place that closes down pretty early. However, it has a certain amount of character and is convenient if you travel by bus. The new city is dominated by big, modern buildings, shopping centers, hidden mansions, and wide avenues like La Reforma, which separates Zonas 9 and 10. And Zona 10's "Zona Viva" is packed with fancy restaurants, bars, and discos that are busy until the wee hours, when the old city sleeps. The ideal thing would be to spend some time in each one, but the search for either comfort or low-budget digs tends to keep the luxury seekers in the new city and the deal seekers in the old. As far as the "foreign" experience goes, Zona 1 is definitely Guatemala, whereas the new city often seems more like the United States or Canada.

Arriving and Departing

La Aurora Airport, which is *too* close to the city—less than a mile from the heart of Zona 9 or 10—is where most tourists arrive and depart. But all roads lead to Guate, or so it would seem, so if you enter by land it's easy to drive or hop a bus to the capital (*see* Staying in Guatemala, *above*). A taxi to the airport from the heart of the city should run you about $5–$7.

Getting Around

It's an easy enough city to find your way around in if you stick to the central zones, where the *avenidas* (avenues) run north and south and the *calles* (streets) run east and west, Zona 4 being a bit of an aberration (streets here run at a 45° angle to the rest of the city). The major arteries of the city are 6 and 10 avenidas: 6 Avenida runs through the center of Zona 1, via Zona 4, into the heart of Zona 9, passing three series of identically numbered calles; 10 Avenida runs through Zonas 1 and 4 and becomes La Reforma. Most streets and avenues are numbered, and addresses are usually given as a numbered avenida or calle followed by two numbers separated by a dash, the first number being that of a nearby cross street or avenue, the second being that of the specific residence or business. Thus, 9 Avenida 5–22 is on 9 Avenida between 5 and 6 calles, and 9 Avenida 5–74 is on the same block, only closer to 6 Calle. A word of warning: Make sure you're in the right zone; different zones often contain identical addresses.

By Bus Guatemala City's bus system seems rather chaotic, but the buses are cheap and plentiful, and the locals are usually happy to point you to the one you need. The No. 82 route is an essential one for travelers: It connects the new city and old city by running down La Reforma and through the heart of Zona 1. Other buses also service La Reforma and will say REFORMA on the windshield; likewise, buses that say TERMINAL all pass by the main bus station in Zona 4. Some of the No. 83 buses go to the airport, but only the ones that are marked AEROPUERTO.

By Taxi Taxis park throughout the city, usually near major hotels, parks, or intersections, but they don't cruise the main roads, as in most large cities. Guatemalan taxis—usually beat-up ramshackle cabs of every conceivable size, make, and color—don't have meters, so it's best to negotiate your fare before getting in. To summon a cab by phone, call 203–42, 288–34, or 533–152 in Zona 1 or 312–867, 371–748, or 335–765 in Zonas 9 or 10.

Important Addresses and Numbers

Tourist Information INGUAT, Guatemala's government tourist office, (7 Avenida 1–17, Zona 4, tel. 311–339) is on the south end of a plaza containing modern government buildings. The office is open weekdays 8–4 and Sat. 8–1.

Consulates **U.S. Embassy** (Avenida La Reforma 7–01, Zona 10, tel. 311–541). **Canadian Embassy** (13 Calle 8–44, Zona 10, Edificio Edyma Plaza, 8th Floor, tel. 336–102). **U.K. Embassy** (7 Avenida 5–10, Zona 4, Centro Financiero Torre II, 7th floor, tel. 321–604).

Emergencies **Police** (tel. 120); **Red Cross** (ambulance) (tel. 125); **Fire Department** (tel. 122 or 123).

Hospital Hospital Herrera Llerandi, 6 Avenida 8–71, Zona 10, tel. 345–942 or 345–959. **Centro Médico** (6 Avenida 3–47, Zona 10, tel. 323–555).

Pharmacies When closed, all pharmacies should have a sign indicating which pharmacy in the area is *en turno* (open all night) that week. The following pharmacies are open 24 hours a day: **Farmacia San José,** 5 Avenida 16–56, Zona 1, tel. 25314; **Farmacia Exclusiva,** 7 Avenida 3–28, Zona 1, tel. 535–767; **El Sauce Las Americas,** Avenida Las Americas and Calle 23, Zona 13, tel. 315–996.

English-language Bookstores The bookstore in the **Camino Real** hotel has a small selection of English-language books, as do the bookstores **Cervantes** (Avenida La Reforma 13–70, Zona 9) and **La Plazuela** (12 Calle 6–14, Zona 9), which also sells used novels. **Vista Hermosa** (2 Calle 18–50, Zona 15) has a good selection of bird guides. The gift shop of the **Popol Vuh**

Museum has some interesting books, and there's a big collection of paperbacks that can be bought or borrowed from a bar by the name of **El Establo** (Avenida La Reforma 14–34, Zona 9). The **IGA** (Instituto Guatemalteco Americano, Ruta 1, 4–05, Zona 4, tel. 310–022) has an extensive English-language library, which is open to the public.

Guided Tours

Many major tour operators offer half- and full-day city tours, or day trips to nearby sites and cities, including **ATC Tours and Travel** (tel. 25–921), **Turansa** (tel. 953–575), **Jaguar Tours** (tel. 340–421), and **Tropical Tours** (tel. 345–893).

Exploring Guatemala City

Highlights for First-time Visitors

Cathedral (*see* Tour 1: The Old City)
Central Market (*see* Tour 1: The Old City)
Ixchel Museum (*see* Tour 2: New City and Museums)
National Museum of Archaeology and Ethnology (*see* Tour 2: New City and Museums)
Popol Vuh Museum (*see* Tour 2: New City and Museums)
Presidential Palace (*see* Tour 1: The Old City)

Numbers in the margin correspond to points of interest on the Guatemala City map.

As the capital is easily divided into two parts, two tours make sense for exploring it. The old city tour begins in the heart of town and works its way south toward the new city. The new city tour begins at the northern end of Zona 10 and ventures south to the museum complex in Aurora Park, at the southern end of Zona 9. The old city tour can be easily walked, but the new city's attractions are so spread out that either buses, taxis, or a car will be needed. Since quite a distance separates the old and the new, and few attractions appear in the distance between, drive or ride your way between them.

Tour 1: The Old City

The old city is centered on the Parque del Centenario and adjacent Plaza de las Armas, located between 6 and 8 calles and 7 and 5 avenidas, Zona 1. The park is dominated by a huge band shell, where military bands and musical artists perform. The plaza is basically an expanse of cement, with a parking garage underneath. To the north of the plaza stands the grandiose **Palacio Nacional** (National Palace), which was built by President Jorge Ubico between 1939 and 1943 and now houses the offices of the president and his ministers. The ornate stairways, stained glass, fountains, and quiet courtyards provide a pleasant contrast to the city beyond its walls. *Admission free. Open weekdays 8–4:30, Sat. 8–noon.*

To the east of the plaza stands the intriguing **Catedral Metropolitano** (Metropolitan Cathedral). Constructed from 1782 to 1868, it houses ornate altars, statues, and colonial religious art. *Admission free. Open daily 9–6.* To the west of the park is the modern National Library and military offices. To the south of the plaza is the Portal Comercio, an arcade packed with vendors, and behind the cathedral is the underground **Mercado Central** (Central Market), where handicrafts from throughout the country are hawked from overstocked stalls that line a seemingly endless maze of passages.

If you've got time, head one block north and a few to the east to the neoclassical church of **La Merced.** Walk inside to see the baroque-style interior of this church, which was consecrated in 1813, and wit-

Guatemala City

ness the array of elaborate paintings and sculptures, many of which once decorated the original La Merced church in Antigua. *11 Avenida and 5 Calle. No phone. No admission fee. Open 6 AM–7 PM.*

From here, return to the plaza, and head south on 6 Avenida. Lined with shops and restaurants, it's a good area to stop for a meal.

Time Out   The restaurant **Rey Sol** (8 Calle 5–36, Zona 1) offers amazingly inexpensive buffet-style vegetarian lunches in a pleasant cafeteria setting. Specialties include spinach lasagna and stuffed chilies. It also has freshly baked breads and cakes, soy milk, and fruit juices.

❺ One block to the east of 6 Avenida at 12 Calle is one of the city's prettier buildings—the big pink **Edificio de Correos Central** (Main Post Office), which deserves a visit even if you've got nothing to drop in the slot. It's open weekdays 8–7 and Sat. 8–3. On the corner of 6

❻ Avenida and 13 Calle stands the church of **San Francisco,** constructed between 1800 and 1851, with its ornate wooden altar and small museum. To the south, notice the **Cuartel General de la Policía** (Police Headquarters), a massive medieval-looking structure that seems an appropriate metaphor for the state of the Guatemalan justice system.

A couple of blocks to the south is a small park, which is a good spot to get a taxi. If you want to continue walking, stay on 6 Avenida. You'll pass the old Tipografía Nacional, the government's press center, a few blocks down, and beyond that, the main food market. Beyond the

❼ long, blue building atop a hill on the right is the **Miguel Angel Asturias Culture Center** (tel. 240–44). It houses several theaters and a small museum of antique arms. On the left, on 7 Avenida just south

❽ of the railroad bridge, is the **Tourist Office** (tel. 311–339; open weekdays 8–4, Sat. 8–1), which carries maps and brochures and dispenses invaluable advice. Buses to the new city stop on 6 Avenida below the Culture Center; take one that says REFORMA.

Tour 2: New City and Museums   If you've got the time, start with a visit to the **Jardines Botánico** (Botanical Gardens), a small but lovely garden with an impressive collection of plants and a little Natural History Museum, all run by the

❾ University of San Carlos. *Just off the Avenida La Reforma on Calle 0, at the northern end of Zona 10. Admission: 5¢. Open weekdays 8–4.*

From the Botanical Gardens, head south on La Reforma, the wide boulevard that separates Zonas 9 and 10. Even though it is just a few blocks, you may want to take a taxi west to the end of 6 Calle, a steep

❿ hill that bottoms out into the new **Museo Ixchel.** This modern museum is probably the city's best, with extensive exhibits on the country's indigenous population, especially on its weaving and traditional costumes. In addition to an impressive collection of native textiles, the museum contains art exhibits, photos of religious processions, and an anthropology library. *6 Calle Final, Zona 10, tel. 313–792. Admission: $2. Open weekdays 8–5, Sat. 9–1.*

Once back on La Reforma, head south three blocks, then cross the street to the south of the Edificio Galerías, a large, modern building

⓫ in which the sixth floor houses the **Museo Popol Vuh.** Though smaller than the National Archaeology Museum, the Popol Vuh is much more informative and displays its collection of Maya artifacts masterfully. *Admission: $1. Open Mon.–Sat. 9–5.*

⓬ Another block south of the museum, on the other side of La Reforma, marks the beginning of the **Zona Viva,** the area between La Reforma and Zona 10's 4 Avenida and 10 and 14 calles. This posh area of shops, restaurants, bars, and dance clubs is the liveliest part of the country on weekend nights and is fun to visit anytime.

Time Out **La Tertulia** (Avenida La Reforma 10–31, Zona 10, tel. 64–057) is at the edge of the Zona Viva. It serves international cuisine at very reasonable prices. Daily lunch and dinner specials are a steal.

From the Museo Popol Vuh, you'll need a taxi to reach the museums of Aurora Park, to the southwest. The most important of these is the

⑬ **Museo Nacional de Arqueología y Etnología** (National Museum of Archaeology and Ethnology), a large museum dedicated to the ancient and modern Maya. It features an impressive collection of Mayan artifacts—pottery, jewelry, and clothing—as well as models of the ancient cities themselves. Across the street is the **Museo de Arte Moderno** (Modern Art Museum), which has some interesting works by Guatemalan artists, and nearby is the **Museo Nacional de Historia Natural** (National Museum of Natural History), with a long-neglected collection of old stuffed animals, plants, and minerals. *All these museums charge a small admission. All museums open Tues.–Fri. 9–4, weekends 9–noon and 2–4.*

Off the In Zona 2's Minerva Park, you'll find the **Relief Map**—an immense
Beaten Track cement map of Guatemala depicting the country's precipitous topography. Constructed in 1904, this map is so large, it must be viewed from observation towers.

Kaminaljuyú (in the heart of Zona 7) is the site of an early Maya city, which flourished from 300 BC to AD 900. Though little survives of the city that was once home to some 50,000 people (most of it is buried beneath the urban sprawl), the site offers a glimpse of the area's prehistory, and some of the objects found here can be seen at the Archaeological and Popol Vuh museums. To get here, take Bus 32A from Zona 1.

Shopping

Antiques **Casa San Antonio** (2 Avenida 12–75, Zona 10), **Centro Comercial de las Máscaras** (13 Calle 2–01, Zona 10), **El Patio** (12 Avenida 3–39, Zona 1), and **Collection 21** (13 Calle 2–75, Zona 10) are all good bets. Be advised that it's illegal to take pre-Columbian and colonial artifacts or antiques out of Guatemala. Post-colonial works—anything made after 1820–can be exported.

Jewelry The cheapest jewelry is sold in the **Central Market** and in the stores that line the passages south of the Plaza de Armas. You'll find mostly hand-crafted silver embellished with local stones. Designs range from Maya reproductions to modern. The city's better jewelers include **El Angel Diamantino** (Geminis Mall, Zona 10), **Jades S.A.** and **La Esmeralda** in the Camino Real Hotel, **El Sol** (13 Calle 2–75, Zona 10), and **Sombol** (Avenida La Reforma 14–14, Zona 9).

Leather For inexpensive leather goods, check out the **Central Market.** Shops selling fine leather products include **Arpiel** (Avenida La Reforma 15–54, Zona 9; Avenida Americas 7–20, Zona 13; 11 Calle 5–38, Zona 1), **Boutique Mariano Riva** (12 Calle 1–28 and Avenida La Reforma 15–54 in Zona 9), and **Tata** (Avenida La Reforma 12–81, Zona 10).

Típica The best selection and prices for handicrafts can be found in the **Central Market,** behind the cathedral, though some people might feel claustrophobic in its narrow, crowded passageways. An above-ground alternative is the **Handicrafts Market** on 6 Calle in La Aurora Park. A number of stores in the city sell handicrafts and European styles mixed with traditional weaving. **Sombol** (corner of 14 Calle and Avenida La Reforma, Zona 9) has an impressive collection of clothing, textiles, jewelry, and paintings. The smaller **El Gran Jaguar** (14 Calle 7–49) is across the street and down a bit. **Típicos Reforma Utatlán** (14 Calle 7–77) and **Galerías La Montaña** (2 Calle 6–26, Zona 13) are on the same block. Across La Reforma, in Zona 10, there are several small típica shops at the corner of 1 Avenida and 13 Calle. One block south is **Bizzarro** (14 Calle 0–61, Zona 10). **Galería El Dzunun** (1 Avenida 13–29) incorporates traditional weaving into elegant women's clothing, and **Belloto** (Avenida La Reforma 11–07) has a creditable selection. In Zona 1, try **Mayatex** (11 Avenida 4–50, Zona 1), **Yaman Munil** (12 Calle "A" 0–10), **La Momosteca** (7 Avenida 14–48), **Maya Modern** (corner of 7 Avenida and 9 Calle), **Lin Canola** (5 Calle 9–60), and **Maya Sac** (6 Avenida "A" 10–39, 2nd Floor).

Sports

The hotels Camino Real, Guatemala Fiesta, and El Dorado all have tennis courts, workout rooms, saunas, Jacuzzis, swimming pools, and massage therapy. El Dorado also has squash and racquetball courts. Hotel Las Américas has a swimming pool as well, and a public pool is located in Minerva Park. The best area for jogging is La Aurora Park.

Dining

Being the largest city in the country, the capital has the best selection of good restaurants and the widest variety of specialty cuisines. Inexpensive restaurants are mainly in Zona 1, Expensive ones in Zonas 9 and 10. If you are dining at an expensive restaurant, reservations are recommended on weekend nights. Dress is informal across the board—even the more expensive establishments don't require jacket and tie. The following is a sampling of what the capital has to offer.

New City Dining
$$$

El Pedregal. When one steps into this premier restaurant, the modern atmosphere of the Zona Viva seems to fade away. The main dining room of El Pedregal is an enclosed courtyard, with a fig tree at its center and gardens lining the edges, which soften an atmosphere dominated by stone. Leather chairs lend to the elegant gaucho ambience, and a small fountain babbles at one end of the room. In the back are two smaller dining rooms, and the one on the left opens onto a garden courtyard with a fountain. The cuisine is unmistakably Mexican, but the menu ranges from the traditional fajitas to *camarones especiales* (shrimp marinated in cognac, stuffed with cheese, and tied in bacon strips). Service is impeccable. *1 Avenida 13–42, Zona 10, tel. 680–663. AE, DC, MC, V.*

★ **Jake's.** Owner and chef Jake Denburg is a painter who has turned his creative powers to cooking. A converted old farmhouse with hardwood ceilings and tile floors is the setting for his complex, carefully prepared meals. The Italian and international menu is augmented by 25 daily specials, ranging from handmade tortellini filled with smoked chicken and spices to *robalo* (snook) in a green-pepper sauce. Jake has focused much of his artistry on fish; his crowning achievement is the *robalo Venecia royal*, which comes in a creamy shrimp sauce over a bed of spinach. All of the vegetables are organically grown here—one of the few places in Guatemala where a traveler can enjoy a salad without fear. *17 Calle 10–40, Zona 10, tel.*

680–351. Reservations advised. AE, DC, MC, V. Closed Sun.-Tues.

★ **Jean François.** Although this restaurant does not identify itself with a sign, it's been full since the day it opened. Inside the main dining room, chairs embroidered with flower patterns, hand-carved wooden cherubs on the walls, and gold stars on the ceiling give the restaurant an easy charm. For a more intimate setting, candlelit tables are set in an outside patio. The rich Provençal cuisine features mouthwatering appetizers such as shrimp soufflé in a spinach jacket, and chicken mousse with lemon, blue cheese, and nuts. For a main course, try the ravioli filled with mushrooms and chicken or the *robalo le clasique*, a delicate fish fillet sautéed in butter, fresh green herbs, and spices. *Diagonal 6, 13–63, Zona 10, tel. 334–785. Reservations advised. DC, MC, V. Closed Sun. and dinner Sat.-Tues.*

La Cúpula. The colonial-style building looks a bit out of place in Zona 9, but once inside, you'll leave the city far behind. The *cúpula*, a sort of chimney, rises out of the center of the restaurant where the cooking area would traditionally be but instead is filled with the verdure of potted plants. The white stucco walls parade the work of Guatemalan artists, and antique silver trays and pitchers rest on wooden ledges. Figure on predominantly Italian foods, with items like *gnocchi* (dumplings) in pepper cream sauce, but you can also eat seafood such as lobster Thermidor and shrimp Veracruz. *7 Avenida 13–01, Zona 9, tel. 319–346. AE, DC, MC, V. Closed Sun.*

Mario's. Owner and chef Mario Morillo is a Spaniard who moved to Guatemala 10 years ago after quitting his post as head chef at one of Madrid's best clubs. The menu is one of the more varied and original in the country, ranging from appetizers like garlic mushrooms to entrées such as roast suckling pig and the traditional paella. Mario's robalo is a standout—the premier local fish served with a special mushroom sauce. *1 Avenida and 13 Calle, Zona 10, tel. 321–079. AE, DC, MC, V. Closed Sun.*

Romanello's. A quiet but popular spot in the heart of the Zona Viva, Romanello's serves a limited but well-prepared selection of the country's best meat and seafood. The restaurant has a simple but elegant decor, with pink stucco walls, wooden floors, arched doorways, and a few antiques. One table at the back overlooks an attractive shopping area with a small garden. There is no menu, but guests usually choose from tenderloin, robalo, lobster, and a pasta dish, all of which can be prepared to order with a number of sauces. *1 Avenida 12–70, Zona 10, no phone. AE, DC, MC, V. Closed Sun.*

$$ **Don Emiliano.** This small steak house at the edge of the Zona Viva is popular with the locals, thanks to the quality and quantity of its servings. The restaurant looks like a log cabin from the outside, and the inside sustains the pioneer motif with lots of varnished wood, a palm-bark ceiling, and western posters on the walls. Two floors of tables accommodate the customers, who head here for the steaks, barbecued ribs, shrimp, and chicken. *4 Avenida 12–70, Zona 10, tel. 326–467. DC, MC, V.*

El Parador. Traditional Guatemalan cuisine is served at two locations in Zona 9, with a menu that includes lots of grilled meat, served with *elote* (corn on the cob) and guacamole, plus items like chili relleno (stuffed pepper) and enchiladas. The 12 Calle restaurant has a rustic ambience, with a high thatched roof, several small gardens along the edges, and a woman cooking tortillas near the entrance. The Reforma locale has a mahogany ceiling, white-stucco walls, and colorful woven tablecloths. Both restaurants offer marimba music at mealtimes. *12 Calle 4–09 and Avenida La Reforma 6–70, Zona 9, tel. 320–062. AE, DC, MC, V.*

Excellent. One of the city's best Chinese restaurants, this place has a relatively small but resourceful menu, with items like beef with mango sauce, green peppers stuffed with shrimp, and conch with cashews. The decor is nothing to write home about, but the food makes up for any lack of ambience. *Corner of 2 Avenida and 13 Calle, Zona 10, tel. 364–278. AE, DC, MC, V.*

★ **Olivadda.** In this ideal lunch spot, tasty Mediterranean cuisine is served in a tranquil patio setting, with a melodic fountain surrounded by flowers and hummingbirds. Traditional Middle Eastern appetizers such as tabuleh, babghanouj, and falafel can be followed by a chicken-breast sandwich with cumin dressing or kafta in pita, delicately spiced beef patties served in pita bread with tahini dressing. For dinner, don't miss the *linguini à la Cataflana*, linguini with clams simmered in white wine, Spanish sausage, and tomatoes. Finish your meal with a baked apple stuffed with almond and cinnamon and baked with orange juice and honey—a delicious apple pie without the calories. *12 Calle 4–21, Zona 10, tel. 310–421. AE, DC, MC, V.*

Pizzeria Vesuvio. The best pizza in Guatemala City can be found here, baking in open-brick ovens. Vesuvio has three locations in the city, but this one, in Zona 10, is the most comfortable. In a family living-room atmosphere with scenes of Naples on the walls, diners can choose from a variety of pizza toppings or one of several pasta dishes. All of the pasta is made in-house. A grand pizza, sufficient for two people, ranks as one of the best cheap meals in the city. *18 Calle 3–36, Zona 10, tel. 371–697. DC, MC, V.*

Old City Dining
$$
★

Altuna. This popular restaurant in an old house a block off 6 Avenida serves a predominantly Spanish menu in a pleasantly hustle-bustle atmosphere. Waiters move briskly about in white jackets and ties in the main dining area—a covered courtyard surrounded by a wooden railing and potted plants—or in several adjacent rooms decorated with Iberian paintings, photographs, and posters. The menu is fairly limited: Consider the calamare, filet mignon with mushroom sauce, or paella. Prices lean toward the low end of the moderate price range. *5 Avenida 12–31, Zona 1, tel. 20–669. AE, DC, MC, V. Closed Mon.*

Arrin Cuan. Guatemalan cuisine typical of the Cobán area is served from these two restaurants located just half a block apart. The 5 Avenida restaurant is the more pleasant of the two: Its walls are drenched with brightly colored, handwoven fabrics, wooden masks, and Guatemalan art. Harp or marimba music plays, and every table is set with flowers in soda-bottle vases. The 4 Calle locale lacks much of the charm of the one around the corner (you'll miss out on the dulcet tones of live music here). Both serve the same extensive menu, with items such as *kak-ik* (a spicy turkey stew) and *gallo en chicha* (chicken in a slightly sweet sauce). *5 Avenida 3–27 and 4 Calle 4–79, Zona 1, tel. 80–242. DC, MC, V.*

El Gran Pavo. You can't miss this pink building topped with neon. You'll soon discover that the inside is just as flashy as the facade. Bright colors bedazzle the innocent initiate; a few mirrors and plants, Mexican hats, and blankets bestow the walls with even more spirited brilliance. The food is authentic Mexican, with the standard *taquitas* (tacos), enchiladas, and moles, but you'll also run across items like *aujas nortenas* (grilled beef strips covered with a red sauce and surrounded by avocado slices) and *camarones siempre joven* (shrimp in a spicy black chili sauce). It's open past midnight and has live music as well as mariachis who often perform private concerts for a small fee. *13 Calle 4–41, Zona 1, tel. 29–912. AE, DC, MC, V.*

Los Cebollines. A wide selection of delicious Mexican food is the attraction at Los Cebollines, which has, however, a rather banal decor. Two menus—a drink menu that includes cocktails, Mexican beers, and sangria; and a food menu that lists traditional tacos, burritos, fajitas, and, less predictably, *caldo tlalpeno de pollo* (a chicken stew with chick peas and avocado)—are available. *6 Avenida 9–75, Zona 1, tel. 27–250. AE, DC, MC, V.*

$ **Café de Imeri.** This elegant establishment across the street from Godspell is about as different from its neighbor as it can get. The old house with barrel-tile roof and wooden balcony has seating in an indoor setting or in a luxuriantly planted courtyard with a small fountain at one end. The menu is light—mostly sandwiches and soups—but has some wonderful cakes, pies, and coffee for dessert. *6 Calle 3–34, Zona 1, tel. 23–722. No credit cards. Closed Sun.*

El Mesón de Don Quijote. A colorful restaurant in the heart of the old city, Don Quijote not only serves respectable food at reasonable prices but is a favorite late-night spot of older Guatemalans, and it obliges them by staying open until 2 AM. The restaurant has a long bar and several adjacent rooms for dining. Live music plays at night, and an organist entertains the lunchtime crowd. The menu is large: Choose from fried fish, liver and onions, Spanish tortillas, lentils with sausage, and paella (for four people or more). *11 Calle 5–27, Zona 1. DC, MC, V. Closed Sun.*

Europa Bar and Restaurante. This second-floor bar has long been a hangout for travelers and members of the American expatriate community. The owner, Oregon native Judy Strong, creates a pleasant and welcoming atmosphere where customers can relax, play backgammon, or watch a sports event on cable TV. There's a functional American menu with mainstays like hamburgers, chili, *pollo migado* (breaded chicken), and mashed potatoes, and a U.S. diner-style breakfast of pancakes or bacon, eggs, and hash browns. *11 Calle 5–16, Zona 1, tel. 534–929. No credit cards. Closed Sun.*

Godspell. Despite its unlikely name, this restaurant serves typical Guatemalan food at incredibly low prices. The decor is very basic, and the blaring stereo may put you off, but the menu is honest-to-goodness Guatemala, with dishes like *pollo pepian* (chicken in a dark sauce), chili relleno (stuffed pepper), or *marrano* (roast leg of pork). Boquitas (hearty snacks) come with every drink. *6 Calle 3–49, Zona 1, tel. 84–770. No credit cards. Closed Sun.*

Lodging

New City Lodging $$$$

Camino Real. With luxurious rooms, several restaurants and bars, a shopping arcade, and an array of services, the Camino Real is comfortable, convenient, and cosmopolitan. One enters the hotel through a foyer with a low wooden ceiling and wood-and-mirror walls, which leads to a more spacious lobby with a view of the main swimming pool and a series of passageways heading off to bars, restaurants, shops, galleries, and the spa. Carpeted rooms are done in green and brown pastels and furnished with stately carved wooden pieces. All units have electronic locks, tiled baths, cable TV, and a minibar. *14 Calle and Avenida La Reforma, Zona 10, tel. 334–633, fax 374–313. 378 rooms. Facilities: 2 restaurants, bar, disco, 2 pools, spa with sauna and massage, 2 tennis courts, shopping arcade. AE, DC, MC, V.*

El Dorado. Though its exterior is hardly attractive, El Dorado looks quite different inside. A small lounge to the right of the lobby offers rest to the weary: Guests plop down in the couches and armchairs and order cocktails each evening when jazz is played. Beyond the lobby are the bar, restaurants, shops, offices, and the Cabana Club, an extensive spa and sports facility open to all guests. Rooms are carpeted, with pink, purple, and green floral patterns on the drapes and bedspreads. All have small balconies, cable TV, and tiled baths. *7 Avenida 15–45, Zona 9, tel. 317–777, fax 321–877. 259 rooms with bath. Facilities: 2 restaurants; bar; disco; pool; spa with sauna, Jacuzzi, and massage; tennis, racquetball, and squash courts. AE, DC, MC, V.*

★ **Hotel Las Americas.** Built in 1993, this is the most modern luxury hotel in Guatemala City. Conveniently located just 3 kilometers (2 miles) from the Aurora Airport, it displays a splendid vista of the surrounding volcanoes. Two giant glass elevators in the middle of the atrium-style lobby ascend to a dizzying view of the city and adjacent residential areas. The rooms on the south side of the hotel offer the most impressive views of the airport, with Agua and the active Pacay volcanoes in the background. The bright, modern rooms are decorated with pale-green carpeting and walls of whitewashed wood; all have a minibar and a cable TV. The hotel is located near several shopping centers, bars, and restaurants. *Avenida Las Americas 9–08, Zona 13, tel. 390–666; in U.S., 800/327–3573; fax 390–690. 200 rooms with bath. Facilities: restaurant, bar, pool spa with sauna, Jacuzzi, art gallery, shopping arcade. AE, DC, MC, V.*

$$$ **Hotel Pan American.** Some people may be put off by this hotel's location on the busy 6 Avenida in the heart of Zona 1, but to step into the lobby of this traditional inn is to leave the confusion of the city behind. The lobby is a spacious covered courtyard, half of which holds tables from the restaurant, where waiters and waitresses dressed in traditional costumes serve the guests. Rooms are small but attractive, with tile floors, soft beds covered with highland blankets, cable TVs, and walls decorated with traditional weavings and paintings. *9 Calle 5–63, Zona 1, tel. 26–807, fax 26–402. 60 rooms. Facilities: restaurant, cable TV. AE, DC, MC, V.*

Residencia Reforma. Also known as the Casa Grande, this comfortable hotel in a stately former residence is a wonderful alternative to the modern lodgings that predominate in the new city. One enters the grounds through iron gates: Both the classical statue at the center of the circular driveway and the manicured lawn and gardens enhance the beauty of the white mansion before you. A comfortable lounge with a fireplace is situated just past the reception area. The restaurant is in the former courtyard, with cast-iron chairs surrounded by stout pillars and arches and the verdure of dangling philodendron against the white walls. The rooms have tile floors and white walls decorated with Guatemalan art; they are furnished with antiques and antique reproductions. In front, units open onto a balcony, but the back rooms are quieter. Numbers 13 and 16 are next to a small garden courtyard. *Avenida La Reforma 7–67, Zona 10, tel. 317–893. 28 rooms with bath. Facilities: restaurant, parking, gardens. AE, DC, MC, V.*

Villa Expanola. This popular hotel combines a motel-style design with Spanish architectural elements like barrel-tile roofs, white-stucco walls, and lots of arches. Three stories of rooms face a cobbled parking area, the far side of which is lined by a tiled wall, fountain, and small garden. The rooms are fairly small and are furnished with colonial reproductions. Rooms on upper floors open onto wide balconies where you might hear a few parrots competing with the sound of nearby traffic from their perches by the garden. A restaurant is located in the basement. *2 Calle 7–51, Zona 9, tel. 323–381, fax 365–515. 63 rooms with bath. Facilities: restaurant, cable TV, parking. AE, DC, MC, V.*

$$ **Hotel Plaza.** This place was designed in the '60s and seems to have changed little since; it bears a distinct resemblance to a chain motel in the midwestern United States. Located at an unlikely junction between the old and new cities, this is an excellent family hotel, because the rooms surround a swimming pool and enclosed patio. The adjacent restaurant—which looks like a coffee shop in Anywhere, USA—and guarded parking lot all add to the convenience. Rooms have well-worn parquet floors, beige walls decorated with a few tourism posters, large private baths, and cable TV. *7 Via 6–16, Zona 4, tel. 310–396. 64 rooms with private bath. Facilities: restaurant, bar, cable TV, swimming pool, parking. AE, DC, MC, V.*

Old City Lodging
$$

Hotel Colonial. Though the rest of this hotel doesn't live up to the expectations raised by its outward appearance, it's a pleasant place with a few exceptional rooms. The reception overlooks an enclosed patio full of potted plants, and to the right of the entrance is a small lounge furnished with antique reproductions. The rooms have red-tile floors and colonial-style decor, with modern baths and optional cable TV. A small restaurant at the back of the hotel is open for breakfast only. *7 Avenida 14–1, Zona 1, tel. 26–722. 32 rooms with bath. Facilities: restaurant, cable TV. No credit cards.*

Hotel Sevilla. This new hotel in the heart of the old city is a comfortable spot with reasonable rates. The lobby is graced by a small tile fountain, but the decor of this establishment is predominantly modern, with carpeted rooms, small private baths, and cable TV. Not terribly attractive, it's clean, and there are a sauna and a small restaurant and bar. *9 Avenida 12–29, Zona 1, tel. 82–226, fax 28–431. 80 rooms with bath. Facilities: restaurant, bar, sauna, cable TV. AE, DC, MC, V.*

★ **Hotel Spring.** This Spanish colonial–style hotel offers inexpensive and moderately priced rooms. The moderate rooms are small and neat, with floral-print bedspreads and cable TV. Most of the other rooms in the two-story building face a large courtyard filled with potted plants and cast-iron tables and chairs, where guests can escape the downtown bustle and soak up the afternoon sun. Rooms have high ceilings, carpeting, and firm beds. There's a small café behind the courtyard, and side-street rooms on the second floor share a balcony that overlooks the avenue. Although this hotel is a good value, note that the shelter next door is a refuge for street children, most of whom are excellent thieves, so hang on to your wallets as you head in and out. *8 Avenida 12–65, Zona 1, tel. 26–637, fax 20–107. 43 rooms, 23 with bath. DC, MC, V.*

★ **Posada Belem.** This little bed-and-breakfast on a quiet side street in Zona 1 is an exceptional place, thanks to the couple that runs it. The hotel is the family's former residence, built in 1873, and has been renovated just enough to combine traditional charm with modern comfort. Rooms have tile floors and walls decorated with Guatemalan painting and weaving, handwoven rugs and blankets, and modern private baths. The Posada has a small library and collection of pre-Columbian artifacts, and family-style meals can be cooked to order. The owners are a fount of information for visitors and even make travel arrangements for guests. *13 Calle "A" 10–30, Zona 1, tel. 29–226, fax 513–478. 9 rooms with bath. Facilities: dining room, library, travel service. AE, DC, MC, V.*

$ **Hotel Ajau.** This very basic hotel is built in the Spanish style, with an inside courtyard and three floors of rooms with balconies. The rooms are clean, with tile floors and a couple of pieces of cheap wood furniture. Rooms with a bath also have cable TV. To avoid noise, ask for a room that does not face the street. *8 Avenida 15–62, Zona 1, tel. 20–488, fax 518–097. 38 rooms, 19 with bath. No credit cards.*

Hotel Chalet Suizo. This quiet hotel has been a favorite with budget travelers for 35 years, and the property has been recently remodeled and expanded to meet the growing demand. Rooms are found on two stories and most of them face a series of small courtyards. The rooms themselves are pretty basic, with tile floors and small beds with thin mattresses, but the place is clean, the staff is friendly, and the management is willing to store extra baggage for guests while they travel around the country. A small café sits to the right of the entrance, and a little courtyard behind the reception desk has a marble floor, carved wooden pillars, and a few chairs and tables for guests. *14 Calle 6–82, tel. 513–786. 44 rooms, 13 with bath. Facilities: restaurant. No credit cards.*

Hotel Hernani. This traditional hotel is run by an older Basque couple, and the walls of the small lobby are decorated with posters and paintings from their homeland. Rooms are located along a series of dark hallways on the second floor, and each room has a private bath across the hall. Most rooms have high ceilings, aging wallpaper, and wooden floors. *15 Calle 6–56, Zona 1, tel. 25–522. 16 rooms with bath. No credit cards.*

Nightlife

The **Zona Viva** is the liveliest part of town at night, with everything from quiet bars to fashionable discos. Popular bars include **Shakespeare's** (13 Calle 1–51) and **Stratos,** next door; both are dark bars with stereo-driven pop music. You'll find young to middle-aged patrons here. For live music, try **Steps** (upstairs at 1 Avenida 12–70)—the music doesn't blare, much to the relief of a slightly older crowd—or **Bar El Lugar,** downstairs in the Geminis Mall, for a younger, livelier clientele. Good discos include **Dash** (downstairs in Geminis), **Le Pont** (13 Calle 0–48), **Bacos** (Avenida La Reforma at Calle 16), **Fridays** (1 Avenida 11–40), and **El Establo** (Avenida La Reforma 14–32), a good place to meet foreigners and members of the American expatriate community. There are a number of new bars on Avenida Las Americas between 4 and 9 Calles that are hip and youthful without being sophomoric. For dancing in Zona 1, try the colorful **El Gazabo** (6 Calle at 3 Avenida) or **La Taberna** (basement of the Hotel Ritz Continental). Poetry readings and concerts are held at **La Bodeguita del Centro** (12 Calle 3–55), a popular gathering spot for intellectuals. **El Mesón de Don Quijote** (11 Calle 5–27), a popular late-night spot, has live music that draws an older crowd.

Antigua

In Antigua, you will find a city that combines the amenities of the modern world with both the charmed remnants of its colonial past and living proof of Guatemala's colorful indigenous culture. Although Indians cannot afford to live here, many travel to the city daily to sell their wares. The architectural beauty of this city of 44,000 has attracted increasing numbers of tourists over the years, and the influx of visitors has led to the development of an array of services. The city now has some of the country's finest hotels and restaurants, a plethora of shops and galleries, and several dozen language schools that attract students from all over the world.

During the 200 years that Antigua was the Central American capital, it was one of the three great cities of the Americas (with Lima and Mexico City). Sadly, most of its early, major structures were demolished by earthquakes, but the cobblestone streets—remaining much as they were centuries ago—and vine-covered ruins offer a glimpse of the city's former grandeur.

Founded in 1543, after the original capital was destroyed by a landslide, the city was called Saint James, or Santiago, and became the capital of an area that encompassed what is today Central America and the Mexican state of Chiapas. Destroyed by earthquakes and rebuilt several times, by the late 18th century Santiago had become a major political, religious, intellectual, and economic metropolis, with 32 churches, 18 convents and monasteries, a university, seven colleges, five hospitals, beautiful private mansions, wide cobblestoned boulevards, and many small parks with fountains. But again, powerful tremors struck the city: Late in 1773, much of Santiago's painstakingly restored elegance was reduced to rubble. Reluctantly, the government relocated to a safer site in the Ermita Valley, where the country's capital, Guatemala City, is found today.

Razed and haggard as it was, Santiago was further violated by the relocation project. Gradually, all that could be stripped and carried—art, furniture, doors, tiles, columns—was moved to the new capital; even the city's name was lost, and it has since been known officially as Antigua Guatemala, the old capital, and commonly referred to simply as Antigua.

Ironically, it is because Antigua was abandoned that it retains so much of its colonial charm. Only its poorest inhabitants stayed put after the capital was moved, but being of such limited means, they could only repair the old structures, not build anew. In the 1960s protective laws took effect, and in 1972 the National Council for the Protection of Antigua Guatemala was formed to restore ruins, maintain monuments, and rid the city of such modern intrusions on its landscape as billboards and neon signage. Though the 1976 quake set its restoration work back, the Council continues its efforts to rescue the city's colonial charm from centuries of neglect.

The most spectacular time to be in Antigua is Semana Santa (Holy Week), which lasts from Palm Sunday to Easter Sunday and features a series of vigils, colorful processions, and reenactments of Christ's last days in Jerusalem. You'll see Roman centurions charging on horseback through the streets, boulevards carpeted with colored sawdust and flowers, and immense hand-carried floats winding their way through throngs of thousands. The tourist office has schedules and maps with procession routes; just be aware that Antigua's hotels are booked up months ahead of time for this event.

Arriving and Departing by Bus, Taxi, and Car

No air or rail service is available to Antigua.

By Bus A daily shuttle service runs between Guatemala City and Antigua. After stopping at Guatemala City's major hotels, vans leave the Aurora International Airport around 7:15 AM and 6:15 PM for Antigua. Coming back, the Guatemala City–bound shuttle picks up at Antigua's big hotels at around 4:45 AM and 3 PM. Tickets ($10) can be purchased at major hotels in both cities (tel. 322–928 in Antigua, tel. 953–575 in Guatemala City).

Buses leave Guatemala City for Antigua every 15 minutes from 6 AM until about 6 PM from 18 Calle and 4 Avenida or from 15 Calle between 3 and 4 avenidas, in Zone 1. From Antigua, buses depart (when they're full) from the market area on a similar schedule. The trip takes about an hour, though it is slower and the buses are more crowded in the evening.

By Taxi A taxi between the two cities should cost about $25. Regular service is available between Aurora Airport and Antigua. As usual, you'll have to haggle with drivers. To call a taxi, *see* Getting Around Guatemala City, *above.*

By Car To reach Antigua, drive west out of Guatemala City via the Calzada Roosevelt, which becomes the Interamerican Highway, winding up into pine-covered hills with excellent views. At San Lucas, turn right off the highway and drive south to Antigua. If you're coming from the western highlands to Antigua, turn right off the highway just after passing Chimaltenango. Car-rental offices in Antigua include **Avis** (5 Avenida Norte 22, tel. 322–692) and **Budget** (in the Ramada, tel. 320–013).

Getting Around

By Bus Buses to surrounding villages leave Antigua from behind the mar-
Outside ket (departing whenever the bus is full enough), with hourly ones
the City making the hour-long trip to Chimaltenango, where buses to most highland destinations can be flagged down on the Interamerican Highway. Hourly service begins at 5 AM and ends at 6 PM. Shuttles leave Antigua for Panajachel every Tuesday, Thursday, Friday, and Saturday at 8:30 AM, arrive in Panajachel at 10:30, and return at noon.

In the City Antigua is not a large city and has no intracity service. People walk or take taxis, which are plentiful and cheap and easy to flag down or get in the Parque Central near the bus station. Remember to do a bit of haggling before beginning your ride.

Guided Tours

The tourist office in Antigua can find you a qualified tour guide (*see* Important Addresses and Numbers, *below*).

One travel agency is **Turansa** (Ramada Hotel, tel. 322–928).

Important Addresses and Numbers

Tourist The **Tourist Office** (tel. 320–763) is located south of Central Plaza on
Information the east end of the Palace of the Captains General, and is open daily 8–noon and 2–6. The INGUAT representatives can provide you with a map, hotel list, and information on local sights and excursions. They can also contact a licensed tour guide. Bulletin boards covered with flyers describing excursions, entertainment, travel deals, and tourism services appear all over town; the best ones are in Doña Luisa's restaurant (*see* Dining, *below*) and the Casa Andinista book-store.

Emergencies **Police** (tel. 320–251); **Hospital** (Pedro de Bethancourt, tel. 320–301); **Pharmacy:** Farmacia Roca (4 Calle Poniente 11, tel. 320–612).

Exploring Antigua

Both voices and colors can seem subdued and tranquil here—often the splashing water of a nearby fountain is the loudest assault on the ears. As you wander the city's ancient avenues, you will continually be surprised by the restrained pace of the city and the discoveries of tiny, private nooks and sanctuaries, picturesque corners, and views—past the whitewash and barrel tiles—of volcanoes that command the horizons. If you plan to spend much time in Antigua, Elizabeth Bell and Trevor Long's book, *Antigua Guatemala*, is an excellent guide and can be purchased in most of the city's book-stores. Note that all ruins are closed on Monday.

Numbers in the margin correspond to points of interest on the Anti-gua map.

1 The best place to begin any exploration is the **Plaza Central,** a well-tended park that is a favorite hangout of locals and visitors alike. To
2 the east stands the **Catedral.** Only two chapels serve as the cathedral today, since most of the city's original cathedral, completed in 1680, was destroyed in 1773. As in most other colonial cities, the church was built with the cross and altar to the east so that parishioners face the Holy Land. *No admission fee.*

3 To the south stands the **El Palacio del Capitán General** (Palace of the Captains General), which housed royal offices during colonial times and contains the police department, army barracks, tourist office, and other government headquarters today. North of the plaza is the
4 **Ayuntamiento** (City Hall), which was the seat of the city council in colonial times, and remains so today. The Ayuntamiento houses two museums: **Museo de Santiago** and **Museo del Libro Antiguo.** The for-mer contains a collection of colonial art and artifacts, with the old city jail at the back; the latter displays Central America's first print-ing press and a collection of ancient manuscripts. *Museum admis-sion: 5¢. Open Tues.–Fri. 9–4, weekends 9–noon and 2–4.*

The western boundary of Central Plaza is 5 Avenida, which is lined with shops and restaurants for several blocks. Head north on this street toward the beautiful yellow arch that spans it. The only rem-nant of the once immense **Santa Catalina Convent,** the arch was built to connect the buildings that flanked the road so that the sisters could pass from one part of the convent to the other without being seen.

Time Out | On the right, before the arch, is the **Posada Don Rodrigo,** a colonial mansion that is now a first-class hotel. Even if you don't stay here, it's worthwhile to wander around its courtyards and gardens and visit the restaurant for a meal or drink.

To the left and across the street, as you enter the intersection of 5
5 Avenida and 1 Calle, stands **La Merced,** the ancient church and mon-astery of the Mercedian fathers. One of the newer churches in town, La Merced wasn't inaugurated until 1767, only six years before the city was destroyed and abandoned. Designed by architect Juan Luis de Dios Estrada after several previous Mercedian churches had been flattened by quakes, this one has a squat appearance, with thick walls and small, high windows that enabled it to survive the 1773 quake intact. La Merced is noted for its beautiful interior, stuc-co facade, and the immense fountain in the monastery, which stands to the left of the church. *Admission: 5¢. Open Tues.–Sun. 8–noon.*

From La Merced, head east on 1 Calle for four blocks to 2 Avenida, where you turn right and walk one block. On the corner of 2 Calle
6 and 2 Avenida are the ruins of **Las Capuchinas,** the former convent of the Capuchin nuns, which was built in the mid-1700s. The ruins in-clude a small museum, a lovely garden, former bathing halls, and a round tower lined with the nuns' cells, two of which have been re-stored to illustrate concretely the nature of 18th-century cloistered life. Although gaudily restored in part by ex-president Jorge Serrano Elias, this is still probably Antigua's finest ruin. *Admis-sion: 5¢. Open daily 9–5.*

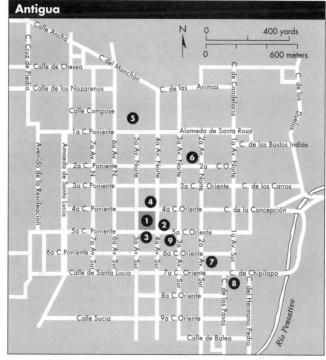

Ayuntamiento, **4**
Catedral, **2**
La Merced, **5**
Las
Capuchinas, **6**
Museo de Arte
Colonial, **9**
Palacio del
Capitán
General, **3**
Plaza Central, **1**
San Francisco, **8**
Santa Clara, **7**

Time Out A few blocks away from Las Capuchinas are the ruins of the **Santo Domingo Monastery.** A restaurant by the name of **Casa Santa Domingo** (3 Calle Oriente 28, tel. 320–140), built within ancient ruins, is one of the most inspiring places in the city to have a meal. Walk one block south on 2 Avenida, left on 3 Calle, and it's a couple of blocks east, on the left side.

Continue south on 2 Avenida from Las Capuchinas for four blocks to 6 Calle and the ruins of **Santa Clara** convent. Founded in 1699, it was eventually home to 46 nuns. Once a large and elaborate complex, it was destroyed by an earthquake in 1717, subsequently rebuilt with intentions of exceeding, in terms of size and complexity, its former glory, only to suffer violent tremors again in 1773. The convent collapsed and was finally abandoned. Roam the arches and garden courtyards of the ruins first, then cross the street to a beautiful palm-lined park to the west—you'll find an assortment of handicrafts vendors and a public laundry area. *Admission: 5¢. Open Tues.–Sun. 9–5.*

From Santa Clara, head south to 7 Calle, turn left, and walk a block to the ruins of **San Francisco,** which contain the most impressive church in the city. Work on San Francisco began in 1579; over the centuries, an assembly of structures that contained a college, church, hospital, and monastery grew to cover four city blocks. The church houses some interesting religious carvings, and the view of Antigua and environs from the second story of the ruins should not be missed. *Admission: 5¢. Open Tues.–Sun. 9–5.*

From San Francisco, head north on 1 Avenida for two blocks, to the beautifully restored colonial mansion **Casa Popenoe** (5 Calle and 1

Avenida, no phone; open Mon.–Sat. 3–5). From Popenoe follow 5
❾ Calle west three blocks to the **Museo de Arte Colonial,** across the
street from the cathedral. Housed in the former site of the University of San Carlos, this museum features a collection of mostly colonial
religious paintings and statues and a display on the city's Holy Week
celebrations. *Admission: 5¢. No phone. Open Tues.–Fri. 9–4,
weekends 9–noon and 2–4.*

Short Excursions from Antigua

Cerro de la Cruz, a small park on a hill just north of town, affords an
excellent view of Antigua and volcanoes Agua, Fuego, and
Acatenango. Tourists have been robbed here in the past; check the
tourist office for a park schedule and recent reports of any problems.
San Felipe de Jesús, just north of Antigua, has a small church with a
famous Christ figurine and a silver factory. It is the site of a saint's-
day celebration on August 30 as well. A short drive southwest of
town will take you to **San Antonio Aguas Calientes,** a dusty little Indian village built around an ancient church; this is a good spot to
shop for típica. **San Juan del Obispo,** on the slopes of Agua to the
south, is the site of a mansion built by Bishop Marroquín in the 16th
century (only sporadically open to visitors); consider the stop just
for the view of the valley below. Head a little farther up the hill to
Santa Maria de Jesús, and you'll be privy to an even more spectacular
view. Buses to these towns regularly leave from behind the market,
or you can haggle with a taxi driver in the Central Plaza for a trip to
several of them in one day.

Shopping

Handicrafts can be purchased from stalls in or near the main market, off Calzada de Santa Lucia. A permanent outdoor típica market
has been created along 4 Calle by the **Companía de Jesus Church** and
in its front courtyard. Countless shops are scattered throughout the
city, and the following offer the most interesting selections. **Jade
S.A.** (4 Calle Oriente 34) is a small shopping complex that features
jade and silver jewelry, clothing, temple rubbings, and handicrafts.
Al Pie del Volcano is a three-store emporium that offers gifts made
by artisans using traditional mediums in modern and sophisticated
ways. **La Boutique** (5 Calle Poniente 13) offers a variety of clothing
styles made from typical weaving patterns and techniques. **Textiles
Plus** (6 Calle Poniente and Calle de Santa Lucía) has everything from
bolts of fabric to pottery. **The Gift Shop** (3 Calle Poniente 3b) carries
a full range of kitchenware, from ceramics to beautiful hand-blown
glassware. Also worth checking out are **Ojalá** (4 Calle Oriente 35);
Ixchel (4 Calle Oriente 20), which specializes in hand-spun wool rugs
and blankets; and **Colibrí** (4 Calle Oriente 3), for nice embroidery
work. A number of foreign-owned shops specialize in taking local
fabrics and designs and adapting them to sophisticated North
American and European tastes; among them are **Casa de Artes** (4
Avenida Sur 11), **Armario** (5 Avenida Sur at 6a Calle Poniente), and
IMGUASA (3 Calle Poniente 5).

Books   Due to a sizeable expatriate resident population, Antigua has the
country's best selection of English-language reading material. The
city's bookshops include **Casa Andinista** (4 Calle Oriente 5), which
sells some hard-to-find titles, note cards, and posters and also rents
paperbacks. **Rainbow Reading Room** (7 Avenida Sur 8), **La Gallería,**
(5 Avenida Sur 4), and the smaller **Un Poco de Todo** (5 Avenida Sur
10), the last two on the west side of Central Plaza, sell a good selec-

tion of English titles. **El Pensativo** (5 Avenida 29), a few blocks to the north, carries mostly Spanish-language merchandise.

Galleries **El Sitio** (5 Calle Poniente 15), **Gallería de Artes Integradas "Los Nazarenos"** (6 Calle Poniente 13), **Estípite** (3 Avenida el Desengaño 22).

Jewelry Two jade shops stand out: Antigua's **Platería Típica Maya** (7 Calle Oriente 9) and **La Antigüeña** in the nearby town of San Felipe de Jesús. Smaller jade emporiums—jade is mined country-wide but worked mostly in Antigua—include **Casa del Jade** (4 Calle Oriente 3) and **Jade's J.C.** (9 Calle Oriente 2).

Sports

The **Hotel Ramada** has tennis courts, a spa, and swimming pools that can be used by nonguests for a small fee. Horses can be rented from a private farm at 2 Calle Poniente 31. Mountain-bike tours are arranged from apartment 9 of El Rosario, at the southern end of Avenida 5. If you wish to tour by motorcycle, you can rent one at 7 Calle Poniente 11. Expeditions up nearby volcanoes are organized by **Club de Andinismo Chicag** (6 Avenida Norte 34, tel. 323–343). **Casa Andinista** (4 Calle Oriente 5) rents camping equipment.

Dining

If you don't want a meal, but simply want to rest and sip coffee and relish a sweet treat, try **La Cenicienta** (5 Calle Norte 7), **Las Americas** (6 Avenida Sur at 5 Calle Poniente), or **Cafe Condesa** (5 Avenida Norte 4).

Count on an informal dress code wherever you eat, but it's a good idea to book reservations at the expensive establishments on weekends.

$$$ **El Sereno.** This exclusive restaurant serves fine food in the elegant atmosphere of a restored colonial house. Ring the bell at the entrance and you'll be led to a table in a small garden courtyard or to one of two rooms with corner fireplaces and walls adorned with paintings by local artists. The menu, which features a variety of dishes leaning toward a French or Italian influence and a few Guatemalan items, is changed weekly. Selections include filet mignon with mushroom sauce, chicken pesto, fettuccini with a ham and cream sauce, and robalo in various guises. This spot is not suitable for children. You can count on impeccable service. *6 Calle Poniente 30, tel. 320–073. AE, MC, V. Open Wed.–Sun. noon–3 and 6:30–9:30.*

El Picarón. This new restaurant-gallery is an attempt to create Guatemalan nouvelle cuisine, with the chef using local products in original and sophisticated ways. Although the menu changes every 10 days, there are a few standards: Seafood bouillabaisse, which is cooked in a slightly spicy tomato sauce, and steak tenderloin with chiltepe sauce are two standouts. El Picarón is located in a renovated colonial house with fountains and mauve and peach walls lined with rotating exhibitions of photos and paintings. *Callejón de la Concepción No. 7, tel. 320–219. DC, MC, V. Closed Mon.*

★ **Welten.** Welten's owner says she wants her customers to feel as if they're guests in her home, and until the bill arrives, you can easily fall under the illusion. Guests have their choice of seating locales: on a plant-filled patio with hammocks and cascading orchids, by a small pool and garden in the back, or in a couple of elegant dining rooms. Homemade pasta, like fettuccine with walnut sauce, and fish and meat dishes complemented by an assortment of sauces are served. Save room for dessert. *4 Calle Oriente 21, tel. 320–630. AE, DC, V. Closed Tues.*

$$ El Capuccino. This Italian restaurant doesn't look like much from the street, but it is the city's best of its kind. Pasta and pizza are the principal fare in this large dining room filled with red-and-white covered tables. *6 Avenida Norte 8, no phone. No credit cards. Closed Mon.*

Fonda de la Calle Real. An old Antigua favorite, this place now has two locations serving the same menu of Guatemalan and Mexican cuisine. The old restaurant is just off the plaza at 5 Avenida Norte 5 and has upstairs seating with pleasant views, but the space is slightly cramped and dingy. The new restaurant around the corner, at 3 Calle Poniente 7, is more spacious and attractive as it's located in a large colonial home with both indoor and outdoor seating. The mutual menu includes *queso fundido* (melted cheese with condiments and tortillas) and *claldo real* (a hearty chicken soup). Live music plays on weekends. *3 Calle Poniente 7, tel. 320–507; and 5 Avenida Norte 5, tel. 322–696. No credit cards.*

Katok. Katok is a small corner restaurant with a bar whose picture window looks right onto the street. Grilled beef is the mainstay here, and service is friendly and efficient. *4 Avenida Norte 7, no phone. AE, MC, V.*

★ **El Oasis del Perigrino.** This out-of-the-way place, located in a comfortable old colonial home, resembles an expensive restaurant in everything but the price. The international menu reflects a strong German influence but serves pasta and vegetarian dishes as well. Guests may sit in the dining rooms decorated with traditional weaving or in a lush outdoor courtyard. *7 Avenida Norte 96, no phone. No credit cards. Closed weekday lunches and Wed. dinner.*

$ Café Flor. This cheerful Mexican restaurant with friendly service has a standard menu at low prices. Breakfast is served, too. *4 Avenida Sur 1, no phone. No credit cards. Closed Sun.*

Caffé Opera. Walking into this restaurant is like stepping into a fanciful pop-art version of an Italian café. The walls are lined with posters of European opera and film stars, the floors covered in large black and white tiles. If you order anything from the ample menu of specialty coffees, sandwiches on fresh-baked bread, or exotic desserts (including homemade ice cream), you will not be disappointed. The coffee is the best in Antigua. *6 Avenida Norte 17, tel. 320–727. No credit cards.*

★ **Doña Luisa's.** The best breakfast spot in town, Doña Luisa's has become a bit of a local institution. A multitude of tables are scattered throughout a dozen rooms and on the balcony and terrace of this former colonial residence, but it's still not easy to get a seat. In addition to early-morning specialties like fruit salad, pancakes, and freshly made pastries from the in-house bakery, there are plenty of sandwiches and sundry light fare for lunch and dinner patrons. Incidentally, the bulletin board is a great information resource for travelers. *4 Calle Oriente 11, no phone. No credit cards.*

Quesos y Vino. This small Italian restaurant serves homemade pasta, pizzas baked in a wood-burning oven, and a variety of cheeses and home-baked breads. Choose from an impressive selection of imported wine sold by the bottle. *5 Avenida Norte 32, no phone. No credit cards. Closed Tues.*

Sueños del Quetzal. This two-story vegetarian restaurant off the main plaza is a great place to sit on a balcony, sip a drink, and watch the world go by. Inside is a relaxing loft of hardwood floors and high ceilings that sport hanging fans. Wall collages of clowns and a couple of giant fabric toucans and macaws give the place a touch of frivolity. Sueños's menu of international breakfasts, served until 11, ranges from New York bagels and cream cheese to Mexican tofu ranchero, beans, wheat tortillas, and avocado. Sueños also has one of the best desserts in town: *pie de lodo* (mud pie), a decadently rich heated chocolate brownie topped with coffee ice cream and chocolate syrup. *5 Avenida Norte 3, tel. 322–676. No credit cards.*

Lodging

$$$$ **Casa Santo Domingo.** A new hotel has been established amid the
★ ruins of the ancient Santo Domingo Monastery. This hotel captures the past without losing any modern luxuries. Dark, carved-wood furniture, yellow stucco walls, and iron sconces preserve the monastic atmosphere. Fountains, hanging plants, and colonial furniture decorate the public rooms. Guest rooms are the ultimate in comfort, with cable TV, hair dryers, fireplaces, and deep bathtubs with Jacuzzis. *3 Calle Oriente 28, tel. 320–140, fax 320–102. 24 rooms with bath. Facilities: restaurant, bar, pool, spa, cable TV. AE, MC, V.*

★ **Hotel Antigua.** As a tastefully rendered design combination of colonial elegance and modern comfort, this property succeeds where others fail. Guest rooms are furnished with fireplaces and cable TV and surround a large lawn and pool. The oldest part of the hotel is a colonial-style building that houses a restaurant, small bar, and sitting room (with a view of the ancient San José el Viejo Church). *3 blocks south of the plaza, between 4 and 5 avenidas, tel. 320–331, fax 320–807. 60 rooms with bath. Facilities: bar, restaurant, pool. AE, DC, MC, V.*

$$$ **Posada Don Rodrigo.** A night spent in this restored colonial mansion—constructed some 250 years ago—is like stepping back in time. All the rooms have high ceilings and are furnished with antiques, while two lovely courtyards and several small gardens enhance the grounds. The restaurant consists of an ancient dining hall with a tile fountain, fireplace, and terrace whose garden is lit at night. Marimba music enlivens every meal. Light sleepers, beware: The festivities here go long and lively into the night. *5 Avenida Norte 17, tel. 323–080, fax in Guatemala City 316–838. 33 rooms with bath. Facilities: restaurant, parking. AE, DC, MC, V.*

Ramada. Just outside town on 9 Calle (a short walk will get you here), the Ramada is Antigua's most modern accommodation. Spacious, carpeted rooms furnished adobe-style have balconies or patios that border the handsome grounds. The Ramada boasts the most extensive facilities in the city—fireplaces, cable TV, spa with sauna and massage, spacious tiled bathrooms, two swimming pools, tennis courts, and a bar and disco—but it lacks the colonial charm of other properties. The restaurant is adequate, but you'll find better food in town. Ask about special rates. *9 Calle Poniente, tel. 320–013 or 800/ 228–9898 in the U.S., fax 320–237. 156 rooms with bath. Facilities: parking, 2 pools, tennis courts, spa with massage and sauna, restaurant, bar/disco. AE, DC, MC, V.*

$$ **Hotel Mesón Panza Verde.** This is one of the prettiest and most com-
★ fortable hotels in Antigua. The main entrance, carpeted with pine needles, opens up to a fountain, a garden, and an elegant restaurant. In back are the rooms, three of which are suites with fireplaces and shared patio; they are furnished with deep bathtubs and down comforters. Suites can sleep up to six with folding beds. *5 Avenida Sur 19, tel. and fax 322–925. 6 rooms with bath. Facilities: restaurant. DC, MC, V.*

Hotel Aurora. This family-run, 16-room pension, located in the heart of the city, is slightly overpriced. Comfortable colonial-style rooms with tiled floors face a garden courtyard, surrounded by a tiled portico equipped with plenty of chairs for quiet repose. The hotel is still run by the same family that opened it in 1923, and although it's a little run-down, the garden is beautiful, the service attentive, and the location unbeatable. A small restaurant serves breakfast. *4 Calle Oriente 16, tel. 320–217. 16 rooms with bath. Facilities: breakfast café. No credit cards.*

★ **Hotel Convento Santa Catalina.** This hotel, aptly named, is built amid the ruins of the old convent, which is famous for its yellow arch that spans the street. Spacious rooms face a verdant courtyard with an ancient fountain; for those who wish to sip a drink at leisure in this tranquil setting, a smattering of tables and chairs in the courtyard offer sweet repose. *5 Avenida Norte 28, tel. and fax 323–080. 10 rooms with bath. Facilities: restaurant. No credit cards.*

Posada San Sebastián. Here are two pleasant hotels with simple but comfortable rooms. The 7 Avenida hotel is more attractive (it is located in an older, colonial home and has a colorful bar), but the other, more modern establishment benefits from its central location on 3 Avenida. *3 Avenida Norte 4, tel. 322–621, 7 rooms with bath; or 7 Avenida Norte 67, tel. 320–465, 6 rooms with bath, 3 without bath. AE, MC, V.*

$ **Hospedaje Santa Lucia.** Beyond this, there's not much to say: You'll be right near the bus station, and you won't wear a hole in your pocket for what amounts to a basic, clean, well-run hotel. All rooms have private baths. *Calzada Santa Lucia 5, no phone. 12 rooms with bath. No credit cards.*

Posada Asjemenou. You may not want to hear about yet another charming hotel in a former colonial residence, but the difference here is this one's a true bargain. The rooms are clean and comfortable, the staff friendly and eager. A small café in the hotel serves breakfast and snacks, and if you hanker for more substantial victuals, the owners run a larger restaurant off the Central Plaza that specializes in pizza. *5 Avenida Norte 31, tel. 322–832. 8 rooms, 4 with bath. V.*

★ **Villa San Francisco.** A block east of Santa Clara Ruins, this old hotel is a great value for the money. The atmosphere is relaxed and quiet. There is a garden in the back and an upstairs patio with a magnificent view of the San Francisco church and all three volcanoes. The modest rooms are clean, and two of them have televisions. Both shared and private baths are available. *1 Avenida Sur 15, tel. and fax 323–383. 12 rooms. AE, DC, MC, V.*

The Arts and Nightlife

The Arts The **Biennial Culture Festival,** which takes place in February every odd-numbered year (preparations for 1995 were in the works as of press time), is a relatively new venture but should become an important event. During the rest of the year, various musical and artistic events take place in the city's ruins, churches, and galleries. Check the tourist office for current listings.

Nightlife Interestingly enough, video parlors—like **Cafe Flor Cinema** (4 Avenida Sur 1), **Cinemala** (3 Avenida Norte 9), and **Cine Geminis** (5 Calle Oriente 11A)—are a popular diversion in Antigua, since the local movie theater tends to run horrendous films. They serve refreshments and alcohol, and weekly schedules are posted on the town's many community bulletin boards.

You won't have trouble finding a bar in Antigua—many operate out of the above-mentioned restaurants. Others include **La Chimenea** (4 Calle at 7 Avenida), a popular space affording a little area for dancing to rock and pop music; **Jazz Gruta** (Calzada Santa Lucía Norte 17), an intimate jazz club where good music can be heard Monday through Saturday; and **Latinos** (7 Avenida Norte 16), which features live music but is closed Sunday. Farther down 7 Avenida are bars that cater to young tourists, the best of which is **Picasso's.** On 5 Avenida Norte across from the Don Rodrigo is **Macondo,** which is frequently and festively crowded. If you want to stay up late and dance the night away, try the Latin and rock rhythms at **Moscas y Miel** (5 Calle Poniente 6). Please note that many bars and clubs do not have telephones.

The Western Highlands

The Western Highlands (*Altiplano* in Spanish) are home to the majority of Guatemala's Indians, most of whom live in small villages scattered across the isolated valleys that punctuate this rugged region. The villages themselves are colorful agricultural communities, integrated into a rural economy that functions through a series of weekly markets; the inhabitants maintain traditions that have dominated the lives of their people for centuries. In addition to being the home of a striking and intriguing people, the highland villages are invariably surrounded by a spectacular scenery of volcanic cones, granite peaks, pine-draped hillsides, pastoral plains, and lush tropical valleys.

The highlands are bounded in the south by a chain of volcanoes that begins near Guatemala City and stretches northwest toward Mexico, and in the north by a series of mountain ranges that tower above the rest of the country, where most villages are accessible only by foot or on horseback. Though the precipitous terrain and lack of infrastructure make it difficult to visit the majority of the highland villages, some are quite easy to reach, and the particular beauty and uniqueness of both the area and its inhabitants are guaranteed to reward any extra effort required to explore the region's farther reaches.

The highland climate is pleasant, with cool nights and warm afternoons, and no doubt inspired a European traveler more than a century ago to dub the country "the land of eternal spring." Temperatures often reach 70°F–80°F (21°C–26°C) in the afternoon, but it can drop to 40°F–50°F (4°C–10°C) at night, so a sweater or warm jacket is essential for the evenings. Travel in the highlands tends to be cheaper than in the rest of the country; there are no Very Expensive hotels and only a handful of Expensive ones, in Atitlán, Chichicastenango, and Quezaltenango. Most villages offer only Inexpensive, often rustic lodging, so all but the hardiest travelers will want to base themselves in the few cities and tourist towns, and explore the region's more remote reaches through a series of day trips. What's more, the road system doesn't lend itself to touring—most of the more charming villages are found along roads that end in the mountains, which implies a lot of doubling back.

The best time of the week to visit any highland village is on its market day, when the streets are packed with families from the surrounding countryside (*see* Shopping in Staying in Guatemala, *above*). But the liveliest time of year for each town is the week or several days of its annual festival, which surrounds the feast day of the town's patron saint. The festivals are an interesting mixture of religious ritual and carnival commotion, with processions, live music, and traditional dancers in costumes that depict animals, gods, and conquistadors.

Important highland festivals occur in **Panajachel** (annual festival honoring St. Francis, Oct. 1–7); **Santiago Atitlán** (July 23–27 and Holy Week from Palm Sunday to Easter Sunday); **Chichicastenango** (Dec. 18–21); **Santa Cruz del Quiché** (Aug. 14–19); **Nebaj** (Aug. 12–15); **Quezaltenango** (Sept. 9–17); **Zunil** (Nov. 22–26); **Totonicapán** (Sept. 24–30); **Momostenango** (last week in July); **Huehuetenango** (July 12–17); and **Todos Santos** (Oct. 21–Nov. 1).

Arriving and Departing by Car, Bus, and Boat

By Car   The Interamerican Highway—more country road than highway, really—heads northwest out of Guatemala City, where it is called the Calzada Roosevelt. It passes through Chimaltenango (Km 56) to a crossroads called Los Encuentros (Km 127), which is marked by a two-story blue traffic-police tower, and where the road to El Quiché splits off the highway to the right, leading to **Chichicastenango,** Santa Cruz del Quiché, and the Ixil Triangle. Veering left at Los Encuentros, the Interamerican Highway skims the turnoff to Sololá and **Panajachel,** 3 kilometers (about 2 miles) down on the left. The highway skims over some impressive ridges and then descends to a crossroads called Cuatro Caminos, about 200 kilometers (125 miles) from the capital, where the road to **Quezaltenango,** 27 kilometers (17 miles) south, heads off to the left. The short dirt road to **Huehuetenango** appears on the right of the highway about 60 kilometers (38 miles) north of Cuatro Caminos. Roads to the north of Huehuetenango and Santa Cruz del Quiché are unpaved and pretty rough—this is nerve-racking mountain driving relieved intermittently by memorable views.

By Bus   From Guatemala City, bus service supplies the following highland
From   cities:
Guatemala
City to   Panajachel: **Transporte Rebuli** (tel. 513–521) has daily bus service
Highland   leaving from Zona 1 at 21 Calle 1–34 in Guatemala City, with depar-
Towns   tures at 5:30 and 6:15 AM, then hourly from 7 AM to 4 PM. Buses leave
Panajachel at 5, 7, and 8 AM, then hourly from 9:30 AM to 2:30 PM. Count
on a four-hour trip.

Chichicastenango and Santa Cruz del Quiché: From the capital, **Veloz Quichelense** (no phone) operates hourly buses, departing on the half-hour between 5 AM and 6 PM from the Terminal in Zona 4, and returning from Santa Cruz on a similar schedule.

Quezaltenango: **Galgos** (7 Avenida 19–44, Zona 1, tel. 23–661) buses leave Guatemala City at 5:30, 8:30, and 11 AM, and 12:30 PM, every hour until 5:30 PM, and then at 7 PM, and they depart Quezaltenango at 12:30 PM every hour until 4:30 PM. The trip takes four hours.

Huehuetenango: Choose from two bus services for the five-hour run from Guatemala City to Huehuetenango: **Los Halcones** (7 Avenida 15–27, Zona 1, tel. 81–979), with departures at 7 AM and 2 PM; or **Rapidos Zaculeu** (9 Calle 11–42, Zona 1, no phone), with departures at 6 AM and 3 PM.

Inter-highland   For inter-highland service from Antigua, take a bus to Chimal-
Service   tenango first, then wave down a bus on the Interamerican Highway; anything heading north stops at Los Encuentros, where it's easy to transfer. The shuttle service between Panajachel and Antigua leaves Antigua about 8:30 AM and Panajachel around noon every

Wednesday, Friday, and Sunday. Tickets can be purchased at the big hotels (tel. 322–928 in Antigua). Daily buses also leave Panajachel for Chichicastenango at 7, 8, 9, and 10:30 AM, and 1 PM; for Quezaltenango at 5:30 and 11:30 AM, and 2:30 PM; for San Lucas Tolimán at 6:30 AM and 4 PM; and for Santa Catarina and San Antonio Palopó at 9 AM. Hourly buses operate between Quezaltenango and Huehuetenango (a 2½-hour trip), and sporadic service is available between Quezaltenango and Chichicastenango, but it's often quicker to switch buses at Los Encuentros. Buses leave Quezaltenango for Panajachel at 6 AM, noon, and 1. Buses to the Ixil Triangle leave Santa Cruz around 8 and 9 AM and return at 12:30 and 3 AM. There is also early-morning bus service between Huehuetenango and Sacapulas. Buses leave Huehuetenango for Todos Santos from 1 Avenida and 4 Calle at 11:30 AM and 12:30 PM, returning at 5 and 6 AM, or you can hike down to the Interamerican Highway via San Juan or Jacaltenango and catch one of the regular buses coming from the Mexican border.

By Boat A variety of ferries and private boats ply the waters of Lake Atitlán. Daily boats leave Panajachel for Santiago Atitlán at 8:30 AM, 9 AM, 9:30 AM, 10 AM, 4 PM, and 5 PM, returning at 6 AM, 11:45 AM, 12:30 PM, 1 PM, 2 PM, and 5 PM, and for San Pedro La Laguna at 8:20 AM, 10 AM, noon, 2 PM, 4 PM, and 7:30 PM, returning at 4:45 AM, 6 AM, 8 AM, 10 AM, noon, 2 PM, and 5 PM. Several boats per day also travel between Santiago and San Pedro, and a daily excursion leaves Panajachel at 9 AM for San Pedro, Santiago, and San Antonio Palopó, stopping for about an hour at each village and returning around 4 PM. There are also plenty of smaller boats that offer private tours of the lake.

Emergencies **National Police** (tel. 2569); **Hospital** (tel. 2471); **Farmacia Nueva Pharmacy** (Calle 6 Avenida 10, Zona 1, tel. 4531).

Exploring the Western Highlands

Highlights for First-time Visitors Chichicastenango (*see* Tour 1: Atitlán and Chichicastenango)
Lake Atitlán (*see* Tour 1: Atitlán and Chichicastenango)
Momostenango (*see* Tour 2: Quezaltenango and Huehuetenango)
San Francisco el Alto (*see* Tour 2: Quezaltenango and Huehuetenango)
Santiago Atitlán (*see* Tour 1: Atitlán and Chichicastenango)
Zunil (*see* Tour 2: Quezaltenango and Huehuetenango)

Tour 1: Atitlán and Chichicastenango *Numbers in the margin correspond to points of interest on the Western Highlands map.*

Lake Atitlán, which lies at the foot of three volcanoes at the southern end of the highlands, is an awesome sight that has impressed many a visitor over the centuries. The conquistador Pedro Alvarado stopped between battles to marvel at the area's timeless beauty, and since his day the lake has inspired the likes of John L. Stephens and Aldous Huxley. Atitlán means "place of the great waters" in Nahuatl, the language of Alvarado's Mexican troops, and the lake's cool depths are both inviting and impressive: On a moonlit night or early in the morning the water can be as smooth as glass, like an immense liquid mirror reflecting massive volcanic cones. But in the early afternoon, a regular wind known as the *xochomil* blows across the lake, and the surface turns choppy and defiant. The xochomil can turn Atitlán's waters violent in a hurry, creating dangerous currents, so water sports and trips in small boats are advisable only during the morning.

The lake measures about 13 by 17 kilometers (8 by 11 miles), its surface is at some 1,576 meters (5,200 feet) above sea level, and it is more than 300 meters (1,000 feet) deep, though in some parts its depth has yet to be determined. Its volcanic origin is apparent from the steep ridges that surround it. From the southern shore rise three massive volcanoes. Viewed from the town of Panajachel, San Pedro Volcano (3,006 meters, or 9,920 feet) is on the right, Tolimán (3,133 meters, or 10,340 feet) is on the left, and Atitlán (3,506 meters, or 11,560 feet) is behind Tolimán. Both Tolimán and San Pedro volcanoes are extinct, and Atitlán has been dormant since 1853.

The lake also has its mysteries: Not only was the expedition that attempted to map its bottom unsuccessful in determining the depth at some points, but because the lake is surrounded by hills, it pours into no rivers and must instead be drained by underground passages. During the 1976 earthquake, the level of the lake dropped about 2 meters (6½ feet), a shift that is still visible on some parts of the shore.

Complementing the natural beauty of the lake are 13 charming villages that stand on its shores. The towns are predominantly quiet agricultural communities, rich in indigenous culture. Most women and many men wear traditional costumes, which vary from town to town, and nearly everybody speaks one of two Mayan languages: Tzutujil to the south and Cakchiquel to the north. The inhabitants of the area are a proud, independent, and conservative people whose traditions should be respected. Though the lake is ideal for swimming, such things should never be done in the nude, and when walking in the villages, make sure you're decently dressed.

❶ Panajachel is a popular base for exploring Lake Atitlán, since it's easy to reach and has a wide selection of hotels and restaurants. Located on the northern shore of the lake, Panajachel was just a quiet Cakchiquel village a few decades ago, but it has since grown into a sprawling tourist town and hippie hangout with little character. The old part of town, though, up toward the valley, hasn't lost its charm, and during Sunday markets it looks much like any other highland village.

Time Out | **The Deli 2,** by the lake at the end of Calle Santander, the main drag, is a great spot for breakfast or lunch, with good coffee, fresh bagels, pastries, and a rather unique menu, including falafel and humus.

The **tourist office** (tel. 9/621–392), marked by a blue sign sporting a white *i*, is on the right side of the road as one enters Panajachel. It's open Wednesday–Sunday 8–noon and 2–6, and Monday morning 8–noon. The next right is Santander Street—you'll find a bank on the left and, a little farther down, the Guatel office, where you can make long-distance calls. Santander leads to the waterfront and is lined with restaurants, shops, and street vendors. Shortly after Santander, Avenida Los Arboles heads off to the left. The next right is the road to Santa Catrina, the first right from which is Calle Rancho Grande, which leads to the public beaches, docks, and the Hotel Del Lago.

❷ Santiago Atitlán is a large and fascinating village across the lake from Panajachel. It is the capital of the Tzutujile Indians, a proud people who have long resisted political domination. The town is famous for the quality of its weaving, and most people still wear their striking traditional costume, which includes a women's headdress that resembles a bright red halo. It is also one of the few places where people actively worship Guatemala's cigar-smoking saint, Maximón, who is actually a Mayan god masquerading as a Catholic

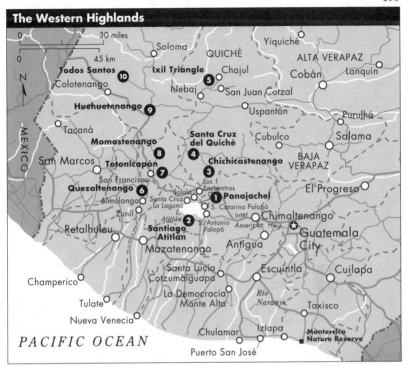

The Western Highlands

saint. Though it is invaded by tourists daily, and the locals have become aggressive hawkers, Santiago Atitlán remains a lovely village.

Of the remaining towns of Lake Atitlán, three are well worth a visit: Santa Catarina Palopó, San Antonio Palopó, and Santa Cruz la Laguna. Each of these quiet, traditional indigenous villages provides another perspective on the striking beauty of the lake and its majestic volcanoes. All three towns have excellent, moderately priced hotels and can be reached by boat.

Santa Cruz la Laguna is a small village perched on a hill about a 40-minute boat ride west of Panajachel. One highlight is a small but beautiful adobe church whose walls are lined with carved wooden saints. Another reason to visit this village is the Arca de Noé, a small, rustic hotel with magnificent views and wonderful home-cooked food (*see* Dining and Lodging, *below*). Visitors can swim right off the hotel's dock or hike to nearby towns. Four hours west of Santa Cruz by foot is San Marcos de la Laguna; the wonderfully scenic walk guides travelers past several tiny mud villages where women sit and weave in front of their houses.

Santa Catarina Palopó is about 6½ kilometers (4 miles) east of Panajachel on a dirt road. Visitors are surrounded by the brilliant blues and greens of traditional native blouses as they walk down the cobblestoned streets of this picturesque town. The hotel Villa Santa Catarina (*see* Dining and Lodging, *below*), at the lakeside entrance to town, boasts magical views of the water and volcanoes and offers waterskiing and windsurfing.

The road ends another 6½ kilometers (4 miles) east in the slightly larger **San Antonio Palopó**. This hill town has the feel of a quiet fishing village. Women dress in white blouses with stripes of color, and men wear headdresses and checkered shirts. A drive along the beach on Calle de la Playa brings you to the pleasant and basic hotel Terrazas del Lago (*see* Dining and Lodging, *below*).

❸ Chichicastenango is one of the most colorful and accessible highland towns, just a 1½-hour drive from Panajachel. Return to Los Encuentros via Sololá, and turn left to drive north for less than an hour. The main attraction in this town is the market, which is one of the largest in the country and is held every Thursday (5:30 AM and 1:30 PM) and Sunday (5:30 AM and 3 PM). Like all other highland markets, Chichicastenango's was originally the basis of local commerce, but since its fame has grown, the local market has been pushed into the periphery. The bulk of the business is now between tourists—arriving en masse twice weekly—and Indian merchants from throughout the highlands, who come to sell their wares to the foreigners. The night before market day is in many ways more intriguing than the event itself, as vendors set up their stalls with pleasant anticipation and the town still belongs to the Indians.

Though the buying and selling may steal the show, Chichicastenango would be well worth visiting if there were no market at all. The quiet town, which stands on a hill surrounded by pine forest, is still tradition-bound in many respects: The Indians proudly worship Christian and pagan deities side by side. This mixing of Catholicism and Mayan ritual can be witnessed at **Santo Tomás Church,** located on the main plaza in the heart of the market. Built in the mid-1500s on the site of a Mayan altar, Santo Tomás is busy with devotees all day and late into the night. Its steps are usually engulfed in a cloud of copal incense, which worshipers burn while performing rituals before entering the church. Visitors may enter through a door on the right side of the church, and they must refrain from taking photographs while inside. Across the plaza stands **Capilla de Calvario** (Calvary Chapel), which doesn't attract such devotion but affords a nice view of the market. If you face San Tomás, the building to the right houses a little museum of pre-Columbian artifacts. And on a hill a short walk out of town is **Pascual Abaj,** a Mayan shrine where pagan rituals are regularly performed. If you don't want to pay a local to take you to Pascual Abaj, just follow 9 Calle out of town and look for the mask-shop signs on the left, which mark the footpath up the hill.

Adventurous travelers may want to continue north from Chichicastenango for further glimpses of the department of El Quiché, which offers more fine scenery and traditional villages. A half-hour **❹** north of Chichicastenango lies **Santa Cruz del Quiché,** the provincial capital, which isn't as attractive as Chichicastenango but has inexpensive accommodations, a bank, and several restaurants on the main plaza. The nearby ruins of **Utatlán** haven't been restored, but they are frequently used for traditional ceremonies.

An interesting although somewhat inaccessible part of El Quiché is **❺** the **Ixil Triangle,** which comprises the villages of **Nebaj, San Juan Cotzal,** and **Chajul** and is a fantastic area for hiking. The Triangle is located about five hours by bus from Santa Cruz del Quiché. Nebaj is the most accessible of the three, but Cotzal is serviced by sporadic buses, and Chajul can be hiked or driven to. The Ixil Triangle is the home of the Ixil Indians, a proud and beautiful people who speak a unique language and preserve a rich culture. The area was the scene of intense combat during the early 1980s, when the army razed dozens of villages, and though things are quiet now, a frightening number of widows and orphans populate the area. You'll discover that the friendly nature of the locals here belies the nightmare they lived just a decade ago.

Tour 2:
Quezaltenango
and
Huehuetenango
❻

Continuing northwest from Los Encuentros on the Interamerican Highway, you pass over a ridge and then descend into a valley to reach **Quezaltenango,** which is 20 minutes south of a crossroads called Cuatro Caminos. Although it is Guatemala's second-largest city, Quezaltenango is little more than an overgrown town. Surrounded by rich farmland, the city has long had agriculture as the basis of its economy, but it is also a significant industrial center known especially for its textiles. While considered a sprawling minimetropolis with few attractions of its own, it is located near some charming highland villages and is thus a good base for exploring the region.

The city received its name, which means "place of the quetzal," from the language of the Mexican warriors who fought with Alvarado. The conquistador defeated the great Indian warrior Tecún Umán in the area and destroyed the nearby Quiché city of Xelaju. But local Indians have never gotten used to that foreign name and instead refer to Quezaltenango as **Xela** (pronounced *shayla*), which is the name you'll find on buses.

There are a number of language schools in Xela, as it is a popular alternative to Antigua for studying Spanish. Most tourists stay in Zone 1 in an area near the grandiose Parque Centro América, the city's central plaza, which is surrounded by government buildings and banks (most open 9 to 7) and the cathedral. The Tourist Office is on the south end of the park, and the Guatel telephone office is on the southwest end. Guatemala Unlimited Travel Bureau (tel. 061–6043), a few blocks away at 12 Avenida and 1 Calle, can arrange local tours. The bus lines Rutas Lima, Galgos, and Lineas Americas are all off the Calzada Independencia in Zone 2, while buses to most other towns leave from the terminal in Zone 3.

Time Out

Just off the plaza, on the corner of 13 Avenida and 5 Calle, is the inexpensive **Cafe Baviera,** with an ample selection of excellent coffees and a relaxing atmosphere. Treats like fresh pastries, quiches, and hot croissant sandwiches are also served.

The real attraction of Quezaltenango is the area that surrounds it. In **Almolonga,** 5 kilometers (3 miles) south of Xela, you'll find women wearing bright orange *huipiles* (embroidered blouses) and beautiful headbands, and there are busy markets on Wednesday and Saturday. A few kilometers beyond Almolonga are several hot springs where private tubs can be rented for a few dollars. **Zunil,** 9 kilometers (5½ miles) south of Xela on the same road, is one of the most picturesque villages in the region. Set at the end of the valley, above which a river plunges into a massive cascade, Zunil's colorful presence is enhanced by the purple costumes worn by local women. Market day is Monday, and Zunil is another town where Maximón is actively worshiped—his image is in the basement of a building just down the hill from the church—and if you want to visit him be sure to bear gifts: money, alcohol, and cigarettes are most welcome. Buses to both towns regularly leave from the area behind Xela's Quezaltenango cathedral, in Zone 1.

High in the hills above Zunil, tucked back in a lush valley, are the **Fuentes Georginas** hot springs. The local municipality has a restaurant and bungalows, also called Fuentes Georginas (*see* Dining and Lodging, *below*), and though the cabins are run-down, they have fireplaces and private tubs, which can sometimes be filled from the springs. The main pool is cleaned on Mondays, but there's a smaller one by the entrance. A dirt road to Georginas heads up from the road between Zunil and Cantel, and pickup taxis take people there from Zunil for a couple of dollars a head.

❼ Totonicapán, some 14 kilometers (8¾ miles) east of Cuatro Caminos, is a traditional village famous for its handicrafts; the tourist office in Xela has maps with all the workshops listed. Totonicapán's market day is Saturday; hop a bus from behind the cathedral in Xela to get there.

San Francisco el Alto, just north of Cuatro Caminos, features the country's largest market, held every Friday, and has great views of **❽** the valley below. **Momostenango** is an extremely traditional village just an hour's drive north on a dirt road from San Francisco. The center of an important wool-producing region, Momostenango displays its wares at a Sunday market. Buses to both San Francisco and Momostenango leave Xela from the Minerva bus station in Zone 3.

❾ Huehuetenango is a quiet town at the foot of the massive Cuchumatanes mountain range, the country's highest. Though Huehuetenango's only real attraction is Zaculeu, a nearby Mayan ruin, it is the gateway to the magnificent Cuchumatanes and the isolated villages scattered across them. The town is centered on a large plaza, surrounded by government offices and a few banks, with a band shell. A couple of blocks to the east is the central market, where local handicrafts can be purchased, and if you're headed for Mexico, the Mexican consulate is in the building of Del Sid pharmacy, on the corner of 5 Avenida and 4 Calle. Direct buses to Guatemala City leave from **Los Halcones** (7 Avenida 3–62) and **Rápidos Zaculeu** (9 Calle 11–42), and both Guatel and the post office are on 2 Calle between 3 and 4 Avenidas.

The ruins of **Zaculeu,** a few kilometers outside town, hardly constitute one of the country's most spectacular archaeological sites, but they are well worth a short visit. In the postclassical period (AD 900–1200), Zaculeu was the capital of the Mam, one of the predominant highland tribes at the time of the conquest but about which little is known. It was conquered by Spanish troops led by Pedro de Alvarado's brother, Gonzalo, and surrendered only after enduring a 45-day siege. The United Fruit Company restored the ruins in the 1940s but did a pretty heavy-handed job and left the site looking rather artificial. Nevertheless, it's a tranquil spot with views of the surrounding pine-draped hills, and a modest museum offers some small insight into the world of the Mam. Minibuses leave for the ruins from the corner of 3 Avenida and 4 Calle in Huehuetenango.

A short drive north of town, the dirt road begins to wind its way up into the **Cuchumatanes Mountains,** where traditional villages are set between massive, rocky peaks. This region offers only budget accommodations and very limited dining options, but if you're willing to rough it a little, you will be well rewarded by your experience here; those who aren't can drive to Todos Santos and return in one day. There's a *mirador* (scenic view) near the town of Chiantla, 6 kilometers (3¾ miles) from Huehuetenango. From there it's up, up, up for quite a while. The most frequently visited mountain village is **❿ Todos Santos,** which can be reached by turning left at the Paquix junction, some 20 kilometers (12½ miles) out of Huehuetenango. Traditional male garb—bright red pants and shirts with oversized red collars—is still commonly worn in this small highland village. Market day is Saturday. The town is also a popular base for hiking to nearby villages, like San Juan Atitán, Santiago Chimaltenango, San

Martín, or Jacaltenango. If you're adventurous, head farther north to **Soloma,** a larger town with markets on Thursdays and Sundays, or on to **San Mateo Ixtatán,** a small village known for its traditional Chuj Indian inhabitants and a small Mayan site nearby. Market days—Thursdays and Sundays—are the best time to visit San Mateo. **Barillas,** to the east, is where the mountains begin to drop down toward the rain forests.

Shopping

The highlands are where nearly all of Guatemala's handicrafts come from, and the region is consequently a shoppers' paradise. The country is most famous for its handwoven fabrics, and in every highland village women can be seen weaving the traditional patterns of that area. But there are countless other kinds of handwork created by Guatemala's indigenous population, and as each region has its traditional fabrics, each one has its other specialties, such as baskets, statues, bags, or hats. The highland town most famous for its shopping is Chichicastenango, but if you plan to visit other villages, remember that the lowest prices are usually found in the areas where the handicrafts are made.

Chichi-castenango Though the selection of goods from around the country at this town's Thursday and Sunday markets is overwhelming, the prices rise the moment the first tour bus rolls into town. If possible, do your purchasing the evening before, when the merchants are setting up, or in the early morning or late afternoon of market day, when the big spenders have moved on. The key to getting a deal in Chichicastenango is hard bargaining.

Panajachel Buying and selling is almost as popular in Panajachel as it is on Wall Street, and everywhere one looks, someone is hawking típica. Local merchants have assembled an impressive array of goods from throughout Guatemala as well as from around the lake, and prices are competitive. Calle Santander is lined with vendors who hang their wares from fences and makeshift stalls. **Casa Alegri,** a large boutique on the east side of Calle Santander, has an interesting selection and good prices, as does **Mayan Relics,** on Monte Rey Street. **Mayan Palace,** on the main street, has an amazing collection of antiques, although prices are high and the authenticity of some goods may be questionable.

Quezaltenango Handiwork from most of the villages in the region can be found in the new market on 15 Avenida and 1 Calle in Zone 3, and since there are few shoppers, prices tend to be low. The other market, near the plaza in Zone 1, has a limited selection of típica. **ADEPH,** an outlet for a local artisans' association, is on Rodolfo Robles Calle 15–63 in Zone 1. Other típica shops include **Salsa Limitada** (12 Avenida 1–40, Zone 1), where you can have clothes custom-made, and **AJ Pop** (14 Avenida "A" 1–26).

Totonicapán All the villages in the Quezaltenango have weekly markets where típica can be purchased, but Totonicapán is full of factories where a wide variety of handicrafts are produced. The tourist office (tel. 9/ 621–392), located on the corner opposite the Hotel Maya Palace, produces a brochure about Totonicapán with a map of all the típica factories and outlets.

Sports

Boating There are a variety of boating options on Lake Atitlán, where ferries run regularly between major towns, small motor boats with drivers can be hired, and plastic "kayaks," pedal boats, and Windsurfers can be rented at the public beach.

Fishing Lake Atitlán is stocked with black bass, but no one rents fishing equipment here, so you'll have to bring your own.

Hiking The Cuchumatanes Mountains are an excellent area for hiking, especially in the area of Todos Santos and the Ixil Triangle. Most of the small villages in those areas can be reached only by foot or horseback, and many of them have rustic hotels for overnights. Topographical maps can be obtained from the **Instituto Geográfico Militar,** in Guatemala City (Avenida de las Américas 5–7, Zona 13, tel. 2/363–281), but the army won't release maps of many areas.

Horseback Riding The **Hotel Vision Azul** (tel. 621–426) in Panajachel has a small ranch from which horses can be rented by the hour.

Swimming It is popular to swim in the brisk waters of Lake Atitlán, but beware of currents: Don't enter the lake during strong winds, and swim upstream of towns to avoid raw sewage. Many Expensive and Moderate hotels have pools.

Volcano Climbing It's best to climb with a guide, or consult one before ascending, since some of the country's volcanoes harbor bandits (*see* Security in Before You Go, *above*). The volcanoes of **Santa Maria** (3,772 meters, or 12,372 feet) and **Tajamulco** (4,210 meters, or 13,809 feet, Guatemala's highest), located near Quezaltenango, are the two best volcanoes for climbing. Both are strenuous ascents and are best done in two days. When the weather is clear, one can see most of the country's other volcanoes from either summit, including nearby Santiaguito, which is frequently erupting. Several tour companies arrange volcano trips.

Dining and Lodging

Dining Panajachel has an impressive selection of quality restaurants and may well have more exceptional eateries than are found in all the rest of the Western Highlands. Unfortunately, few of the town's good restaurants are near the beach, so it can be difficult to enjoy a good meal with a view of the lake. Nevertheless, fine dining is one of the attractions in Panajachel.

Dining options are rather limited in Chichicastenango, with the best food being served in the restaurants of the finer hotels. Quezaltenango has a fair selection of quality restaurants, all in the Inexpensive and Moderate ranges, but the food in the rest of the highlands, though hearty, will elicit little enthusiasm from gourmets.

Lodging Accommodations are distributed through the Western Highlands in much the same way that restaurants are. Panajachel has the widest and best selection; Chichicastenango and Quezaltenango can claim a few creditable establishments; and little else exists beyond that. Chichicastenango's hotels tend to fill up on Wednesday and Saturday nights, so it's best to have reservations. Holy Week is very busy in both Chichicastenango and Atitlán.

Chichicastenango Dining **El Torito.** This second-floor restaurant has an immense dining room that gets packed on market days. It is primarily a steak house, but the menu also features chicken, pork, and some seafood. All meals include a bowl of soup. *Giron Shopping Arcade, no phone. No credit cards. $*

Tziguan Tinamit. This corner restaurant is probably the best of Chichicastenango's meager selection of eateries. Both the decor and the menu are pretty basic: You can count on a selection of beef, chicken, or fish served with rice, beans, and a salad. The most interesting item is pizza, which isn't half bad. *1 block north of the plaza, no phone. No credit cards. $*

Dining and Lodging

Hotel Santo Tomás. A newer hotel built in the Spanish style, this is Chichicastenango's second best. Rooms are spacious and decorated with traditional textiles and antique reproductions, and each one has a fireplace. The back of the hotel is quieter, whereas front rooms overlook the town. Attendants wear traditional costumes, but service is less personalized than it is at the Mayan Inn. To the left of the reception desk is an unmarked room full of masks, statues, and pottery. The large restaurant features a lunch buffet on market days, and on the upper level of the hotel are a heated pool and small spa. *2 blocks east of the plaza, tel. 561–316 or 602–13 in Guatemala City, fax 561–306. 43 rooms with bath. Facilities: bar, restaurant, heated pool, sauna, Jacuzzi, exercise room. DC, MC, V. $$$*

★ **Mayan Inn.** The Mayan Inn has been operating since 1932 and can still be classified as one of the most charming hotels in the country. Rooms are furnished with fireplaces, antiques, and Guatemalan weavings and art. They surround a series of beautifully maintained garden courtyards, and the newer ones look onto the forested hills around town. Highly recommended are the units across the street from the office, in the same compound as the bar and restaurants. They are set in a series of levels built into the hillside, and the lower the level you choose, the more likely you'll have a view of the town's cemetery (not as lugubrious as it sounds) and the surrounding pine forests. Service is excellent, with an attendant in traditional costume assigned to each room who does everything from lighting the fire to serving dinner. Meals are served in stately old dining halls with fireplaces, with a set menu that is changed daily. The restaurant is open to nonguests, with meals served from 7 to 9 AM, noon to 2 PM, and 7 to 9 PM. *1 block west of the plaza, behind Calvario Church, tel. 561–176, 310–215 in Guatemala City, fax 561–212. 30 rooms with bath. Facilities: bar, restaurant. AE, DC, MC, V. $$$*

Lodging

Hotel Villa Grande. This large new luxury hotel at the entrance of town boasts the modern amenities absent from most other Chichicastenango hotels. The hotel consists of three separate buildings, and a fourth is under construction. Guest rooms, with peach walls and típica bedspreads, have a panoramic view of the town. The suites have fireplaces. *Tel. and fax 561–053. 40 rooms with bath. Facilities: health spa, Jacuzzi, pool. No credit cards. $$*

Pension Chiuguila. This pleasant little hotel is located in an older building a few blocks north of the plaza. A variety of rooms face a cobblestoned courtyard, which is used for parking. The tiled portico that most rooms lead off of has some chairs, tables, and potted plants, and there is also a small restaurant with a limited menu. Rooms with shared or private baths are available; the more expensive ones have fireplaces, including a couple of suites with little sitting rooms. *Tel. and fax 561–134. 21 rooms, 16 with bath. No credit cards. $$*

El Salvador. This colorful budget hotel is three blocks south of the plaza, down the hill from the Santo Tomás Church. Rooms surround a large cobblestoned courtyard decorated with statues and potted plants, and facing the entrance is a small shrine shared by the Virgin Mary and a Mayan god. The rooms are a bit musty, the beds are a bit old, and hot water is only available for a couple hours in the morning, but what El Salvador lacks in comfort, it compensates for with low rates and character. *No phone. 22 rooms, 10 with bath. No credit cards. $*

Huehuetenango
Dining

Jardin Café. This colorful little corner restaurant serves decent food in a bright, friendly atmosphere, and consequently it's popular with the locals. It opens daily at 6 AM for breakfast (pancakes are a possibility), and the lunch and dinner menu includes basic beef and chicken as well as a few Mexican dishes. *Corner of 6 Avenida and 4 Calle, no phone. No credit cards. $*

Las Brasas. This little steak house is probably Huehuetenango's best restaurant. The decor is unassuming enough, with lots of wood and simple red-and-white tablecloths, but since it's the only restaurant in town that has anything remotely resembling atmosphere, it is a fairly reassuring sight. The house specialty is grilled meat, but the menu is fairly ample and even includes Chinese food, which you sure won't find anywhere else in town. *Corner of 4 Avenida and 2 Calle, no phone. No credit cards. $*

★ **Pizza Hogarena.** You can build your own pizza from a long list of fresh ingredients, or opt for spaghetti, grilled meat, or sandwiches. *6 Avenida 4–49, no phone. No credit cards. $*

Lodging

Hotel Los Cuchumatanes. Two kilometers (1¼ miles) outside of town, this hotel is ideal for those traveling with a car. Located on an old plantation, it is clean with a modern, motellike feel. The hotel has a swimming pool and a terrace that overlooks a garden. The owners are constructing tennis courts. *Zona 7, tel. 641–951, fax 642–816. Facilities: bar, cable TV, pool. 22 rooms with bath. AE, DC, MC, V. $$*

Hotel Zaculeu. This older hotel off the main square has long been Huehuetenango's most charming inn, but recent expansion and remodeling have made it the city's most comfortable one as well. The entrance leads into a lush garden courtyard, which is surrounded by a portico and the hotel's older rooms. A passage on the other end of the courtyard leads to the new rooms, which are built on two levels and surround an enclosed parking area. Take your pick: Older rooms are graced with local weavings and other handicrafts, but the newer ones have wall-to-wall carpeting, modern bathrooms, and TVs; older rooms have more character but can be noisier, especially those along the street, while the newer units are more expensive. *5 Avenida 1–14, tel. 641–575. 38 rooms with bath. No credit cards. $$*

Hotel Mary. This four-story hotel in the heart of town offers comfortable, clean accommodations at a good price, but not much more. Though not terribly attractive, Hotel Mary is conveniently located across the street from the post and Guatel offices. *2 Calle 3–52, tel. 641–618. 25 rooms, 11 with bath. $*

Panajachel
Dining

Casablanca. This restaurant has a reputation for serving some of the best food in town, and you'll find it right on the main street across from the Maya Inn. Seating is in a wood-trimmed and white-walled dining room, with windows overlooking the street and artwork by Guatemalan talent enhancing the simple, tasteful decor. Or you may elect to sit upstairs at one of the few tables on the more private upper level. Occasionally the management hires musicians for entertainment. The menu is ample—more European than Guatemalan, actually—including a selection of soups and salads, pasta, meat dishes, and seafood. *Calle Santander, no phone. DC, MC, V. Dinner only. $$$*

Al Chisme. This popular restaurant owned by an American woman serves good food in a relaxed atmosphere. Seating is on a covered terrace or in the main dining room, decorated with black-and-white photos of some of Panajachel's more interesting faces. There's usually rock and roll playing on the stereo, and many of the regulars are a testament to the town's reputation as a hippie hangout. As a popular breakfast spot, Al Chisme serves homemade bagels and pastries, but the lunch and dinner menu is even better, with a selection rang-ing from chicken cordon bleu to shrimp curry crepes to three-cheese lasagna. *Avenida de los Arboles, no phone. No credit cards. Closed Wed. $$*

★ **El Bistro.** This small Italian restaurant, among the best Panajachel has to offer, is hidden behind a low wall and iron gate where the main drag hits the lake. A couple of tables are set up in a garden, where hummingbirds dart among flowering vines. Inside are two cozy, in-timate dining rooms. All of the simple but delicious food, from the tasty bread to the fresh pasta, is homemade. Two standout special-ties are the fettuccine arrabiata with a slightly spicy tomato sauce and the steak au poivre cooked in a wine sauce and served with fresh vegetables. *Final de la Calle Santander, no phone. No credit cards. Closed Tues. $$*

La Laguna. A comfortable restaurant in a former residence, La La-guna is set off the main street and surrounded by a large lawn. Seat-ing is on the porch or in a scattering of rooms in the old house, which is decorated with wooden masks and other local handicrafts. The slightly dark, candlelit interior and mellow jazz or Latin American music on the stereo make it the perfect place for a romantic dinner. The selection at this lunch and dinner restaurant ranges from the traditional *pepian de pollo* (chicken in a spicy sauce) to the Spanish rice and seafood dish, paella, which must be ordered two hours in advance. *Located on the south side of the street just east of Calle Santander, tel. 621–231. DC, MC, V. $$*

El Patio. Across the street and north of the Guatel building, this res-taurant can be recognized by the patio to which it owes its name. Though the patio itself is a pleasant spot to sit and watch the world go by, most of the restaurant's seating is indoors, in a large dining room with little ambience. It's a fairly popular spot for breakfast, but the lunch and dinner menu offers greater variety, with items like filet mignon, chicken à la king, roast pork, and a barbecue spe-cial on Sundays. *Calle Santander, no phone. No credit cards. $*

Dining and Lodging ★ **Hotel Atitlán.** As you take the main road out of town, you'll come to a fork in the road with a sign marked HOTEL. Located on a quiet cove about a mile east of town, this is the area's most luxurious and ex-pensive hotel. An older, Spanish-style inn, it consists of a main building—with reception, bar, restaurant, conference rooms, and gift shop—flanked by two-story wings that form a semicircle around the pool and gardens. The hotel was designed so that all the rooms have a view of the lake, and the extensive grounds include a long stretch of beach and a wooded region traversed by footpaths. The rooms themselves have a colonial decor, with tile floors, carved wooden furniture, and handwoven blankets and rugs; each unit has a balcony or patio with a view of the tropical gardens and lake. Even if you don't stay there, it's worth stopping by for a meal or drink in the bar or restaurant, as the view of the water from both is wonderful, especially at sunset. *1 mile east of Panajachel, tel. and fax 621–441 or 372–557 in Guatemala City. 64 rooms with bath. Facilities: res-taurant, bar, conference rooms, heated swimming pool, tennis court. AE, DC, MC, V. $$$$*

Cacique Inn. This quiet hotel is located one block off the main street, and though it doesn't have a view of the lake, it has an excellent res-taurant, a swimming pool, and a lovely garden. Spacious though sparsely decorated rooms with private baths are located in two-sto-ry buildings, and large sliding-glass doors open onto terraces that look onto the garden. The rooms may seem a bit cool with their tile floors and small rugs, but they all have fireplaces that can warm them up quickly if need be. The hotel grounds are surrounded by a wall, which makes the terraces and patio by the pool good private havens for relaxing. The Cacique's restaurant is one of the best in town, offering an ample selection of international and Guatemalan cuisine. Cacique's agreeable chefs will sometimes even prepare dishes that aren't on the menu. *Calle del Embarcadero, tel. and fax 621–205. 33 rooms with bath. Facilities: restaurant, bar, pool. No credit cards. $$$*

Lodging **Hotel del Lago.** This six-story building behind the public beach is Panajachel's biggest and most modern hotel. It may not look like much from outside, and the colorful contemporary interior is a far cry from those of more traditional hotels, but it is comfortable, conveniently located, and offers first-class services and some great views of the lake. Rooms feature wall-to-wall carpeting, firm double beds, cable TV, large bathrooms, and either balconies or patios (first floor) with Atitlán vistas. There's an airy bar with a verdant backdrop, and the adjacent restaurant that looks onto the pool is immense. *Calle Rancho Grande, tel. 621–555 or 334–633 in Guatemala City, fax 621–562. 100 rooms with bath. Facilities: restaurant, bar, pool, Jacuzzi, sauna, massage, conference rooms, games room. AE, DC, MC, V. $$$*

Hotel Vision Azul. Located on the road to the Hotel Atitlán, this place seems to be a smaller, cheaper version of that venerable hotel—not as nice but at half the price. Rooms in the main building are decorated in the colonial style, with antique reproductions and traditional weavings, and each one opens onto a small porch or balcony with a distant view of the lake. A series of simple bungalows, with three beds each, sits along the road, and while they're not as attractive as the main rooms, they are very private. The hotel's extensive grounds include a long stretch of waterfront, but all the rooms are set several hundred feet off the lake, on the south side of the road. For equestrian spirits, the hotel also owns a small ranch that rents horses and arranges guided trail rides. *Tel. and fax 621–426. 25 rooms and 8 bungalows, all with bath. Facilities: restaurant, bar, pool, beach, stables. AE, DC, MC, V. $$–$$$*

Hotel Monterrey. This is the least expensive hotel on the waterfront, and though the rooms themselves don't look like much, the view from their windows easily makes up for it. The two-story cement building isn't attractive by any standards, and the rooms lack decor, but wait! Every single unit is clean and has a bathroom and a view of the lake. The large swimming pool is surrounded by a deck and lawn, and there's also a private beach and a little restaurant. *Waterfront between Embarcadero and Santander streets, tel. 621–126. 30 rooms with bath. Facilities: restaurant, pool, beach. No credit cards. $$*

Hotel Regis. Hotel Regis isn't quite as attractive or quiet as Rancho Grande (*see below*), but it's less expensive. A group of bungalows is spread out around verdant grounds, where there's a small playground and a Jacuzzi. The decor of the rooms is an attempt at the popular colonial motif. Several bungalows have fireplaces, and a couple that have kitchens can sleep six. Though the grounds aren't terribly large, they are well tended, and the hotel is conveniently located in the heart of town. *Calle Santander, across from Guatel, tel. 621–149, fax 621–152. 19 rooms with bath. Facilities: restaurant, Jacuzzi, parking, playground. MC, V. $$*

Rancho Grande. About halfway between the beach and old town is Rancho Grande, a series of bungalows that flank the street of the same name. This bed-and-breakfast was opened around 1950 by German immigrant Milly Schleisier, who melded the designs of country houses in her homeland with the colorful culture of her adopted residence. Since 1975 it has belonged to Marlita Hannstein, who has maintained the level of comfort and service established by Schleisier. Every room is unique, but all are spacious, with wood ceilings, white stucco walls, tile floors, and locally woven rugs and bed covers. Some bungalows sleep five, the suite has a fireplace and cable TV, and all units have porches and are separated by lawns and gardens. *Calle Rancho Grande, tel. 621–554, fax 622–247. 12 rooms with bath. Facilities: breakfast room, parking, lawns, gardens. DC, MC, V. $$*

Hotel Galindo. This conveniently located hotel is in the heart of town on the main street, behind its own spacious restaurant. Rooms are small and haven't been decorated, but they surround a lush garden courtyard. Behind the courtyard are several suites, which are considerably larger with separate sitting rooms and fireplaces; if you can afford it, a suite is certainly worth the extra money. The restaurant is airy and attractive, but better food can be found nearby. *Calle Principal, tel. 621–168, fax 621–178. 18 rooms with bath. DC, MC, V. $*

Hotel Maya Kanek. Located on the main street at the edge of the old town, this place is in a quiet area with fewer foreigners than in the tourist side of town. The Maya Kanek is arranged like a miniature motel, with rooms surrounding a paved parking area. The rooms themselves are rather small, with little decor to speak of, but they are clean and have new, firm bed mattresses. The owner is a friendly fellow, and he has assembled a thorough list of local boat and bus schedules in the lobby. *Calle Principal, tel. 621–104. 26 rooms with bath. No credit cards. $*

Quezaltenango
Dining
★

Casa Grande. This new restaurant located in a former residence in Zone 3 has filled a void in this city of few fine dining options. The "Big House" is an impressive white edifice of modern Spanish design across the street from Benito Juárez Park. Seating is in the foyer and in several simple but elegant rooms decorated with a bit of contemporary art. An interesting array of Continental cuisine is served, ranging from filet mignon to shrimp scampi to cheese fondue. Sit back and enjoy the dinner music on Thursday through Saturday nights; Sunday lunches are enlivened by marimba. A rather plush lounge, paneled in mahogany, is attached to the restaurant. If you're feeling less hungry or fancy, go for the inexpensive café on the second floor, where you can sit outdoors and munch on an afternoon snack. *Corner of 4 Calle and 16 Avenida, Zona 3, tel. 612–601. AE, DC, MC, V. $$*

Royal Paris. This smaller restaurant half a block from the Casa Grande isn't nearly as impressive as its neighbor, but it offers a limited menu of interesting dishes, like chicken curry and vegetarian sandwiches. You'll find a dark, slightly bohemian feel here. The ambience is definitely imported, with some Parisian scenes on the walls and jazz playing on the stereo. In back of the restaurant is a small bar, which is popular with foreigners who come to Xela to study Spanish. *16 Avenida 3–05, Zona 3, no phone. No credit cards. Open for dinner only. $$*

El Kopetin. Aside from the two big hotels, this restaurant serves the best food in Zone 1. It's not large or fancy, but El Kopetin is somehow comforting, with its wood paneling and long polished bar. The menu has a number of appetizers, like *queso fundido* (melted cheese served with condiments and tortillas), and a selection of meat and seafood dishes, some of which get smothered in rich sauces. Good food and service at reasonable prices have made El Kopetin popular with the locals, so it can be tough to get a seat later in the evening. *14 Avenida 3–51, Zona 1, tel. 612–401. No credit cards. $*

Dining and Lodging
★

Hotel Villa Real Plaza. Across the plaza from the Bonifaz is Quezaltenango's other first-class hotel, which was recently remodeled and renamed by new management. The Villa Real is centered around a spacious covered courtyard, topped by skylights. Rooms are large and modern, with wall-to-wall carpeting, double beds, and fireplaces. The restaurant has an interesting selection that ranges from cordon bleu to a variety of stews and pastas, plus a small sampling of vegetarian dishes. The hotel also has a large bar that changes into a disco on weekends. *4 Calle 12–22, Zona 1, tel. 616–270, fax 616–780. 34 rooms with bath. Facilities: cable TV, restaurant, bar, parking. AE, DC, MC, V. $$$*

Pension Bonifaz. Don't be fooled by the term "pension" in its name—this is Quezaltenango's most upscale hotel. Inside a stately old yellow edifice by the northeast corner of the Central Plaza, the Bonifaz's interior isn't quite as grand as its exterior, but it is a comfortable, well-run establishment. Rooms are large and carpeted, with a fairly modern decor. The nicest rooms are in the older building—the hotel was expanded years ago—and if you don't mind a little noise, the ones on the street have little balconies that offer some pleasant views of the central plaza. The rooftop garden is a quiet spot for soaking up the afternoon sun. A small café serving sandwiches and Mexican fare and a sizable restaurant are located in the covered courtyard that is also the lobby. The restaurant offers an extensive menu of Continental cuisine, and it has one of the better kitchens in town. The café and the restaurant share a devilishly tempting pastry cart. *4 Calle 10–50, Zona 1, tel. 614–241 or 612–959. 63 rooms with bath. Facilities: cable TV, restaurant, café, bar, roof garden, parking. AE, DC, MC, V. $$$*

Lodging

Hotel Centroamericano. This modern, comfortable hotel is located in Zone 3, which is on the periphery of the city but is closer to the main bus terminal and near several worthy restaurants. The Centroamericano resembles a North American motel; its decor is something like '70s Wisconsin, with lots of wood, spacious rooms, new furniture, and ample parking. The key here is comfort, with firm beds and large, modern bathrooms. The hotel has a large restaurant, but with two excellent restaurants a few blocks away, by Benito Juárez Park, there's no reason to eat anything but breakfast here. *Corner of 4 Calle and 14 Avenida, Zona 3, tel. 630–261. 14 rooms with bath. DC, MC, V. $$*

Hotel Modelo. Founded in 1883, the Modelo is a small, family-run establishment that over the years has maintained a distinguished appearance and a tradition of good service. Rooms face a couple of small courtyards with porticoes leading off the lobby, which also adjoins a fine little colonial-style restaurant. Much of the hotel's furniture is antique, and the rooms have wooden floors and stucco walls decorated with traditional weavings. There's also a nearby annex, which has some newer rooms that rent for less. *Located a few blocks from the plaza, between Avenidas 14 and 15, 14 Avenida "A" 2–31, Zona 1, tel. and fax 612–529. 24 rooms with bath. AE, MC, V. $$*

Casa del Viajero. It's a bit of a walk from the plaza, but this is one of Xela's best bets for budget travelers. Casa del Viajero is clean, comfortable, and safe. A small restaurant serves standard Guatemalan fare, and rooms with either private or shared bath are available. There are also a few two-room apartments available, with small kitchens, which cost little more than the hotel rooms. *8 Avenida 9–17, Zona 1, tel. 614–594, fax 630–743. No credit cards. $*

Casa Kaehler. This quiet pension a few blocks off the plaza is run by a friendly family of German descent and is a popular spot with budget travelers. Rooms are on two floors of a converted residence and face a small, plain courtyard. Though the rooms are simple, they are clean, and the hotel has a separate lounge where guests gather to read, relax, or chat. There's only one room with a private bath and a double bed, but the shared baths are well maintained and have plenty of hot water. *13 Avenida 3–33, Zona 1, tel. 612–091. 7 rooms, 1 with bath. No credit cards. $*

Fuentes Georginas. The local municipality has a dozen bungalows and a restaurant at these lovely hot springs high in the mountains above Zunil. The cabins are a bit run-down, and in recent years there has been a dearth of water at times, but the area presents a wonderful example of cloud-forest ecology, there are some nice walks, and the restaurant is decent. Since there's no phone, you're stuck if you arrive and they're full, but the risk is usually confined to weekends. Turn left after passing Zunil, then right on the first dirt road; from there it's about a 20-minute drive into the hills. Or take the bus to Zunil and pay a couple of dollars for a ride up in one of the pickup taxis that park by the main road. *No address or phone. 12 bungalows with baths. Facilities: hot springs, restaurant, parking. No credit cards. $*

San Antonio Palopó
Lodging

Terrazas del Lago. This very basic hotel on the town's public beach is decorated with floral-patterned stone tiles. Guest rooms have stone walls, wood tables, and iron candlesticks; rooms in front have patios with lake vistas. Breakfast and sandwiches can be prepared for guests in a tiny kitchen in the back. *Calle de la Playa, tel. 621–288. 14 rooms with bath. No credit cards. $$*

Santa Catarina Palopó
Dining and Lodging

Villa Santa Catarina. This hotel, housed in a long, two-story yellow building with adobe tile roof, offers spectacular views of the lake and volcanoes. Guest rooms are small, with hardwood floors and ceilings, peach walls, and *típica* bedspreads; each has a private balcony. The restaurant serves typical Guatemalan dishes such as *pepian* (chicken in a spicy gravy) and fresh *robalo* (snook). It has a large pool and offers waterskiing and windsurfing. *Calle de la Playa, tel. in Guatemala City 348–136. 33 rooms with bath. Facilities: restaurant, bar, pool, games room, laundry, waterskiing and windsurfing equipment. AE, DC, MC, V. $$$*

Santa Cruz la Laguna
Dining and Lodging

Arca de Noé. This rustic lakeside hotel boasts magnificent views, friendly owners, and delicious home cooking. The guest rooms, housed in several attached wood and stone bungalows, are small but neat, with low ceilings. Electricity is solar-powered, and there is no hot water. Meals are served family-style in the main building, which resembles a New England farmhouse. The menu changes constantly, but each meal comes with fresh vegetables and bread right out of the oven. *Main dock, tel. and fax 621–196. 8 rooms, 5 with bath. Facilities: restaurant, swimming, canoe rental. No credit cards. Closed May 10–31. $$*

Santiago Atitlán
Dining and Lodging
★

Posada de Santiago. This fabulous hotel is sandwiched between two volcanoes on the shores of the lagoon at the south edge of town. The owners have brought the friendliness of northern California as well as incredible cooking to this old-fashioned Indian village. The bungalows have carved-wood doors, stone walls, fireplaces, and thick wool blankets on the beds. There is a small store on the premises, and canoe and mountain-bike rentals are available. The restaurant serves exquisite specialties such as smoked chicken *píbil* in a tangy red sauce and Thai coconut shrimp; it also boasts an extensive wine list. *Tel. and fax 627–167. 6 bungalows with bath. Facilities: restaurant, shop, sports-equipment rentals. No credit cards. $$*

Nightlife

Chichi- Chichicastenango has few night spots—the hotel bars are as good as
castenango it gets. The best entertainment on a Wednesday or Saturday night is
to wander around town, visit the church, and watch the vendors set
up their stalls.

Panajachel This resort town probably has the liveliest nightlife in the highlands, which doesn't mean much. The **Circus Bar,** on the Calle de los
Arboles, is a popular night spot that also serves good food.
Chapiteau, across the street, is a large bar and disco that sometimes
offers live music. For a more sedate evening, try the video lounges at
the **Zanahoria Chic restaurant,** on Avenida de los Arboles, and at the
Grapevine, on Calle Santander, which has a happy hour from 7 to 9.

Quezaltenango Besides the lounges in the big hotels, there are few night spots in
this town. But a luxurious little bar operates at the **Casa Grande** hotel, which sometimes has live music on weekends. **Royal Paris,** down
the block, also has a quiet bar (*see* Dining and Lodging, *above*). If
you're in the mood for dancing, try **El Garage Club** on Boulevard
Minerva.

The Verapaces and Atlantic Lowlands

From the misty mountains of Alta Verapaz to the torrid beaches of
the Caribbean coast, this region's natural bounty unfolds in the
caves and pools near Lanquín, the lush forests of the Quetzal Reserve, the languid waters of the Dulce River, and the ancient Mayan
city of Copán, just over the border in Honduras. The eastern departments of Alta Verapaz and Baja Verapaz are rich in beauty, culture,
and history, but they are missed by the majority of visitors to Guatemala who spend their entire vacations in the highlands or El Petén.

Here is a mountainous verdant region covered with lush forests and
coffee plantations, drained by wild rivers, and pierced by deep caverns. The smaller Baja Verapaz, to the south, is drier than Alta
Verapaz, where deluges are common and mist-covered mountains
the norm. The area's humid climate has made it the cradle of
Guatemala's coffee production, but is also responsible for the lush
tropical forests that drape uncultivated hillsides and the crystalline
rivers that flow between them, some of which are perfect for white-
water rafting.

The region's inhabitants are predominantly Pokomchí and Kekchí
Indians, who over the years have lost much of their territory to expanding coffee plantations and have abandoned some of their traditional ways. There is also some lingering remnant of the culture
imported by German immigrants, most of whom were expelled
years ago. The region's largest city is Cobán, which doesn't have
many attractions of its own but is a good base for exploring surrounding villages and natural wonders, like the emerald pools of
Semuc Champey and the grottos of Lanquín.

Guatemala's small stretch of Caribbean coast and its hinterlands are
sparsely inhabited, hot, and humid, and are covered in many areas
with luxuriant tropical forests. Though the indigenous culture is not
as striking as what one encounters in the highlands, the coast today
has Guatemala's only representation of Afro-Caribbean culture, and
in times past the region was an important part of the ancient Maya

empire, as is attested by the presence of some important archaeo-logical sites. The area's numerous attractions include the spectacu-lar Dulce River, the typically Caribbean town of Livingston, and the impressive ruins of Quiriguá. The Atlantic region is also on the way to El Petén, if you brave the overland route.

Arriving and Departing

By Car The Atlantic Highway leaves Guatemala City from the north end of town, at Calle 5 in Zone 2. It heads northeast, first through some mountains, later descending into the desert region of Zacapa and then through the lush Caribbean lowlands to Puerto Barrios. At El Rancho (K 84), the road to the left heads toward the mountains of Baja and Alta Verapaz. The Quetzal Reserve is about 75 kilometers (46½ miles) north of El Rancho, and Cobán is another 50 kilometers (31 miles) north of the reserve. Lanquín Caves are located some 63 kilometers (39 miles) to the northeast of Cobán on a rough road, and Semuc Champey is about 10 kilometers (6 miles) beyond Lanquín, but a four-wheel-drive vehicle is needed for that stretch. If you con-tinue northeast on the Atlantic Highway, the turnoff for Quiriguá, a dirt road on the right, is at Km 205, shortly after Los Amates. The road to the Dulce River heads off to the left at Km 245, shortly after the road to Morales. Copán, in Honduras, 238 kilometers (149 miles) from Guatemala City, can be driven to via the Atlantic Highway to Río Hondo, then south past Chiquimula to Vado Hondo, where a dusty road heads off to the left to the border post of El Florido, and on to the nearby ruins.

By Bus Regular bus service links Guatemala City (**Transportes Escobar/ Monja Blanca,** 8 Avenida 15–16, Zona 1, tel. 511–878) and Cobán (4 Avenida and 0 Calle, no phone), with departures every hour or so from 4 AM to 4 PM at both ends of the route, and includes comfortable Pullman direct buses. All buses pass the Quetzal Reserve, and the trip to Cobán takes four hours. Regular buses leave Cobán for San Pedro Carchá, which operates sporadic service to Cahabón via Lanquín. Buses also leave Cobán at 5, 8, and 11 AM for the seven-hour trip to El Estor, on Lake Izabal, which has a budget hotel and ferry service at 5 AM to Mariscos, with bus connections to Puerto Barrios or Guatemala City.

Comfortable buses run the route between the capital and Puerto Barrios, with hourly departures from 6 AM to 5 PM, but be sure to ask for the direct bus (**LITEGUA,** 15 Calle 10–40, Zona 1, tel. 538–169). The ruins of Quiriguá are 3 kilometers (2 miles) south of the highway around Km 205, and there is sporadic bus or prompt motorcycle-taxi service to and from the site and the highway. If you're headed for Fronteras, you'll want to get off at Ruidosa junction and catch a minibus north, but if you're on a late bus (leaving after 1 PM) you'll have to hitch. **Izabal Adventures** (tel. 340–323) runs a convenient and comfortable Río Dulce shuttle with door-to-door service to El Relleno on Monday, Wednesday, Friday, Saturday, and Sunday. The van departs Antigua at 5 AM ($32 one way) and Guatemala City at 6 AM ($23). The ride includes a side trip to Quiriguá. Reservations are required. All Flores-bound buses pass through Fronteras, but they are slower than the Puerto Barrios buses. Hourly buses leave Guatemala City in Copán for Chiquimula from 18 Calle and 9 Avenida in Zone 1; from Chiquimula, buses regularly leave for El Florida, and a variety of transportation services the route between the border and Ruinas de Copán. Many Guatemala City travel agencies offer one- or two-day tours to Copán.

By Boat Daily ferry service between Puerto Barrios and Livingston leaves Puerto Barrios at 10:30 AM and 5 PM and Livingston at 5 AM and 2 PM. The mail boat carries passengers up and down the Dulce River between El Relleno (south side of the bridge) and Livingston on Tuesday and Friday mornings. There are also plenty of private boats on both ends that will make the trip for a fee. Or you can rent a 46-foot Polynesian catamaran that sleeps 10 people for trips from the Dulce River to the Belizean cays. Contact **Tivoli Travel** in Antigua (5 Avenida Norte 10A, tel. 323–041).

Exploring the Verapaces and Atlantic Lowlands

Though these two eastern regions are very similar in the dampness of their climates and the verdant hue of their scenery, the Verapaces are a predominantly mountainous region whereas the Atlantic zone is comparatively flat. They are also very separate regions: Most travelers enter and leave the Verapaces by the same route, and though there is more room to move around in the Atlantic zone, most visitors arrive and depart here via the Atlantic Highway.

Highlights for **Livingston** (*see* Tour 2: The Atlantic Lowlands)
First-time **Quetzal Reserve** (*see* Tour 1: Baja and Alta Verapaz)
Visitors **Quiriguá Ruins** (*see* Tour 2: The Atlantic Lowlands)
Río Dulce (*see* Tour 2: The Atlantic Lowlands)

Numbers in the margin correspond to points of interest on the Verapaces and Atlantic Lowlands map.

Tour 1: Seventy-five kilometers (46½ miles) north of El Rancho is the **Baja and Alta** **Quetzal Reserve,** a 1,154-hectare (2,849-acre) tract of cloud forest **Verapaz** along the road to Cobán, just south of the village of Purhulhá (*see* ❶ Chapter 3, National Parks and Wildlife Reserves). The reserve was created to protect Guatemala's national bird, the resplendent quetzal, which is endangered by the indiscriminate destruction of the country's forests. It is also called the Mario Dary Reserve, after the Guatemalan ecologist who fought for its creation and was a victim of the political violence of the early 1980s.

The elusive but beautiful quetzal has been revered since the days of the ancient Maya, who called it the winged serpent. Though the Maya often captured quetzals to remove their tail feathers, which grow back, killing one was a capital offense. The quetzal has long symbolized freedom, since it is said that the bird cannot live in captivity. While the female quetzal is attractive, the male is as spectacular a creature as ever took to the air, with its crimson belly, bright green back, and long-flowing tail feathers. Its unforgettable appearance notwithstanding, the quetzal remains difficult to spot within the mist and lush foliage of the cloud forest.

The reserve has several well-kept trails that wind through the forest, and the 3⅝-kilometer (2¼-mile) Musgos trail passes a lovely waterfall. Since it is easier to spot quetzals around dawn or dusk, it's worth spending a night in the area. Even if you don't catch a glimpse of the legendary quetzal, there are plenty of other species to be spotted, and the luxuriant verdure of the cloud forest is gorgeous in its own right.

Time Out Even if you don't plan to spend a night near the Quetzal Reserve, the **Posada Montaña del Quetzal** (*see* Chapter 3, National Parks and Wildlife Reserves), a few kilometers south of the reserve, has a couple of inexpensive restaurants, which makes it the perfect stop for a meal or snack.

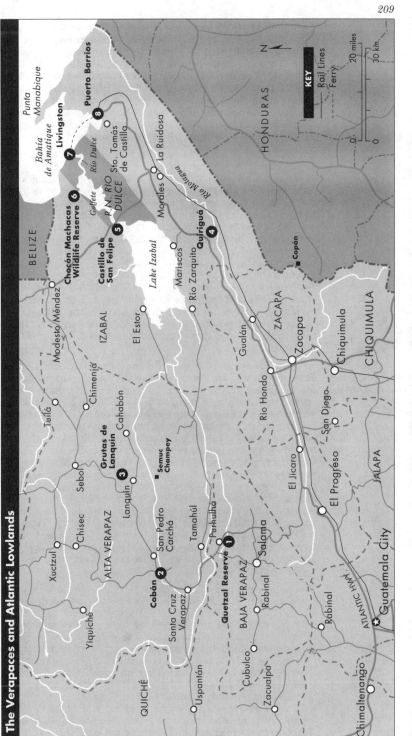

The Verapaces and Atlantic Lowlands

KEY
Rail Lines
Ferry

N

20 miles
30 km

HONDURAS

BELIZE

Punta Manabique
Bahía de Amatique
Puerto Barrios
Livingston
Río Dulce
Sto. Tomás de Castilla
P.N. RÍO DULCE
Golfete
Chocón Machacas Wildlife Reserve
Castillo de San Felipe
La Ruidosa
Morales
Quiriguá
Río Zarquito
Mariscos
El Estor
Lake Izabal
Modesto Méndez
IZABAL
Chimenjá
Cahabón
Copán
Gualán
ZACAPA
Tuilá
Sebol
Grutas de Lanquín
Semuc Champey
Zacapa
CHIQUIMULA
Chisec
Xuctzul
Lanquín
San Pedro Carchá
Tamahú
Río Hondo
San Diego
Chiquimula
Yiquiché
ALTA VERAPAZ
Cobán
Tamahú
Purulhá
El Jicaro
El Progreso
JALAPA
QUICHÉ
Santa Cruz Verapaz
Quetzal Reserve
Salamá
BAJA VERAPAZ
Rabinal
Rabinal
Uspantán
Cubulco
Zacualpa
Chimaltenango
Guatemala City
ATLANTIC HWY.

Continue north from the reserve for another 50 kilometers (31 miles) to the city of **Cobán.** The principal city of the Verapaces, Cobán is in many ways the city that coffee built. During the 19th-century coffee boom, Cobán functioned almost independently of Guatemala City, exporting its products and dealing directly with Germany, whence most of its prominent citizens came. Though German influence declined during World War II, when the U.S. government pressured Guatemala to expel most of the region's German residents, traces of their influence remain. The city has an attractive plaza and cathedral, as well as a selection of hotels and restaurants.

San Pedro Carchá, 6 kilometers (3¾ miles) east of Cobán, is a traditional little town with an interesting daily market. Nearby Las Islas, with a waterfall and pool, is a popular spot for picnics and swimming. The village of Lanquín, a couple of hours' drive to the northeast, is near some impressive caves called **Grutas de Lanquín.** Stop by the municipal offices in Lanquín and arrange to have someone turn the lights on and let you into the caves, for which there is a small charge. They can describe the way to **Semuc Champey,** a natural arch topped by a series of emerald pools that are perfect for swimming and are surrounded by dense forest. Semuc Champey is a spectacularly beautiful spot and is only 10 kilometers (6 miles) to the south on a dirt road, but you'll need a four-wheel-drive vehicle to reach it. The **Cahabón River,** which pours into a sinkhole nearby, is popular for white-water rafting farther downstream. Rafting trips on the Cahabón, which last one to three days, can be arranged through Maya Expeditions (*see* Tour Companies in Staying in Guatemala, *above*).

Tour 2: The Atlantic Lowlands As you head east on the Atlantic Highway, past the turnoffs for the Verapaces and Copán, the ancient Mayan ruins of **Quiriguá** stand a few kilometers to the south of the road. This important Mayan trading center originally stood on the banks of the Motagua River, which has since changed its course and was closely linked to Copán for many years. It is famous for its beautiful and intricate carving, which is similar to that of Copán, and especially for its massive stelae, which are the largest in the Mayan world. The stelae depict Quiriguá's most powerful chiefs, especially Cauac Sky, who was probably the city's most influential leader. Several monuments, covered with interesting zoomorphological figures, still stand, and the remains of an acropolis and other structures have been partially restored. The site is located 3 kilometers (2 miles) south of the Atlantic Highway, around Km 205, in the heart of banana country. The ruins are surrounded by a lush stand of rain forest—an island of untouched wilderness in a sea of agricultural production—and is an excellent spot for birding as well as for the area's obvious archaeological assets.

Continuing east on the highway, past the turnoff to Morales, you'll reach the junction called Ruidosa, where a road heads north toward El Petén. Some 30 kilometers (19 miles) north of the junction, the road crosses the **Río Dulce** (Dulce River), a short but significant waterway that is well worth exploring. The wide, jungle-lined Dulce River drains Lake Izabal, Guatemala's largest, and flows slowly into the Caribbean next to the colorful community of Livingston, just 37 kilometers (23 miles) to the east. The river was an important Mayan trade route and later became the colony's link with Spain. Because Spanish ships regularly exported Guatemala's products via the river, it was also frequented by pirates, who attacked both the ships and the warehouses on the shore of the lake. In hopes of curtailing these forays, the colonists built a series of forts during the 17th cen-

tury on the north bank of the river by the entrance to the lake. These
❺ forts, called **Castillo de San Felipe,** were repeatedly razed by the pirates only to be rebuilt bigger and better. In the 1950s the Guatemalan government reconstructed the ruined castle to resemble its last
version, and the result is an attractive landmark located in a small
national park, which can be reached by road or a short boat ride from
El Relleno, the town on the south end of the bridge. The castle is
located on the river's north bank at the entrance to Lake Izabal, a
few kilometers west of the massive cement bridge that spans the river and connects the town of Fronteras, on the north bank, to El
Relleno, on the south. East of the bridge, the river is lined with an
odd mixture of Ladino communities, luxury homes and hotels, and
Kekchí Indian villages. Traffic on the river includes yachts, fancy
motor boats, and a variety of dugout canoes called *cayucas*. Trips
down the river can be arranged through most of the area's hotels or
with the **Río Dulce Travel Warehouse** (can be reached through Izabal
Adventures, tel. 340–323), in El Relleno near the water, under the
concrete bridge. The company also offers trips to **Finca Paraíso**
(Paradise Farm) on Lake Izabal. An hour's boat ride takes you to the
farm; from there, you can walk 45 minutes or hire a tractor to a river
with a fabulous hot-springs waterfall set in a secluded spot in the
forest. The owners of the farm charge $1 to visit the site. They make
excellent lunches and have several rustic cabins available for rent.

Time Out   If you take a boat to see the ruins, you may want to work a stop at
Suzanna's Laguna into the trip. This moderately priced restaurant
is excellent but can only be reached by water. It's hidden in a cove
across from the castle, but the boat pilots know how to find it. You
should bargain the lunch stop into the price of a river tour before embarking.

The farther you get from the bridge, the fewer fancy homes you'll
see, and the river soon widens into a small lake known as the
Golfete. The northern side of the Golfete is covered by the 7,205-
❻ hectare (17,790-acre) **Chocón Machacas Wildlife Reserve** (*see* Chapter 3, National Parks and Wildlife Reserves), which includes
stretches of virgin rain forest and an extensive mangrove swamp
that is frequented by manatees—shy marine mammals also known
as sea cows. East of the Golfete, the river narrows and passes
through a spectacular forest-draped gorge before pouring into the
Caribbean next to the funky town of Livingston.

❼ **Livingston** can be reached only by water, either by traveling down
the river from El Relleno, or by ferry from Puerto Barrios or Belize.
It is a charming little beach town that resembles Belize much more
than anything else you'll find in Guatemala. Its main inhabitants are
Garífuna, descendants of renegade slaves who migrated there from
the island of Roatan, off the coast of Honduras. Their language is a
strange mixture of African and European tongues, and their life-
style is more outdoor-oriented, laid-back, and freewheeling than
that of Guatemala's other ethnic groups, which are also represented
within the town. The narrow beach that stretches north from the
river mouth is lined with shacks for several kilometers and is not
very clean near town. But a 1½-hour walk or short boat ride to the
north takes you to a gorgeous little river with a series of deep pools
and rainy-season waterfalls called **Siete Altares**, which is ideal for
swimming and is near a pleasant beach and restaurant. Don't leave
things unguarded at the falls, since the forest sometimes harbors
thieves, and avoid walking on the beach late at night. Day trips from
Livingston up the Dulce River to the wildlife reserve or Punta

Manabique can be arranged through the Tucán Dugú (*see* Dining and Lodging, *below*) or Casa Rosada hotel, or with the **Río Dulce Travel Warehouse** in El Relleno.

❽ If you're driving and want to visit Livingston, you're probably best off leaving the car at one of the hotels in **Puerto Barrios** and taking the ferry, or staying at the Cayos del Diablo hotel, which offers excursions to Livingston and the Dulce River. The port town of Barrios has little to offer tourists, but if you're headed to or from Belize, Livingston, or Punta Manabique, you may want to spend a night there. Though low on attractions, Barrios has plenty of hotels and restaurants.

Off the Beaten Track The ancient Mayan city of **Copán** is in Honduras, very close to the Guatemalan border, and is easy to visit. Comprising a spectacular set of ruins, Copán is famous for its remarkably well preserved ornate carvings adorning an expansive central plaza, its group of temples, and its residential area. The site's many attractions include impressive stelae and a hieroglyphic staircase that contains the longest Mayan epigraph discovered to date. The city reached its apex during the 8th century, when it controlled much of the southern realm of the Maya and experienced a bloom in artistic development, the remnants of which can be seen today. The site is 238 kilometers (149 miles) from Guatemala City; the nearby town of Ruinas de Copán offers a variety of accommodations.

Dining and Lodging

Livingston Dining and Lodging **Hotel Tucán Dugú.** Livingston's only first-class hotel, the Tucán Dugú sits on a hill in the heart of town and consequently has some great views of the Caribbean. The hotel has extensive grounds,
★ which stretch over the hillside and are largely covered with lush tropical foliage. Units are located in a long, two-story, thatched-roof building, and all of them are spacious and have views of the gulf. Several suites are available, and some smaller "bungalows," which are actually just rooms, offer a good value. The pool, a large bar, a grassy area, and a private beach are down the hill. The restaurant serves an array of international dishes plus local seafood, like coconut shrimp and robalo. Trips up the Dulce River and to spots around the bay can be arranged. *Main Street in Livingston at the top of the hill, tel. and fax 481–572 or 345–242 in Guatemala City. 38 rooms with bath. Facilities: pool, restaurant, bar. DC, MC, V. $$–$$$*
African Place. This mosquelike building houses a restaurant on the second floor and hotel rooms down below. The rooms face a small patio that leads to a garden with benches and a shallow pool, and they are decorated with tiled floors and antique reproductions; the restaurant serves the best food in town. Lots of fresh seafood as well as some more unusual dishes such as Nigerian chicken are the menu's strong points. *West of the school, past the Catholic church, no phone. 11 rooms, 6 with bath. Facilities: restaurant, gardens. No credit cards. $*

Puerto Barrios Dining and Lodging **Cayos del Diablo.** A new first-class hotel on Amatique Bay, Cayos del Diablo blends luxury accommodations into a spectacular natural setting. Rooms are in a series of thatched bungalows, with colorful decor, air-conditioning, and cable TV. The grounds are dotted with tropical gardens and surrounded by rain forest, and directly behind the hotel is a forest-draped hill with a small waterfall. The hotel has a pool, a large restaurant, and private beach, and trips on the bay and up the Dulce River can be arranged. *Located 13 km (8 mi) west of Puerto Barrios, near Santo Tomás de Castilla, tel. 482–361 or*

315–720 in Guatemala City, fax 482–364. 50 rooms with bath. Facilities: bar, restaurant, beach, water sports. AE, DC, MC, V. $$$$

Hotel Puerto Libre. This place stands at the crossroads outside of town and resembles a U.S. motel, with large, modern, simply furnished rooms built around a parking area and swimming pool. Since the noise of traffic can rattle the light sleeper, it's worth noting that units in the far left corner have views of some woods and a small stream and are quieter. The small restaurant and rooms are air-conditioned. You can leave your car here if you overnight in Livingston. *Crossroads for Santo Tomás de Castilla, tel. 483–066, fax 483–065. 30 rooms with bath. Facilities: pool, parking, restaurant. AE, DC, MC, V. $$*

Hotel Henry Berrisford. A three-story building in town, the Berrisford doesn't look like much, but it offers decent rooms and a pool at a good price. The rooms are rather plain but clean; air-conditioning or a fan keeps units cool, but alas, there is no hot water. A large restaurant is located by the swimming pool in back. *9 Avenida and 17 Calle, tel. 481–557. 32 rooms with bath. Facilities: restaurant, pool. D, MC, V. $-$$*

Hotel del Norte. This old waterfront hotel has what the other Puerto Barrios lodges lack: ambience and a view. A two-story, cream-colored, wooden building with venerable Caribbean character, the hotel has small rooms with high ceilings, soft but small beds, creaky and uneven floors, and porches with wonderful views of the bay. An unattractive cement annex with air-conditioned rooms is available for those who suffer the heat badly. The restaurant downstairs is charming, with its old pictures, uniformed waiters, and big windows facing the sea, and they serve some good seafood and local specialties here, like *tapado* (a seafood stew). *At the end of 7 Calle, tel. 480–087. 38 rooms, 20 with bath. Facilities: restaurant, parking. No credit cards. $*

Punta Manabique
Dining and Lodging

Pirate's Point. You can get away from it all, after all. An hour's boat trip from either Livingston or Puerto Barrios will bring you to this remote and rustic collection of palm-leaf huts on the beach of Punta Manabique. Sound intriguing? For a boat ride to this secluded spot, contact Cafeteria Cony in Livingston or Kentucky BBQ in Barrios. Now you're *really* curious. *Tel. 946–950. 3 bungalows (each sleeps two to three people). Facilities: restaurant. No credit cards. $*

Río Dulce
Dining and Lodging
★

Catamaran Island. This hotel complex is located on the north bank of the river a few miles east of the bridge and is accessible only by water. Catamaran Island takes advantage of its waterfront location with a series of one-room bungalows and a restaurant built right over the water. The bungalows, albeit a bit tired and weather-worn, are nonetheless spacious and insect-proof, and they take solid advantage of the breezes that blow off the river (when the breeze fails, turn on the fan). The nicest aspect of the cabins are their porches, which are perfect for sitting and watching the varied boat traffic that plies the river. Cheaper rooms, which aren't nearly as nice as the bungalows, are a more landlocked option. The restaurant and bar are in an immense, open, thatched building with lovely views. The restaurant serves a variety of Continental cuisine, but among the specialties are steaks and grilled fish, including the delicious *robalo* (snook), which is common in the river. The hotel arranges boat trips to the surrounding attractions and to Livingston. When it's time to cool off, jump in the pool—it's at the center of the grounds—or in the river. *North bank of Dulce River, 5 km (3 mi) east of bridge, tel. and fax 364–450 in Guatemala City. 11 rooms with bath. Facilities: restaurant, bar, pool, boat trips arranged. DC, MC, V. $$*

Hotel Izabal Tropical. A pleasant collection of bungalows located a short walk from the castle, the Izabal Tropical sits at the eastern end of Lake Izabal, which provides it with a wonderful view and an almost constant breeze. The bungalows, little thatched houses with bamboo walls, have tiled baths and porches with hammocks. Several bungalows—the ones with the best views and ventilation—sit near the water, and all of them are surrounded by manicured grounds full of lush vegetation and bright flowers. The swimming pool, waterfront bar, and restaurant are added perks. Consult the management if you're interested in renting a houseboat (they're anchored nearby), or if you would like to arrange a river trip on a Polynesian catamaran that sleeps 10 people and offers trips to the cays of Belize. *Reached by following a dirt road on the left, just north of the bridge, tel. 478–115, fax 371–451 in Guatemala City. 10 rooms with bath. Facilities: restaurant, bar, pool, parking, docks, river tours. AE, DC, MC, V. $$*

Marimonte Inn. This large hotel on the river's south bank was recently remodeled and expanded, and now it has the largest variety of accommodations in the area. Though the Marimonte has less character than the competition—sparse grounds and simple rooms—it is easy to reach and less expensive. Rooms surround a large pool, and a three-story bar-and-restaurant complex overlooks the water. Many new buildings a good distance from the river contain several modern rooms each, but the older bungalows, which are slightly run-down, have much better views of the river. Windsurfers are available for rent, and river trips can be arranged through the management. *Located on the south bank, 1½ km (1 mi) east of El Relleno, tel. and fax 478–585 or 344–965 in Guatemala City. 24 rooms with bath. Facilities: bar, restaurant, pool, docks, parking, boat trips. AE, DC, MC, V. $$*

Hotel Don Humberto. This low-budget hotel offers nothing but the basics, but it offers them at an excellent location—at the northern edge of the tiny national park that surrounds the castle—and with friendly service. Rooms are small cement boxes facing a little courtyard, but they all have private baths and are fairly clean. There's also a small restaurant serving a limited selection of Guatemalan cuisine. *Reached via the road to the castle or by a quick boat ride from El Relleno, no phone. 11 rooms with bath. Facilities: restaurant. No credit cards. $*

The Verapaces
Dining and
Lodging

Hotel El Recreo Lanquín Champey. This large hotel at the entrance to the Lanquín caves across the road from the Lanquín River is a good place for swimming. Lodgings are in clean, concrete rooms in the main building and in several bungalows in back. The restaurant was built with the expectation of more tourists than usually visit; it serves decent, typical Guatemalan food. *Tel. 512–160, fax 512–333. Facilities: restaurant, parking. AE, DC, MC, V. $$*

Hotel La Posada. This traditional old inn near Central Park is a tasteful, comfortable spot—definitely the nicest place to stay in Cobán. Rooms have wood floors and beamed ceilings, and they are furnished with antiques and decorated with Guatemalan handicrafts, as are the porticoes and hallways. The hotel has a beautiful little garden and a cozy restaurant with a fireplace that serves mostly Guatemalan food. For entertainment, a TV lounge and ping-pong table suffice. *1 Calle 4–12, Zona 2, Cobán, tel. and fax 511–495. 14 rooms with bath, 2 with fireplaces. Facilities: restaurant, café, TV room, gardens. No credit cards. $$*

★ **Posada Montaña del Quetzal.** This comfortable country lodge is located on the road to Cobán near the Quetzal Reserve and is the best hotel in the region. Guests may choose from small rooms within the main building and spacious bungalows, each with two bedrooms, a sitting room, and a fireplace. The restaurant overlooks the swimming pool and serves a limited selection of Guatemalan and Continental cuisine. Wander the trails nearby—you might catch a glimpse of a quetzal. *4 km (2½ mi) south of the Quetzal Reserve, tel. 351–805 in Guatemala City. 10 bungalows and 8 rooms with bath. Facilities: restaurant, pool, hiking trails, parking. DC, MC, V. $$*

Ranchito del Quetzal. Just north of the Quetzal Reserve is this rustic lodge, a super-budget affair that consists of two cabins packed with beds and a tiny eatery. You're just a step above camping here, so be prepared. The food at the restaurant is laughable and the service is sporadic at best, but the location is good and the rates are low. *1½ km (1 mi) north of the Quetzal Reserve, no phone. 2 bungalows. Facilities: restaurant. No credit cards. $*

Tikal and El Petén

El Petén's position as both an archaeological and a biological wonderland makes it especially attractive to the traveler, and though many of the region's sites are difficult to reach, a growing supply of services makes traveling here easier than it used to be. In fact, the difficulty in reaching some sites merely enhances the feeling of adventure. Though the ancient ruins are the focus of most expeditions, they often become secondary to the exotic scenery and rare tropical species you'll witness along the way, or to the excitement of the river, horseback, and jeep trips required to reach them. Whatever a traveler's primary interest, exploring the remnants of the ancient Mayan civilization and observing the complexity of the tropical rain forest go hand in hand. A visit to the top of Temple IV is an experience you will not soon forget: The sunrise illuminates other temples that pierce the thick jungle canopy, howler monkeys scream call and response, and toucans fly below.

What is now the jungle department of El Petén was once the heartland of the Mayan civilization, but for the past millennium it has been a sparsely populated backwater in which nature reigns. In recent decades the Guatemalan government has attempted to settle this modern-day frontier, but much of the province still remains the realm of the monkey and the macaw. Covering about a third of Guatemala's territory, El Petén is home to less than 3% of its population. The region is rapidly being inhabited and developed, at the cost of its wilderness, but the natural and anthropological wonders that it contains remain ample inspiration for extensive travel.

The high point of any trip to El Petén is Tikal, a former city of the ancient Maya, where majestic temples tower above pristine rain forest. The view from the top of any of those temples is an unforgettable sight, with the gray roof cones of other reconstructed pyramids protruding out of the green sea of the rain forest's canopy. Though the forest that surrounds those ruins is today the home of the hummingbird and the jaguar, the area was covered with villages and farms 1,500 years ago, when an estimated 75,000 people lived here. What remains of that metropolis is an extensive series of impressive ruins, and two museums filled with smaller monuments and artifacts that archaeologists have recovered from the jungle. The beauty and intrigue of Tikal warrant at least a two-day visit, though it is possible to see them in a day. El Petén also has other ruins that are well worth visiting, the best of which is Ceibal on the Pasión River, including sites like Dos Pilas, Uaxactun, and Yaxja.

Arriving and Departing by Plane

The hub of this region is Flores, which is best reached from Guatemala City by plane; flights last less than an hour and cost about $50 each way. Several daily flights leave the capital early in the morning and return late in the afternoon, so it is possible to visit the ruins of Tikal in a single day. Plane tickets can be purchased at any travel agency. Airlines that fly to Flores daily include **Aviateca** (tel. 81–415), **Aerovias** (tel. 319–663), **Tapsa** (tel. 314–860), and **Tikal Jets** (tel. 345–631). The airport, known as the **Flores airport,** is about a mile outside town. Taxis meet every plane and charge about $2 to take you into Flores.

From Flores there are regular flights to Belize City and several Mexican cities, and daily bus service to Belize, Tikal, Poptún, and Sayaxché (*see* By Bus, *below*). Flights from Flores to Belize City on **Aerovias** leave at 9:30 AM Mon., Wed., Fri., Sat., and Sun. Flights to the Mexican city of Chetumal on **Aerovias** leave at 9:30 AM on Mon., Wed., and Fri. Flights to the Mexican resort of Cancún on **Aviateca** leave at 9:30 AM on Tues. and Sat.; **Aerocaribe** flies there at 6:45 AM on Mon., Wed., and Sat. Aerocaribe also flies to Villahermosa, near the Mayan ruins of Palenque, at 11 AM on Mon., Wed., and Sat. Call 500–042 in Flores for information.

Arriving and Departing by Bus and by Boat

By Bus Bus service to Flores from Guatemala City takes between 10 and 20 hours, and the trip is one of the most uncomfortable in the Western world. Unless you're on an incredibly tight budget, you'll want to fly at least one way. It's best to break the bus trip up with a stop in Poptún. Bus companies serving El Petén are **Fuentes del Norte** (17 Calle 8–47, Zona 1, tel. 513–817), with departures from Guatemala City to Flores at 1, 2, 3, and 7 AM and 9 PM; **Maya Express** (17 Calle 9–36, Zona 1, tel. 21–914), with departures at 4, 6, and 8 AM and 8:30 PM; and **Petenera** (16 Calle on the corner of 10 Avenida, Zona 1, tel. 296–58), with departures at 4, 6, and 8 PM. Direct buses, which have fewer stops, cost about $10 each way, and reservations are required.

San Juan Travel (tel. 500–042), in Santa Elena, runs minibus service to Belize City, Chetumal, and Tikal, and it rents four-wheel-drive jeeps and vans. **Hertz** (tel. 500–204) also rents jeeps in El Petén from an office in the Camino Real Tikal. **Koka** (tel. 501–232) rents four-wheel-drive vehicles at the airport.

By Boat Another option for traveling to Mexico is by boating down the Usumacinta River. For river trips out of Sayaxché, talk to Julio Mariona at La Montaña restaurant, Jorge Mendez, or his brother Pedro Mendez, who has an office by the river but is expensive. A river trip to one of the ruins should cost $30–$60, depending on the number of passengers. Bargain before you travel!

Getting Around

Most hotels in El Petén arrange trips to nearby archaeological sites and natural wonders in cooperation with the hotels in Flores and boat operators who dock near the causeway and provide boat trips on Lake Petén Itza.

By Car If you're not on a tour, the best way to get around El Petén is by renting a four-wheel-drive vehicle. All the major car-rental companies have offices at the airport. You can also call ahead to reserve a car from **Budget** (tel. 500–741), **Koka** (tel. 501–232), or **Hertz** (tel.

500–204), which also has an office in the Camino Real Tikal hotel, or **San Juan Travel** (tel. 500–042), located in the Hotel San Juan in Santa Elena. San Juan Travel runs a daily minibus service to Tikal, with departures at 6, 8, and 10 AM and returns at 2, 4, and 5 PM.

By Taxi Taxis can be hired at the airport to take you about anywhere in the region, but tours are often cheaper. Local buses are inexpensive but very slow.

By Bus The Hotel San Juan, in Santa Elena, is the local bus terminal, with service to the following destinations: Tikal, 6:30 AM and 1 PM (the trip takes 2 hours); Poptún, 5 and 10 AM, 1 and 3:30 PM; Melchor Menos (border with Belize), 5, 7, 10, 11 AM and 3 PM.

Important Addresses and Numbers

Tourist Information The tourist office for both Flores and El Petén is located in Flores (tel. 500–533). The INGUAT office at the airport is open sporadically.

Arcas (Calle El Remolino, Flores, tel. 500–566; open daily 9–7), an organization that takes animals captured from poachers and releases them back into the wild, is a great resource on the flora and fauna of El Petén as well as a good source of information on ecotours. It has a tremendous nature library that is open to the public.

Emergencies Medical facilities in El Petén are primitive at best. If you are really sick, get on the next plane back to Guatemala City.

Police (tel. 501–365); **Hospital** (tel. 500–619); **Pharmacies:** Farmacia Nueva (Avenida Santa Ana, Flores, tel. 501–387) and Farmacia San Carlos (2 Calle 727, Zona 1, Santa Elena, tel. 500–701).

Tour Operators

Toucan Tours (tel. 501–380); **Maya Expeditions** (tel. 947–951); **Jaguar Tours** (tel. 340–421); **Intertours** (tel. 315–421); **Expedition Panamundo** (tel. 317–641). The environmental group **ProPetén** (tel. 501–370), a Nature Conservancy affiliate that seeks economic alternatives for Petén residents to cutting down the rain forest, is planning to offer in-depth adventure trips led by rubber tappers who once worked in the forest.

Exploring Tikal and El Petén

Highlights for First-time Visitors Flores
La Pasión River
Lake Petén Itzá
Ceibal
Tikal

Numbers in the margin correspond to points of interest on the Tikal and El Petén map.

Rain-forest travel is about as difficult as it gets, and reaching many of these sites means driving down muddy roads that require four-wheel drive, river trips, or hiking. It consequently takes a while to get from one place to the next, and after so much effort, it's nice to be able to spend some time here. The only sites that are easy to visit are Tikal and the Cerro Cahui Wildlife Reserve, both of which are connected to the airport by the department's only paved road. Everything else is off the beaten track but well worth the trip.

No one should miss Tikal. Though it can be visited in one day, you should spend at least two days here and, if possible, a night. If you have three days, options include visiting Uaxactún, exploring the area around Lake Petén Itzá, or heading south to Ceibal. Though Ceibal is the second-best site in the region, it should only be visited if you have three or more days in the Petén region because it takes almost four hours to reach from Flores. This tour runs backward, in that the most important site, Tikal, is at the end, but since it is the most spectacular spot in the region, it should be saved for last. Your tour should be tailored to your time limitations, but keep in mind that the following itinerary should take more than a week to complete and that there are options to keep one exploring the area for several weeks.

1 From Flores head south down a bumpy dirt road to **Sayaxché,** a muddy frontier town on the southern bank of La Pasión River that is the best base for exploring the southern Petén. Sayaxché offers basic accommodations and services, and La Pasión and nearby Petexbatún rivers lead to a number of important ruins and flow past numerous wonders of tropical nature.

2 Up river from Sayaxché is **Ceibal,** the region's second most impressive ruin. Though its structures could never rival those of Tikal, it is a beautiful and inspiring site. One interesting aspect of Ceibal is the number of anomalies found in its monuments, which hint at profound foreign influence. Ceibal's beauty has much to do with its jungle surroundings, which offer visitors glimpses of the rain forests' seemingly infinite web of life. The site's archaeological attractions include several restored temples, plazas, and intricately carved stelae. Though it can be driven to, Ceibal is best reached by an hourlong boat ride on La Pasión River, followed by a half-hour ascent through the forest.

Two hours by boat from Ceibal lies Lake Petexbatún, an impressive rain-forest lagoon that was once an important area for the Maya and **3** is consequently near several significant ruins. **Dos Pilas,** which is reached by a three-hour hike or a horseback trip from the Petexbatún River, is a site of significant recent archaeological finds indicating that continual warfare may have caused an ecological imbalance that led to the collapse of Mayan civilization. This ancient city's attractions include a staircase covered with hieroglyphics, and **4** the surrounding forest. **Aguateca,** on the southern shore of the lake, is a smaller site that is beautiful but largely unrestored. It does have a few nice stelae, and the trip there is a wonderful river adventure. The smaller site of **Punta Chimino,** on the lake, has little to see but is the location of a wonderful hotel, the Posada de Matéo.

La Pasión River flows into the Usumacinta, and the two of them wind for countless miles through the rain forest. Both rivers are popular for expeditions, which can last from one day to more than a week; that way, you can catch a glimpse of the area's many animal inhabitants, including turtles, crocodiles, and a vast array of birds. The rivers were important trade routes of the ancient Maya and thus pass archaeological sites, like the impressive Yaxchilán, down the Usumacinta on the Mexican side of the river. River trips are organized by several tour companies in the capital. *See* Tour Operators, *above.*

Heading north on the same road that brought you to Sayaxché, you'll return to the muddy villages of San Benito and Santa Elena and the **5** more interesting **Flores.** The last outpost of the Mayan civilization to be conquered by the Spanish in Guatemala, this island city didn't fall

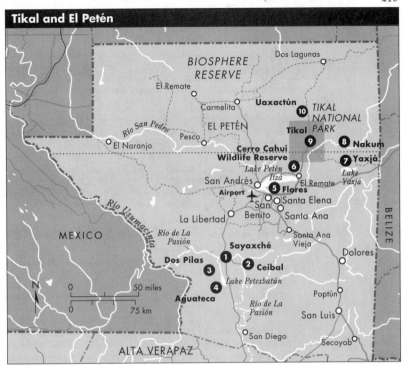

Tikal and El Petén

to the European invaders until 1697. Today the island is connected to the mainland by a causeway, and the city of Flores is a colorful provincial capital surrounded by the waters of Lake Petén Itzá. Though most of the area's population and commerce are located in San Benito and Santa Elena, Flores is a much more attractive town where visitors will want to spend more time. There are banks in both Santa Elena and Flores, and gas stations in Santa Elena—don't leave town with less than a full tank. Boat trips on **Lake Petén Itzá** can be arranged through hotels in Flores or by haggling with boat owners found near the causeway: The view from Mirador San Miguel is nice, and though the Petencito Zoo is sad, the nearby slide is a great spot for a swim. Flores has no sewage-treatment system, so it is inadvisable to swim close to town. There are several caves in the hills behind Santa Elena, the easiest to visit being **Aktun Kan**, just south of town.

The eastern edge of Lake Petén Itzá is an area called El Remate, which is near several hotels and the **Cerro Cahui Wildlife Reserve** (*see* Chapter 3, National Parks and Wildlife Reserves), a good spot for a nature hike or a swim in the lake. The reserve comprises more than 1,500 acres of rain forest and a stretch of lakefront. A hike on the 3-kilometer (2-mile) trail that enters the woods near the ranger station offers a chance to see ocellated turkeys, toucans, parrots, spider monkeys, and a wealth of other tropical critters. The paved road continues north from El Remate to Tikal National Park. A dirt road, however, heads east to Belize—if you take this route and drive for about two hours, you'll hit another dirt road on the left that leads to the ruins of Yaxjá and Nakum, which can be reached by four-wheel-drive jeep, on horseback, or by hiking. Though these ruins

❼ are covered by rain forest, **Yaxjá** overlooks a beautiful lake of the same name, where the island ruins of Topoxte can be visited by boat from El Campamento del Sombrero (contact Juan de la Hoz, tel. 505–196), a rustic lodge. Surrounded by virgin rain forest, Lake
❽ Yaxjá is a fine spot for bird-watching. **Nakum** lies deep within the forest, farther to the north, and is connected to Tikal via jungle trails that are sometimes used for horseback expeditions.

❾ The country's most famous and impressive Mayan ruin, **Tikal** has an array of well-restored structures, including the tallest pyramid in the western hemisphere. The ruins of this ancient city are the high point of any trip to El Petén, so if you plan on visiting other archaeological sites, save Tikal for last. As it is near the center of the forest-covered, protected Tikal National Park, Tikal facilitates wildlife observation as well as archaeological exploration (*see* Chapter 3, National Parks and Wildlife Reserves). Commonly seen critters include spider monkeys, deer, coati mundis, toucans, parrots, scarlet macaws, and ocellated turkeys.

The ruins are reached via the only paved road in El Petén and are just over an hour's drive northeast from Flores. The park headquarters, near the ruins, has two archaeological museums, three hotels, and a few small restaurants. Tikal deserves more than one day. If you want to see wildlife, it's best to stay in the park and get moving before dawn. For a truly stirring experience, park visitors are allowed to stay two hours past closing time on full-moon nights, when all the tour buses are gone, to view the moonrise (bring a flashlight). The following is a brief description of the site, but for more information on the ruins, William Coe's book *Tikal: A Handbook of the Ancient Maya Ruins* is a good source and can be purchased in the airport, at the area's larger hotels, and sometimes at the park entrance.

Though the area had Mayan communities by 600 BC, Tikal's civilization didn't reach its height until around AD 600. During the Classic Period (AD 250–900), Tikal was an important religious and administrative center, with a population estimated between 50,000 and 100,000. The great temples that still tower above the jungle were at that time covered with stucco and painted bright colors, and a hierarchy of priests and dynastic rulers used them for elaborate ceremonies meant to please the gods and thus assure prosperity for the city. What makes those structures even more impressive is the realization that the Maya had no beasts of burden, never used the wheel for anything but children's toys, and possessed no metal tools to aid them in construction.

The city of Tikal thrived for more than a millennium, trading and warring with city-states both near and far. It probably exerted considerable influence over other cities in the area, only to be heavily influenced itself by the northern civilization of Teotihuacán, which dominated the entire region during the latter half of the Classic Period. But by AD 900, Tikal was in a state of chaos as the entire Mayan empire began its mysterious decline and the process of depopulation had begun. Though the site may have been sporadically inhabited for centuries that followed, the civilization of the Maya throughout the region suffered a rapid decline.

As you enter the site, you are walking toward the west; if you keep to the middle trail, you'll arrive at Tikal's ancient center with its awe-inspiring temples and intricate acropolises. The pyramid you approach from behind is called Temple I, or Temple of the Giant Jaguar, after the feline represented on one of its carved lintels. Facing it, to the east, is Temple II, or Temple of the Masks, dubbed for the decorations on its facade. The North Acropolis, to the right, is a mind-boggling conglomeration of temples that were built over layers and layers of previous construction. Excavations have revealed that the base of this structure is more than 2,000 years old. Be sure to see the stone mask of the rain god at Temple 33. The Central Acropolis, south of the plaza, is an immense series of structures that are assumed to have been palaces and administrative centers.

If you climb one of the pyramids, you'll see the roof combs of Temple V to the south and Temple IV to the west, both rising above the rain forest but still trapped within it, waiting to be restored to some memory of their former grandeur. Temple IV is the tallest known structure built by the Maya, and though the climb to the top is difficult and involves some scrambling up the roots and rocks, the view is spectacular. To the southwest of the plaza lie the South Acropolis, which hasn't been reconstructed, and the Lost World complex, with its 32-meter-high (105-foot-high) pyramid, similar to those at Mexico's Teotihuacán. A few trails through the jungle offer opportunities to see spider monkeys and toucans. One is the marked interpretative trail called **Trail Benil-Ha.** Outside the park, a somewhat overgrown trail halfway down the old airplane runway on the left leads to the remnants of old rubber-tapper camps and is a good bird-watching spot.

⑩ **Uaxactún,** to the north of Tikal, is a good day trip from the park center with a four-wheel-drive vehicle. Though unrestored, the city is an important site that contains an observatory and includes construction that is 4,000 years old. Both the ruins and the road here are surrounded by the natural wonders of the rain forest, so the trip can be an ecological excursion as well. The track to Uaxactún heads out of Tikal between the old museum and the Jungle Inn, and if current roadwork is successful, it may become possible to make the trip without a four-wheel-drive vehicle in the near future.

Shopping

There are several stores in Flores that sell típica, which you can find just as easily and buy even cheaper in the rest of the country. What is unique to El Petén are the beautiful wood carvings of **El Remate.** More than 70 families in this small town dedicate themselves to this artistry. Their wares should not be missed and are on display on the side of the highway right before the turnoff for the Camino Real hotel on the road to Tikal.

Dining and Lodging

Restaurants serving traditional cuisine in rustic ambience include **El Jacal** and **El Faisan,** due west of the causeway, and **Mesa de los Maya, La Jungla, Gran Jaguar,** and **Palacio Maya,** all one block off the lake, west of the causeway.

All restaurants listed serve beef and chicken dishes. Several **Flores** restaurants have menus that concentrate on rain-forest game, like *venado* (venison) and *tepezcuintle,* a nocturnal mammal found in the rain forest that has become a threatened species. Keep in mind that the more tourists who order these dishes, the farther the locals will go into the forest to kill the animals and the more difficult they become to see in the wild.

Dining options are limited in Tikal National Park. Besides the restaurants in the hotels, there is one next to the big museum, and a few simple restaurants across the street, all of which are inexpensive.

El Remate/
Tikal
Dining and
Lodging
★

Camino Real Tikal. This is El Petén's premier hotel, and first-class it is. Among its myriad virtues are a top-notch restaurant, a bar, and a swimming pool. The list goes on—large, colorful rooms are equipped with cable TV, minibar, and balcony or patio; all rooms have a spectacular view of Lake Petén Itzá. Located at the eastern end of the lake, within the Cerro Cahui Wildlife Reserve, the hotel grounds are surrounded by wilderness, and it's just a half-hour drive from the ruins of Tikal. *West of El Remate, on the dirt road to the Cerro Cahui Wildlife Reserve, tel. 500–207 or 500–208, fax 500–222, or call Camino Real in Guatemala City, tel. 334–633. 120 rooms with bath. Facilities: bar, restaurant, pool, games room, car rental, excursions. AE, DC, MC, V. $$$$*

El Gringo Perdido. Fortunately for those on tighter budgets, there's another option for staying in the beautiful Cerro Cauhi area: this collection of cabins in the forest called The Lost Gringo. The accommodations are dorm-style, with a number of bunk beds packed into each room. The location compensates for any minor discomfort: The lake sits literally at your doorstep, and the forest surrounds you. Trails run through the nearby reserve, and it's a great spot for swimming in the lake. Camping is allowed for a few dollars, and a dining hall with a menu that changes daily is located on the property. *Located west of El Remate, by the reserve, tel. 20–605 or 25–811 in Guatemala City. 40 beds. Facilities: open-air restaurant, parking. No credit cards. $$*

Lake
Petenchel
Dining and
Lodging
★

Villa Maya. Big, bright rooms in a series of bungalows along beautiful Lake Petenchel enable guests to bird-watch from their beds (some 50 species of birds populate the lake region). A troupe of seven semitrained spider monkeys roam the grounds. What's more, the hotel owns and protects some 101 hectares (250 acres) of rain forest surrounding the lake. Rooms are spacious and tastefully ornamented—mahogany floors and white walls are decorated with colorful weavings and paintings—but the best part of every room is the view of the lake and surrounding jungle, all of which can be explored by following a trail around the lake or renting a rowboat. There are a small zoo on the grounds, a swimming pool, and an open-air restaurant. The hotel also has several vans and offers daily trips to Tikal. *A short drive north of the paved road, 12 km (8 mi) east of Santa Elena, tel. and fax 319–872 in Guatemala City. 44 rooms with bath. Facilities: restaurant, TV lounge, pool, boat rental, zoo. AE, DC, MC, V. $$$$*

Santa Elena
and Flores
Dining

Maya International. This hotel's restaurant, in a round, thatched building with a wooden floor, is built over the water and thus offers a great view of the lake by which to enjoy your meal. Almost every table is near a window. The menu changes daily, since the supply of groceries is rather sporadic in El Petén, with a set meal and just a few substitutes offered. *East of the causeway, Santa Elena, tel. 510–276. AE, DC, MC, V. $$*

Chal Tun Ha. This little waterfront restaurant, situated on the southwest corner of Flores, is a pleasant alternative to the rustic eateries that abound on the isle. Though the restaurant itself is hardly an inspiring structure—a cement building planted on gravel—its design takes advantage of the location's view with lots of windows, and the limited menu offers simple but well-prepared items, like fish from the lake or the standard stuffed peppers. *Southwest corner of the island, no phone. No credit cards. $*

El Tucán. You'll find this small lakeside restaurant on the southeast corner of Flores. A pleasant patio, which serves as a playground for the owner's pet toucans and parrots, looks onto the water. Or you might opt for the small dining room decorated with highland weavings—if you sit by a window, you'll have a good view of one of Flores's colorful cobbled streets. The menu includes a variety of traditions, though Mexican cuisine is the specialty. Bread is baked in-house. *Turn left off of the causeway, then take the next 2 right turns. Tel. 501–577. No credit cards. $*

Lodging **Hotel del Patio-Tikal.** A barrel-tile roof shelters this modern hotel, built in traditional Spanish style. Porticoes, balconies, and rooms face a large, grassy courtyard that contains a small patio with chairs and a central fountain. You'll find red-tile floors, big bathrooms, closets, ceiling fans, and cable TV in the rooms. *2 Calle and 8 Avenida, Santa Elena, tel. 500–104, fax 501–229. 22 rooms with bath. Facilities: restaurant, cable TV. AE, DC, MC, V. $$$*

Hotel Petén. This newer place run by friendly Pedro Castellanos is one of the best hotels in Flores. Located on the western end of the island, the hotel has great views of the lake from the windows and balconies of most rooms, the restaurant, and the deck out back. Rooms are simple but clean, with good beds, fans, and private baths with hot water. The restaurant serves breakfast and dinner only and has a patio that overlooks a sunning area and the lake. The hotel also arranges trips to Tikal or around the lake. The nearby **Casona de la Isla,** on the same street, is run by the same family and is a simpler, less-expensive version of the Hotel Petén. *West end of island, tel. 501–392, fax 500–662. 21 rooms with bath. Facilities: restaurant, tours. DC, MC, V. $$*

Maya International. This group of thatched bungalows built over Lake Petén Itzá in Santa Elena has some of the best views around. The lake rose several meters in 1979, flooding the bottom floors of the entire hotel, but the top floors are still in good shape and can be reached via a series of pedestrian causeways. The rooms themselves are pretty simple, with twin beds, fans, and private baths, but their private balconies afford some wonderful views, the best ones being units 48 through 54, which are the farthest out. The hotel's pool and grounds having been inundated, the area between bungalows is now covered with water lilies, on which waterfowl forage for dinner. *Santa Elena, a few blocks east of the causeway, tel. 319–876 or 341–927 in Guatemala City. 20 rooms with bath. AE, DC, MC, V. $$*

Savanna Hotel. One of the best hotels on the island, the Savanna has a sun deck, a restaurant, and simple rooms with views of Lake Petén Itzá. *North side of Flores, tel. 811–248. 23 rooms. Facilities: restaurant. No credit cards. $$*

Hotel Yum Kax. This large building stands at the southwest corner of the island, and though it may not be terribly attractive, it has a good supply of inexpensive rooms. The rooms are simple, with fans and private baths, but some of the ones on the upper floor face the lake and thus have decent views. There's a small lounge by the lobby with a TV; behind the lounge is the restaurant, which is best avoided. *West of the causeway, tel. 500–686 or 534–065. 39 rooms with bath. Facilities: restaurant, TV lounge. No credit cards. $*

San Juan. This large hotel offers a variety of decent rooms with private or shared baths. In addition, it is a departure point for a lot of early-morning buses, so eager-beaver travelers can jump out of bed and hop right on their transport. If you want to sleep late, however, get a back room. *Santa Elena, a block in from the causeway. Tel. 500–562. 60 rooms, 35 with bath. Facilities: restaurant, travel agency, bus station. AE, DC, MC, V. $*

Sayaxché Area
Dining and
Lodging
★

Posada de Mateo. This luxury nature lodge is spread out over Punta Chimino, a small peninsula in Lake Petexbatún that archaeologists speculate was once a home for Mayan nobility, which makes it the logical location for an exceptional rain-forest retreat. The Posada consists of a series of bungalows scattered along the peninsula's edges, each unit set amid the rain-forest foliage, with a private view of the lake and jungle beyond. The bungalows are beautiful, with resin-coated hardwood floors, modern bathrooms, and screened walls that make one feel a part of the jungle while keeping its insect inhabitants at a safe distance. Delicious meals are served in an open-air restaurant, and tours of nearby archaeological sites are included in the price of the room. *Tel. 500–505 in El Petén. 6 rooms. Facilities: restaurant, tours. No credit cards. $$$*

La Montaña. This new arrival on the Petexbatún River is a lodging option that lies somewhere between the jungle luxury of the Posada and the cheap accommodations in Sayaxché. Located on a bend in the river, the lodge consists of a series of bungalows built in a clearing hacked out of the rain forest. In each house, you'll find a cement floor, bamboo walls, and a simply appointed private bath. Family-style meals are served in a rustic open-air dining hall. As a guest, you can book a tour of local archaeological sites. *For reservations, contact Julian Mariona at La Montaña Tours in Sayaxché, fax 500–622. 8 rooms. Facilities: dining room, tours. No credit cards. $$*

Lodging

Hotel Guayacan. A simple lodge that stands by the south bank of La Pasión River in the town of Sayaxché, the Guayacan offers basic accommodations at a reasonable price. Rooms are on the second floor of this motellike structure, which is surrounded by mud, and are equipped with decent beds and private or shared baths. There is no decor here to speak of, but the establishment is clean and conveniently located. There is a small parking area, and the owner can arrange boat trips to Mayan ruins. *No phone. 10 rooms. Facilities: tours, parking. No credit cards. $*

La Posada Maya Betal. Located on the banks of the Usumacinta River in the town of Betel, this rustic lodge, basically just hammocks and a thatched roof, is a good jumping-off point for trips to nearby ruins such as Yaxchilán. *Contact Maya Expeditions (tel. 947–951) or Raphael Sagastume at Villa Maya hotel, above (tel. 319–872). No credit cards. $*

Tikal
Dining and
Lodging
★

Jungle Lodge. The largest hotel in the park, the lodge offers rooms with private or shared baths, restaurant, and pool, all of which are surrounded by jungle and only a short walk from the ruins. You might run into some ocellated turkeys or scarlet macaws on the grounds here—keep your eyes open for uncommon surprises like these. *Tikal Park headquarters, no phone. 46 rooms, 34 with bath. Facilities: restaurant, pool. AE, DC, MC, V. $$*

Tikal Inn. This small hotel near the airstrip consists of a series of comfortably rustic bungalows surrounding a pool. The rooms are much more attractive than the Jungle Lodge's, with thatched roofs, white stucco walls, and traditional fabrics. There is also a small restaurant for the guests, with a menu that changes daily. Rates are reasonable and include breakfast and dinner. *Tikal Park headquarters, no phone. 15 rooms with bath. Facilities: restaurant, pool. No credit cards. $$*

Nightlife

Las Puertas, a light and airy bar-café in Flores on a side street across from El Toucano, has live music at night and is a place to sit and talk among friends.

6   Belize

By Simon
Worrall

Simon
Worrall is a
British-born
writer. He
writes
regularly for
the London
Sunday Times
Magazine,
Geo, and
many other
European
and
American
publications
on travel,
technology,
culture, and
politics. He
currently
makes his
home in East
Hampton,
New York.

Clever Belize. In Chicago it's probably snowing, but here you're bouncing over the mint-green water after a day's snorkeling, the white-painted prow of the boat pointing up into the billowing clouds, the base of the sky darkening to a deep lilac, the spray pouring over you like warm rain. To the left, San Pedro's pastel buildings huddle among the palm trees like a detail from a Paul Klee canvas. To the right, the surf breaks in a white seam along the reef. Over the surface of the water, flying fish scamper away like winged, aquatic hares.

Look for a mere geographical sliver wedged between Mexico and Guatemala, 280 kilometers (175 miles) long and 109 kilometers (68 miles) wide at its broadest point, and you will discover Belize. The country occupies a land mass no larger than the state of Massachusetts, but don't let its diminutive status fool you. Within its borders, Belize probably has the greatest variety of landscapes and peoples, of flora and fauna, of any country of equivalent size in the world. In the Maya Mountains, the central highlands that form the watershed for the thousands of streams and rivers that make their way to the sea, there is dense rain forest. In the north is savanna and sugarcane. One moment you can be in pine savanna; the next, in dense equatorial forest. Because it has the lowest population density of any country in Central America—El Salvador, the region's only smaller country, has 10 times as many people—and as Belizeans are by temperament and by tradition town dwellers, most of this green interior remains uninhabited, the home of scarlet macaws, tapir, and jaguars, kinkajous, mountain lions, and howler monkeys. Even reduced to vapid statistics—300 species of birds, 250 varieties of orchids, dozens of species of butterflies—the sheer variety of Belize's wildlife is breathtaking. The same holds for its nearly 600 Mayan ruins, which range from the metropolitan splendor of Caracol to the humble living mounds that you see throughout the country.

Less than an hour's flight from the green heartland is the Barrier Reef, a great wall of coral stretching the length of the coast, from the Yucatán Peninsula in the north to Guatemala in the south. Australia is the only other country that has both landscapes cheek by jowl like this. In Belize you can be scuba diving before breakfast and canoeing in the rain forest after lunch.

Dotting the reef like punctuation marks are the cays, more than 200 in all. Around these cays, and the atolls farther out to sea, are some of the best diving and snorkeling in the world—560 kilometers (350 miles) of coral reef, more than Bonaire, Cozumel, and all the Caymans put together. Some of them are no more than Robinson Crusoe islets of white coral sand and mangroves, inhabited by frigate birds, pelicans, and the occasional fisherman, who will string a sheet of canvas between the trees to sleep under and spend a few days diving for conch and lobster. Others, like Ambergris Cay, are gradually being developed. Their bars, hotels, dive shops, and discos are a source of pride and wealth to the local people.

Belize's peoples are as diverse as its landscape, their history the history of immigration and extraordinarily successful racial integration. To the original inhabitants, the Maya, were added shipwrecked British seamen and liberated African slaves, deported Indian sepoys, and persecuted Black Caribs. In the 19th century mestizos fleeing the Yucatán during the War of the Castes poured into northern Belize; in ours, Mennonites fleeing persecution in Europe settled in the Orange Walk District. All these peoples, like Belize's most recent wave of refugees—the thousands of Salvadorans and Guatemalans who fled the death squads and tor-

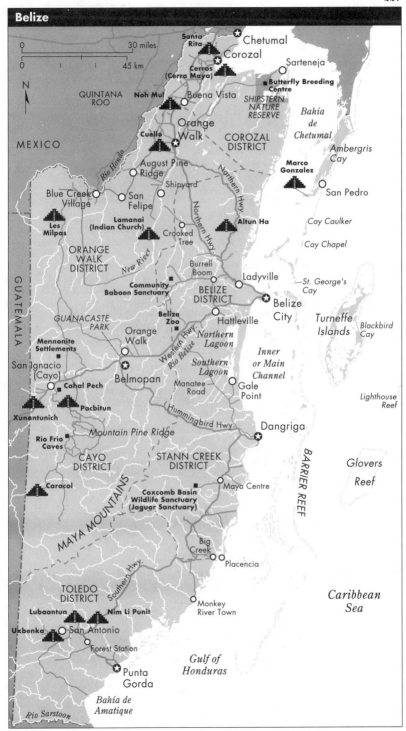

Belize

0 ___ 30 miles

0 _|_|_|_ 45 km

N

Chetumal

Santa Rita

Corozal

Cerros (Cerra Maya)

Sarteneja

QUINTANA ROO

Noh Mul

Buena Vista

Butterfly Breeding Centre

SHIPSTERN NATURE RESERVE

Bahía de Chetumal

MEXICO

Cuello

Orange Walk

COROZAL DISTRICT

Ambergris Cay

Marco Gonzalez

San Pedro

August Pine Ridge

Rio Hondo

Shipyard

Blue Creek Village

San Felipe

Northern Hwy

Cay Caulker

Les Milpas

Lamanai (Indian Church)

Crooked Tree

Altun Ha

Cay Chapel

ORANGE WALK DISTRICT

New River

Burrell Boom

Ladyville

St. George's Cay

GUATEMALA

Community Baboon Sanctuary

BELIZE DISTRICT

Belize City

Turneffe Islands

Blackbird Cay

GUANACASTE PARK

Belize Zoo

Hattieville

Northern Lagoon

Inner or Main Channel

Mennonite Settlements

Orange Walk

Western Hwy. Rio Belize

Southern Lagoon

San Ignacio (Cayo)

Cahal Pech

Belmopan

Manatee Road

Gale Point

Lighthouse Reef

Xunantunich

Pacbitun

Hummingbird Hwy.

Dangriga

Rio Frio Caves

Mountain Pine Ridge

CAYO DISTRICT

STANN CREEK DISTRICT

Glovers Reef

Caracol

MAYA MOUNTAINS

Coxcomb Basin Wildlife Sanctuary (Jaguar Sanctuary)

Maya Centre

BARRIER REEF

Big Creek

Placencia

Caribbean Sea

TOLEDO DISTRICT

Southern Hwy.

Lubaantun

Nim Li Punit

Monkey River Town

Ukbenka

San Antonio

Forest Station

Punta Gorda

Gulf of Honduras

Bahía de Amatique

Rio Sarstoon

ture chambers of their own countries in the '70s to start peaceful new lives in Belize—found in this tiny English-speaking country a tolerant, amiable home. In a country where almost everyone is a foreigner, no one is.

Today, the dominant social and ethnic group of modern Belize, the Creoles, are the offspring of this unique marriage of races. Half African, half Anglo-Saxon, the Creoles consider themselves the heirs of the colonial era. University positions and jobs in the administration, the police, and politics are generally held by them. In Belize City, they form approximately 70% of the population. As there has never been a stigma to racial mixing in Belize, Creoles have never been afflicted by a sense of self-consciousness about their ethnic origins. They are both black and white, like the two men standing under the logwood tree on the national flag. And they're proud of it. The suspicion and hostility that often so disfigure race relations in North America or Europe are much less noticeable in Belize.

For the moment, the British maintain a small military presence that has remained since independence in 1981. To ensure that Belize wasn't jumped by a junta, they have assumed a role not as colonial masters but as partners in deterrence. Now, initiatives like Mundo Maya, a joint effort by Mexico, Guatemala, Belize, El Salvador, and Honduras to coordinate travel to Mayan sites, are paving the way for greater regional cooperation. At any rate, the sight of a detachment of knobby-kneed "squaddies" setting off for a week's jungle bashing or of a Harrier jump-jet hovering like an insect over International Airport is a familiar part of the country's visual scenery.

For many years, Belize was the best-kept secret in travel. Now, word is slowly getting out, and more and more people are making the journey to this tiny country of huge contrasts. Luckily, its government has an enormously enlightened attitude to conservation and the environment. More important, awareness of the fragility of nature has taken root in the hearts of the people, and you will hear fishermen or schoolchildren talking earnestly about the need to protect the environment. As a result there is little industry, and this is not by default but by choice. Instead, ecotourism—getting visitors into nature, and out again, without destroying it—is its fastest-growing source of revenue. Clever Belize.

Before You Go

Government Tourist Offices

In the U.S. and Canada   **Belize Tourist Board** (421 7th Ave., Suite 701, New York, NY 10001, tel. 212/563–6011, fax 212/563–6033).

In the U.K.   **Belize High Commission** (10 Harcourt House, 19A Cavendish Sq., London W1M 9AD, tel. 071/499–9725).

When to Go

Though everyone you'll meet when you're there will tell you otherwise, Belize is not really a year-round destination. Summer in the Northern Hemisphere is the wet season in the Tropics, and though this varies dramatically between the north and south of the country, between May and October you'll need an umbrella. In the far south, you'll need it most of the year (as much as 160 inches of rain falls annually) except for during a brief respite between February and April. On the cays, the wet season is often accompanied by lashing northerly winds known in Creole as Joe North. In a bad year, Joe North can turn into Hurricane Hattie.

Between November and April—the coldest season in North America—you are likely to spend much of your time dreaming up ways to be able to stay in Belize forever. If you're a diver, the water is at its absolute glass-clearest in the spring from April to June.

The following are the average monthly maximum and minimum temperatures for Belmopan, Belize.

Jan.	81F	27C	May	87F	31C	Sept.	87F	31C
	67	19		75	24		74	23
Feb.	82F	28C	June	87F	31C	Oct.	86F	30C
	69	21		75	24		72	22
Mar.	84F	29C	July	87F	31C	Nov.	83F	28C
	71	22		75	24		68	20
Apr.	86F	30C	Aug.	88F	31C	Dec.	81F	27C
	74	23		75	24		73	23

Festivals and Seasonal Events

March 19: Baron Bliss Day hears three cheers for Baron Henry Edward Ernest Victor Bliss, a wealthy English sportsman who endowed Belize with an immense estate in return for a holiday devoted to the traditional pursuits of the gentleman: sailing and fishing.

Summer: The San Pedro Sea & Air Festival, usually held in mid-August, is a multicultural bash held on Ambergris Cay that lasts about four days and features entertainment from Belize and other Central American and Caribbean countries.

September 10: The Battle of St. George's Cay celebrates Belize's romantic beginnings, when in 1798 a motley crew of British settlers, buccaneers, and liberated slaves won a David-and-Goliath victory over the might of the Spanish navy. A week of partying and carnivals keeps the memory alive.

September 21: National Independence Day, during Belize's Carnival month, comes 11 days after the holiday commemorating the early British settlers. The country finally became independent from the motherland on this day in 1981.

November 19: Garifuna Settlement Day marks the arrival of Black Carib settlers, known as Garifuna, from the West Indies in 1823. Processions and traditional dancing abound, above all in Dangriga and the Toledo District.

Belizean Currency

The monetary unit in Belize is the dollar (BZ$). For many years now it has been tied to the U.S. dollar at a rate of BZ$2 per dollar. Most tourist prices are quoted in U.S. dollars, but the smaller restaurants and hotels tend to work in BZ$. Usually, hotels will exchange currency, but large transactions should be made at banks. Note that banking hours in Belize are very different from our own. They are open Monday–Thursday 8 AM–1 PM, and Friday 8 AM–1 PM and 3 PM–6 PM. Major credit cards are accepted at most of the larger hotels and a few restaurants. The rest of Belize is cash country.

What It Will Cost

There are two ways of looking at the prices in Belize: Either it is one of the cheapest countries in the Caribbean, or it is one of the most expensive countries in Central America. A good hotel room for two will cost you upwards of US$100; a budget one, as little as US$6. A meal in one of the more expensive restaurants will cost $25–$35 for one; but you can eat lobster and salad in a small seafood restaurant for as little as $10. Prices are highest in Belize City and Ambergris Cay. In this chapter, prices will be listed in U.S. dollars unless otherwise noted.

Taxes There is a government hotel tax of 6% and an airport departure tax of $10, plus $1.25 security tax, when you leave the country.

Sample Costs Coffee: 50¢; beer $1; sandwich $1.50.

Passports and Visas

No visas are required for U.S., Canadian, and British citizens, but you must have a passport. Citizens of EC countries and the British Commonwealth also require only a passport. Technically, visitors are permitted to stay in the country for only one month. If you're young and you arrive by road from Mexico, you may be asked to prove you have enough money to cover your stay. For more information contact the **Belize Embassy** (3400 International Dr. NW, Suite 25, Washington DC 20008, tel. 202/332–9636).

Customs and Duties

On Arrival U.S., British, and Canadian nationals entering Belize may bring in 3 liters of liquor and one carton of cigarettes duty-free. Laptop computers and other electronic items should be declared. Visitors are allowed to bring in the equivalent of $250 in foreign currency per day of their stay in the country. Any amount above that should be declared.

On Departure There is a BZ$22.50 airport tax on departure. To take home fresh seafood of any kind, you must first obtain a permit from the Fisheries Department; there is a 20-pound limit.

Security

Thousands visit Belize each year and encounter no problems. However, travelers should consult current advisory listings with the Department of State, and call the Citizens' Emergency Center (tel. 202/647–5225) for updates. Belize City, where tourists are mugged occasionally, is the only place in Belize with a high incidence of crime. You should take the same precautions you would take in any large city—leave valuables in a safe place, don't wear expensive jewelry on the street, and always check with your hotel before venturing into any unfamiliar areas.

Language

Unlike all other Central American countries, English is the official language of Belize, making it an easy, hassle-free place to travel in for the non-Spanish speaker. The English spoken here is closely allied to the English of the British Caribbean ("tea" is still used, as it is in the West Indies and cockney London, to refer to just about any meal). Among themselves, many Belizeans also speak Creole patois, a slang English with its own vocabulary and musical rhythms. Spanish is widely spoken in the north, central regions, and south; Mayan is heard mainly in the Toledo District in the south.

Car Rentals

Most of the major international companies are now represented in Belize City, as well as several local operators. Prices vary from company to company, but are all expensive by U.S. standards ($65–$130 per day). Belize is one of the most expensive places in the world to hire cars, and some of the cars run by the local operators—V8 gas-guzzlers driven down from Mexico—will cost you dearly for gas alone. The international agencies have modern, dependable fleets, and prices to match. A four-wheel-drive Suzuki with unlimited mileage from Avis, for instance, will cost about $100 per day, though weekly rates are considerably cheaper. Some companies have a clause relating to cars that are *not* four-wheel-drive vehicles that binds you not to go off the main highways, which gives you an idea of what the roads are like. For serious safaris, a four-wheel-drive vehicle, preferably a Land Rover, is invaluable. All-terrain vehicles with guides are available from most of the major hotels, at a cost of about $200 per day.

National (Philip Goldson International Airport, tel. 02/31586); **Smith & Sons** (1–8 Central American Blvd., Belize City, tel. 02/73779); **Budget** (711 Bella Vista, Belize City, tel. 02/32435); **Avis** (Radisson Fort George Hotel, Marine Parade, Belize City, tel. 02/78637 or 800/828–2131); **Elijah Sutherland** (127 Neal Pen Rd., Belize City, tel. 02/73582); **Crystal Auto Rental** (Mile 1½ Northern Rd., Belize City, tel. 02/31600).

Further Reading

Two histories stand out: *The Making of Modern Belize*, by C.H. Grant, and *A Profile of the New Nation of Belize*, by W.D. Setzekorn. *Jaguar*, by Alan Rabinowitz, an interesting book about the creation of the Coxcomb Basin Jaguar Preserve, unfortunately tells you too much about the man and too little about the cat. Aldous Huxley, who wrote *Beyond the Mexique Bay*, is always hard to beat. If you're interested in the Maya, Ronald Wright's *Time Among the Maya* ties past and present together in one perceptive whole. Classic works on the Maya include *The Maya*, by Michael Coe, a compendious introduction to the world of the Maya, and *The Rise and Fall of the Maya Civilization*, by one of the grand old men of Mayan archaeology, J. Eric S. Thompson. For natural history enthusiasts, three books belong in your suitcase: *A Field Guide to the Birds of Mexico*, by E.P. Edwards; *Guide to Corals and Fishes of Florida, the Bahamas and the Caribbean*, by I. Greenberg; and *An Introduction to Tropical Rainforests*, by T.C. Whitmore.

Arriving and Departing

From North America by Plane

Airports and Airlines International flights arrive at **Philip Goldson International Airport** in Ladyville, 14 kilometers (9 miles) to the north of Belize City ($30 and rising for a cab to town) and probably the only airport in the world with a mahogany roof.

The main airlines serving Belize from the United States are **American** (tel. 800/433–7300), with daily flights from Miami; **Continental** (tel. 800/231–0865), with daily nonstop flights from Houston; and **Taca International** (tel. 800/535–8780), which has flights from New York, Washington, Los Angeles, New Orleans, Miami, and San Francisco. **Tan Sahsa** (tel. 800/327–1225) has flights out of Houston, New Orleans, and Miami. **Taca International** offers special baggage concessions to divers and has the most modern fleet. The snag is that flights are often late in arriving, which can be a nuisance if you have connections to make. **Tropic Air** services Belize from Cancún, Mexico.

Flying Time From Miami it is only 2 hours to Belize; from Houston, 2½ hours; from New York, 5 hours; and from San Francisco, 8 hours.

From the United States by Car, Boat, and Bus

By Car It's a three-day drive from Brownsville, Texas, to Chetumal, Mexico, on the border with Belize, and then about another 3½-hour drive to Belize City. To save time when leaving the country, make sure you get a Temporary Import Permit for your car, and watch out for potholes.

By Boat *See* Belize City, Arriving and Departing, *below.*

By Bus If you want to enter Belize by bus, there are connections from Guatemala City via Flores to Ciudad Melchor de Mencos, the Guatemalan border town (though not in the wet season). From there, you can get a cab or a bus to San Ignacio. This is cheaper early in the day, as many Guatemalans cross the border to work in Belize. From Mexico, there are regular bus connections from Chetumal to Corozal. From there, you can fly to Belize City or San Pedro on Ambergris Cay.

Batty Bros. Bus Services (15 Mosul St., Belize City, tel. 02/72025) covers most northern and western bus routes, with stops in Chetumal, Belmopan, and San Ignacio. For routes south to Belmopan, Dangriga, and Punta Gorda, try **Z-Line Bus Service** (Venus Bus Terminal, Magazine Rd., Belize City, tel. 02/73937). **Venus Bus Service** (Magazine Rd., Belize City, tel. 02/77390 or 02/73354) runs north from Belize City to Orange Walk, Corozal, and Chetumal.

From the United Kingdom by Plane

There are no direct flights from the United Kingdom to Belize. Most travelers connect with U.S. flights (*see* From North America by Plane, *above*).

Staying in Belize

Getting Around

By Plane Like everything good in Belize, flying—in twin-engined island-hoppers—has a bit of adventure attached to it. Most planes flying in-country leave from the **Municipal Airport,** which is only a mile or so from the Belize City center and is therefore more convenient than International. The main carriers are **Tropic Air** (tel. 02/45671, 713/440–1967, or 800/422–3435 in the U.S.) and **Maya Airways** (tel. 02/72312, 02/77215, or 02/44032, fax 02/30585 or 02/30031). Tropic has the largest and most modern fleet. It flies to the cays (Ambergris, Caulker) and does limited runs to the south. Maya Airways flies to San Pedro and to Big Creek, Dangriga, and Punta Gorda in the south. **Island Air** (tel. 02/31140) also flies to San Pedro, and **Skybird** (tel. 02/32596) has a new service to Cay Caulker. **Javier Bosch** (tel. 02/45332), a much-respected local pilot, will take you pretty much anywhere for $150 per hour.

By Bus Though there is no railway in Belize, there is a fairly extensive bus service run by franchised private companies. The quality of the buses and of the roads on which they travel vary considerably (Batty's is the best; points south, the worst). But the buses run according to reliable schedules, are extremely cheap (about $2 to $4 for all you can take), and remain an excellent way of experiencing Belize as the Belizeans do. Outside the cities you can flag them down like cabs. The driver will let you off whenever you want. *See* Arriving and Departing, By Bus, *above*, for bus operators in Belize.

By Car If you're expecting the New Jersey Turnpike, you'll be sorely disappointed. Only the Northern Highway, to Orange Walk and Corozal, and the Western Highway, to Belmopan and San Ignacio, are paved, but even these can be badly potholed after the rains. The Hummingbird Highway, to the south, is a difficult road in any season. In the rain it turns to mango-colored ice cream; in the dry, to bumpy concrete. Once you get off the main highways, distances don't mean that much—it's time that counts. You might have only 20 kilometers (12½ miles) to go, but that can take you 90 minutes. If you bring your own car into the country, you will need insurance bought in Belize. Gasoline costs $2.40 per gallon, and note well: It is *not* unleaded. Fill up whenever you see a gas station.

Telephones

Local Calls Belize has a good nationwide telephone system. Pay phones are on the street in the main centers. Local calls cost BZ25¢; calls to other districts, BZ$1.

International Calls **BTL** (Belize Telecommunications Limited, 1 Church St., Belize City, tel. 02/32868) offices, from which you can call internationally in most towns, are open Monday–Saturday 8 AM–9 PM, Sunday 8–6. To reach an **AT&T Direct** operator, dial 55; for **Sprint International,** dial *4. **MCI** has no service available from Belize.

Mail

The Belizean mail service prides itself on being the best in Central America, and the stamps, mostly of wildlife, are beautiful. An airmail letter takes about a week to the States. Parcels have to be standard-wrapped in brown paper and, if you are in Belize City, sent from a special office on Church Street, next to the BTL offices. It is open Monday–Thursday 8–noon and 1–4:30, Friday 8–noon and 1–4.

You can receive mail sent Poste Restante to the main post office (tel. 02/72201) on Front Street at the northern edge of the Swing Bridge in Belize City, where it will be kept for at least a month (you will need a passport or other ID to pick it up). The post office is open Monday–Thursday 8–5 and Friday 8–4:30. **American Express** (Belize Global Travel, 41 Albert St., Belize City, tel. 02/77185) will handle mail for card-holders free of charge.

Tipping

Tipping is a relatively informal affair in Belize. There is no official service charge set by the government. One is usually expected to tip

10%–15% in most hotel restaurants, and bellhops normally get $1–$3 depending on how many bags they carry. Generally, the more touristed the area or restaurant, the more likely is one should tip. In small, individually operated restaurants tipping is purely optional. Taxi drivers do not expect tips.

Opening and Closing Times

Belize is a very laid-back place, and so shops tend to open according to the whim of the owner. Generally, though, shops are open 8–noon and 3–8. Some shops and businesses work a half day on Wednesdays and Saturdays. On Fridays, many shops close early for the weekend. On Sunday, Belize takes it very easy. Few shops are open. Flights are very limited. Almost all restaurants are closed except those in the major hotels.

Banks Banks are open weekdays 8–1 (Friday also 3–6).

Sports and Outdoor Activities

Belize has rightly been called the "adventure coast," so if you want to play golf, this is not the country for you. But if you want to take a night dive through a tunnel of living coral, ride a horse through jungle loud with the call of howler monkeys, or canoe through the rain forest, you will love it. As in Alaska, much gets organized over the bush-telegraph, and it won't be hard to find someone who can rent you a boat, sail you out to the reef, or teach you how to ride—at a price, of course.

Fishing Some of the most exciting sportfishing in the world is to be had in Belize's coastal waters. Tarpon, snook, bonefish, and permit abound, all of which, when hooked, will make your reel screech and your heart beat faster. Several specialist resorts and fishing camps (*see* The Cays and Atolls, *below*) cater especially to the angler, but most resorts and hotels will be able to organize excellent fishing for you. Note well: In this ecologically minded country, only catch-and-release fishing is allowed.

Horseback Riding In the interior of the country, particularly in the Cayo District, riding has begun to catch on as one of the best ways of seeing the mountainous landscape. Horses tend to be small, tough local breeds (quarter horses often suffer in the climate). Mountain Equestrian Trails and Chaa Creek (*see* Dining and Lodging in The Cayo, *below*) offer three-day horseback excursions to the Mayan ruins at Caracol. For those who prefer trotting along the beach, a new stable called **Isla Equestrian** (Barrier Reef Dr., San Pedro, tel. 026/2895), located right by the airstrip in San Pedro, rents horses by the hour.

Water Sports Belize has some of the finest scuba diving and snorkeling in the world (*see* Diving in The Cays and Atolls, *below*). Some of the resorts also rent Windsurfers and small sailing dinghies. The new Yacht Club (Box 1, San Pedro, Ambergris Cay, tel. 026/2777) has just opened in San Pedro, on Ambergris Cay.

Beaches

Much of the mainland coast is fringed with mangrove swamps and therefore has few beaches. The few that do exist are not spectacular. On the cays, particularly Ambergris, that changes dramatically. Here beaches are not expansive—generally there is a small strip of sand at the water's edge—but with their palm trees and mint-green water, you'll definitely know you're in the Caribbean. The best beach on the mainland is in Placencia, in the south (*see* Placencia and the South, *below*).

Tour Companies

Local tour companies in Belize tend to fall in one of three categories: those based in Belize City, which offer mainly day trips to the nearby Mayan ruins and nature reserves; those in San Pedro and Placencia, offering diving and snorkeling; and those in the Cayo, offering river trips, horseback riding, and tours of the Mountain Pine Ridge area. In Belize City, **Mesoamerica Tours** (tel. 02/30748) is the biggest and most reputable operator; it can arrange tours virtually anywhere in the country. **Mayaworld Safaris** (tel. 02/31063) specializes in trips to nearby Mayan ruins and currently offers the best deal on trips to Lamanai. **S&L Travel Services** (tel. 02/77593) is another well-known and highly reputable operator in Belize City. In San Pedro, **Out Island Divers** (tel. 026/2151 or 800/BLUE–HOLE in the U.S.) offers day and overnight dive trips to the Blue Hole and Lighthouse Reef. **Amigo Travel** (tel. 026/2180) offers mainland and island tours and snorkeling excursions. **Ricardo's Adventure Tours** (tel. 022/2138), based on Cay Calker, offers island-hopping excursions for divers and fishermen. In the Cayo the best way to get in contact with local tour operators is to check in at **Eva's Restaurant** in San Ignacio (22 Burns Ave., tel. 092/2267). Most jungle lodges in the Cayo offer tour-inclusive packages and a full range of day trips. For true adventure travelers and naturalists who want to explore the Cay in depth, **The Divide** (tel. 092/3452) offers three- to seven-day jungle camping trips. In Placencia the **Placencia Tourist Guide Association** (tel. 06/23166) provides assistance with arranging diving, fishing, and jungle excursions.

Dining

Unfortunately, Belize's rich ethnic variety has not found reflection in its cuisine. The basic Creole dish—beans and rice, served with stewed chicken or beef—is dismayingly ubiquitous. The one great exception to this is the seafood. Shrimp, lobster, conch, red snapper, and grouper abound, and whether simply cooked in garlic and butter and served with a slice of fresh lime, or smothered in a rich sauce, they are delicious. During spawning season, from March 1 to June 15, there is no fresh lobster, and conch is off-season July through September.

Most of the best restaurants are in the hotels and resorts. The best of them bear comparison with good, though not first class, restaurants in North America or Europe. It's important in Belize not to judge a restaurant by the way it looks. Some of the best cooking gets done in the humblest-looking cabanas. Follow your nose. Good cooks don't stay a secret for long.

Ratings Prices vary considerably between the interior and Belize City and the cays. Ambergris Cay, because it's the most developed, is the most expensive. A meal for two at one of the best restaurants will cost $40–$60, but you will be able to eat well for much less. Lobster varies between $10 and $15, depending on the restaurant. A fish like grilled grouper usually costs about $7.50; a substantial American-style breakfast, $5; and a hamburger, $3. As there has been a considerable influx of Hong Kong Chinese in the last few years, Chinese food is plentiful and usually cheap. Prices are per person, including first course, entrée, and dessert. Drinks and gratuities are not included. Highly recommended restaurants are indicated by a star ★.

Category	Cost
$$$$	over $50
$$$	$30–$50
$$	$15–$30
$	under $15

Lodging

Little in the way of standardized, Holiday Inn–style accommodations exists in Belize. Large hotels are the exception rather than the rule. The best places in Belize are the small, exclusive resorts that offer personalized service and accommodations. They are strongly shaped by the tastes and interests of the people—mostly American or British—who have created them. Most have traveled widely themselves and are excellent hosts. Because of the salt and the humidity, operating a hotel in the tropics is the closest thing there is to keeping house on the deck of a ship. If there is not constant work going on in the background, paradise quickly rusts and the thatched cabana leaks.

Hardest to find are good, mid-priced accommodations; it tends to leap from tropical Spartan to luxury Caribbean with little in between. The middle ground is often occupied by either grand hotels that have fallen on hard times or small ones that are overcharging. For budget travelers, a wide selection of accommodations are available, ranging from $12 to $15 for a double room, and $6 to $7 for dormitory-style accommodation.

Generally, accommodations are more expensive than in other Central American countries. Put another way, if you check into a moderately priced room in Belize, you will get the sort of amenities that you had in an inexpensive room in Guatemala. Accommodations are most expensive in Belize City and Ambergris Cay, where prices are usually quoted in U.S. dollars. This is also where you generally get the best value for your money because the infrastructure is more developed, and there is more competition among different hotels.

Ratings Prices are for a double room and include 6% tax. Many hotels tack on a 15% service charge. If you pay by credit card, there may be a further 2%–3% fee. Most hotels offer off-season (May–October) reductions of 15%–40%. Highly recommended restaurants are indicated by a star ★.

Category	Cost*
$$$	$90–$195
$$	$45–$90
$	$15–$50

Belize City

Arriving and Departing

By Plane *See* Arriving and Departing, From North America by Plane, *above.*

By Car There are only two highways that lead to Belize City—the Northern Highway, which leads from the Mexican border (165 kilometers, or 103 miles), and the Western Highway (131 kilometers, or 82 miles) from Santa Elena, in Guatemala. These are both paved, though the Northern Highway is frequently potholed. If you arrive from Mexico you will have to hand in your Mexican Tourist Card (and/or car papers, if you have them). On the Belizean side, make sure you get a Temporary Import Permit for your car, or you may be delayed when leaving the country. Money changers at the border give a standard 2 to 1 rate for U.S. dollars. For pesos, wait for a bank in Corozal 172 kilometers (7 miles) away, where the rate is far better.

By Bus Belize City is the hub of the country's fairly extensive bus service. There is daily bus service from the Guatemalan and Mexican borders, though the route from Guatemala is sometimes impassable in the rainy season. Buses from Mexico cross into Belize and stop in Corozal, from where you can take a bus to Belize City. The buses from Guatemala stop at Melchor de Mencos, at the bridge that separates the two countries. Cross the bridge, and take a bus or a taxi on the Belizean side. San Ignacio, the main center for the region, is 13 kilometers (8 miles) away. As many people commute across the border, you will probably be able to share a ride if you arrive early in the day. Otherwise, it costs $15. From San Ignacio, there is regular service to Belize City.

By Boat For the adventurous, there is an irregular, will-it-won't-it ferry service from Puerto Barrios in Guatemala to Punta Gorda, in Belize. The fare for the three-hour trip is $2. Tickets are available—if the boat is running—from the Immigration Office at 9A Calle. From Punta Gorda, there is bus service on a very rough road to Belize City and several flights a day on **Maya Air.**

Getting Around

There is no bus service within Belize City, so the only way to get around is by taxi or on foot, if you don't have your own car.

By Taxi Taxis cost $1.50 for one person between any two points in the city, or $1 per person if there are two or more passengers. Generally, the farther you go, the more you'll be charged. Since there are no meters, always be sure to set a price before going. Taxis are available at Market Square, by the Swing Bridge, or call **Cinderella Taxi** (tel. 02/45240) or **Caribbean Taxi** (tel. 02/45240). For car rental companies, *see* Before You Go, *above.*

Important Addresses

Tourist Information The **Belize Tourist Board** is at 53 Regent St., Box 325, Belize City, tel. 02/77213. It is open weekdays 8–noon and 1–5.

Embassies U.S. Embassy (20 Garbourel La., Belize City, tel. 02/77161). **Canadian Consulate** (29 Southern Foreshore, Belize City, tel. 02/31060). **British High Commission** (Embassy Sq., Belmopan, tel. 08/22146). Note that there is neither a Guatemalan consulate nor embassy in

Belize. Citizens of the United Kingdom, Canada, Ireland, and Australia must apply for visas in Chetumal, Mexico.

Bookstores **Admiral Burnaby's,** in the Radisson Fort George Hotel, run by colorful expatriate American Emory King, is bookshop, art gallery, and coffee shop. **The Book Centre** (144 North Front St., tel. 02/77457) sells magazines and "the classics." **The Belize Bookshop,** on Regent Street (tel. 02/72054), sells magazines, books, and local and U.S. newspapers (it has a half-day on Wednesday).

Emergencies There is a 24-hour emergency room at **St. Francis Hospital and Diag-**
Hospital **nostic Centre,** 28 Albert St. (tel. 02/77068 or 02/75658).

Pharmacies The best pharmacy in Belize City is **Brodie's Pharmacy,** on Regent St. at Market Sq. It is open Mon., Tues., Thurs., and Sat. 8:30–7, Wed. 8:30–12:30 PM; Fri. 8:30–9 PM, Sun. 9 AM–12:30 PM.

Exploring Belize City

Numbers in the margin correspond to points of interest on the Belize City, Corozal, and the North map.

From the air, you realize how small it is—more town than city, with a population of fewer than 60,000 and not many buildings higher than the palm trees. After a few miles, the city simply stops. Beyond it is a largely uninhabited country where animals rather than people still
❶ form the majority of the population. **Belize City** is generally a staging post from which to see these natural wonders.

The British left surprisingly little behind them in their former colony—no parks and gardens, no university, no art galleries or museums. One of the clichés about Belize City used to be that the most exciting thing that happened was the opening of the swing bridge on Haulover Creek twice a day. But if you're prepared to take the time and trouble, Belize City will repay your curiosity. Belizeans are, by temperament, natural city dwellers, and there is an infectious sociability on streets like Albert and Queen, the main shopping areas. The best of the fine British colonial–style houses—graceful, white buildings with wraparound verandas, painted shutters, and fussy Victorian woodwork—are on the North Shore, near the Radisson Fort George. The Governor General's Residence, on the Southern Foreshore, is the largest and best maintained of the many beautiful colonial homes in Belize City. Sadly, many structures that ought to have been preserved as historic sites have been allowed to fester and rot. But before you judge the dilapidation in other parts of the city too harshly, it's worth remembering that Belize is a Third World country where the minimum wage is 60¢ per hour.

What to See and Do with Children

Though Belize as yet offers children little in the way of specific activities, it is one of the best places on earth to give children a sense of the richness and variety of tropical wildlife. Whether you go to the Belize Zoo (*see* Exploring in The Cayo, *below,* and Chapter 3, National Parks and Wildlife Reserves) or head for one of the many nature reserves, whether you go to the cays or travel to the Cayo, children will never be far from the wonders of nature. Show it to them, before it disappears!

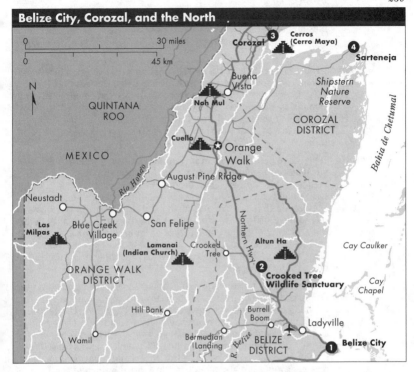

Belize City, Corozal, and the North

0 — 30 miles
0 — 45 km

N

QUINTANA ROO

Corozal **③** Cerros (Cerro Maya)

④ Sarteneja

Buena Vista

Noh Mul

Shipstern Nature Reserve

COROZAL DISTRICT

Bahia de Chetumal

MEXICO

Cuello

Orange Walk

Río Hondo

August Pine Ridge

Neustadt

Blue Creek Village

San Felipe

Las Milpas

Lamanai (Indian Church)

Crooked Tree

Northern Hwy

Altun Ha

Cay Caulker

ORANGE WALK DISTRICT

② Crooked Tree Wildlife Sanctuary

Cay Chapel

Hill Bank

Burrell Boom

Ladyville

Wamil

Bermudian Landing

R. Belize

BELIZE DISTRICT

① Belize City

Belize for Free

Belize is too small and too poor a country to offer the visitor much for free. But there are a few interesting sights that don't cost anything. Try strolling around the Saturday-morning market between Haulover Street and the Swing Bridge, with its colorful displays of tropical fruits and vegetables, or visiting the Bliss Institute, a modest museum-library down the street from the Bellevue Hotel. The opening of the Swing Bridge at 5:45 PM every day, to let through a stream of fishing boats, is not only a good opportunity to learn about mechanics; it also tells you much about the way of life in Belize City.

Excursions to the Community Baboon Sanctuary, Altun Ha, and Lamanai

The Community Baboon Sanctuary This baboon sanctuary (the "baboon" in Belize is actually the black howler monkey), about 50 kilometers (30 miles) from Belize City, is one of the most interesting wildlife conservation projects in Belize. It was established in 1985 by a zoologist from the University of Wisconsin and a group of local farmers, with help from the World Wildlife Federation. Protection of the howler monkey—an agile bundle of black fur with a derriere like a baboon's and a roar that sounds like something between a jaguar and a stuck pig—began after it had already been zealously hunted throughout Central America and was facing extinction. In Belize, it found a refuge. An all-embracing plan, coordinating eight villages, more than 100 landowners, and a 32-kilometer (20-mile) stretch of the Belize River, was drawn up to protect its habitat. Today, there are nearly 1,000 black howler monkeys in the sanctuary, as well as numerous other species of birds and mammals. About 4.8 kilometers (3 miles) of trails run from the small museum and afford visitors an efficient and easily accessible means of exploring the sanctuary. *Tel. 02/44405. Admission free. Open during daylight hours.*

Getting There From Belize City take the Northern Highway to the sign for Burrell Boom, then follow the road west. **Batty Bros. Bus Services** (tel. 02/72025) runs a trip to the sanctuary daily, except Sunday; **International Expeditions** (*see* Tour Companies in Staying in Belize, *above*) runs a boat trip up to the sanctuary. Once there, limited accommodations are available at the visitor center. Early booking is essential.

Altun Ha If you have never visited an ancient Mayan city or want to visit them without too much exertion, a trip to Altun Ha is highly recommended. It is the best-excavated and most accessible major site in Belize and is a great way to spend a half day before heading out to the cays or up to the Cayo. Human habitation at Altun Ha, spans an incredible 2,000 years—its first inhabitants settling shortly before the crowning of the ancient Egyptian king Sheshonk I, in 945 BC, and their descendants finally abandoning the city the year after King Alfred of England died, in AD 900. At its height, Altun Ha was home to 10,000 people.

The team from the Royal Ontario Museum that first excavated the site in the mid-'60s found 250 structures in all, spread over an area covering more than 1,000 square yards. At Plaza B, in the **Temple of the Masonry Altars,** those archaeologists also found the grandest and most valuable piece of Mayan art ever discovered—the head of the sun god **Kinich Ahau.** Weighing 9¾ pounds, it was carved from a solid block of green jade. In the absence of a national museum, it is kept in a solid steel vault in the central branch of the Bank of Belize.

Getting There Altun Ha is about 45 kilometers (28 miles) north of Belize City. Take the Northern Highway until you see a turnoff for the ruins and the Maruba Resort, about 24 kilometers (15 miles) north of the International Airport. This will take you onto the Old Northern Highway, once part of the old Interamerican Highway system. A sign pointing left to the ruins leads about 1½ kilometers (1 mile) down a bumpy dirt road.

Lamanai Lamanai ("submerged crocodile" in Mayan) was the longest-occupied Mayan site in Belize. Unlike all other sites, it was occupied by the Maya until well after Columbus arrived in the New World. Archaeologists have found signs of continuous occupation from 1500 BC until the 16th century. Its people carried on a way of life that had been passed down for millennia until Spanish missionaries arrived to sunder them from their past and lure them to the faith of the popes. The ruins of the church the missionaries built can still be seen at the nearby village of **Indian Church.** In the same village, there is also an abandoned sugar mill from the 19th century. With its immense drive wheel and steam engine, on which you can still read the name of the manufacturer, Leeds Foundry in New Orleans, swathed in strangler vines and creepers, it is a haunting sight.

In all, 50 or 60 Mayan structures are spread over the 950-acre Archaeological Reserve. The largest of them is the largest preclassic structure in Belize, a massive stepped temple built around 200 BC into the hillside overlooking the river; a ball court, numerous dwellings, and several other fine temples also grace the compounds. One of the finest stelae found in Belize, an elaborately carved depiction of the ruler Smoking Shell, can also be seen here.

Many structures at Lamanai have been only superficially excavated. Trees and vines grow from the top of the temples, the sides of one pyramid are covered with vegetation, another rises abruptly out of the forest floor. At Lamanai, there are no tour buses and cold-drink stands: just ruins, forest, and wildlife.

Getting Lamanai is accessible by car (except just after heavy rains); the trip
There takes about 2½ hours from Belize City via Orange Walk and the village of San Felipe (four-wheel-drive vehicle advisable). Make sure you get good directions from someone before leaving Orange Walk, as the turnoff to San Felipe is not well marked. The turnoff to the ruins is in the tiny village of Indian Church, just before the entrance to the Lamanai Outpost Lodge.

The best way to approach the ruins is by river. The Maruba Resort (*see* Dining and Lodging, *below*) runs a boat up the New River. From Belize City, various tour operators run day trips to Lamanai (*see* Tour Companies in Staying in Belize, *above*). Various local operators also offer tours. One is Mr. Godoy, in Orange Walk (tel. 03/22969).

Shopping

Belize City is a good place to kick the consumer habit. There isn't much to buy. Most of the crafts items for sale are from Guatemala. The hotel shops sell a few carvings, mostly of wildlife (jaguars and dolphins) or Mayan themes; they're made of zericote wood, a hardwood native to Belize. The best of them are quite good, though nothing in comparison with African wood carvings. The recently opened **National Handicraft Center** (tel. 02/33833), located on Fort Street just past the Fort Street Guest House, is the best place to check out Belizean-made products of all sorts. You can also find crafts at **Cottage Industries** (26 Albert St., tel. 02/72359), and more colorful T-shirts with Creole slogans are at an array of small shops spread across Albert and Queen streets.

One thing that Belize does have is beautiful stamps, available from the **Philatelic Society** (91 North Front St.). It also produces a few excellent and low-priced rums. **Brodie's** and **Romac's**, the main supermarkets on Albert Street, have good selections. **Go Graphics** (23 Regent St., tel. 02/74082 or 02/75512) has T-shirts for adults and children, and a small selection of crafts.

Dining and Lodging

Dining Most of the best restaurants in Belize City are in the hotels. Belize is a casual place, and little in the way of a dress code exists. The more expensive restaurants prefer, but do not require, a jacket and shirt for men. Otherwise, as long as you don't have bare feet, and have a T-shirt or a shirt on, you will probably get served. Reservations are advisable in the higher price categories. For details and price-category definitions, *see* Dining in Staying in Belize, *above*.

Lodging Belize City offers a wide range of accommodations, from budget hotels for back-packers to luxury hotels. Luxury hotels like the Ramada Royal Reef or the Radisson Fort George offer first-class, international-style accommodations. Budget accommodations can be found for approximately $10 for a single room, $12–$15 for a double. For details and price-category definitions, *see* Lodging in Staying in Belize.

Dining **Chateau Caribbean.** The restaurant is on the second floor, up a flight of wide stairs, and has marvelous views of the ocean and the cays beyond. With its white tablecloths, gleaming cutlery, and abstract art on the walls, it is one of the best-looking places to eat in the city. The menu offers a combination of Chinese and Caribbean dishes. For a sampling of local shellfish, try the seafood combination. *6 Marine Parade, Belize City, tel. 02/30800. AE, MC, V. $$$*

The Grill. This handsome white building is surrounded by a garden overlooking the bay. Run by an Englishman, it's no toad-in-the-hole, but it does serve excellent steaks and grills. *164 Newtown Barracks, tel. 02/45020. AE, MC, V. Dinner only. $$$*

Dit's Saloon. More pastry café than restaurant, this is a real local place, with cheery striped tablecloths and a homey feel. It also shows off a humongous fan—about the size of a Piper Cub propeller. Like many other older Belizean restaurants, it's got the washbasin right in the dining room. The cakes—try the three-milks cake or the coconut tarts—are the best in town. Otherwise, Dit's serves simple food like burgers, fish-and-chips, and tea. *50 King St., tel. 02/73330. No credit cards. $*

★ **GG's.** After 20 years in Los Angeles, George Godfrey decided to come home and open an American-style restaurant with first-rate Belizean food. As well as the best burgers in Belize, he serves T-bone steak, rice and beans with stewed beef or pork, and seafood. The courtyard, with its custard apple tree, traveler's palms, and green-and-white Belikin umbrellas, has an Italian café atmosphere. The rest rooms are spotless and the beer comes in frosted mugs. Here is an excellent value. *2-B King St., tel. 02/74378. No credit cards. Closed Sun. $*

★ **Macy's Café.** On the wall of this cozy restaurant is a letter from the bishop of Belize, congratulating the staff on its catering feats, and a photo of Harrison Ford during the making of *Mosquito Coast* (his was the table by the door). If you're an eco-freak or a vegetarian, Macy's may give you shudders: You've seen the wildlife? Now you can eat it. In other words, it specializes in game animals. Wrap your mouth around stewed armadillo, brocket deer, "royal" gibnut, and, by request, stewed iguana, known locally as "bamboo chicken." Macy, the Jamaican-born proprietor, says it's tough to prepare—it has to be scalded, then washed in lime juice and vinegar—but delicious to eat. Some of you might want to just take her word for it. By the way, bring your own booze. *18 Bishop St., tel. 02/73419. No credit cards. $*

Dining and Lodging

Belize Biltmore Plaza. Along with the Ramada and the Radisson, this place offers the most upscale accommodations in Belize. Rooms feature all the amenities of a deluxe hotel and open onto verandas overlooking the pool and a tropical garden. Because it offers the best meeting and entertainment facilities in Belize, this is a popular hotel for business travelers. *Mile 3, Northern Highway, Belize City, tel. 02/32302, fax 02/32301. 90 rooms with bath. Facilities: restaurant, bar, gift shop, pool, travel agency. AE, MC, V. $$$*

Bellevue Hotel. The oldest of Belize's first-class hotels makes up in character what it lacks in size and modernity. Originally a family home, it still imparts a personal, bed-and-breakfast atmosphere. The second-floor Harbour Room is the best bar in Belize City, with live local music on weekends. *5 Southern Foreshore, Box 428, Belize City, tel. 02/7705, fax 02/73253. 37 rooms with bath. Facilities: restaurant, bar, pool. AE, MC, V. $$$*

★ **Maruba Resort.** Everything done at the Maruba, a resort 64 kilometers (40 miles) outside the city on the Old Northern Highway, is done with style. Succulent food is served on a palm leaf and decorated with hibiscus flowers; the glasses are crystal; the plates are handsome porcelain. Each cabana is individually furnished with

Guatemalan blankets and rugs and decorated with local artwork. A beautiful, small swimming pool with a waterfall and a Jacuzzi (you can steam under the stars at night) graces the property. The convivial center of the resort is the large, circular, thatch-covered restaurant and bar, where you will eat consistently delicious food, imaginatively prepared and served with excellent salads, to the accompaniment of good jazz (a Maruba favorite is the excellent Ladysmith Black Mombasa, at one time featured with Paul Simon). As if that weren't enough, the Maruba also offers an imaginative spa program. If you get tired of all this lavish attention, try an invigorating tour to the Mayan ruins at Altun Ha or a boat trip to Lamanai. *40½ Mile Old Northern Highway, Maskall Village, tel. 03/22199; or Box 300703, Houston, Texas 77230, tel. 713/799–2031. 10 rooms, 1 suite, all with private bath. Facilities: restaurant, bar, health spa, laundry, Jacuzzi, pool. AE, MC, V. $$$*

★ **Radisson Fort George.** The Fort George still breathes an air of British colonial style, though the accommodations—72 air-conditioned rooms, with phone, cable TV, and the best water pressure in town—are among the most modern in the country. The new six-story wing, with its tinted-glass frontage, has marvelous views of the ocean, and the recent addition of the Villa Wing (formerly the Holiday Inn Villa) makes it the second-largest hotel in Belize. Paul Hunt, the English manager, is widely regarded as the best innkeeper in the country. As though that weren't enough, Maxime's, the hotel restaurant, serves excellent fare. Reason enough for Her Majesty, the queen of England, to have eaten here when she came to Belize. Why not try the gibnut? She did. *2 Marine Parade, Belize City, tel. 02/77400 or 800/333–3333, fax 02/73820. 113 rooms. Facilities: restaurant, bar, business center, conference facilities, gift shop, laundry, pool. AE, MC, V. $$$*

Ramada Royal Reef. With 114 deluxe rooms, four suites, a presidential suite, and three large meeting rooms, the Ramada Royal Reef is now the biggest hotel in Belize. Rooms all come with private bathroom, cable TV, and air-conditioning, and the oceanside setting is first class. You can count on skillfully concocted international and local cuisine, like grilled swordfish and grouper, at the restaurant, whose views embrace the ocean and stretch across the bay. *Box 1248, Newtown Barracks, Belize City, tel. 02/32670 or 800/228–9898, fax 02/31649. 114 rooms. Facilities: restaurant, bar, business and conference facilities, gift shop, laundry, pool. AE, MC, V. $$$*

El Centro. The hotel is rather drab, but the restaurant next door, with mirrored panels, is a cool, pleasant place to eat. It is open all day and is one of the few restaurants that still serve cow-foot soup, a working-class specialty from Lancashire, England, that died out in that country long ago but survived in British Honduras. El Centro also serves "reef and beef," a seafood-and-beef kebab. *4 Bishop St., tel. 02/72413, fax 02/74553. 13 rooms with bath. Facilities: restaurant, bar, cable TV. AE, MC, V. Open Mon.–Sat. 11 AM–10 PM. $$*

Fort Street Guest House. A favorite among young travelers, this renovated Victorian house emanates the warm southern hospitality of new owners Hugh and Theresa Parkey, formerly managers of a well-known dive resort. Upstairs, cool pastel grays prevail. Modern paintings decorate the walls. One of the exotic features of the place is that every bed has a baldachin-style mosquito net over it. The downstairs restaurant, cooled by lazy ceiling fans and graced with a full-size poster of Bogart, is a bit of Casablanca in Belize; its menu is inventive and witty. Try Death by Chocolate for dessert or one of the excellent fruit breakfasts. *4 Fort St., Belize City, tel. 02/30116,*

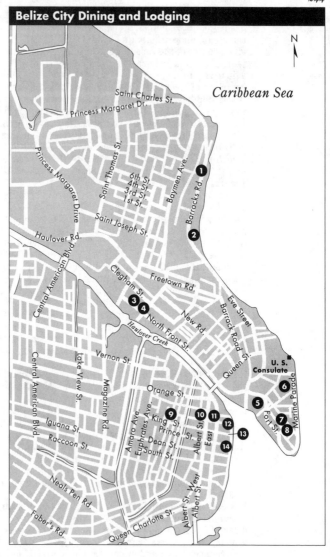

Belize City Dining and Lodging

Dining
Chateau
Caribbean, **6**
Dit's Saloon, **9**
GG's, **12**
The Grill, **1**
Macy's Café, **11**

Lodging
Bakadeer Inn, **3**
Bellevue
Hotel, **13**
Colton House, **7**
El Centro, **10**
Fort Street
Guest House, **5**
North Front
Street Guest
House, **4**
Radisson
Fort George, **8**
Ramada Royal
Reef, **2**
The Seaside, **14**

Caribbean Sea

N

fax 02/78808. 6 rooms. Facilities: restaurant, bar, gift shop, laundry. MC, V. $$

Lodging **Bakadeer Inn.** The surrounding area is drab, but this new, Belizean-run hotel has 12 very agreeable rooms built along a quiet, secure courtyard set back from the street. All rooms have a well-stocked minibar, phone, TV, and private bath. There is a cheery breakfast room and a reassuringly large night watchman. *74 Cleghorn St., Belize City, tel. 02/31400, fax 02/31963. 12 rooms. Facilities: business facilities, laundry, breakfast room, night porter. No credit cards. $$*

★ **Colton House.** Good accommodations in the middle price range are the hardest to find in Belize, so this is a real gem. Tucked in between two of the finest hotels in the city—the Fort George and The Villa—this beautiful colonial house offers excellent value at a central location. You go up the steps onto a crisp, white veranda. Inside, there are fine antiques and cool, polished wooden floors. The English family who run it offer the charm of traditional bed-and-breakfast (unfortunately, without the breakfast). They will also rent you a four-wheel-drive vehicle at a competitive price. As there is only limited space, reservations are essential. *9 Cork St., Belize City, tel. 02/44666. 4 rooms, 2 with bath. No credit cards. $$*

North Front Street Guest House. The sign on the street calls this weathered, clapboard boardinghouse "world famous," a soubriquet earned among the many backpackers and fishermen who have enjoyed its simple but friendly hospitality. The "most fun place in Belize" was how one guest described it. "Pure Steinbeck," chipped in an elderly man from Georgia. Heavy-duty wire fences off the steps up from the street guarantee security. *124 N. Front St., Belize City, tel. 02/77595. 8 rooms. No credit cards. $*

The Seaside. Of the budget hotels, this has by far the best location, opposite two of the grandest villas in the city and not far from the water. The accommodations are dormitory-style, but the house is a good-looking, two-story colonial-style building, and the owner, Philip Ramare, who is from Maryland, is intent on making your stay an agreeable one. *3 Prince St., Belize City, tel. 02/78339. 6 rooms. No credit cards. $*

Corozal and the North

As Belize is only the size of Massachusetts, much of it is within range of Belize City. This is particularly true of the north. Whereas getting to the south involves circuitous routes on bad roads, the north is easily accessible. The landscape is mostly flat—this is sugarcane country—and the Northern Highway is one of the better roads. Although the north has lost out to the Cayo in recent years in terms of visitor numbers, some of Belize's most interesting Mayan sites, as well as several first-class resorts, can be found here.

Arriving and Departing

By Plane **Tropic Air** (*see* Arriving and Departing, *above*) has flights from both San Pedro on Ambergris Cay and Belize City's International Airport to Corozal. The journey takes 20 minutes and costs $95 return, and $52, respectively.

By Bus **Batty Bros.** and **Venus** (*see* Arriving and Departing, *above*) make the three-hour journey from Belize City to Corozal several times a day. Buses also travel on from there to Chetumal, Mexico.

By Car Corozal is the last stop on the Northern Highway from Belize City before you hit Mexico. Due to the variable state of the roads, the 153-kilometer (96-mile) journey will probably take you a good two to three hours, longer if you stop off at the ruins of Altun Ha on the way.

Getting Around If you haven't got your own wheels, you will have a hard time exploring the north, as no cross-country bus services exist, and little traffic means little hitching potential. Taxis are available in Corozal but are costly. There is a large expatriate community in the town, so if you're stuck, try hooking up with them.

Exploring Corozal and the North

If you continue along the Northern Highway from Belize City, you eventually reach Corozal. Before the town of Orange Walk, however, ❷ at Mile 33, a road branches off to the **Crooked Tree Wildlife Sanctuary.** Founded by the Belize Audubon Society in 1984, it encompasses a chain of swamps, lagoons, and inland waterways covering an area of 3,000 acres.

At the center of the sanctuary is **Crooked Tree,** one of the oldest inland villages in Belize, with a population of 800. A church and a school, and even one of the surest signs of civilization in former British territories—a cricket pitch—can be found here. Crooked Tree Resort is a small, low-key complex with seven simple, thatched cabanas with hot and cold water at the edge of one of the lagoons. For details write Box 1453, Belize City, Belize, C.A., tel. 02/77745.

The wildlife sanctuary is one of the most interesting in the country. For bird-watchers it is paradise. There are snowy egrets, snail kites, ospreys, and black-collared hawks, as well as two types of duck—Muscovy and black-bellied whistling—and all five species of kingfisher native to Belize. The sanctuary's most prestigious visitor, however, is the jabiru stork, a kind of freshwater albatross with a wingspan of up to 8 feet; it's the largest flying bird in the Americas.

The best way to tour the sanctuary is by canoe, and there are a number of excellent local guides at the village. You will be rewarded for your adventuresomeness: By boat, you are likely to see iguanas, crocodiles, coatis, and turtles.

❸ **Corozal** is the last town before the Río Hondo, the border separating Belize from Mexico. Like Ambergris Cay, it was originally settled by refugees fleeing south from the Caste Wars of the 19th century. Though still officially English-speaking, Spanish is just as common. The town has been largely rebuilt since Hurricane Janet almost destroyed it in 1955, and consequently it is neat and modern. One of the few remaining historic buildings is a portion of the old fort in the center of the town. Most houses are clapboard, built on wooden piles. Worth visiting is the town hall with its colorful mural depicting local history. Only a few restaurants and bars exist.

Not far from Corozal are several Mayan sites. The closest, **Santa Rita,** is just a few minutes' walk from the center of the town. Only a few of its structures have been unearthed, and it requires imagination to picture this settlement, founded in 1500 BC, as one of the major trading centers in the district. The second site is **Cerros,** a late preclassic center on the coast, south of Corozal. As at Santa Rita, little has been excavated, but the site, which dates from about 2000 BC, includes a ball court, several tombs, and a large temple. The best way to get there is by boat from Corozal.

❹ Also best reached by boat are the village of **Sarteneja** and the **Shipstern Reserve,** though a new road has made them accessible by car or bus from Orange Walk for the first time. The village of Sarteneja is a small community of mestizo fishermen and farmers who make a living from lobster fishing and pineapple production. Traditionally, their links were always north, across the Bay of Chetumal to Mexico, rather than south to Belize, but with the building of the roadway, that is beginning to change.

Situated at the tip of a peninsula jutting into the Bay of Chetumal, the 81 square kilometers (31 square miles) of tropical forest that has now been turned into the Shipstern Reserve is, like the Crooked Tree Reserve, a paradise for bird-watchers. Look for egret (there are 13 species here), American coot, keel-billed toucans, flycatchers, warblers, and several species of parrot. A rich tapestry of animal life also exists, including deer, peccaries, pumas, jaguars, and raccoons, as well as a dizzying variety of insects and butterflies. In fact, at the butterfly farm adjacent to the reserve's visitor center, pupae are hatched for export mainly to Britain, where they are used at tourist sites offering a simulated jungle experience.

Dining and Lodging

$$$ **Adventure Inn.** This little-known gem on the ocean road about 11 kilometers (7 miles) southeast of Corozal offers a relaxing tropical escape with swimming, fishing, sailing, biking, tennis, and caves to explore. Nightlife consists of whatever you and the other guests can arrange at Tiger Lilly's, a dining room–bar that serves up some of the best food in Belize. *Box 35, Corozal, tel. 04/22187, fax 04/22243. 20 rooms with bath. Facilities: restaurant, bar, laundry. No credit cards.*

Chan-Chich Lodge. Whether the spirit of Smoking Shell, Jaguar Paw, or some other fierce Mayan lord will one day take revenge on Barry Owen, Chan-Chich Lodge's owner, for erecting a group of cabanas slap in the middle of a Classic Period (AD 300–900) Mayan plaza remains to be seen. But since it opened in 1988, this off-the-beaten-track resort has established itself as one of the more unusual destinations in Belize. It's a 3½-hour drive to get here from Belize City, unless you fly, but the abundant wildlife and the particular ambience of the place—it's a bit like camping out in a Roman forum—make it worth it. Set in the 250,000-acre Río Bravo Conservation Area and created with the help of the Massachusetts Audubon Society and the distinguished British naturalist Gerald Durrell, the property teems with wildlife and birds. Accommodations are in thatch-covered cabanas with mahogany interiors, priate bathrooms, and queen-size beds. Tours include canoe trips along the river and horseback tours to Mayan ruins that haven't yet been built on. *Chan-Chich Lodge, Gallon Jug, Box 37, Belize City, tel. 02/75634 or 800/451–8017 in the U.S., fax 02/75635. 12 rooms with private bath. Facilities: restaurant, bar, laundry. AE, MC, V.*

Lamanai Outpost Lodge. This new resort, just a few minutes' walk from the Mayan ruins of Lamanai, is rapidly becoming one of Belize's most popular spots. Guest rooms have breathtaking views of the huge New River Lagoon, and the hotel offers a variety of wildlife-viewing excursions, including Belize's only nighttime river safari. *Indian Church, Orange Walk District, tel. 02/33578. 16 thatched cabanas with bath. Facilities: restaurant, bar, canoes. MC, V.*

$$ **Tony's Inn.** Tony's is a smart, white, two-story hotel located a short distance south of Corozal overlooking the bay and the Mayan site of

Cerros beyond. The beach, in a secluded cove, is one of the most pleasant in the north. Visit the cool bar for a refreshing cocktail or the restaurant for such piquant specialties as curried lobster. All rooms are fitted with mahogany and tile floors, and all have private bathrooms. The more expensive units have air-conditioning. *Box 12, Corozal, tel. 04/2055 or 800/633–4734 in the U.S., fax 04/22829. 17 rooms, including 5 singles. Facilities: restaurant, bar, laundry. AE, MC, V.*

$–$$ **Maya Hotel.** The Maya is a small, friendly, family-run hotel at the
★ southern end of Corozal with a restaurant specializing in Mexican and Belizean food. Rooms are clean, cheap, and cheerful and have fans and private baths. *Box 112, c/o Sylvia and Rosita Mai, Corozal, tel. 04/2082. 17 rooms. Facilities: laundry, restaurant, bar. MC, V.*

$ **Caribbean Motel and Trailer Park.** Known simply as Mom's, this is the only place in Belize you'll be able to park an RV with ease. There are also 10 simple cabanas and a decent restaurant. *Box 55, Corozal, tel. 04/22045. Facilities: restaurant, bar, laundry. No credit cards.*

The Cays and Atolls

There can be few moments more thrilling than turning a corner round an outcrop of coral in 70 feet of virgin water and coming upon a fully grown, spotted eagle ray. Nearly 24 meters (8 feet) long and weighing more than 88 kilograms (40 pounds), its fleshy undersides as white as coconut, its back a jaguar-symmetry of dots, it is, with its needlelike tail streaming out behind it and its great wings flapping, sinuous beyond imagination, one of nature's grandest creations.

At the other end of the scale is the feisty little damselfish, a bolt of blue no bigger than your little finger, with sides as smooth as black marble and iridescent blue markings that glitter like the rhinestones in a diva's dress.

These are just two of a cast of aquatic characters awaiting you under the water in Belize. There are bloated blowfish hovering in their holes like nightclub bouncers; lean, mean barracuda patroling the depths like junk-bond dealers; and queen angelfish that shimmy through the water with the puckered lips and haughty self-assurance of a Madison Avenue model. In all, several hundred species of Caribbean tropicals frequent the reef, including 40 kinds of grouper, numerous kinds of cardinal fish, damselfish and wrasses, squirrel fish, butterfly fish, parrot fish, snappers, jacks, pompanos, basslets, and many others.

More than 200 cays (the word comes from the Spanish *cayo* but is pronounced like *key* in Key Largo) dot these waters like punctuation marks in a long, liquid sentence. The vast majority of them are uninhabited except by iguanas and opossums, frigate birds, pelicans, brown- and red-footed boobies, and some very lewd-sounding creatures called wish-willies (actually, a kind of iguana). Most of the cays lie inside the barrier reef, which over the centuries has acted as a breakwater, allowing them to take shape, grow, and develop undisturbed by the tides and the winds that would otherwise sweep them away.

Arriving and Departing by Plane and Boat

Airport and Airlines Except for those to Ambergris Cay and Cay Caulker, there are no scheduled plane connections to the cays. Each resort makes its own arrangements for guests to come out. Lighthouse Reef was, at press time, the only atoll with an airstrip.

To Ambergris Cay As an increasing number of visitors transfer directly to Ambergris Cay on arrival in Belize City, there are regular flights to San Pedro from both the Municipal and International airports. The two airlines that fly to the cay are **Tropic Air** (Box 20, San Pedro, Belize, tel. 026/2012) and **Maya Airways** (6 Fort St., Box 458, Belize City, tel. 02/77215). Fares for the 15-minute flight are $70 (Municipal) and $60 (Intl.) round-trip. **Island Air** (tel. 026/2435 in San Pedro or 02/31140 in Belize City) runs 10 flights per day, from 7:30 AM to 5 PM from the International Airport to San Pedro. The fare is $35 round-trip. The airstrip—it's not an airport—is right in San Pedro, so much so that when you fly in you feel as though the wing tips are going to drag the washing lines from the surrounding houses with them. You'll always find taxis at the airstrip, and the hotels run courtesy coaches. If you are proceeding on foot, it's two minutes, around the edges of the soccer pitch, to the main street. There are no buses.

To Cay Caulker Three airlines now fly to Cay Caulker: **Tropic Air** (tel. 02/45671), **Skybird** (tel. 02/32596), and **Island Air** (tel. 026/2435 in San Pedro or 02/31140 in Belize City). **Skybird Air Services** has a regular service from Municipal Airport. The first flight is at 8:30 AM, the last at 4:30 PM.

By Boat A variety of boats operate between Belize City and Ambergris. The *To Ambergris Cay* most dependable are the *Andrea* and *Andrea II*. They depart from the Southern Foreshore, by the Bellevue Hotel, daily, except Sunday, at 4 PM (1 PM on Saturday) and return from San Pedro at 7 AM Monday–Friday and 8 AM on Saturday. The journey takes 75 minutes and costs $20 round-trip. The *Miss Belize* makes a daily run from Belize City to San Pedro, leaving from the dock by the Bellevue Hotel. The journey takes 75 minutes and costs about $10 one way. Private charter boats also make the round-trip. They leave from the docks around the Swing Bridge. Ripoffs have been known, so only pay the fare once you reach your destination!

To Cay Caulker Boats leave from the dock by the Bellevue Hotel and from the Shell station, near the Swing Bridge. The journey takes 45 minutes. Boats—known locally as skiffs—leave from the dock behind the A&R Shell Service Station on North Front Street in Belize City. Finding them is no problem—the young kids who hustle for the boat owners will find you. The best-known of these boats is the *Soledad*, captained by a well-known local character called Chocolate. Chocolate also runs trips to Goff's Cay, a small island southeast of Belize City.

To get to and from San Pedro and Cay Caulker, take *The Banana Boat*. It does two trips per day on Monday, Wednesday, Friday, Saturday, and Sunday, departing at 9 AM and returning at 3:30 PM from San Pedro, and departing at 9:30 AM and returning at 3:30 PM from San Pedro, and departing at 9:30 AM and returning at 4 PM from Cay Caulker. The 30-minute journey costs $17.50 round-trip. A boat called *The Thunderbolt* (tel. 026/2217) also makes runs to and from Cay Caulker, Monday to Saturday, departing San Pedro at 7:30 AM and returning at approximately 9 AM. Fare: $10. Both boats arrive in Cay Caulker at the Lagoonside Marina.

To the Outer and Southern Cays For travel to the more remote cays, you are basically left to your own resources. There are boats that can be hired for charter, either in San Pedro or Belize City, but they are not cheap. The resorts on the atolls (*see* Dining and Lodging, *below*) run their own flights or boats, but these are not public services.

For the southern cays like Tobacco Reef and South Water Cay, check in Dangriga (*see* Exploring in Placencia and the South, *below*) for availability of boats. The Pelican Beach Hotel has a boat that goes to its resort on South Water Cay. At the Río Mar Hotel you can find out about boats for Tobacco Reef. Both services are not usually available to the general public, but those not staying at the resorts can sometimes catch a ride if there's room.

Important Addresses and Phone Numbers

Ambergris Cay **Police** (tel. 2022); **Fire** (tel. 2372); **Ambulance** (tel. 90).

Pharmacies: Lopez Drugs, Ambergris's drug store, is open Mon.–Thurs. 8–noon and 5:30–9, Fri. 8–2, weekends 7 AM–9 PM.

The **Belize Bank,** on Barrier Reef Drive, is open weekdays 9–3 and Sat. 9–noon.

The post office is located on Barrier Reef Drive. It is open Mon.–Thurs. 8–noon and 1–5, Fri. 8–noon and 1–4:30.

For taxis, call 2089 or 2038.

Cay Caulker The **Cay Caulker Health Centre,** opposite the Marin Hotel, is open weekdays 8–11:30 and 1–4:30.

The telephone office is near the Reef Hotel. It is open weekdays 8–noon and 1–4, Sat. 8–noon.

As there have been a number of incidents, you are advised not to leave anything valuable in your room on Cay Caulker.

There are no banks on Cay Caulker, so either come with ready cash or change traveler's checks at your hotel.

Exploring the Cays and Atolls

❶ Today, **Ambergris Cay** is the most developed of the cays—some would say too developed—and offers the greatest range of accommodations, dining, and diving in Belize. The main town, **San Pedro,** is a hardworking community of fishermen, hoteliers, and tradespeople, and it is rightly proud of its comparative prosperity. The town also has one of the highest literacy rates in the country and an admirable level of ecological awareness about the fragility of the reef from which it now makes its living.

Recently, San Pedro has been written about as though it is a Belizean Cancún, which is absurd. With a population of fewer than 2,000 and little stores and restaurants with names like Lily's, Alice's, Martha's, and Estel's, San Pedro is a small, friendly Caribbean village—a couple of streets of mostly two-story wooden houses, with the ocean on one side and the lagoon on the other. You can walk from one end to the other in 10 minutes and not be out of breath. At night it feels like Spain's Costa Brava must have felt 40 years ago. Old men lean over their balconies to watch the world go by. Teenagers stroll barefoot up and down Front Street. Every now and again a battered American station wagon crawls along the sandy street.

The Cays, Atolls, and Barrier Reef

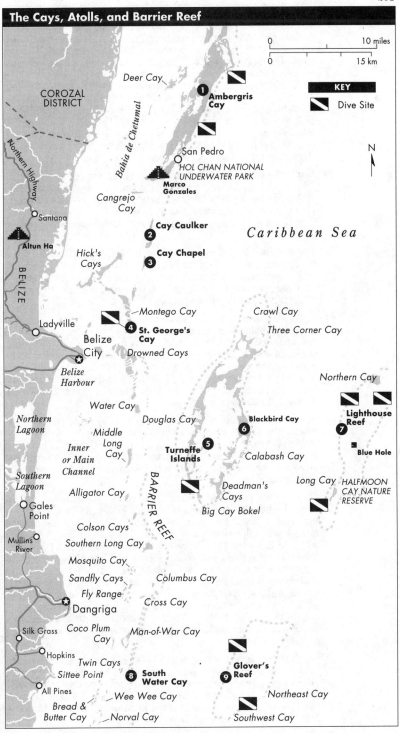

| 0 | | 10 miles |
| 0 | | 15 km |

KEY

Dive Site

N

COROZAL
DISTRICT

Deer Cay

1 **Ambergris Cay**

Northern Highway

Bahia de Chetumal

San Pedro

HOL CHAN NATIONAL
UNDERWATER PARK

Marco Gonzales

Santana

Cangrejo Cay

Altun Ha

BELIZE

Cay Caulker **2**

Caribbean Sea

Cay Chapel **3**

Hick's Cays

Montego Cay

Crawl Cay

Ladyville

4 **St. George's Cay**

Three Corner Cay

Belize
City

Drowned Cays

Belize Harbour

Northern Cay

Water Cay

Northern Lagoon

Douglas Cay

Blackbird Cay **6**

Lighthouse Reef **7**

Middle Long Cay

Turneffe Islands **5**

Inner or Main Channel

Blue Hole

Southern Lagoon

Alligator Cay

BARRIER REEF

Deadman's Cays

Long Cay HALFMOON CAY NATURE RESERVE

Gales Point

Calabash Cay

Mullins River

Colson Cays

Big Cay Bokel

Southern Long Cay

Mosquito Cay

Sandfly Cays

Columbus Cay

Fly Range

Dangriga

Cross Cay

Silk Grass

Coco Plum Cay

Man-of-War Cay

Hopkins

Twin Cays

Sittee Point

All Pines

8 **South Water Cay**

Glover's Reef **9**

Wee Wee Cay

Northeast Cay

Bread & Butter Cay

Norval Cay

Southwest Cay

2 Two signs you often see on **Cay Caulker**—NO SHIRT NO PROBLEM and NO ILLEGAL DRUGS—pretty much sum up the ambience of Ambergris's little southern brother, which is, after it, the most developed of Belize's cays. In recent years, it has received a reputation as a tropical paradise for tightwad travelers. As a result, it has become immensely popular with the backpack-and-Birkenstock brigade, either young and student or old and poor, and Belize's few Rastafarian clones. Actually, it's a bit of a dump. What the Irish playwright Synge said about his own country—that what most people found beautiful about Ireland was actually its poverty—amply applies to Cay Caulker. The colorful water tubs and flowering shrubs give it the illusion of beauty, but the local people live in dilapidated shacks with no running water. Here, even the pelicans look disheveled.

3 Just to the south of Cay Caulker is **Cay Chapel,** owned entirely by the Pyramid Island Resort, which was at one time an exclusive resort with its own airstrip and tennis courts. In recent years it has become very run-down, however. If you come here for the day you are likely to be sharing the island with a group of British officers who use it for R&R.

4 The origins of Belize as a state began in **St. George's Cay,** the site of the first capital of the original British settlement and, subsequently, of the decisive sea battle with the Spanish. The original resort— St. George's Lodge—has long been a favorite with the British because of its proximity to Belize City.

5 Forty kilometers (25 miles) east of Belize City, the **Turneffe Island group** is a chain of tiny islands and mangrove swamps. Most of them are inhabited only by birds and fishermen, but for diving, Turneffe is second only to Lighthouse Reef, with **The Elbow**—probably the most exciting wall-dive in Belize—and several other steep drop-offs in its midst. Only an hour from Lighthouse Reef and 45 minutes from the northern edge of Glover's Reef, the best diving in Belize is within range of a day trip.

6 Part of the Turneffe Island atoll, **Blackbird Cay** is the newest of the resort sites in Belize, the product of a partnership between a Houston businessman and Belizean Ray Lightburn. Originally built as a base camp for scientists researching the marine life, this small, isolated resort has a strong accent on ecotourism and fishing. Access is by boat only.

7 If Robinson Crusoe had been a man of means, and had had his own plane, **Lighthouse Reef** is where he would have gone for a break from his desert island. It's the farthest away of Belize's atolls, but the closest you will get to paradise. The Lighthouse Reef system— which includes the **Half Moon Cay National Monument** (*see* Chapter 3, National Parks and Wildlife Reserves)—has two of the country's five-star dives: the **Blue Hole,** a breathtaking vertical chute that drops several hundred feet through the reef; and the vertiginous walls off **Half Moon Cay.** The nature reserve protects loggerhead turtles, iguanas, and one of the world's two large colonies of red-footed boobies. The only accommodations in the area are at the Lighthouse Reef Resort on Northern Cay (*see* Lodging, *below*).

8 **South Water Cay** is the first cay to have been developed for tourism in the south of Belize. The coral is only a few flipper-beats away and offers good off-the-beaten-reef diving. Nearby, on **Carrie Bow Cay,** is a research institute run by the Smithsonian. Visitors are welcome, by appointment. Since there is no phone, contact the Blue Marlin Lodge (*see* Lodging, *below*) for more information.

❾ Named after the pirate John Glover, **Glover's Reef** is the farthest south of Belize's three atolls, a necklace of coral strung around a 208-square-kilometer (80-square-mile) lagoon. The diving rates as some of the best in Belize, and there is excellent fishing for permit and bonefish. Two resorts now exist on Glover's. The newer and more upscale of the two is the Manta Reef Resort (*see* Lodging, *below*). It is situated on Southwest Cay at the southernmost tip of the atoll.

Scuba Diving

The Barrier Reef, a 320-kilometer-long (200-mile-long) coral necklace stretching from the Yucatán Peninsula in the north to the Guatemalan border in the south, is the longest in the Western Hemisphere. If you add to this the three coral atolls farther out to sea—Lighthouse Reef, Glover's Reef, and Turneffe Islands—there are more than 560 kilometers (350 miles) of reef to be dived in Belize, more than in Bonaire, Cozumel, and all the Caymans put together. The great majority of this is water that has never been dived before.

When to Go Diving is possible year-round in Belize, but it is at its best in the early spring. Between November and February, cold fronts from North America may push southward, producing blustery winds known as "northers." These bring rain and rough weather and tend to churn up the sea, thus reducing visibility. For the rest of the year visibility is glass-clear stunning: usually between 100 and 150 feet. As water temperatures rarely stray from the 80s, many people dive without any sort of wet suit. If you are doing several dives a day, however, you may prefer to use a short suit for the winter and a Lycra skin for the summer.

Dive Sites Dive destinations can be divided into two broad categories—the reef and the atolls. Most of the diving on the reef is done on the northern section, particularly off Ambergris Cay. The reasons for this are twofold. First, the reef is closer, a white seam on the horizon a few hundred yards from the shore, making getting out to your dive site extremely easy. Journey time by boat is usually between 10 minutes and half an hour. This, in turn, means you are not nearly so dependent on the weather. Take out a map of Belize, and you will see that the farther south you go the farther the coast and the coral part company. In Placencia on the mainland, it is more than 33 kilometers (20 miles) out to the reef. This means far longer journeys—an hour or upwards—and far greater weather dependency. In Ambergris you may be prevented from diving by a storm in the morning, but you still have a good chance to get out for an afternoon dive.

Ambergris Cay The people of Ambergris, sensing that the future lay in tourism rather than fishing, were the quickest at setting up the infrastructure for diving, and they remain the best organized. In terms of the number of dive shops, the quality of the dive masters, the range of equipment and facilities, Ambergris Cay remains the most obvious all-around choice as a base for diving. (There is now a hyperbaric chamber in San Pedro, paid for by contributions from all the dive shops and through fees attached to diver insurance, which is highly recommended, since emergency services and transport costs could wipe out your savings in a hurry.) It also offers the greatest variety of accommodations at prices that range from budget to expensive.

Diving is generally done in Ambergris out of fast, maneuverable speedboats. There is no bouncing around in Zodiac boats here: Transports are handbuilt out of solid mahogany. As the boats represent the dive masters' major assets, costing as much as $14,000 each, they are normally lovingly cared for. Power generally comes from two hefty outboards mounted on the back. With the throttle right open, it's an exhilarating ride.

Most of the dive masters are ex-fishermen, local guys from San Pedro who started their diving as an adjunct to their work as lobster fishermen, then went on to get certified as dive masters. The best of them are immensely personable and have an intimate knowledge of the reef and a superb eye for coral and marine life. They also have an unusually developed ecological awareness, knowing as they do that the destruction of the reef would not only be a great tragedy in itself, but economic suicide for them. An example of this is the fact that a group of dive masters have recently created a network of buoys fastened to the bedrock to prevent the further destruction of the coral because of the practice of dropping anchor directly into it. In bad weather, one anchor dragging across the bottom can destroy more coral than a thousand divers.

Most of the dives off Ambergris are one-tank dives at depths of between 15 and 24 meters (50 and 80 feet). This gives you approximately 35 minutes' bottom time. The general pattern is two one-tank dives per day, one in the morning at 9, and one in the afternoon at 2, though this can be varied depending on your budget. The diving is, with slight variations, similar all along Ambergris Cay. You always dive on the windward side of the reef, and the basic form is canyon-diving. For wall-diving, you have to go out to the atolls (*see below*).

Located 20 minutes from San Pedro, at the southern tip of Ambergris Cay, the **Hol Chan Marine Reserve** (*see* Chapter 3, National Parks and Wildlife Reserves) is one of the best dives on the reef. Basically, it is a narrow break in the reef between 6 and 11 meters (20 and 35 feet) deep through which tremendous volumes of water pass with the tides. As well as containing rich marine life and exciting corals, the park has a miniature Blue Hole, a 12-foot-deep cave, the entrance to which is often a favorite spot for fish like the fairy basslet, an iridescent purple-and-yellow fish frequently seen here. Hol Chan is also home to a large population of the gloomily named *Gymnothorax funebris*, or moray eel.

As with other destinations off Ambergris, canyon-diving is the norm at Hol Chan. The canyons lie between buttresses of coral running perpendicular to the reef, separated by white, sandy channels. They vary in depth from 15 to 30 meters (50 to 100 feet). Some sides are very steep, and others comprise gently rolling undulations. In some spots there are tunnellike passageways, which you can dive through, leading from one canyon to the other. The particular pleasure of this kind of canyon-diving is not knowing what is going to be in the next "valley" as you come over the hill.

Fish are abundant in Hol Chan, as they are everywhere else on the reef. You'll identify large numbers of squirrel fish, butterfly fish, parrot fish, and queen angelfish, as well as Nassau groupers, barracuda, and large shoals of yellow-tailed snappers.

The fish are generally in the canyons, and as you pass over you have a bird's-eye view of them. Though the rainbow variety of coral you will find on the Great Barrier Reef in Australia does not exist in Belize— much of it is biscuit-colored here—there is nonetheless plentiful brain, antler, and fan coral. Hol Chan is also one of the best and most popular places to night-dive. As Hol Chan is an open stretch of reef, it does not have opening times as such or admission fees.

The Atolls Having said that Ambergris was the most obvious all-around choice for diving in Belize, now you can be let in on a well-kept secret. It isn't the best. The best diving, and some of the greatest diving anywhere in the world, is off the three coral atolls—**Lighthouse Reef, Glover's Reef,** and **Turneffe Islands**—situated between 48 and 96 kilometers (30 and 60 miles) off the coast.

From the air the atolls look impossibly beautiful. At the center the water is mint-green, and the white sandy bottom reflects the light upwards and is flecked with patches of mangrove and rust-colored sediments. Around the fringe of the atoll the surf breaks in a circular white seam before the color changes abruptly to ultramarine as the water plunges to 915 meters (3,000 feet).

The origin of Belize's atolls is still something of a mystery, but the evidence suggests that unlike the Pacific atolls, which formed by accretion around the rims of submerged volcanoes, these grew from the bottom up as vast pagodas of coral accumulated over millions of years on top of limestone fault blocks. Mayan Indians were probably the first humans to discover and use the atolls, as stopovers on their trading routes. Piles of sea shells and rocks, known as "shell-maidens" and thought to have been placed there as markers, have been found on Turneffe Island.

The battle of nomenclature fought by the Spanish and English on their sea charts reflects the larger frictions that existed over the control of Belize's offshore waters, but with the rout of the Spanish at the Battle of St. George's Cay in 1798, the English names took precedence: Turneffe, for Terre Nef; Lighthouse Reef for Quattro Cayos; Glover's Reef, for Longorif.

Until recently the atolls were sparsely inhabited. Lobster fishing, sponge gathering, and coconut plantations provided a small permanent population with a hard-won living, but it is only with the creation of small dive resorts in recent times that the atolls have begun to revive economically.

In all, there are now five resorts on the atolls (*see* Lodging, *below*): two on Glover's Reef, two on Turneffe, and one on Lighthouse Reef. All of these offer seven-night, eight-day packages. All of them are remote and very quiet. None of them except Lighthouse Reef can be reached without a private charter boat. Though they all cater specifically to divers, they are also marvelous destinations if you simply want to swing in a hammock, snorkel, or read. The bad news is that they all cost $1,200 per week and upwards.

Glover's Reef is the most southerly of atolls. Most of the finest dive sites are along the southeastern limb of the atoll, on the windward side. One exception is Emerald Forest Reef, so called because of the mass of huge green elkhorn coral to be found here. Because the most exciting part of the reef is only 25 feet down, it is excellent for novices and even snorkelers, and it abounds in healthy corals and fish. It also proves an important point: depth is not everything. **Southwest Cay Wall,** close to the Manta Resort, is a typically dramatic drop-off—an underwater cliff that drops quickly to 39 meters (130 feet), is briefly interrupted by a narrow shelf, then continues its near vertical descent to 105 meters (350 feet). As with all wall-dives, where it is easy to lose track of depth and time with the exhilaration of flying in blue space, both ascent and descent require careful monitoring. **Long Cay Wall** is another exciting wall, with a dramatic drop-off to hundreds of feet. Overhangs covered in sheet and boulder coral make it a good place to spot turtles, rays, and barracuda.

The **Turneffe Island** group is the largest of the three atolls and the most centrally placed. Both Glover's and Lighthouse can be reached from here in day trips, as can Belize City. Though it is famous for its spectacular wall-dives, there are dives for every level, including novice. The shallower dives are generally on the western, leeward side of the atoll and are also excellent for snorkeling. Here, the reef is wide and gently sloping. There are large concentrations of tube sponges, soft corals such as forked sea feathers and sea fans, and varied fish, including plentiful permit. Also on the leeward side is the **wreck of the *Sayonara*.** No doubloons to be scooped up here—it was a small passenger and cargo boat that went down in 1985—but it makes a good site for practicing wreck-diving. The highlight of Turneffe, and one of the three best dives in Belize, is **The Elbow,** situated at the southernmost tip of the atoll. Because of the conditions, it is generally considered an advanced dive. Seas are often rough, even on calm days, and strong currents tend to sweep you out toward the deep water beyond the reef. The drop-off is dramatic, and here, if anywhere, you will have the feeling of flying in blue space. Flying with you are likely to be large groups of eagle rays. They regularly visit this area, and sometimes as many as 50 flutter together, a rippling herd of rays that will take your breath away.

Lighthouse Reef is the farthest away and the most accessible of the atolls, thanks to the construction of an airstrip. The atoll is about 29 kilometers (18 miles) long and less than 2 kilometers (1 mile) wide and is surrounded by 67 kilometers (42 miles) of coral reef, with precipitous walls that plummet to 915 meters (3,000 feet) less than 2 kilometers (1 mile) from the atoll. Great depth is not always best, though, and many people say that the best diving is in less than 50 feet of water.

The two most famous dives on Lighthouse Reef are the **Blue Hole** and **Half Moon Cay Wall,** the Grand Canyon and Matterhorn of Belize's underwater world. From the air the Blue Hole looks like a dark-blue eye in the center of the shallow water of the lagoon. Formed in an ice age 15,000 years ago, which exposed the limestone foundations of the reef and created vast subterranean caverns, it was first dived by Jacques Cousteau in 1970 and since then has become a place of pilgrimage for divers.

Just over 305 meters (1,000 feet) wide at the surface, and dropping almost vertically to a depth of 126 meters (412 feet), the Blue Hole offers a diving experience that feels like swimming down a mine shaft. It is the excitement of that feeling, rather than the marine life (of which you will see far more with a snorkel and flippers at the surface), that has made it such a suitcase-sticker destination: "I dived the Blue Hole."

The best diving on Lighthouse is at **Half Moon Cay** at the southeastern tip of Lighthouse Reef, as much because of the presence of the largest colony of red-footed boobies in Belize. In other words, there is nearly as much going on above water as below it. The Half Moon Cay Wall is a classic wall-dive, beginning at 11 meters (35 feet) and dropping almost vertically to blue infinity. Floating out over the edge is a bit like free-fall parachuting. One of the special features here are the magnificent spurs of coral jutting out to the seaward side. Looking like small tunnels, they are fascinating to explore and invariably full of fish. Because of the great variety of bottom types, an exceptionally varied marine life exists around Half Moon Cay. On the gently sloping sand flats behind the coral spurs, a vast colony of garden eels, whose heads can often be seen from a distance protruding from the sand like a field of periscopes, stirs. Spotted eagle rays, turtles, and other pelagics are frequent visitors by the drop-off.

Getting There If you are based on Ambergris Cay, Glover's Reef is out of the question for a day trip by boat. Don't be too optimistic, either, about getting to the Blue Hole. Even when the weather is perfect, it is a two- to three-hour boat trip to Lighthouse Reef. In the winter the weather is usually too unpredictable. Turneffe is more accessible, but even then it is a long and comparatively costly day trip, and you're unlikely to reach the southern tip of the atoll, where the best diving is.

If you are determined to dive the atolls, you basically have three choices. Stay at one of the resorts (*see* Lodging, *below*), go on a live-aboard dive-boat, or do a fly-and-dive trip.

The *Belize Aggressor II* runs a ship-shape, navy-style operation with a crew of four in khaki outfits. It uses a purpose-built, 110-foot cruiser powered by twin 500-HP Detroit Diesels and equipped with the latest communications systems. Weather reports come by fax from Norfolk, Virginia. The schedule—five single-tank dives a day, including one night dive—will leave you begging for mercy. The week-long tours depart from the dock at the Fort George Hotel in Belize City on Saturday night and return from Lighthouse Reef on the following Friday. Scheduled stops are made at all three atolls, but most diving is on the southeast corner of Lighthouse Reef. *Aggressor Fleet, Drawer K, Morgan City, LA 70381, tel. 504/385–2416 or 800/348–2628 in the U.S.*

A similar operation, *Wave Dancer,* also operating from the dock of the Fort George Hotel, is run by the well-known diver Peter Hughes, and diving is done out of a 120-foot cruiser, with smart accommodation and the latest equipment. *Wave Dancer, Waterway II, Suite 2213, 1390 S. Dixie Hwy., Coral Gables, FL 33146, tel. 305/669–9391 or 800/932–6237 in the U.S.*

As both of the above operations run at about the same price as a week in one of the atoll resorts ($1,200–$1,400), it is not for everyone's pocket. An excellent, budget alternative is the **Out Island Diving** operation run by Ray Bowers, a gangly, Hemingwayesque type originally from New Jersey. On his 39-foot boat, *Reef Roamer II,* based in San Pedro on Ambergris Cay, he offers two- and three-day trips to the atolls. Accommodation is simple and is often supplemented by a night's camping on a cay. He also operates the only **Fly-and-Dive Tour,** a one-day, into-the-water, out-of-the-water trip to Lighthouse Reef starting at the crack of dawn in San Pedro and getting back to Ambergris at sunset: a subaqua version of helicopter skiing. *Out Island Divers, Box 7, San Pedro, tel. 026/2151 or 303/586–6020 in the U.S.*

Costs The following were the prices at press time for diving and snorkeling from Ambergris Cay. **Snorkeling:** $15–$20 for two hours or $10–$55 for a day trip with lunch. **Diving:** $20–$35 for a single-tank dive, $35–$50 for a double-tank dive, and $30–$40 for a single-tank night dive. Day trips, with two-tank dives, cost $75 to Cay Caulker, $100 to Turneffe Island, and $150 to the Blue Hole.

Many resorts offer **diving courses.** A one-day basic familiarization course will cost $125. A four-day PADI certification course costs $300. A popular variant is a referral course, in which you do the academic and pool training at home, then complete the diving section here. The cost, for two days, is $250.

Dive Operators Most of the dive shops on the cays are attached to the hotels (*see* Dining and Lodging, *below*). They can vary considerably in terms of the quality of the dive masters, the equipment, and facilities. The following is a checklist of the better ones. Those marked with a star are particularly recommended.

Ambergris Cay ★ Captain Morgan's, Holiday Hotel, Milo's Hotel, Paradise Resort, ★ Ramone's Village, Ruby's Hotel, Spindrift Hotel, Sun Breeze Hotel, ★ Victoria House.

Other Cays Caye Caulker: Belize Diving Services. St. George's Cay: St. George's Lodge. Glover's Reef: Manta Resort, Glover's Reef Resort. Lighthouse Reef: ★ Lighthouse Reef Resort. South Water Cay: ★ Blue Marlin Lodge. Turneffe Island: Turneffe Island Lodge. Placencia: ★ Kitty's Place, The Paradise Vacation Resort.

Dining

Except for those in resorts, all restaurants in Ambergris Cay listed below are in San Pedro. As most of them are on the two main streets, they are easy to locate. Reservations are advised in the high season, from November to April. Dress is casual.

Ambergris Cay ★ **Elvi's Kitchen.** When Elvi, a smiling Creole woman in her late fifties, started her restaurant in 1964, she had a few tables on the sidewalk under a flamboyant tree. Nearly 30 years on, the tree is still there, now pollarded to fit inside the roof and hung with painted wooden parrots. The floor is still sand, but the restaurant now has doors of massive carved mahogany and 22 staff members in snappy black-and-white dress. Harrison Ford ate here when he visited. It is, indeed, "Di Place for Seafood," as it says on Elvi's letterhead. *Halfway down Middle St. Tel. 026/2176. AE, MC, V. $$*

Little Italy. If you read in the local paper that Umberto Eco will be reading from his novels here, or Cicciolina will be waitressing topless, don't believe it. But if you want snapper scaloppine—thin slices of snapper, sautéed in olive oil with lime juice, garlic, and herbs—then Mary Ellen, from Memphis, Tennessee, will serve it with fresh pasta and homemade garlic bread. Try the conch ceviche. *Front St., San Pedro, tel. 26/2866. AE, MC, V. $$*

★ **Estel's.** Estel's father-in-law was a World War II flier with a squadron called "Di Nah Might"—his flying jacket and an old photo are up on the wall—so not surprisingly, this is one of the best places in town to get an American-style breakfast. She also makes burgers, sandwiches, and excellent seafood. The little white-and-aqua building with a sand floor and porthole-style windows is right on the beach. Outside there is a terrace where you can sit under a palapalai and watch the pelicans splat into the water. *Front St., tel. 26–2019. No credit cards. $*

Cay Caulker **Marin's Restaurant.** Marin's, the best restaurant on Cay Caulker, serves good seafood. You can't miss it: Head one block back from Main Street, and you'll know it by its distinctive black-and-red exterior. *One block west of the Tropical Paradise Hotel, tel. 022/2104. MC. $$*

Aberdeen Chinese Restaurant. It's halfway down Main Street and is the most popular eating house for young people. Burgers, sandwiches, and Chinese dishes, particularly lobster combinations like chow mein and sweet and sour, fill the menu. *Next door to Hotel Jimenez, tel. 022-2127. MC, V. $*

Lodging

The accommodations on Ambergris fall basically into two categories—those in the town, and those outside it. Most of the hotels in town are on San Pedro's main street, a sandy lane running parallel to the sea. Officially it is known as Barrier Reef Drive, but everyone calls it Front Street. It is the commercial center of the town, with the two banks, gift shops, and most of the restaurants.

Accommodations in town are generally simpler and cheaper, with a different ambience. Rooms on the main street can be noisy, for instance—not so much with cars as with late-night revelers. Prices range from as little as $10 to about $100.

If you like some action at night and don't want to spend too much, a hotel in San Pedro is ideal. If you want silence and sand, blue water and palm trees, you have to go out of town, either to the north or south. This is also where the larger, resort-style accommodations are situated. Generally, whether in town or out, all hotels offer snorkeling and fishing tours. Many have their own dive shops.

In recent years, small resorts have begun to open on more of the cays, and on atolls farther out to sea. Because of logistical realities—power, water supply, transportation—some of these are very basic, with no electricity and Spartan accommodations. Others are turning increasingly to an exclusive clientele. If you want a real castaway experience, this is where to find it. If you like a bit of nightlife and sociability, you might go stir-crazy. Most of the resorts lie in the upper price range. Because of their isolation, many do only eight-day, seven-night packages. As all have only limited space, early booking, particularly between November and March, is essential.

Ambergris Cay
In San Pedro Town

Sunbreeze Beach Resort. This resort hotel, which sits just on the edge of town next to the airstrip, has been extensively refurbished over the last few years. Grouped around a large, plant-filled central courtyard, the rooms all have air-conditioning and television. *Box 14, San Pedro Town, Ambergris Cay, tel. 026/2347, fax 026/2346. 34 rooms with bath. Facilities: restaurant, bar, dive shop, fishing boats, laundry service. AE, MC, V. $$$*

★ **San Pedro Holiday Hotel.** This group of four colonial-style houses, with their cheery pink-and-white trim and seaside ambience, is the closest you will get to a resort in the center of town. It is slightly overpriced, but there is an excellent dive shop, with some of the best air in town. Ceili's, on the property, is one of the better restaurants. *Box 1140, Belize City, tel. 026/2014 or 02–44632 in Belize City, fax 026/2295. 15 rooms and 2 apartments, some with air-conditioning. Facilities: restaurant, bar, beach, dive shop, laundry, gift shop. AE, MC, V. $$–$$$*

Rock's Inn. Built in an E-shape around a pretty central garden, with a little strip of sand in front and a view across the water, this small, modern guest house on two floors offers self-catering apartments with well-equipped kitchenettes at reasonable prices. Most rooms have an extra bed, and each additional person costs only $10. Children under 12 are free. *Rock's Inn, San Pedro Town, tel. 026/2326, fax 026/2358. 9 rooms. Facilities: laundry, baby-sitting services. AE, MC, V. $$*

Spindrift Hotel. Centrally located, this family-run hotel is something of a meeting-place for local people (a hilariously funny local game, known as Chicken Drop, is played on the beach outside on Wednesdays) and is a favorite with divers. The rooms, some of which overlook the ocean, are grouped around an inner courtyard and vary considerably in price. *Spindrift Hotel, San Pedro Town, tel. 026/*

2174, fax 026/2251. 24 rooms, including 2 apartments with kitchenettes, and a large suite. Facilities: laundry, dive shop. AE, MC, V. $$

Martha's. Backpackers favor this large white house on Middle Street, upstairs from a grocery store two blocks back from the sea. *Box 27, San Pedro Town, tel. 026/2053, fax 026/2589. 16 rooms. MC, V. $*

★ **San Pedrano.** Painted mint-green, blue, and white, with crisp linen provided and spotless rooms, this is the cheeriest of the budget hotels in San Pedro. The Gonzalez family, who owns it, is friendly and hardworking and maintains a gift shop downstairs. *San Pedrano Hotel, San Pedro Town, tel. 026/2054. 7 rooms and 1 apartment. No credit cards. $*

Ambergris **Belize Yacht Club.** It will be some time before there are the sloops
Cay and the society that the name implies. But what you can rely on is a
Outside San group of attractive, Spanish-style villas at the water's edge, all with
Pedro Town air-conditioned bedrooms, kitchenettes, and verandas specially angled to look over the ocean. For sea dogs, there is a dock with fueling facilities; for those who want to pump iron, probably the best-equipped gym in Belize is at your disposal. *Box 1, San Pedro, Ambergris Cay, tel. 026/2777, fax 026/2768. 22 apartments. Facilities: gym, laundry, dock. AE, MC, V. $$$*

★ **Captain Morgan's Retreat.** "An island feeling, with American amenities" is how Frank, the manager from Ohio, described this excellently run resort, which is 20 minutes by speedboat to the north of San Pedro. What that means is that the handsome thatched cabanas dotted along 244 meters (800 feet) of white coral sand give you the feeling of being on a desert island, while the efficiency and hard work of the management ensure that there will be no glitches in paradise. Not everyone will like the "captain's table" seating arrangements—guests eat all together at long mahogany tables—but it is typical of the down-home conviviality that Captain Morgan's specializes in. Elmer "Patojo" Paz, the dive master, is one of the best on Ambergris Cay. *c/o Magnum Americas, 718 Washington Ave., Box 1560, Detroit Lakes, MN 56502, tel. 218/847–3012 or 800/447–2931, fax 026/2616. 21 rooms. Facilities: restaurant, bar, beach, dive shop, laundry, pool. AE, MC, V. $$$*

★ **Caribbean Villas.** Before they decided to build these two graceful, white villas on a secluded stretch of beach 3 kilometers (2 miles) south of San Pedro, Wil Lala had been a dentist and his wife, Susan, was an interior decorator. The result of their collaboration is state-of-the-art island architecture, incorporating Caribbean and Spanish styles in an undisturbed setting. Lots of intelligence and creativity has gone into the design—like the luggage niches under the built-in sofas, and the spacious sleeping lofts—so these self-catering apartments, which range from single rooms to two-bedroom suites with sleeping loft, feel larger than they are. The owners offer wildlife, fishing, and snorkeling tours. *2 miles south of San Pedro, tel. 026/2715, fax 026/2885. 7 units. loft, which sleeps 6. AE, MC, V. $$$*

El Pescador. Owners Juergen Krueger and his Wisconsin-born wife, Kathleen, were the first people to build on the northern part of the cay; and though they tend to refer to El Pescador as a "fishing camp," it is in fact a handsome colonial-style house. El Pescador offers a week-long fishing package, which includes round-trip airfare from Belize City to Ambergris Cay, three meals a day, and the sole use of a boat and guide for six days of fishing, eight hours a day. Tours also go outside the reef for sailfish, barracuda, wahoo, and tarpon. Accommodations are basic but comfortable. *Box 793, Belize*

City, tel./fax 026/2398. 11 rooms. Facilities: dining room, fishing. No credit cards. $$$

Ramon's Village. The pink-and-blue Mayan warrior's head over the entrance—the largest neon sign in San Pedro—is a landmark on the road south from the town. Inside, the 60 cabanas, many of them two-story, are thatch to thatch, but with their mahogany floors and fittings, views of the ocean, and hibiscus plants, they are extremely pleasant. As the atmosphere is lively and sociable, Ramon's is not for people seeking quiet and seclusion. The clientele is mostly young and active, and the place remains popular with divers. *Ramon's Village Resort, Ambergris Cay, tel. 026/2071, fax 026/2214. 61 rooms with private bath. Facilities: restaurant, bar, dive shop, laundry, pool. $$$*

★ **Victoria House.** This grand colonial-style house a few miles south of San Pedro, with its airy verandas and mature gardens planted with bougainvillea, hibiscus, and oleander, has the style and seclusion of a diplomatic residence. The dining room, with its carved mahogany doors, tiled floor, and blue tablecloths, serves excellent buffet meals that combine the best local seafood with imaginative salads and side dishes. Guests like to linger at a large bar in the garden. The stone-and-thatch cabanas all have private verandas overlooking the sea. Chris Berlin and Rebecca Johnson run the best dive shop on the cay; sea kayaks, catamarans, and Windsurfers are available. *Box 22, San Pedro Town, tel. 026/2067, fax 026/2429 or c/o Box 20785, Houston, TX 77225, tel. 713/662–8000 or 800/247–5159. 26 rooms with shower. Facilities: restaurant, bar, dive shop, gift shop, laundry. AE, MC, V. $$$*

Blackbird Cay **Blackbird Cay Village.** Blackbird Cay is part of the Turneffe Island group. Originally, the four, frond-roofed cabanas were built for scientists to research the reef and its wildlife, particularly dolphins, and ecotourists looking for an alternative to bustling, commercial San Pedro. Kent Leslie, who runs the place, is also a passionate angler, and the Blackbird offers some of the best sport-fishing on the nearby Calabash Cay Flats. A generator supplies power. The food is Belizean—conch fritters, barracuda steaks, or grilled snapper—and the ambience, desert-island-quiet. *c/o Blackbird Cay Ltd., 1415 Louisiana, Suite 31000, Houston, TX 77002, tel. 713/658–1142. 10 thatched cabanas. MC, V. $$$*

Cay Caulker **Jimenez Cabanas.** These four simple but pleasant thatched cabanas are set on a small plot of land on the lagoon side of the cay. They are set in a pretty garden with flowerbeds edged with conch shells. Each cabana has one or two double beds, and a very basic bathroom (cold water only). One disadvantage is the bugs that breed in the lagoon. *Tel. 022/2175. 4 thatched cabanas (or 8 rooms). No credit cards. $$*

★ **The Tropical Paradise.** The Tropical Paradise is the best bet in town, with simple but clean rooms in a small cluster of cabanas at the south end of the town. It also has one of the better restaurants on the cay. *Tel. 022/2124, fax 022/2225. 18 rooms with bath. No credit cards. $$*

Rainbow Hotel. This is a large, concrete building painted mint-green and blue, at the northern end of the Main Street. The rooms are Spartan but cheerful, and the management is friendly. Rooms overlooking the sea are more expensive. *Tel. 022/2123. 8 rooms, all with private showers. $*

Glover's Reef **Manta Reef Resort.** This fishing and diving resort is located on the
★ southern tip of Glover's Reef. Accommodations are in mahogany-fitted cabanas. Each cabana has a private bath, with a shower, a small porch, a hammock to swing in, and daily maid service. There is a res-

taurant and bar on a pier overlooking the lagoon, which offers good home-cooking (and even chocolate chip cookies). The eight-day, seven-night packages are, as much as possible, tailored to suit individual needs, whether diving, fishing, or simply lolling in a hammock. Transport to and from the reef is by boat and takes four hours. *c/o 102 Laurelwood, San Antonio, TX 78213, tel. 512/344–6428 or 800/342–0053, fax 02/31895. 9 rooms with private bath. AE, MC, V. $$$*

Lighthouse Reef ★ **Lighthouse Reef Resort.** If you want to get blissed out in Belize, this is the place to do it. Once a spartan dive camp for aficionados of the reef, it has gradually been transformed into one of the most exclusive resorts in Central America. Luckily, small is beautiful seems to be the guiding principle of the development. No clutter, and no noisy generators will be found here. You always have the feeling that you are the only person on the island. As well as the five original brick cabanas, two handsome, new, British-colonial–style villas have just been completed. Each villa is tastefully furnished in Queen Anne style and has a modern, well-equipped kitchenette. Two more villas were under construction at time of writing. The setting—white coral sand, palm trees, mint-green water—is breathtaking. The diving, under expert and friendly supervision, is as good as any in the world. If you are lucky, you may even meet Peeto, a bottle-nose dolphin that lives in the bay. Whatever happens, you will never want to leave. *Lighthouse Reef Resort, Northern Two Caye, Box 26, Belize City; or Box 1435, Dundee, FL 33838, tel. 813/439–1486 or 800/423–3114, fax 02/31205. 9 rooms with private bath. Facilities: restaurant, diving, fishing. 8-day, 7-night packages only. AE. $$$*

St. George's Cay **Cottage Colony.** A brand new resort and an island dependence of Bellevue Hotel in Belize City, Cottage Colony offers colonial-style beachfront cottages that opened in 1991. *Cottage Colony, c/o The Bellevue Hotel, Box 428, Belize City, tel. 02/33571, fax 02/73253. 11 units. Facilities: dive instruction, water-sports facilities. AE, D, MC, V. $$$*

St. George's Lodge. Only 15 kilometers (9 miles) from Belize City, and once the capital of the country, this small, relaxed cay is steeped in history. It has long been a favorite haunt of Her Majesty's Forces. There are 12 rooms in the main building, all constructed of beautiful Belizean hardwood (the bar is made of rosewood), and four thatch cottages by the water. Electricity is provided by the lodge's own windmills. Shower water is solar heated. In the restaurant, you can enjoy grilled snapper or grouper. *Box 625, Belize City, tel. 02/44190 or 800/678–6871, fax 02/30461. 12 rooms and 4 cabanas, all with private bath. $$$*

South Water Cay **The Blue Marlin Lodge.** Situated on South Water Cay, on the southern portion of the reef—access is from Dangriga—this picture-postcard resort makes an excellent base for fishing excursions and dive trips. The reef is only 50 yards away, and famous sites like the Blue Hole and Glover's Reef are also accessible. There are 15 double rooms and six cabanas, close enough to the sea to hear it, all with private bath, hot water, and electric fans. A restaurant and bar tops off the amenities. *Blue Marlin Lodge, Box 21, Dangriga, Belize, tel. 05/22243 or 800/798–1558, fax 02/22296. 15 double rooms, 6 cabanas, all with private bath. AE, MC, V. $$$*

Turneffe Islands ★ **Turneffe Islands Lodge.** The only resort on Cay Borkel, it's at the southern edge of the atoll and is run by Americans Dave and Jill Bennett. It offers rooms overlooking the water and an easygoing atmosphere. For those suffering from castaway syndrome, there are planned evening activities. Only eight-day, seven-night packages are offered. Guests must transfer from Belize City by boat. *Turneffe Islands Lodge, 11904 Hidden Hills Dr., Jacksonville, FL 32225, tel. 904/641–4468 or 800/338–8149, fax in the U.S. 904/641–5283. 8 rooms with private bath. Facilities: restaurant, bar, gift shop. AE, MC, V. $$$*

The Cayo

With more than 5,200 square kilometers (2,006 square miles) of rugged, mountainous land but fewer than 15,000 inhabitants, the Cayo—originally, the word referred to the peninsula of land between the Macal and Mopan rivers on which San Ignacio grew up, and not to the district—is both the largest district in Belize and one of the least populated. As in all of Belize, the land is never still for long: The Cayo is full of sudden, surprising contrasts. During a trip to the Mountain Pine Ridge area you can drop, ecologically speaking, from South Carolina to Brazil, in the space of a few miles. One minute you're in pine savanna; the next, in lush subtropical rain forest.

Ten years ago, when the first jungle lodges began to open in the Cayo, no one believed that this wild, western district straddling the border with Guatemala could become an attractive destination for travelers. It seemed too remote, the roads were too bad, the weather was too unpredictable. But today, more than half of all visitors to Belize go to the Cayo, making it the most popular destination in the country.

Indeed, it is still remote. As soon as you enter it, things change: electric to hurricane lamps, telephones to two-way radios, two-wheel drive to four-wheel-drive. The rewards, however, far outweigh the inconveniences. Most of the wildlife featured on Belize's 20-dollar bill can be found in the Cayo—mountain lions, jaguars, and their diminutive cousins—the beautiful, shy ocelot and the even smaller margay. There are majestic, haunting ruins where the lost world of the Maya seems to come alive even today. And for those who want it, there are more strenuous pursuits like cave exploring, jungle hiking, and horseback riding. In the Cayo, anyone can be Indiana Jones for a while.

Tour Operators Elvin Holland, of **Hinterland Tours,** in San Ignacio, does excellent guided tours of the region (tel. 092/2559).

Arriving and Departing

By Bus **Novelo's** and **Batty Bros.** (*see* Staying in Belize, *above*) run frequent services to Belmopan and San Ignacio from Belize City. The journey takes three hours and costs only $2. There are also services from Belmopan.

By Car Follow the Western Highway from Belize City.

Getting Around

There is limited bus service between the main centers in the Cayo, but this is wild country and the best way to get around in it is by four-wheel-drive vehicles. Because of the numerous rivers, touring by canoe is also a good way of seeing the country. Most of the resorts have vehicles.

Important Addresses and Numbers

Police (tel. 2022).

Eva's Restaurant in San Ignacio is the Cayo's bulletin board. You can find out where to hire a canoe, how to get to Caracol, where to rent a horse, or find a room. *22 Burns Ave., San Ignacio, tel. 092/2267.*

Exploring the Cayo

Leaving Belize City on the Western Highway (the only fast, well-paved road in Belize), you will appreciate the smooth ride. At Mile 30, before Belmopan, is the **Belize Zoo and Tropical Research Education Center** (*see* Chapter 3, National Parks and Wildlife Reserves). The visitor center at the entrance is named after the famous and very funny British naturalist Gerald Durrell, who was an adviser on the zoo's planning and conception (one of the young directors of the zoo also trained at Durrell's zoo on Jersey, in the Channel Islands). Here, you will be able to see all the wildlife that you are very unlikely to see in the wild—April the tapir, a favorite with Belize's schoolchildren; a pair of jaguars; scarlet macaws; crocodiles; gibnut; and all the rest. As this zoo was designed with the animals' welfare, not yours, in mind, you will probably spend most of your time bent over, peering into the lush, green undergrowth in the spacious enclosures trying to spot the animal. Don't worry, they're in there somewhere. As the zoo is also the flagship of Belize's forward-thinking conservation policies, great emphasis is placed on education. Little green panels next to the cages give short sound bites on ecology and the threat posed to its inmates by creatures like us. *Admission: $5. Open daily 10–5.*

The best way to see **Belmopan,** the capital of Belize, is through the rearview mirror heading out. Indeed, the only reason to go to the city, a dreary cluster of concrete office buildings with all the charm of a shopping center in Shanghai, is to see the **Archaeological Vault.** It is literally a vault, secured by a huge, old-fashioned Chubb lock from England, and is one of the only hands-on museums in the world. Not that you will be allowed to touch. But once you have made an appointment, one of the friendly, well-informed staff will be more than happy to hold priceless Mayan vases or strings of jade necklaces up for you to see—all over a solid concrete floor. *Dept. of Archaeology, Belmopan, Belize, tel. 08/2216 for appointment. Admission free. Open Wed. 1:30–4:30.*

Also worth a quick visit on the way out of Belmopan is the **Guanacaste Park nature reserve,** named after the huge guanacaste tree that grows there. There is also a rich population of tropical birds and plants. *Donations accepted. Open daily 9–3:30.*

A few miles west of Belmopan, you will know you are entering the Cayo. Having run along the side of the Belize River, the road winds out of the valley. The road then heads into a series of sharp bends and passes a low, granite wall, probably the first stone wall you will have seen in Belize. It is a safety barrier and confirms your transition from one kind of landscape to another. In a few minutes you will see horses flicking their tails and cattle grazing on steep hillsides. If it weren't for the banana palms, you could be in the Auvergne, in France.

When you hear a clattering like an express train signaling the crossing of the Hawkesworth Bridge, you will know you are entering **San Ignacio,** the social and administrative center of the Cayo. Built in

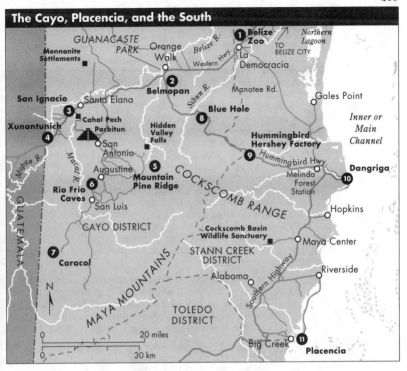

The Cayo, Placencia, and the South

1941 by the British to span the Macal River, the Hawkesworth is the only suspension bridge in Belize. At night you can hear the rattling of vehicles on its metal flanges from 5 kilometers (3 miles) away. Even louder is the incredible commotion of the grackles in the trees in the town square at sunset. It's worth standing for a moment to listen to this eerily beautiful sound.

With its well-preserved vernacular architecture, bustling Spanish ambience, and dusty charm, San Ignacio is one of the few towns in Belize where you might wish to linger. The evenings are cool and mosquito-free. There are a few funky and interesting bars, and a few good restaurants. And for exploring the Cayo, it is by far the best place to base yourself. The majority of accommodations are either in or close to the town.

The population of San Ignacio is typically mixed: Mestizo and Maya dominate, as does the Spanish language (although almost everyone speaks English), but there are also Creoles, Mennonites, Chinese, a few Lebanese, and one charming restaurateur from Sri Lanka. The town was once the center of the chicle and mahogany trades that flourished in this part of Belize, and it remains an important agricultural center for the surrounding district.

An excellent introduction to the Cayo, and a chance to make the acquaintance of the Cayo's two biggest rivers, is the 20-minute walk to Branch Mouth, where the Macal and the Mopan join to form the Belize River. A track leads north out of town past the soccer field. Immediately you are in a world of rich tropical vegetation, birds, and butterflies, of which there are clouds everywhere you go in the Cayo. The merging of the waters, with parrots flying overhead and swallows skimming the water for insects, is a fitting prelude to the sights and sounds that await you.

Back on the Western Highway, heading toward the town of Benque Viejo on the Guatemalan border, you will get to the village of **San José Succottz** on the bank of one of those rivers, the Mopan. The walk up the hill from the river, through shady forest, is extremely pleasant. Butterflies flit through the air. Maidenhair ferns grow in profusion in the limestone rocks. Near the top, a magnificent avenue of cahoune palms announces your approach to the site. **Xunantunich** (pronounced Shoo-nan-too-nitch), an important ceremonial center in the Mayan classical period, is not as well excavated as Altun Ha, in the north, but the view from the top of the main pyramid, a 360-degree panorama over Guatemala and the Mopan River valley, is one of the finest in Central America. The pyramid, built on a leveled hilltop visible from 48 kilometers (30 miles) around offers a startling view that is particularly breathtaking at sunset. At the very top, on the eastern wall of the pyramid, you will find some of the finest Mayan sculpture in Belize, a long, white frieze decorated with jaguar heads, human faces, and abstract geometric patterns. Pan along the frieze with your eyes, then out across the jungle. It is one of the great sights in Belize.

Nothing could more dramatically illustrate both the achievements of the Maya and the modesty of modern Belize than the fact that until recently, El Castillo, the massive 37-meter-high (120-foot-high) pyramid that soars over the grassy plazas of Xunantunich like a Mayan Caernarvon Castle, was the tallest building in the country.

If you are determined to get to Caracol, then you first have to go up into the Mountain Pine Ridge area, which is an adventure in itself. From San Ignacio, you take the road southeast toward San Antonio. As you wind up from the Macal Valley, you will pass fertile farming country, with corn, peanuts, and beans growing in small clearings at the side of the road. A few miles beyond the village of Christo Rey, the road swings south-southeast away from the river, and the vegetation becomes wilder. Cahoune palms, trumpet trees, wild papayas, and strangler vines grow in a riot, with here and there a crop of banana or corn cut into the hillside between them.

Shortly before San Antonio, you emerge onto a flat, plateaulike area with fine views of the Maya Mountains in the distance. **San Antonio,** a cluster of brightly painted wooden houses clinging to the side of a hill at 300 meters (1,000 feet), seems, with its sheep, goats, and orange trees, like a tropical version of a Greek hilltop village. It is home to the **Garcia Sisters,** five bright Mayan siblings with clever hands and an eye for business who became something of a local legend when they set up their own crafts shop and museum. At the other end of the village, the **Magana family** has also recently opened an arts-and-crafts shop, so you may want to visit both before buying anything.

Not far from San Antonio you'll pass a small house on stilts that had been built on a Mayan living mound. Behind it you see the top few feet of a small stepped pyramid, now overgrown with jungle, an extraordinary juxtaposition of worlds centuries apart in time but mere feet apart in space.

About 3 kilometers (2 miles) beyond San Antonio there is a T-junction. To the left the road goes back down 15 kilometers (9 miles) to Georgeville and Mountain Equestrian Trails. The road to follow bears right, and from now on you'll be climbing and climbing—the earth ascending and growing steadily redder until it is the color of

mango; the driving, more and more challenging. You may find yourself slipping and sliding through the mud like a drunken figure
skater.

A barrier across the road is the sign that you are entering the nature
⑤ reserve proper, namely **Mountain Pine Ridge.** A few minutes later,
you will see your first yellow pines, marking a sudden transition in
terrain from lush tropical forest to pine savanna. From now on you
will be driving on forest tracks that circle the western slopes of the
mountains. Some of them have names, yet most are simply algebraic
formulations like A10. Baldy Beacon, at just over 915 meters (3,000
feet) (the height of Ben Nevis in Scotland), lies to the east.

With the Cockscomb Basin Wildlife Sanctuary and the ruins at
Lamanai, this mountainous, 780-square-kilometer (300-square-
mile) nature reserve, a rugged dome of granite and limestone containing some of the most ancient rocks in Central America, will be a
highlight of any journey to Belize.

As you enter the savanna, the flora changes dramatically. You will
see lilac-colored mimosa, St. John's wort, occasionally a garish, red
flower known as hotlips. There is also a huge variety of ferns, ranging from the tiny maidenhair fern to giants the size of small coconut
trees. A fair selection of Belize's 154 species of orchids can also be
found in the Mountain Pine Ridge area. Look out, too, for a wild tree
called craboo. A brandylike liqueur believed to have aphrodisiac
properties is made from the berries. As the birds also love to eat the
tree's fruit, any craboo is a good place to look for the orioles and
woodpeckers.

After the heat and humidity of lowland Belize, the cooler air, the
smell of pine resin, and the shady pine woods are both enormously
refreshing and totally unexpected. It could be Georgia. It could be
the country above Saint-Tropez. It isn't at all what you might have
imagined in Belize. The best way to see it, of course, is not bouncing
around in an Isuzu Trooper but with what the Chinese call the Number 11 bus: your own two feet.

The road gets steepest, albeit downhill, just before the **Hidden Valley Falls,** also known as the Thousand Foot Falls. In fact, they are
nearly 400 meters (1,600 feet) high, making them the highest in Central America. A thin plume of spray plummets over the edge of a
rock face into a seemingly bottomless gorge below. If it were China,
there would be poems carved into the rocks nearby. As there is a
shelter and some benches, this is an excellent place to eat a sandwich
and soak in the setting. A rest room is available to the public.

Back on the move, head southwest to the Rio On River, where you
will find caught among flat, granite boulders, a series of crystal-
clear pools and mini-waterfalls that combine to create one of the
most invigorating experiences on earth (and it's only a two-minute
walk from the road). Next comes the village of **Augustine.** This is the
headquarters for the forest reserve, a small cluster of government-
built houses set in a shady clearing with its own school for the few
children who live here. If you are thinking of camping, this is the
only place you can do it. By the sign for the school, turn right. If you
go straight, you will—well, you might—get to Caracol.

From Augustine, it is a few miles down a steep red-dirt track to the
⑥ **Río Frío Caves**—a few miles, but ecological light-years, away, because on the way you drop from cool pine savanna to lush tropical
forest. Nothing in this small country of huge contrasts so clearly
shows the extraordinary variety of Belize's landscapes than this

startling transition. Also, nowhere gives you a better sense of where you are than does the interior of this ancient swallow-filled cave where at night, ocelot and margay pad silently across the cold sand floor in search of their slumbering prey. A river runs right through the center of it, and over the centuries it has carved the rock into fantastic shapes. From the cool, dark interior of the cave, the light-filled world of mosses, birds, and plants outside seems even more intense and beautiful than ever. Bisecting the circle of light and rising vertically through the mouth of the cave, like a spar propping up the whole mountain, is a giant hardwood tree, *Pterocarpus officialis*, its massive paddle-shaped roots anchored in the sandy soil of the river-bank and its green crown straining toward the blue sky above.

❼ Caracol ("the snail" in Spanish) was a Mayan metropolis, with five plazas and 32 large structures, covering nearly a square mile. The latest evidence suggests that it gained a crushing victory over the great city of Tikal in the mid-6th century AD, something that Guatemala has still not quite gotten used to. For centuries, until a group of *chicleros* stumbled on it in 1936, it was buried under the jungle of the remote Vaca Plateau. The great pyramid of Canaa is now officially the tallest structure in Belize. In fact, once Caracol has been fully excavated, it may dwarf even Tikal, which lies only a few dozen miles across the Guatemalan border. The road to Caracol is now officially open, and many Cayo resorts and tour operators are running day and overnight tours there. If you want to drive on your own, be sure to inquire about road conditions first.

Dining and Lodging

In the Cayo, you may be out in the bush, but you won't be roughing it. Indeed, you will find here some of the most pleasant accommodations in Belize. It varies from simple cabanas to beautifully landscaped properties. As usual in Belize, each of these places is highly individual, with a unique ambience created by its owners. All of them, however, place special emphasis on ecotourism. Nearly all of them are also out on what must surely soon be christened Safari Strip—the western highway heading out of San Ignacio toward the Guatemalan border.

Belmopan
Dining and
Lodging
★

Banana Bank Ranch. The Carr family—she is a painter from Kansas; he, a rancher from Montana (and, incidentally, the first person the reviewer had shaken hands with who was wearing spurs)—make excellent hosts. Both of them came to Belize in the late '50s, love the country, know it extremely well, and are happy to share their knowledge at the communal evening meal. The thatched cabanas, with their curving internal walls and split-level layout, are simple but extremely pleasant. The setting, on the bank of Belize's Mississippi, the Belize River, is heavenly. *Box 48, Belmopan, tel. 08/23180, fax 08/22366. 9 rooms with shower. Facilities: 8" Meade telescope to view the night sky, a remuda of 25 saddle horses for exploring the property's 4,000 acres of land, expert guides, excursions, laundry. No credit cards. $$*

Crystal Paradise. Located on the Macal River in the village of Cristo Rey, this newly opened resort is one of the few locally owned operations in Cayo. And what a family this is! Victor and Teresa Tut (pronounced *toot*) and their 10 children are about an equal mix of three of Belize's main cultures: Creole, Mayan, and Spanish. Eldest son Jeronie can identify more than 200 bird species and is a medicinal-plant expert; along with younger brother Evrald, he knows the surrounding jungle about as well as anyone else. The Tuts offer a variety of very reasonably priced tours, including jungle camping, river excursions, and horseback trips to Caracol. *Cristo Rey, Cayo District, tel. 092/2823, fax 092/3075. 4 cabanas with shower. Facilities: restaurant, bar, excursions. No credit cards. $*

Cristo Rey **Blancaneux.** This new resort, one of the most upscale and expensive in the country, is owned by film director Francis Ford Coppola, and it certainly upholds his reputation for perfectionism. The cabanas dot a landscaped hill located in the Mountain Pine Ridge nature reserve, overlooking the Privassion River, which has a lovely progression of pools and waterfalls that make for excellent swimming. The spacious, thatched-roof cabanas are luxuriously furnished in a Mayan motif, with carvings, figurines, masks, and handwoven bed and chair covers. Although you probably won't see Francis, you can at least enjoy his personal recipes for pizza and pasta. *Box 281, Belize City, tel. and fax 092/3878. 8 cabanas, 2 family-size cabanas with living room. Facilities: restaurant, bar, laundry, excursions. AE, MC, V. $$$*

San Ignacio **Chaa Creek.** Martha Gellhorn raved about it. The BBC has filmed it.
Dining and This is the queen of the jungle resorts. The owners, Mick and Lucy
Lodging Fleming, lived in Africa for many years, and there is a feel of the
★ lodges in the Kenyan Highlands about the place. The simple but luxurious stone cottages with thatched roofs, set on a grassy slope above the Macal River, are decorated with Guatemalan crafts and intentionally have no phones, electricity, or air-conditioning. In the day, you can canoe down the river or visit Mayan ruins in a Land Rover. At night you can sit on the bar's mahogany deck and watch the stars. The 300-acre property also features jungle trails, campsites, Mayan ruins, Belize's only natural-history museum, and a butterfly breeding center. *Box 53, San Ignacio, Cayo District, tel. 092/2037, fax 092/2501. 16 rooms with shower. Facilities: restaurant, bar, laundry, room service, safari tours. AE, D, MC, V. $$$*

Du Plooys. By canoe, this ranchlike ensemble of buildings is only a few minutes upstream from Chaa Creek. By road you have to drive for 15 minutes over a bumpy track. The bush feeling, however, stops at the gate. The setting—above a bend of the Macal River known as Big Eddy—is spectacular. From the new deck, suspended on piles 9 meters (30 feet) above the forest, you look straight out to a dramatic sweep of limestone cliffs. Below, there is a sandy beach where you can swim and dive off the rocks into the Macal River. The cottages are pleasant and airy, and there are now bed-and-breakfast accommodations for the budget traveler. *San Ignacio, Cayo District, tel. and fax 092/3301. 9 rooms with showers. Facilities: restaurant, bar, room service, laundry, safari tours. MC, V. $$$*

★ **Mountain Equestrian Trails (MET).** The name makes it sound forbiddingly one-sided. But even if you can't ride, this is a gorgeous place to stay. Two attractive two-room cabanas are decorated with Guatemalan furnishings and mahogany fittings; and the setting, in the bottom of a lush valley on the western flank of the Mountain Pine Ridge, with horses grazing in the fields, orange trees, and jungle-covered mountains, is second to none. If you want to ride, the 97 kilometers (60 miles) of jungle trails the Bevis family have cleared will take you to breathtaking locations. *Mountain Pine Ridge Rd., Central Farm Post Office, Cayo District, tel. 092/3310, fax 082/3235. 2 cabanas with bath. MC, V. $$*

San Ignacio Hotel. Here you'll find by far the nicest accommodations in San Ignacio—and very reasonably priced. Don't let the modest exterior fool you; the rooms are large and comfortable, and each has a veranda overlooking the jungle. The hotel is just a few yards up the hill from town on the Western Highway. *Box 33, San Ignacio, Cayo*

District, tel. 092/2034, fax 092/2134. 24 rooms. Facilities: restaurant-bar, pool, gift shop, laundry. AE, DC, MC, V. $$

Windy Hill. When you see the sign that reads GRACELAND over the entrance, you wonder if you have seen right. You have. The owner, an ex-marine with impressive arm tattoos, is a devoted Elvis fan. With its pool, pool table, white plastic chairs, air-conditioned cabanas, and rest rooms marked cowgirls and cowboys, this is a bit of Memphis transported south of the Tropic of Cancer. *Graceland Ranch, San Ignacio, tel. 092/2017, fax 092/3080. 19 cabanas with private bath. Facilities: restaurant, bar, excursions, camping and horseback tours, laundry, pool. AE, MC, V. $$*

Belmoral Hotel. Like cow-foot soup, the name of this funky wooden building slap in the center of town is a curious reminder of British colonial occupation (though Her Majesty's Scottish estate is, of course, spelled *Balmoral*). With the address, you might expect haggis and tartan. Don't. It's basic Belizean. *17 Burns Ave., San Ignacio, tel. 092/2024. 15 rooms with shared bath. No facilities. No credit cards. $*

★ **Nabitunich.** This ranch and cottage colony is a friendly, laid-back bit of paradise on the banks of the Mopan River. At sunset, you can see the Mayan ruins of Xunantunich, which is within walking distance, outlined in flame-colored light on a hill nearby. The cabanas are simple but very pleasant; the atmosphere, English bed-and-breakfast. This is an excellent value. *San Lorenzo Farm, San Ignacio, tel. 093/2309. 8 rooms with shower. Facilities: restaurant, laundry, excursions. No credit cards. $*

Parrot Nest. Fred Prost, creator of the Seaside Guesthouse in Belize, one of Belize City's top travel values, has done it again, this time with a hotel 5 kilometers (3 miles) outside San Ignacio amid tropical forest on the banks of the Mopan River. Parrot Nest consists of four simple thatched-roof cabanas, each with two single beds, built up into the trees surrounding the main house. At just $18 a night for two, this is one of the best values in Belize, and good meals are available at very reasonable prices (but bring your own liquor). *5 km (3 mi) outside San Ignacio, just past the village of Bullet Tree Falls. c/o 3 Prince St., Belize City, tel. 092/3702. 4 cabanas with shared bath. Facilities: restaurant, excursions. No credit cards. $*

Placencia and the South

The southern portion of Belize is the least commercialized, and most remote, part of the country. In what is locally known as "the Deep South," tourism is still in its infancy, and little in the way of a hotel or restaurant infrastructure exists. For those who like their traveling rough and adventurous, it is the place to go—though definitely not in the rainy season (as much as 160 inches of rain falls annually) unless you like traveling with galoshes and an umbrella.

Belize's southernmost town is Punta Gorda, which is still in the early stages of developing tourism attractions and infrastructure. Most visitors to "PG" go either to catch the ferry to Guatemala (*see* Arriving and Departing in Belize City, *above*) or to take part in the Mayan Village Guesthouse Program (*see* Fodor's Choice).

The most "developed" area—it's a very relative term in this context—is the area around Placencia. A new airstrip is being built here, and in 10 years the place will almost certainly be transformed to a new Ambergris Cay.

Arriving and Departing by Plane

Flying is the best way to get to the south. The trip provides marvelous views of the Maya Mountains and the Cockscomb Range. **Maya Airways** (tel. 02/44032) has several flights daily from Belize City to Placencia, Big Creek, and Punta Gorda.

Arriving and Departing by Car and Bus

By Car Placencia is a little more than 160 kilometers (100 miles) south of Belize City. If you do drive, check on the state of the Hummingbird Highway first. Even in the dry season, it is a notoriously bad road. The last bit of the journey, on the Southern Highway, is a boneshaker. All-terrain vehicles are strongly advised.

By Bus Take the **Z-Line** or **James** bus (tel. 02/73937) from Belize City. It is a long, hard road. There is also a bus from Dangriga that leaves daily at 3 PM from the Hub Guest House.

Exploring Placencia and the South

Traveling in Belize is never a question of simply going from A to B. There is always a bit of adventure involved, and a few detours to Y or Z. And so it is with the south. To get there by car from Belize City, the first thing you do is set off southwest to **Belmopan.** From there, you head southeast on the **Hummingbird Highway.**

Don't be fooled by the name. This is a seriously rough road, and you are best advised to use a four-wheel-drive vehicle even in the dry season. Despite this, the journey is well worth the effort. To the right rise the jungle-clad slopes of the Maya Mountains, mostly free of signs of human habitation except for the occasional clearing of corn and beans.

8 About 20 kilometers (12½ miles) south of Belmopan you will come to the **Blue Hole,** a cool turquoise pool surrounded by mosses and lush vegetation, which is excellent for a cool dip (after an hour on the Hummingbird, you'll need one). It is, in fact, part of an underground river system. On the other side of the hill you will find **St. Herman's Cave,** once inhabited by the Maya. A path leads up from the highway, just by the Blue Hole. It is quite steep and is difficult to pass unless it is dry. To explore the cave, it's best to wear sturdy shoes and bring a flashlight. Note well: In recent years, the Blue Hole, because of its isolation, has been the scene of numerous car break-ins and even a rape. At press time an attendant was on duty at the site, but you should check on the situation before you go. If you want to go directly to Placencia, missing the Blue Hole and St. Herman's Cave, take the turnoff at Mile 30 on the Western Highway for Dangriga and the south.

9 Farther south, toward Dangriga, you may smell chocolate. This will be a sign that you have arrived at the **Hummingbird Hershey Factory.** If you want to be Charlie in the Chocolate Factory for an hour or two, the management will be happy to let you walk around. Visitors are welcome. No admission fee.

Soon after this the view rolls back to the horizon, and you find yourself driving down to a flat plain dotted with baby orange trees. As always in Belize, the transition from one landscape to another—in this case, from uninhabited mountain country to the fertile **Stann Creek Valley**—is swift and startling. Equally startling, if you are coming from the Cayo, is the ethnic contrast: Whereas San Ignacio is strongly Spanish in feeling, this area is strongly Afro-Caribbean. Originally, bananas were produced here, but a blight all but eliminated the crops in 1906. Today, the citrus plantations, which account for 10% of the nation's production, are touted as one of the country's great success stories, though the fishing community of Dangriga shunned the project with a "bring me the tree and I'll pick it for you" attitude. As a result, the labor force is made up largely of migrant workers from Guatemala. Their simple shacks are visible from the road. The resplendent three-story villa of one of the main plantation owners, Eugene Zabanay, whose brother was involved in a drug-smuggling scandal in Miami, is on the right just before you arrive in Dangriga.

⑩ With a population of 10,000, **Dangriga** is the largest town in the south, home to the **Garifuna,** or Black Caribs, as they are also known, the most exotic and unusual of the many ethnic groups that have found peace and asylum in this tiny country. Their story is a bizarre and moving one, an odyssey of exile and dispossession in the wake of the confusion wrought on the New World by the Old. They are descendants of a group of black slaves from Nigeria who were shipwrecked on the island of St. Vincent in 1635 en route to slavery in America. At first the Caribs, St. Vincent's indigenous inhabitants, fiercely resisted their presence, but understanding conquered fear and racial antipathy, and a new addition to the family of man was born.

In the eyes of the British colonial authorities, the new race was an illegitimate and troublesome presence in one of the Crown's dominions. Worse still, they sided with, and were succored by, the French. After nearly two centuries of guerrilla warfare, the British decided that the best way to solve the problem was to deport them en masse. After a circuitous and tragic journey across the Caribbean during which thousands perished of disease and hunger, the exiled finally arrived in Belize.

Half Amerindian, half African, the Garifuna, as they came to be known, have their own belief systems, a potent mixture of ancestor worship and Catholicism; their own dialect and music, African-style drumming with a modern disco variant known as punta rock, which you can hear everywhere in Belize; and their own clannish social structure—Garifuna seldom marry outside their own race. The day this proud, independent people celebrate their arrival in Belize and remember their roots is November 19, Garifuna Settlement Day, when Dangriga cuts loose with a week of Carnival-style celebrations.

The town of Dangriga, however, is not as compelling as the history of its residents. Imagine a few of the more dilapidated districts of Belize City being towed down the coast and dumped here, and you've got Dangriga. Much—too much—has been written about the Garifuna. Unless you're an ethnographer, or regard going off the beaten track as an excuse to gate-crash someone else's culture, you're best heading on to Placencia.

⑪ **Placencia** is a bit of the South Seas in Belize: a balmy fishing village set in a sheltered half-moon bay, with crystal-clear green water and almost 5 kilometers (3 miles) of palm-dotted white sand. Originally founded by pirates and today peopled with an extraordinary mélange of races (it is one of the few places in the world where you will find blacks with blue eyes), it is the sort of hideaway that Robert Louis Stevenson would have chosen if he hadn't ended up in Tahiti. To the west the Cockscomb Range ruffles the tropical sky with its jagged peaks. To the east, seaward, there is a line of uninhabited cays moored on the horizon like beached oil tankers overgrown with vegetation. There are tours off into the jungle or to the Mayan ruins at Lubantuun, diving, and some of the best sportfishing in the country, but once you get here you will probably just want to lie in a hammock under a palm tree, read, sleep, and swim.

Indeed, Placencia is the best place to get blissed out in Belize. It is so small it doesn't even have a main street. It has a sidewalk or concrete path, just big enough for two walking hand in hand, that sets off purposefully from the south end of town by the generator, meanders through everybody's backyard, passes wooden cottages on stilts overrun with bougainvillea and washing lines sagging with laundry, then peters out abruptly in a little clearing of coconut palms and white morning glory as though it had forgotten where it was headed in the first place. That's the sort of place Placencia is. Along the path are most of the village's guest houses and cafés. Walk the sidewalk, and you've seen the town.

Sports and Outdoor Activities

Diving and Snorkeling
The biggest drawback is this: Whereas farther north the Barrier Reef is right off Ambergris Cay, by the time you get this far south, coast and coral have drifted as much as 35 kilometers (22 miles) apart. This means long boat rides (45 minutes to an hour) to get to the dive sites, which in turn makes you much more weather-dependent. As there are not as many cuts and channels through the reef as in the north, it is also more difficult to get out to the seaward side, the best one for diving. As a result, most of the diving is done off the cays lying off the coast. They have minireefs around them, usually with gently sloping dropoffs of about 24–31 meters (80–100 feet). For example, off Moho Cay, southeast of Placencia, the visibility may be poor due to bad weather, but you will see much marine life and brilliant red and yellow corals that are rarely seen elsewhere in Belize.

One bonus in Placencia is that the diving is cheaper, $40 for a two-tank dive with a couple of people in the boat, compared with $55 in Ambergris, including all the gear. Snorkeling is also considerably cheaper, $20–$25 per day.

Sportfishing
The fly-fishing on the flats off the cays east of Placencia is some of the best in Belize. You will encounter plentiful tarpon—at times, they flurry 10-deep in the water—as well as permit fish, bonefish, and snook, all of which will have your reel screeching and your heart beating once you hook them. Most of the better hotels can arrange guides. Otherwise, try **P&P Enterprise** (tel. 06/23132 or 800/333-5961) or **Joel Westby** (tel. 06/23138), who has more than 30 years of experience as a guide.

Dining and Lodging

Dangriga
Dining and Lodging
Pelican Beach Resort. This rather lugubrious hotel-resort is a misnomer here: Far from catering to all your needs, the management seems to take very little interest in its guests at all. It might remind you of a tropical version of a Maine boardinghouse in the low season. It's the best in Dangriga, though, and the restaurant is decent. It is also convenient for tours to the Cockscomb Jaguar Reserve. And there are baths, not just showers, a delicious rarity for Belize. *Box 14, Dangriga, tel. 05/22044, fax 05/22570. 20 rooms with private*

bath. Facilities: restaurant, bar, excursions, laundry. AE, D, MC, V. $$

Placencia
Dining

BJ's. From the outside it looks plain enough—a thatched cabana with a cafélike interior—but you may be lucky enough to run into Betty, a big, smiling Placencian mama who will prepare *serre*, a local dish made with coconut cream, cassava, and lobster. She also makes fresh-squeezed juices from the fruit of her own trees. *About ¼ mi north of town, tel. 06/23108. No credit cards. $*

Tentacles. The ne plus ultra of Placencia—the town stops here—this busy restaurant, with its pleasant deck overlooking the water and palapa-covered bar at the end of the dock, is a favorite meeting place for the reef-and-sail crowd. Open daily for breakfast, lunch, and dinner. *Tel. 06/23254. No credit cards. $*

Dining and Lodging
★

Rum Point Inn. When they came here in the late '50s, George and Carol Bevier had to cut their way through the undergrowth to find the old colonial-style house they had purchased. Today, Rum Point Inn, located 5 kilometers (3 miles) from Placencia on its own beachfront property, is one of the finest of the highly personalized, small-scale resorts that make traveling in Belize such a pleasure. The feeling you have walking into one of the eight domelike villas is of space, light, and air, as though only a thin, tentlike membrane separates you from the sea, the sky, and the palm trees. Each is luxuriously but simply furnished with Guatemalan fabrics and mahogany. Each has a unique arrangement of windows and skylights. Some are portholes; others, geometric patterns cut in the walls. In the day, they dapple the walls with light and give you cutout glimpses of the surroundings; at night, they make the buildings look from the outside like Halloween pumpkins. Food is cooked by two charming Belizean girls who learned to make such tidbits as lobster and eggplant on English muffins, topped with a layer of grilled Parmesan, from old issues of *Gourmet* magazine. The well-stocked library has one of the best collections of books on the Maya in Belize; and in case you get cultural cold turkey, there's an excellent selection of compact discs and videos. What more could you want? *Rum Point Inn, Placencia, tel. 06/22017 or 800/747–1381 in the U.S., fax 504/464–0325. 8 rooms with private bath. Facilities: restaurant, bar, excursions, laundry. AE, D, MC, V. $$$*

Kitty's Place. Even paradise needs a generator, and you can hear Kitty's half a mile away. Accommodations are in a weathered oceanside colonial-style house and two cabanas, 3 kilometers (2 miles) from the village on the ocean. The restaurant serves good pasta, and there's a funky upstairs bar. Because Kitty, a native of Colorado, has one of the only two dive shops in Placencia, her place is always full of divers. Sea kayaking and sportfishing are also popular here. *Box 528, Belize City, tel. 062/2027. 6 rooms, 4 with bath. Facilities: restaurant, bar, dive shop, excursions, laundry. AE, MC, V. $$*

★ **Ranguana Lodge.** In the center of the village but still on the beach, these five white cabanas, with green shutters and trim and mahogany fittings, are the most pleasant mid-priced accommodations in Placencia. It is also popular with fishermen. *Ranguana Lodge, Placencia, tel. 06/23112. 5 rooms. No credit cards. $$*

★ **The Paradise Vacation Resort.** At the south end of the sidewalk, just back from Tentacles restaurant, you'll find this large house on stilts. As it has its own compressor, a good dive master, and a dock, it is popular with divers looking for a cheap alternative to Ambergris Cay. As far as lodging goes here, basic is the byword. *The Paradise Vacation Resort, Ltd., Placencia, tel. 06/23179. 16 rooms with shared bath. Facilities: dive shop, excursions. No credit cards. $*

The Sea Spray. The rooms are fairly basic, but the management is friendly. The location—on the sidewalk's major intersection, with restaurants nearby—is convenient. *The Sea Spray, Placencia, tel. 06/23148. AE, MC, V. $*

Excursion to the Cockscomb Basin Wildlife Sanctuary

One of the highlights of any journey to Belize will be a trip to the **Cockscomb Basin Wildlife Sanctuary** (*see* Chapter 3, National Parks and Wildlife Reserves). It can be reached from Dangriga—which is slightly closer to it than Placencia—but Placencia is a far better place to be based. Either way, it is an overland trip. Take the road back up the peninsula until you meet the Southern Highway, then head north to the village of Maya Centre. The track leading into the reserve is off to the right, but you have to register in a hut by the entrance before proceeding (there is also a small gift shop selling woven baskets and fine embroideries of the Mayan calendar). From here, it is 8 kilometers (5 miles) up to the reception center. The road climbs up through dense vegetation—splendid cahoune palms, purple mimosa, orchids, and big-leafed plantains—and as you go higher the marvelous sound of tropical bird song, often sounding like strange wind-up toys, grows stronger and stronger.

It is definitely four-wheel-drive terrain. You may have to ford several small rivers as well as negotiate deep, muddy ruts. At the top, you will find a very pleasant clearing with hibiscus and bougainvillea bushes, a little office where you can buy maps to the nature trails (notice the marvelous Oripendula nests hanging from the rafters), rest rooms, and several picnic tables. If you do plan to have a picnic, make sure you have some serious bug spray with you—the Cockscomb is alive with no-see-ums (tiny biting flies) and mosquitoes.

In a vain, misguided attempt by an American naturalist to track the jaguars' movements in the 1980s, seven were caught and tagged with radio collars. To catch them, special steel cages were built— the animals smashed several wooden ones to pieces—using a live pig placed behind a grille as bait. The jaguar would enter the cage to catch the pig, trip a door behind it, and find itself captive. What followed was a conflagration of fur and fury of almost unbelievable proportions. Jaguars are so powerful that in their desperate attempts to escape, the captured animals threw the 300-pound cages around like matchboxes. They sheared off most of their teeth in the process as they tried to bite through the steel. Within a year, all seven had died.

Today it is estimated that there are between 25 and 30 jaguars— eight to 10 mature males; nine to 10 adult females, and the rest, young animals—spread over an area of about 400 square kilometers (152 square miles). It is the largest jaguar population in the world and one of Belize's most significant contributions to conservation (the jaguar was hunted to extinction in the United States by the late 1940s).

Up to 2 meters (6 feet) long and weighing in just below Mike Tyson, the jaguar is nature's great loner, a supremely free creature that shuns even the company of its own kind, except during a brief mating period and the six short months the female spends with her cubs before turning them loose in the green wilds. The rest of the time, they roam the rain forest in splendid isolation, sunning themselves to sleep by day and, by night, stalking gibnut, armadillo, and curassow, a kind of wild turkey, with the deadly efficiency of a serial killer and a call you will grow to recognize as you walk through the reserve. To the ancient Maya, the jaguars were intermediaries between this world and the world of the gods.

You will almost certainly not see a jaguar, as they have exceptionally good hearing and sense of smell. If you do, you'll be far too close for comfort. But walking along the well-marked nature trails is one of the most pleasant ways to spend a day in Belize. Most of them are loops of 1 to 2 kilometers (.6–1.25 miles), so you can do several in a day. The most strenuous takes you up a steep hill from the top of which there is a magnificent view of the entire Cockscomb basin.

In addition to the jaguar, the Cockscomb has a wonderful selection of Belize's wildlife, including the other cats—pumas, margays, and ocelots—plus coatis, kinkajous, deer, peccaries, and, last but not least, tapir. Also known as the "mountain cow," this shy, curious creature appears to be half horse, half hippo, with a bit of cow and elephant thrown in.

Nearly 300 species of birds have been identified in the Cockscomb, including the keel-billed toucan, the king vulture, several species of hawks, and the scarlet macaw. And everywhere you walk there is the lush, riotous growth of the rain forest. The Cockscomb is an immense botanical garden, heated seemingly to the temperature of a sauna.

Spanish Vocabulary

Note: *Mexican Spanish differs from Castilian Spanish.*

Words and Phrases

	English	*Spanish*	*Pronunciation*
Basics	Yes/no	Sí/no	see/no
	Please	Por favor	pore fah-**vore**
	May I?	¿Me permite?	may pair-**mee**-tay
	Thank you (very much)	(Muchas) gracias	(**moo**-chas) **grah**-see-as
	You're welcome	De nada	day **nah**-dah
	Excuse me	Con permiso	con pair-**mee**-so
	Pardon me/what did you say?	¿Como?/Mánde?	pair-**doan**/**mahn**-dey
	Could you tell me?	¿Podría decirme?	po-**dree**-ah deh-**seer**-meh
	I'm sorry	Lo siento	lo see-**en**-toe
	Good morning!	¡Buenos días!	**bway**-nohs **dee**-ahs
	Good afternoon!	¡Buenas tardes!	**bway**-nahs **tar**-dess
	Good evening!	¡Buenas noches!	**bway**-nahs **no**-chess
	Goodbye!	¡Adiós!/¡Hasta luego!	ah-dee-**ohss**/**ah**-stah-**lwe**-go
	Mr./Mrs.	Señor/Señora	sen-**yor**/sen-**yore**-ah
	Miss	Señorita	sen-yo-**ree**-tah
	Pleased to meet	Mucho gusto	**moo**-cho **goose**-to you
	How are you?	¿Cómo está usted?	ko-mo es-**tah** oo-**sted**
	Very well, thank you.	Muy bien, gracias.	**moo**-ee bee-**en**, **grah**-see-as
	And you?	¿Y usted?	ee oos-**ted**?
	Hello (on the telephone)	Bueno	**bwen**-oh
Numbers	1	un, uno	oon, **oo**-no
	2	dos	dos
	3	tres	trace
	4	cuatro	**kwah**-tro
	5	cinco	**sink**-oh
	6	seis	sace
	7	siete	see-**et**-ey
	8	ocho	**o**-cho
	9	nueve	new-**ev**-ay
	10	diez	dee-**es**
	11	once	**own**-sey
	12	doce	**doe**-sey
	13	trece	**tray**-sey
	14	catorce	kah-**tor**-sey
	15	quince	**keen**-sey
	16	dieciséis	dee-es-ee-**sace**
	17	diecisiete	dee-**es**-ee-see-**et**-ay
	18	dieciocho	dee-**es**-ee-**o**-cho
	19	diecinueve	**dee-es**-ee-new-**ev**-ay
	20	veinte	**vain**-tay
	21	veinte y uno/veintiuno	**vain**-te-oo-no

30	treinta	**train**-tah
32	treinta y dos	train-tay-**dose**
40	cuarenta	kwah-**ren**-tah
43	cuarenta y tres	kwah-**ren**-tay-**trace**
50	cincuenta	seen-**kwen**-tah
54	cincuenta y cuatro	seen-**kwen**-tay **kwah**-tro
60	sesenta	sess-**en**-tah
65	sesenta y cinco	sess-**en**-tay **seen**-ko
70	setenta	set-**en**-tah
76	setenta y seis	set-**en**-tay **sace**
80	ochenta	oh-**chen**-tah
87	ochenta y siete	oh-**chen**-tay see-**yet**-ay
90	noventa	no-**ven**-tah
98	noventa y ocho	no-**ven**-tah **o**-cho
100	cien	see-**en**
101	ciento uno	see-en-toe **oo**-no
200	doscientos	doe-see-**en**-tohss
500	quinientos	keen-**yen**-tohss
700	setecientos	set-eh-see-**en**-tohss
900	novecientos	no-veh-see-**en**-tohss
1,000	mil	meel
2,000	dos mil	dose meel
1,000,000	un millón	oon meel-**yohn**

Colors	black	negro	**neh**-grow
	blue	azul	ah-**sool**
	brown	café	kah-**feh**
	green	verde	**vair**-day
	pink	rosa	**ro**-sah
	purple	morado	mo-**rah**-doe
	orange	naranja	na-**rahn**-hah
	red	rojo	**roe**-hoe
	white	blanco	**blahn**-koh
	yellow	amarillo	ah-mah-**ree**-yoh

Days of the Week	Sunday	domingo	doe-**meen**-goh
	Monday	lunes	**loo**-ness
	Tuesday	martes	**mahr**-tess
	Wednesday	miércoles	me-**air**-koh-less
	Thursday	jueves	who-**ev**-ess
	Friday	viernes	vee-**air**-ness
	Saturday	sábado	**sah**-bah-doe

Months	January	enero	eh-**neh**-ro
	February	febrero	feh-**brair**-oh
	March	marzo	**mahr**-so
	April	abril	ah-**breel**
	May	mayo	**my**-oh
	June	junio	**hoo**-nee-oh
	July	julio	**who**-lee-yoh
	August	agosto	ah-**ghost**-toe
	September	septiembre	sep-tee-**em**-breh
	October	octubre	oak-**too**-breh
	November	noviembre	no-vee-**em**-breh
	December	diciembre	dee-see-**em**-breh

Useful phrases	Do you speak English?	¿Habla usted inglés?	**ah**-blah oos-**ted** in-**glehs**?

I don't speak Spanish	No hablo español	no **ah**-blow es-pahn-**yol**
I don't understand (you)	No entiendo	no en-tee-**en**-doe
I understand (you)	Entiendo	en-tee-**en**-doe
I don't know	No sé	no **say**
I am American/ British	Soy americano(a)/ inglés(a)	soy ah-meh-ree-**kah**-no(ah)/ in-**glace**(ah)
What's your name? My name is . . .	¿Cómo se llama usted? Me llamo . . .	**koh**-mo say **yah**-mah oos-**ted**? may **yah**-moh
What time is it?	¿Qué hora es?	keh **o**-rah es?
It is one, two, three . . . o'clock.	Es la una; son las dos, tres	es la **oo**-nah/sone lahs dose, trace
Yes, please/No, thank you	Sí, por favor/No, gracias	**see** pore fah-**vor**/no **grah**-see-us
How?	¿Cómo?	**koh**-mo?
When?	¿Cuándo?	**kwahn**-doe?
This/Next week	Esta semana/ la semana que entra	es-tah seh-**mah**-nah/lah say-**mah**-nah keh **en**-trah
This/Next month	Este mes/el próximo mes	es-tay mehs/el **proke**-see-mo mehs
This/Next year	Este año/el año que viene	es-tay **ahn**-yo/el **ahn**-yo keh vee-**yen**-ay
Yesterday/today/ tomorrow	Ayer/hoy/mañana	ah-**yair**/oy/mahn-**yah**-nah
This morning/ afternoon	Esta mañana/tarde	es-tah mahn-**yah**-nah/**tar**-day
Tonight	Esta noche	es-tah **no**-cheh
What?	¿Qué?	keh?
What is it?	¿Qué es esto?	keh es **es**-toe
Why?	¿Por qué?	pore **keh**
Who?	¿Quién?	kee-**yen**
Where is . . . ? the train station? the subway station? the bus stop? the post office? the bank? the . . . hotel? the store?	¿Dónde está . . . ? la estación del tren? la estación del Metro? la parada del autobús? la oficina de correos? el banco? el hotel . . . ? la tienda . . . ?	**dohn**-day es-**tah** la es-tah-see-**on** del **train** la es-ta-see-**on** del **meh**-tro la pah-**rah**-dah del oh-toe-**boos** la oh-fee-**see**-nah day koh-**reh**-os el **bahn**-koh el oh-**tel** la tee-**en**-dah

the cashier?	la caja?	la **kah**-hah
the . . . museum?	el museo . . . ?	el moo-**seh**-oh
the hospital?	el hospital?	el ohss-pea-**tal**
the elevator?	el ascensor?	el ah-**sen**-sore
the bathroom?	el baño?	el **bahn**-yoh
Here/there	Aquí/allá	ah-**key**/ah-**yah**
Open/closed	Abierto/cerrado	ah-be-**er**-toe/ ser-**ah**-doe
Left/right	Izquierda/derecha	iss-key-**er**-dah/ dare-**eh**-chah
Straight ahead	Derecho	der-**eh**-choh
Is it near/far?	¿Está cerca/lejos?	es-**tah sair**-kah/ **leh**-hoss
I'd like . . .	Quisiera . . .	kee-see-air-ah
a room	un cuarto/una habitación	oon **kwahr**-toe/ **oo**-nah ah-bee- tah-see-**on**
the key	la llave	lah **yah**-vay
a newspaper	un periódico	oon pear-ee-**oh**- dee-koh
a stamp	un timbre de correo	oon **team**-bray day koh-**reh**-oh
I'd like to buy . . .	Quisiera comprar . . .	kee-see-**air**-ah kohm-**prahr**
cigarettes	cigarrillo	ce-gar-**reel**-oh
matches	cerillos	ser-**ee**-ohs
a dictionary	un diccionario	oon deek-see-oh- **nah**-ree-oh
soap	jabón	hah-**bone**
a map	un mapa	oon **mah**-pah
a magazine	una revista	**oon**-ah reh-**veess**-tah
paper	papel	pah-**pel**
envelopes	sobres	**so**-brace
a postcard	una tarjeta postal	**oon**-ah tar-**het**-ah post-**ahl**
How much is it?	¿Cuánto cuesta?	**kwahn**-toe **kwes**-tah
It's expensive/ cheap	Está caro/barato	es-**tah kah**-roh/ bah-**rah**-toe
A little/a lot	Un poquito/ mucho . . .	oon poh-**kee**-toe/ **moo**-choh
More/less	Más/menos	mahss/**men**-ohss
Enough/too much/too little	Suficiente/de- masiado/muy poco	soo-fee-see-**en**-tay/ day-mah-see-**ah**- doe/**moo**-ee **poh**-koh
Telephone	Teléfono	tel-**ef**-oh-no
Telegram	Telegrama	teh-leh-**grah**-mah
I am ill/sick	Estoy enfermo(a)	es-**toy** en-**fair**-moh(ah)

Please call a doctor	Por favor llame un médico	pore fa-**vor ya**-may oon **med**-ee-koh
Help!	¡Auxilio! ¡Ayuda!	owk-**see**-lee-oh/ ah-**yoo**-dah
Fire!	¡Encendio!	en-**sen**-dee-oo
Caution!/Look out!	¡Cuidado!	kwee-**dah**-doh

On the Road

Highway	Carretera	car-ray-**ter**-ah
Causeway, paved highway	Calzada	cal-**za**-dah
Route	Ruta	**roo**-tah
Road	Camino	cah-**mee**-no
Street	Calle	**cah**-yeh
Avenue	Avenida	ah-ven-**ee**-dah
Broad, tree-lined boulevard	Paseo	pah-**seh**-oh
Waterfront promenade	Malecón	mal-lay-**cone**
Wharf	Embarcadero	em-bar-cah-**day**-ro

In Town

Church	Templo/Iglesia	**tem**-plo/e-**gles**-se-ah
Cathedral	Catedral	cah-tay-**dral**
Neighborhood	Barrio	**bar**-re-o
Foreign Exchange Shop	Casa de Cambio	**cas**-sah day **cam**-be-o
City Hall	Ayuntamiento	ah-yoon-tah-mee **en**-toe
Main Square	Zócalo	**zo**-cal-o
Traffic Circle	Glorieta	glor-e-**ay**-tah
Market	Mercado (Spanish)/ Tianguis (Indian)	mer-**cah**-doe/ tee-**an**-geese
Inn	Posada	pos-**sah**-dah
Group taxi	Colectivo	co-lec-**tee**-vo
Group taxi along fixed route	Pesero	pi-**seh**-ro

Items of Clothing

Embroidered white smock	Huipil	whee-**peel**
Pleated man's shirt worn outside the pants	Guayabera	gwah-ya-**beh**-ra

Leather sandals	Huarache	wah-**ra**-chays
Shawl	Rebozo	ray-**bozh**-o
Pancho or blanket	Serape	seh-**ra**-peh

Dining Out

A bottle of . . .	Una botella de . . .	**oo**-nah bo-**tay**-yah deh
A cup of . . .	Una taza de . . .	**oo**-nah **tah**-sah deh
A glass of . . .	Un vaso de . . .	oon **vah**-so deh
Ashtray	Un cenicero	oon sen-ee-**seh**-roh
Bill/check	La cuenta	lah **kwen**-tah
Bread	El pan	el pahn
Breakfast	El desayuno	el day-sigh-**oon**-oh
Butter	La mantequilla	lah mahn-tay-**key**-yah
Cheers!	¡Salud!	sah-**lood**
Cocktail	Un aperitivo	oon ah-pair-ee-**tee**-voh
Dinner	La cena	lah **seh**-nah
Dish	Un plato	oon **plah**-toe
Dish of the day	El platillo de hoy	el plah-**tee**-yo day oy
Enjoy!	¡Buen provecho!	bwen pro-**veh**-cho
Fixed-price menu	La comida corrida	lah koh-**me**-dah co-**ree**-dah
Fork	El tenedor	el ten-eh-**door**
Is the tip included?	¿Está incluida la propina?	es-**tah** in-clue-**ee**-dah lah pro-**pea**-nah
Knife	El cuchillo	el koo-**chee**-yo
Lunch	La comida	lah koh-**me**-dah
Menu	La carta	lah **cart**-ah
Napkin	La servilleta	lah sair-vee-**yet**-uh
Pepper	La pimienta	lah pea-me-**en**-tah
Please give me	Por favor déme	pore fah-**vor** **day**-may
Salt	La sal	lah sahl
Spoon	Una cuchara	**oo**-nah koo-**chah**-rah
Sugar	El azúcar	el ah-**sue**-car
Waiter!/Waitress!	¡Por favor Señor/Señorita!	pore fah-**vor** sen-**yor**/sen-yor-ee-**tah**

Index

Personal Itinerary

Departure *Date*

Time

Transportation

Arrival *Date*   *Time*

Departure *Date*   *Time*

Transportation

Accommodations

Arrival *Date*   *Time*

Departure *Date*   *Time*

Transportation

Accommodations

Arrival *Date*   *Time*

Departure *Date*   *Time*

Transportation

Accommodations

Personal Itinerary

Arrival *Date*   *Time*

Departure *Date*   *Time*

Transportation

Accommodations

Arrival *Date*   *Time*

Departure *Date*   *Time*

Transportation

Accommodations

Arrival *Date*   *Time*

Departure *Date*   *Time*

Transportation

Accommodations

Arrival *Date*   *Time*

Departure *Date*   *Time*

Transportation

Accommodations

Personal Itinerary

Arrival *Date*   *Time*

Departure *Date*   *Time*

Transportation

Accommodations

Arrival *Date*   *Time*

Departure *Date*   *Time*

Transportation

Accommodations

Arrival *Date*   *Time*

Departure *Date*   *Time*

Transportation

Accommodations

Arrival *Date*   *Time*

Departure *Date*   *Time*

Transportation

Accommodations

Personal Itinerary

Arrival	*Date*	*Time*
Departure	*Date*	*Time*
Transportation		
Accommodations		

Arrival	*Date*	*Time*
Departure	*Date*	*Time*
Transportation		
Accommodations		

Arrival	*Date*	*Time*
Departure	*Date*	*Time*
Transportation		
Accommodations		

Arrival	*Date*	*Time*
Departure	*Date*	*Time*
Transportation		
Accommodations		

Addresses

Name	*Name*
Address	*Address*
Telephone	*Telephone*
Name	*Name*
Address	*Address*
Telephone	*Telephone*
Name	*Name*
Address	*Address*
Telephone	*Telephone*
Name	*Name*
Address	*Address*
Telephone	*Telephone*
Name	*Name*
Address	*Address*
Telephone	*Telephone*
Name	*Name*
Address	*Address*
Telephone	*Telephone*
Name	*Name*
Address	*Address*
Telephone	*Telephone*

Addresses

Name	*Name*
Address	*Address*
Telephone	*Telephone*
Name	*Name*
Address	*Address*
Telephone	*Telephone*
Name	*Name*
Address	*Address*
Telephone	*Telephone*
Name	*Name*
Address	*Address*
Telephone	*Telephone*
Name	*Name*
Address	*Address*
Telephone	*Telephone*
Name	*Name*
Address	*Address*
Telephone	*Telephone*
Name	*Name*
Address	*Address*
Telephone	*Telephone*

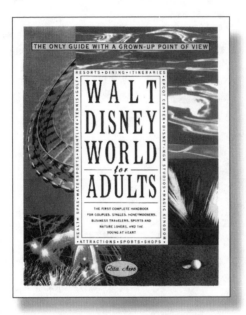

Fodor's Travel Guides

Available at bookstores everywhere, or call 1–800–533–6478, 24 hours a day.

U.S. Guides

Alaska

Arizona

Boston

California

Cape Cod, Martha's Vineyard, Nantucket

The Carolinas & the Georgia Coast

Chicago

Colorado

Florida

Hawaii

Las Vegas, Reno, Tahoe

Los Angeles

Maine, Vermont, New Hampshire

Maui

Miami & the Keys

New England

New Orleans

New York City

Pacific North Coast

Philadelphia & the Pennsylvania Dutch Country

The Rockies

San Diego

San Francisco

Santa Fe, Taos, Albuquerque

Seattle & Vancouver

The South

The U.S. & British Virgin Islands

USA

The Upper Great Lakes Region

Virginia & Maryland

Waikiki

Walt Disney World and the Orlando Area

Washington, D.C.

Foreign Guides

Acapulco, Ixtapa, Zihuatanejo

Australia & New Zealand

Austria

The Bahamas

Baja & Mexico's Pacific Coast Resorts

Barbados

Berlin

Bermuda

Brittany & Normandy

Budapest

Canada

Cancún, Cozumel, Yucatán Peninsula

Caribbean

China

Costa Rica, Belize, Guatemala

The Czech Republic & Slovakia

Eastern Europe

Egypt

Euro Disney

Europe

Florence, Tuscany & Umbria

France

Germany

Great Britain

Greece

Hong Kong

India

Ireland

Israel

Italy

Japan

Kenya & Tanzania

Korea

London

Madrid & Barcelona

Mexico

Montréal & Québec City

Morocco

Moscow & St. Petersburg

The Netherlands, Belgium & Luxembourg

New Zealand

Norway

Nova Scotia, Prince Edward Island & New Brunswick

Paris

Portugal

Provence & the Riviera

Rome

Russia & the Baltic Countries

Scandinavia

Scotland

Singapore

South America

Southeast Asia

Spain

Sweden

Switzerland

Thailand

Tokyo

Toronto

Turkey

Vienna & the Danube Valley

Special Series

Fodor's Affordables

Caribbean

Europe

Florida

France

Germany

Great Britain

Italy

London

Paris

Fodor's Bed & Breakfast and Country Inns Guides

America's Best B&Bs

California

Canada's Great Country Inns

Cottages, B&Bs and Country Inns of England and Wales

Mid-Atlantic Region

New England

The Pacific Northwest

The South

The Southwest

The Upper Great Lakes Region

The Berkeley Guides

California

Central America

Eastern Europe

Europe

France

Germany & Austria

Great Britain & Ireland

Italy

London

Mexico

Pacific Northwest & Alaska

Paris

San Francisco

Fodor's Exploring Guides

Australia

Boston & New England

Britain

California

The Caribbean

Florence & Tuscany

Florida

France

Germany

Ireland

Italy

London

Mexico

New York City

Paris

Prague

Rome

Scotland

Singapore & Malaysia

Spain

Thailand

Turkey

Fodor's Flashmaps

Boston

New York

Washington, D.C.

Fodor's Pocket Guides

Acapulco

Bahamas

Barbados

Jamaica

London

New York City

Paris

Puerto Rico

San Francisco

Washington, D.C.

Fodor's Sports

Cycling

Golf Digest's Best Places to Play

Hiking

The Insider's Guide to the Best Canadian Skiing

Running

Sailing

Skiing in the USA & Canada

USA Today's Complete Four Sports Stadium Guide

Fodor's Three-In-Ones (guidebook, language cassette, and phrase book)

France

Germany

Italy

Mexico

Spain

Fodor's Special-Interest Guides

Complete Guide to America's National Parks

Condé Nast Traveler Caribbean Resort and Cruise Ship Finder

Cruises and Ports of Call

Euro Disney

France by Train

Halliday's New England Food Explorer

Healthy Escapes

Italy by Train

London Companion

Shadow Traffic's New York Shortcuts and Traffic Tips

Sunday in New York

Sunday in San Francisco

Touring Europe

Touring USA: Eastern Edition

Walt Disney World and the Orlando Area

Walt Disney World for Adults

Fodor's Vacation Planners

Great American Learning Vacations

Great American Sports & Adventure Vacations

Great American Vacations

Great American Vacations for Travelers with Disabilities

National Parks and Seashores of the East

National Parks of the West

The Wall Street Journal Guides to Business Travel

At last — a guide for Americans with disabilities that makes traveling a delight

0-679-02591-X $18.00 ($24.00 Can)

This is the first and only complete guide to great American vacations for the 35 million North Americans with disabilities, as well as for those who care for them or for aging parents and relatives. Provides:

- Essential trip-planning information for travelers with mobility, vision, and hearing impairments

- Specific details on a huge array of facilities, along with solid descriptions of attractions, hotels, restaurants, and other destinations

- Up-to-date information on ISA-designated parking, level entranceways, and accessibility to pools, lounges, and bathrooms

  At bookstores everywhere, or call **1-800-533-6478**